AndEngine for Android Game Development Cookbook

Over 70 highly effective recipes with real-world examples to get to grips with the powerful capabilities of AndEngine and GLES 2

Jayme Schroeder

Brian Broyles

[PACKT] open source
PUBLISHING   community experience distilled

BIRMINGHAM - MUMBAI

AndEngine for Android Game Development Cookbook

First published: January 2013

Production Reference: 1070113

Published by Packt Publishing Ltd.
Livery Place
35 Livery Street
Birmingham B3 2PB, UK.

ISBN 978-1-84951-898-7

www.packtpub.com

Cover Image by Jayme Schroeder (jayme.schroeder@gmail.com)

Credits

Authors
Jayme Schroeder
Brian Broyles

Reviewers
Mateusz Mysliwiec
Sergio Viudes Carbonell
Jafar Abdulrasoul [Jimmar]

Acquisition Editor
Kartikey Pandey

Lead Technical Editor
Sweny M. Sukumaran

Technical Editors
Sharvari Baet
Dominic Pereira

Project Coordinator
Priya Sharma

Proofreader
Kevin McGowan

Indexer
Rekha Nair

Graphics
Aditi Gajjar

Production Coordinator
Shantanu Zagade

Cover Work
Shantanu Zagade

About the Authors

Jayme Schroeder was introduced to computers at a very young age. By 11, he had started creating modifications and level packs for his favorite game. By age 16, he had found his true passion in game development and network programming in C++ and OpenGL. In early 2011, Jayme had received an Android smartphone and immediately fell in love with the development experience. Since then, he has been researching and developing for the Android platform on a daily basis.

There are many people I would like to thank for the opportunity to write this book and also thank those who helped me out every step of the way.

First and foremost, I would like to thank Packt Publishing for the acceptance of *AndEngine for Android Game Development Cookbook* and Amber D'souza for first approaching me with the opportunity to write this book. I would also like to thank Kartikey Pandey, Michelle Quadros, Sweny Sukumaran, Priya Sharma from Packt Publishing who all played a large part in making the writing process much easier than anticipated and comfortable for me. I would also like to thank Dominic Pereira and Sharvari Baet for the effort they've put in throughout the production stage and the suggestions they've made.

I would like to thank Nicolas Gramlich for creating AndEngine. Not only has he created an amazing engine for novice and advanced developers alike, but he's created a great community for Android developers to both learn and strengthen their development skills relating to game development.

I would like to also thank my co-author, Brian Broyles, for his contributions and commitment
to the book. It's been an honor to share the experience with him.

Finally, I would like to thank all of my family and friends who showed their support and provided feedback during this experience. More specifically, I would like to thank Kent and Judy Schroeder; my parents, Shannon, Hollie, Taylor, and Brittanie; my brothers and sisters and my girlfriend, Krystal Guevremont. Of my friends, I would like to specifically thank Leo Wandersleb and Jordi Puigdellívol, with whom I've spent many days discussing the finer details of AndEngine which greatly helped to improve my knowledge.

Brian Broyles is a freelance programmer and 2D/3D graphic designer with over 12 years of experience. Before entering the mobile development industry in 2010 as the lead programmer of IFL Game Studio, he designed advanced artificial intelligence systems and graphical effects for interactive PC applications. In addition to his vast programming and design experience, he is also a commercial pilot, instrument flight instructor, and advanced instrument ground instructor.

I'd like to thank my amazing, beautiful wife, Bethany, for her support and enthusiasm as well as my family for encouraging me in all of my endeavors.

About the Reviewers

Mateusz Mysliwiec was born 1993 in Tarnow, Poland, graduating from high school in 2012. He currently lives in England. During his last year of high school, he decided that he would like to study Software Engineering or a different subject connected with math, programming, and engineering. He is also an independent game developer. In his free time, he develops professional mobile games focusing especially on the Android platform. His goal is to permanently impact the global mobile gaming industry in the near future. He is active in a variety of projects, including open source. His passions away from game development are sports and recreation such as football, skydiving, and jogging. His family and friends are the important aspects of his life.

Sergio Viudes is a 30 years old software developer from Elche (Spain). He works developing commercial web apps, and develops video games for Android in his free time.

He likes to play video games since childhood. He started playing with his brother's Spectrum when he was 5 years old. When he bought his first PC (well, his parents did), he was 14 years old, and started learning computer programming, computer drawing, and music composing (using the famous "FastTracker 2"). When he finished high school, he studied Computer Science at the University of Alicante.

His interest in mobile devices started with his first smart phone, ten years ago (2002), when he bought the first Symbian device from Nokia, the Nokia 7650. He really liked the idea that he could develop software that could run everywhere. So, along with his studies and his job, Sergio started creating simple mobile apps for his phone. About two years ago he decided to create his first video game for mobile devices. He really enjoys developing for mobile devices, he likes to compose music, he likes to draw, and, of course, he likes to play video games. So he decided to put all his hobbies together and develop his first video game for his favorite mobile platform—Android.

So far Sergio has released 3 games and he continues developing apps and games for Android as a hobby. He wishes that someday it will be his job, not just a hobby.

Jafar Abdulrasoul—a graduate from the Kuwait University—is a Computer Engineer and an Android game enthusiast who wrote a couple of excellent tutorials on his blog about creating games using AndEngine. He is known online by the name Jimmar.

My gratitude goes to my mother who tries to support me in everything I do, so thank you mama!

www.PacktPub.com

Support files, eBooks, discount offers and more

You might want to visit www.PacktPub.com for support files and downloads related to your book.

Did you know that Packt offers eBook versions of every book published, with PDF and ePub files available? You can upgrade to the eBook version at www.PacktPub.com and as a print book customer, you are entitled to a discount on the eBook copy. Get in touch with us at service@packtpub.com for more details.

At www.PacktPub.com, you can also read a collection of free technical articles, sign up for a range of free newsletters and receive exclusive discounts and offers on Packt books and eBooks.

http://PacktLib.PacktPub.com

Do you need instant solutions to your IT questions? PacktLib is Packt's online digital book library. Here, you can access, read and search across Packt's entire library of books.

Why Subscribe?

- ▸ Fully searchable across every book published by Packt
- ▸ Copy and paste, print and bookmark content
- ▸ On demand and accessible via web browser

Free Access for Packt account holders

If you have an account with Packt at www.PacktPub.com, you can use this to access PacktLib today and view nine entirely free books. Simply use your login credentials for immediate access.

Table of Contents

Preface

AndEngine is an excellent, full-featured, free, and open source 2D framework for the Android platform. It is one of few 2D frameworks for the Android platform which is consistently being used to create stylish and fun games by both independent and professional developers alike, and has even been used in some of the most successful games on the market to date. However, it takes more than just using a specific framework to achieve success.

AndEngine for Android Game Development Cookbook provides many informative walkthroughs relating to the most important aspects of AndEngine at a general game-programming level. The book covers everything from the life cycle of an AndEngine game to placing sprites on the scene and moving them around, all the way through to creating destructible objects and raycasting techniques. Even more importantly, this book is entirely based on AndEngine's latest and most efficient Anchor-Center branch.

What this book covers

Chapter 1, AndEngine Game Structure, covers the important aspects of game development with AndEngine regarding the core components that most games need to survive. Everything from audio, textures, the AndEngine life cycle, saving/loading game data, and more, are covered in this chapter.

Chapter 2, Working with Entities, begins to familiarize us with AndEngine's `Entity` class as well as its subtypes, such as sprites, text, primitives, and more. The `Entity` class is the core component of AndEngine that allows objects in code to be displayed onscreen. More specifically, this chapter includes a list of the most important methods included in the `Entity` class in order to allow us to take full control over how our entities act, react, or simply what they will look like.

Chapter 3, Designing Your Menu, introduces some of the more common aspects of menu design in mobile games. The topics covered in this chapter include creating buttons, adding theme music to the menu, creating parallax backgrounds, and menu screen navigation. The topics found within this chapter can easily be used in other areas of a game as well.

Chapter 4, Working with Cameras, discusses the various options included in AndEngine when it comes to how the game camera and engine view the game's scene. We begin by going over the different types of camera objects available to us in order to give us a proper understanding of the benefits of each for an informative decision. From there, we continue on to cover camera movement and zooming, creating extra large backgrounds, creating a heads-up-display, and even go as far as introducing the split screen game engine for more complex game design.

Chapter 5, Scene and Layer Management, shows how to create a robust scene manager framework that incorporates scene-specific loading screens and animated layers. The managed scenes in this chapter utilize a resource manager and are extremely customizable.

Chapter 6, Applications of Physics, explores the various techniques used to create an AndEngine physics simulation with the Box2D physics extension. The recipes in this chapter cover the basic setup for a Box2D physics world: body types, category filtering, bodies with multiple fixtures, polygon-based bodies, forces, joints, rag dolls, rope, collision events, destructible objects, and raycasting.

Chapter 7, Working with Update Handlers, demonstrates the use of update handlers that are called once per engine update. The recipes in this chapter show how to register entity-based update handlers, conditional updating, and the creation of a game timer.

Chapter 8, Maximizing Performance, introduces some of the most beneficial, high-level practices to follow when it comes to improving the performance of any Android game. This chapter covers optimization techniques involving audio, graphical/rendering, and general memory management to help alleviate performance issues where necessary.

Chapter 9, AndEngine Extensions Overview, is where we discuss some of the more popular AndEngine extensions which can be beneficial to a project, depending on the game. These extensions may not be for everyone, but for those interested, this chapter includes insight on how we can go about creating live wallpapers, multiplayer components via networking servers and clients, creating high resolution SVG textures, and color mapping textures.

Chapter 10, Getting More From AndEngine, provides several useful recipes that expand upon the concepts presented in the previous chapters. The recipes in this chapter include batch texture-loading, textured meshes, autonomous shadows, moving platforms, and rope bridges.

Appendix A, Source Code for MagneTank, outlines the game, MagneTank, with class-by-class descriptions to show how a full game made with AndEngine can be set up. The game includes many of the recipes found throughout the chapters, and the source code is available with the bundled code.

Appendix B, Additional Recipes, is not present in the book but is available as a free download from the following link: `http://downloads.packtpub.com/sites/default/files/downloads/8987OS_AppB_Final.pdf`.

What you need for this book

AndEngine for Android Game Development Cookbook is useful for the majority of AndEngine developers. Starting with the first few chapters, the reader will begin to work with the basics of AndEngine, and even intermediate developers will find useful tips throughout these chapters. As the reader progresses through the chapters, topics that are more difficult will be covered so it is important that beginners do not skip ahead. Additionally, intermediate developers who have not yet made the transition to AndEngine's latest development branch will find useful information throughout the book on the differences between the GLES1/GLES2 branches versus the Anchor-Center branch discussed in this book.

A fundamental understanding of the Java programming language is suggested.

The software required in order to execute the various topics in this book include the Eclipse IDE for building and compiling the code, GIMP for image drawing/editing, and Inkscape for SVG drawing/editing. Please feel free to use alternatives to these products if you are more comfortable with them. Additionally, this book assumes the reader has obtained the required libraries, including AndEngine and its various extensions prior to working with the recipes.

Who this book is for

AndEngine for Android Game Development Cookbook is geared toward developers who are interested in working with the most up-to-date version of AndEngine, sporting the brand new GLES 2.0 Anchor-Center branch. The book will be helpful for developers who are attempting to break into the mobile game market intending to release fun and exciting games while eliminating a large portion of the learning curve that is otherwise inevitable when getting into AndEngine development.

Conventions

In this book, you will find a number of styles of text that distinguish between different kinds of information. Here are some examples of these styles, and an explanation of their meaning.

Code words in text are shown as follows: " To start with the absolute most basic `Entity` method, we will attach an `Entity` object to a `Scene` object."

A block of code is set as follows:

```
float baseBufferData[] = {
    /* First Triangle */
    0, BASE_HEIGHT, UNUSED, /* first point */
    BASE_WIDTH, BASE_HEIGHT, UNUSED, /* second point */
    BASE_WIDTH, 0, UNUSED,    /* third point */

    /* Second Triangle */
    BASE_WIDTH, 0, UNUSED, /* first point */
```

```
      0, 0, UNUSED, /* second point */
      0, BASE_HEIGHT, UNUSED, /* third point */
};
```

> Warnings or important notes appear in a box like this.

> Tips and tricks appear like this.

Reader feedback

Feedback from our readers is always welcome. Let us know what you think about this book—what you liked or may have disliked. Reader feedback is important for us to develop titles that you really get the most out of.

To send us general feedback, simply send an e-mail to feedback@packtpub.com, and mention the book title via the subject of your message.

If there is a topic that you have expertise in and you are interested in either writing or contributing to a book, see our author guide on www.packtpub.com/authors.

Customer support

Now that you are the proud owner of a Packt book, we have a number of things to help you to get the most from your purchase.

Downloading the example code

You can download the example code files for all Packt books you have purchased from your account at http://www.PacktPub.com. If you purchased this book elsewhere, you can visit http://www.PacktPub.com/support and register to have the files e-mailed directly to you.

Errata

Although we have taken every care to ensure the accuracy of our content, mistakes do happen. If you find a mistake in one of our books—maybe a mistake in the text or the code—we would be grateful if you would report this to us. By doing so, you can save other readers from frustration and help us improve subsequent versions of this book. If you find any errata, please report them by visiting `http://www.packtpub.com/support`, selecting your book, clicking on the **errata submission form** link, and entering the details of your errata. Once your errata are verified, your submission will be accepted and the errata will be uploaded on our website, or added to any list of existing errata, under the Errata section of that title. Any existing errata can be viewed by selecting your title from `http://www.packtpub.com/support`.

Piracy

Piracy of copyright material on the Internet is an ongoing problem across all media. At Packt, we take the protection of our copyright and licenses very seriously. If you come across any illegal copies of our works, in any form, on the Internet, please provide us with the location address or website name immediately so that we can pursue a remedy.

Please contact us at `copyright@packtpub.com` with a link to the suspected pirated material.

We appreciate your help in protecting our authors, and our ability to bring you valuable content.

Questions

You can contact us at `questions@packtpub.com` if you are having a problem with any aspect of the book, and we will do our best to address it.

1
AndEngine Game Structure

In this chapter, we're going to take a look at the main components needed for structuring a game in **AndEngine**. The topics include:

- ▶ Know the life cycle
- ▶ Choosing our engine type
- ▶ Selecting a resolution policy
- ▶ Creating object factories
- ▶ Creating the game manager
- ▶ Introducing sounds and music
- ▶ Working with different types of textures
- ▶ Applying texture options
- ▶ Using AndEngine font resources
- ▶ Creating the resource manager
- ▶ Saving and loading game data

Introduction

The most appealing aspect of AndEngine is the incredible ease of creating games. The possibility of designing and coding a game in a matter of weeks after first looking into AndEngine is not too farfetched, but that's not to say it will be a perfect game. The coding process can be a tedious task when we do not understand how the engine works. It is a good idea to understand the main building blocks of AndEngine and the game structure in order to create precise, organized, and expandable projects.

In this chapter, we're going to go over a few of the most necessary components of AndEngine and general game programming. We're going to take a look at some classes that will aid us in quickly and efficiently creating a foundation for all sorts of games. Additionally, we'll cover some of the differences between resources and object types, which play the biggest role in shaping the overall look and feel of our games. It is encouraged to keep tabs on this chapter as reference if needed.

Know the life cycle

It is important to understand the order of operations when it comes to the initialization of our games. The basic needs for a game include creating the engine, loading the game's resources, and setting up the initial screen and settings. This is all it takes in order to create the foundation for an AndEngine game. However, if we plan on more diversity within our games, it is wise to get to know the full life cycle included in AndEngine.

Getting ready

Please refer to the class named `PacktRecipesActivity` in the code bundle.

How to do it...

The AndEngine life cycle includes a few methods that we are responsible for defining directly. These methods include creating the `EngineOptions` object, creating the `Scene` object, and populating the scene with child entities. These methods are called in the following order:

1. Define the `onCreateEngineOptions()` method:

```
@Override
public EngineOptions onCreateEngineOptions() {

  // Define our mCamera object
  mCamera = new Camera(0, 0, WIDTH, HEIGHT);

  // Declare & Define our engine options to be applied to our
Engine object
  EngineOptions engineOptions = new EngineOptions(true,
      ScreenOrientation.LANDSCAPE_FIXED, new
FillResolutionPolicy(),
      mCamera);

  // It is necessary in a lot of applications to define the
following
  // wake lock options in order to disable the device's display
  // from turning off during gameplay due to inactivity
```

```
engineOptions.setWakeLockOptions(WakeLockOptions.SCREEN_ON);

    // Return the engineOptions object, passing it to the engine
    return engineOptions;
}
```

2. Define the onCreateResources() method:

```
@Override
public void onCreateResources(
    OnCreateResourcesCallback pOnCreateResourcesCallback) {

    /* We should notify the pOnCreateResourcesCallback that we've
finished
     * loading all of the necessary resources in our game AFTER
they are loaded.
     * onCreateResourcesFinished() should be the last method
called.  */
    pOnCreateResourcesCallback.onCreateResourcesFinished();
}
```

3. Define the onCreateScene() method:

```
@Override
public void onCreateScene(OnCreateSceneCallback
pOnCreateSceneCallback) {
    // Create the Scene object
    mScene = new Scene();

    // Notify the callback that we're finished creating the scene,
returning
    // mScene to the mEngine object (handled automatically)
    pOnCreateSceneCallback.onCreateSceneFinished(mScene);
}
```

4. Define the onPopulateScene() method:

```
@Override
public void onPopulateScene(Scene pScene,
    OnPopulateSceneCallback pOnPopulateSceneCallback) {

    // onPopulateSceneFinished(), similar to the resource and scene
callback
    // methods, should be called once we are finished populating the
scene.
    pOnPopulateSceneCallback.onPopulateSceneFinished();
}
```

How it works...

The code found in this recipe's class is the foundation for any AndEngine game. We've set up a main activity class which serves as the entry point into our application. The activity contains the four main methods included in AndEngine's activity life cycle that we are responsible for, beginning with creating the `EngineOptions` options, creating the resources, creating the scene, and populating the scene.

In the first step, we are overriding the Engine's `onCreateEngineOptions()` method. Inside this method, our main focus is to instantiate our `Camera` object as well as our `EngineOptions` object. These two object's constructors allow us to define the display properties of our application. Additionally, we've disabled the screen from automatically turning off during application inactivity via the `engineOptions.setWakeLockOptions(WakeLockOptions.SCREEN_ON)` method call.

In step two, we continue to override the `onCreateResources()` method, which gives us a specified method for creating and setting up any resources needed within our game. These resources may include textures, sounds and music, and fonts. In this step and the following two, we are required to make a call to the respective method callbacks in order to proceed through the application's life cycle. For the `onCreateResources()` method, we must call `pOnCreateResourcesCallback.onCreateResourcesFinished()`, which should be included at the end of the method.

Step three involves instantiating and setting up the `Scene` object. Setting up the Scene can be as simple as displayed in this recipe, or for more complex projects, it may include setting up touch event listeners, update handlers, and more. Once we've finished setting up the Scene, we must make a call to the `pOnCreateSceneCallback.onCreateSceneFinished(mScene)` method, passing our newly created `mScene` object to the Engine to be displayed on the device.

The final step to take care of includes defining the `onPopulateScene()` method. This method is in place specifically for attaching child entities to the Scene. As with the previous two steps, we must make a call to `pOnPopulateSceneCallback.onPopulateSceneFinished()` in order to proceed with the remaining AndEngine life cycle calls.

In the following list, we will cover the life cycle methods in the order they are called from the start up of an activity to the time it is terminated.

The life cycle calls during launch are as follows:

- `onCreate`: This method is the Android SDK's native application entry point. In AndEngine development, this method simply calls the `onCreateEngineOptions()` method in our `BaseGameActivity` class then applies the returned options to the game engine.

- ▶ onResume: This is another Android SDK native method. Here, we simply acquire the wake lock settings from our EngineOptions object and proceed to call the onResume() method for the engine's RenderSurfaceView object.

- ▶ onSurfaceCreated: This method will either call onCreateGame() during the initial startup process of our activity or register a Boolean variable as true for resource reloading if the activity had previously been deployed.

- ▶ onReloadResources: This method reloads our game resources if our application is brought back into focus from minimization. This method is not called on the initial execution of an application.

- ▶ onCreateGame: This is in place to handle the order of execution of the next three callbacks in the AndEngine life cycle.

- ▶ onCreateResources: This method allows us to declare and define our application's initial resources needed during the launch of our activity. These resources include, but are not limited to, textures, sounds and music, and fonts.

- ▶ onCreateScene: Here, we handle the initialization of our activity's Scene object. It is possible to attach entities to the Scene within this method, but for the sake of keeping things organized, it's usually best to attach entities within onPopulateScene().

- ▶ onPopulateScene: In the onPopuplateScene() method of the life cycle we are just about finished setting up the scene, though there are still a few life cycle calls which will be handled automatically by the Engine. This method should be used to define the visual result of the Scene when our application first starts up. Note that the Scene is already created and applied to the Engine at this point. It is possible in some cases to see the entities being attached to the Scene if there is no loading screen or splash screen in place and if there are a large number of entities to attach.

- ▶ onGameCreated: It signals that the onCreateGame() sequence has finished, reloading resources if necessary, otherwise doing nothing. Reloading resources depends on the Boolean variable briefly mentioned in the onSurfaceCreated method five life cycle calls back.

- ▶ onSurfaceChanged: This method is called every time our application's orientation changes from landscape to portrait mode or vice versa.

- ▶ onResumeGame: Here we have the final method call which takes place during an activity's startup cycle. If our activity reaches this point without any problems, the engine's start() method is called, bringing the game's update thread to life.

The life cycle calls during minimization/termination are as follows:

- ▶ onPause: The first method call when an activity is minimized or terminated. This is the native android pause method which calls the pause method for the RenderSurfaceView objects and reverts the wake lock settings applied by the game engine.

- **onPauseGame**: Next, AndEngine's implementation of `onPause()` which simply calls the `stop()` method on the Engine, causing all of the Engine's update handlers to halt along with the update thread.

- **onDestroy**: In the `onDestroy()` method, AndEngine clears all graphical resources contained within `ArrayList` objects held by the Engine's manager classes. These managers include the `VertexBufferObjectManager` class, the `FontManager` class, the `ShaderProgramManager` class, and finally the `TextureManager` class.

- **onDestroyResources**: This method name may be a little misleading since we've already unloaded the majority of resources in `onDestroy()`. What this method really does is release all of the sound and music objects stored within the respective managers by calling their `releaseAll()` methods.

- **onGameDestroyed**: Finally, we reach the last method call required during a full AndEngine life cycle. Not a whole lot of action takes place in this method. AndEngine simply sets an `mGameCreated` Boolean variable used in the Engine to `false`, which states that the activity is no longer running.

In the following image, we can see what the life cycle looks like in action when the game is created, minimized, or destroyed:

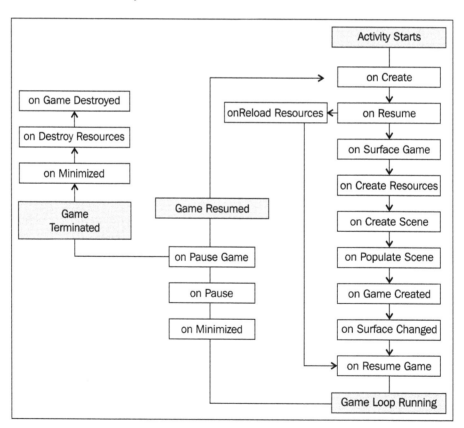

Due to the asynchronous nature of the AndEngine life cycle, it is possible for some methods to be executed multiple times during a single startup instance. The occurrence of these events varies between devices.

There's more...

In the previous section of this recipe, we covered the main `BaseGameActivity` class. The following classes can be used as alternatives to the `BaseGameActivity` class, each providing their own slight differences.

The LayoutGameActivity class

The `LayoutGameActivity` class is a useful activity class that allows us to incorporate the AndEngine scene-graph view into an ordinary Android application. On the other hand, with this class we are also able to include native Android SDK views, such as buttons, seek bars, spinners, additional layouts, or any other view into our game. However, the most popular reason for using this sort of activity is to allow easy implementation of advertisements into games for a means to gain revenue.

There are a few additional steps for setting up a `LayoutGameActivity` class.

1. Add the following line to the project's default layout XML file. This file is usually called `main.xml`. The following code snippet adds the AndEngine `RenderSurfaceView` class to our layout file. This is the view that will display our game on the device:

   ```
   <org.andengine.opengl.view.RenderSurfaceView
   android:id="@+id/gameSurfaceView"
   android:layout_width="fill_parent"
   android:layout_height="fill_parent"/>
   ```

2. The second and final additional step for this activity type is to reference the layout XML file and `RenderSurfaceView` in step one, in the `LayoutGameActivity` overridden methods. The following code is assuming the layout file is called `main.xml` in the `res/layout/` folder; in which case they can be copied/pasted into our `LayoutGameActivity` class after step one has been completed:

   ```
   @Override
   protected int getLayoutID() {
     return R.layout.main;
   }

   @Override
   protected int getRenderSurfaceViewID() {
     return R.id.gameSurfaceView;
   }
   ```

The SimpleBaseGameActivity and SimpleLayoutGameActivity classes

The SimpleBaseGameActivity and the SimpleLayoutGameActivity classes, as suggested, make the overridden life cycle methods somewhat easier to deal with. They do not require us to override the onPopulateScene() method and on top of that, we are not required to make calls to the method callbacks when we are finished defining the overridden methods. With these activity types, we can simply add the unimplemented life cycle methods and AndEngine will handle the callbacks for us.

The SimpleAsyncGameActivity class

The final game activity class we will talk about is the SimpleAsyncGameActivity class. This class includes three alternative life cycle methods called onCreateResourcesAsync(), onCreateSceneAsync(), and onPopulateSceneAsync() along with the usual onCreateEngineOptions() method. The main difference between this activity and others is that it provides us with loading bars for each of the "Async" methods. The following snippet shows how we can increment the loading bar in the event of a texture being loaded:

```
@Override
public void onCreateResourcesAsync(IProgressListener
pProgressListener)
    throws Exception {

  // Load texture number one
  pProgressListener.onProgressChanged(10);

  // Load texture number two
  pProgressListener.onProgressChanged(20);

  // Load texture number three
  pProgressListener.onProgressChanged(30);

  // We can continue to set progress to whichever value we'd like
  // for each additional step through onCreateResourcesAsync...
}
```

Downloading the example code

You can download the example code files for all Packt books you have purchased from your account at http://www.PacktPub.com. If you purchased this book elsewhere, you can visit http://www.PacktPub.com/support and register to have the files e-mailed directly to you.

Choosing our engine type

Before we start programming our game, it is a good idea to come up with the performance needs of the game. AndEngine includes a few different types of engines we can choose to use, each with their own benefits. The benefits, of course, depend on the type of game we plan to create.

Getting ready

Carry out the *Know the life cycle* recipe in this chapter to get a basic AndEngine project set up in our IDE, then continue on to the *How to do it...* section.

How to do it...

In order for us to properly define a specific `Engine` object for our game to use, we must override the `onCreateEngine()` method, which is part of AndEngine's startup process. Add the following code to any base AndEngine activity in order to handle the Engine's creation manually:

```
/* The onCreateEngine method allows us to return a 'customized' Engine
object
* to the Activity which for the most part affects the way frame
updates are
* handled. Depending on the Engine object used, the overall feel of
the
* gameplay can alter drastically.
*/
@Override
public Engine onCreateEngine(EngineOptions pEngineOptions) {
  return super.onCreateEngine(pEngineOptions);
  /* The returned super method above simply calls:
      return new Engine(pEngineOptions);
  */
}
```

How it works...

The following is an overview of the various `Engine` objects available in AndEngine, as well as a brief code snippet displaying how to set up each of the `Engine` objects:

- ► `Engine`: First and foremost, we have the ordinary `Engine` object. The `Engine` object is not ideal for most game development as it has absolutely no limitations in regards to frames per second. On two separate devices, it is very likely that you will notice differences in the speed of the game. One way to think of this is if two separate devices are watching a video which was started at the same time, the faster device is likely to finish the video first rather than both finishing at the same time. For this reason, noticeable issues can arise in devices which might not run as fast, especially when physics are a big part of the game. There are no extra steps involved in incorporating this type of engine into our game.

▶ `FixedStepEngine`: The second type of engine we have at our disposal is the `FixedStepEngine`. This is the ideal engine used in game development as it forces the game loop to update at a constant speed regardless of the device. This is done by updating the game based on the time passed rather than the device's ability to execute code faster. `FixedStepEngine` requires us to pass the `EngineOptions` object, as well as an `int` value, in that order. The `int` value defines the number of steps per second that the engine will be forced to run at. The following code creates an engine that will run at a constant `60` steps per second:

```
@Override
public Engine onCreateEngine(EngineOptions pEngineOptions) {
  // Create a fixed step engine updating at 60 steps per second
    return new FixedStepEngine(pEngineOptions, 60);
  }
```

▶ `LimitedFPSEngine`: The `LimitedFPSEngine` engine allows us to set a limit on the frames per second that the Engine will run at. This will cause the Engine to do some internal calculations, and if the difference between the preferred FPS is greater than the current FPS that the Engine is achieving, the Engine will wait a fraction of a second before proceeding with the next update. `LimitedFPSEngine` requires two parameters in the constructor, including the `EngineOptions` object and an `int` value specifying the maximum frames per second. The following code creates an engine that will run at a maximum of 60 frames per second:

```
@Override
public Engine onCreateEngine(EngineOptions pEngineOptions) {
  // Create a limited FPS engine, which will run at a maximum of
60 FPS
    return new LimitedFPSEngine(pEngineOptions, 60);
}
```

▶ `SingleSceneSplitScreenEngine` and `DoubleSceneSplitScreenEngine`: The `SingleSceneSplitScreenEngine` engine and `DoubleSceneSplitScreenEngine` engine allow us to create a game with two separate cameras, either with a single scene, most generally used for single player games, or two scenes for multiplayer games on a single device. These are just examples, however, but these two engine's can have a wide range of uses, including mini-maps, multiple perspectives, menu systems, and much more. See *Chapter 4, Creating a Split-screen Game*, for more specific details on setting up these types of `Engine` objects.

Selecting a resolution policy

Choosing a resolution policy can be a sensitive topic, especially since we're dealing with a platform which currently runs on devices ranging from 3-inch displays up to 10.1-inch for the most part. Generally developers and users alike prefer that a game takes up the full width and height of the device's display, but in some cases our resolution policy may need to be carefully selected in order to properly display our scenes as we—the developer—see fit. In this recipe, we're going to discuss the various resolution policies included in AndEngine, which will help us decide which policy might best fit our application's needs.

How to do it...

The resolution policy that we choose to adhere to must be included as a parameter in the `EngineOptions` constructor which is created in the `onCreateEngineOptions()` method of AndEngine's life cycle. The following code creates our `EngineOptions` object using the `FillResolutionPolicy` class, which will be explained later in the chapter:

```
EngineOptions engineOptions = new EngineOptions(true,
    ScreenOrientation.LANDSCAPE_FIXED, new FillResolutionPolicy(),
    mCamera);
```

We can select a different resolution policy by simply passing another variation of the resolution policy classes to this constructor.

How it works...

The following is an overview of AndEngine's `BaseResolutionPolicy` subtypes. These policies are used to specify how AndEngine will handle our application's display width and height based on various factors:

- ▶ `FillResolutionPolicy`: The `FillResolutionPolicy` class is the typical resolution policy if we simply want our application to take up the full width and height of the display. While this policy allows our application to run in true full screen mode, it may cause some noticeable stretching in order for our scene to take up the full available dimensions of the display. We can select this resolution policy by simply including `new FillResolutionPolicy()` as our resolution policy parameter in the `EngineOptions` constructor.

- ▶ `FixedResolutionPolicy`: The `FixedResolutionPolicy` class allows us to apply a fixed display size for our application, regardless of the size of the device's display or `Camera` object dimensions. This policy can be passed to `EngineOptions` via `new FixedResolutionPolicy(pWidth, pHeight)`, where `pWidth` defines the final width that the application's view will cover, and `pHeight` defines the final height that the application's view will cover. For example, if we pass a width of `800` and a height of `480` to this policy-types constructor, on a tablet with a resolution of 1280 x 752, we'd be left with an empty black area since there will be no compensation between the resolution policy and the actual display size.

- ▶ `RatioResolutionPolicy`: The `RatioResolutionPolicy` class is the best choice for resolution policies if we need to obtain the maximum display size without causing any distortion of sprites. On the other hand, due to the wide range of Android devices spanning many display sizes, it is possible that some devices may see "black bars" either on the top and bottom, or left and right sides of the display. This resolution policy's constructor can be passed either a `float` value, which defines a preferred ratio value for the display dimensions, or a width and a height parameter from which a ratio value will be extracted by dividing the width by the height. For example, `new RatioResolutionPolicy(1.6f)` to define a ratio, or `new RatioResolutionPolicy(mCameraWidth, mCameraHeight)`, assuming `mCameraWidth` and `mCameraHeight` are the defined `Camera` object dimensions.

- ▶ `RelativeResolutionPolicy`: This is the final resolution policy. This policy allows us to apply scaling, either larger or smaller, to the overall application view based on a scaling factor with `1f` being the default value. We can apply general scaling to the view with the constructor—`new RelativeResolutionPolicy(1.5f)`—which will increase the scale of both the width and height by `1.5` times, or we can specify individual width and height scales, for example, `new RelativeResolutionPolicy(1.5f, 0.5f)`. One thing to note with this policy is that we must be careful with the scaling factors, as scaling too large will cause an application to close without warning. Try to keep the scaling factor to less than `1.8f`; otherwise make sure to do extensive testing on various devices.

Creating object factories

Object factories are a useful design pattern used in all sorts of areas in programming. In game development specifically, a factory might be used to spawn enemy objects, spawn bullet objects, particle effects, item objects, and much more. In fact, AndEngine even uses the factory pattern when we create sounds, music, textures, and fonts, among other things. In this recipe, we'll find out how we can create an object factory and discuss how we can use them to provide simplicity in object creation within our own projects.

Getting ready

Please refer to the class named `ObjectFactory` in the code bundle.

How to do it...

In this recipe, we're using the `ObjectFactory` class as a way for us to easily create and return subtypes of the `BaseObject` class. However, in a real-world project, the factory would not normally contain inner classes.

1. Before we create our object factory, we should create our base class as well as at least a couple subtypes extending the base class:

```
public static class BaseObject {

   /* The mX and mY variables have no real purpose in this recipe,
however in
    * a real factory class, member variables might be used to
define position,
    * color, scale, and more, of a sprite or other entity.   */
   private int mX;
   private int mY;

   // BaseObject constructor, all subtypes should define an mX and
mY value on creation
   BaseObject(final int pX, final int pY){
      this.mX = pX;
      this.mY = pY;
   }
}
```

2. Once we've got a base class with any number of subtypes, we can now start to consider implementing the factory design pattern. The `ObjectFactory` class contains the methods which will handle creating and returning objects of types `LargeObject` and `SmallObject` in this case:

```
public class ObjectFactory {

   // Return a new LargeObject with the defined 'x' and 'y' member
variables.
   public static LargeObject createLargeObject(final int pX, final
int pY){
      return new LargeObject(pX, pY);
   }
```

```
    // Return a new SmallObject with the defined 'x' and 'y' member
    variables.
    public static SmallObject createSmallObject(final int pX, final
int pY){
        return new SmallObject(pX, pY);
    }
}
```

How it works...

In the first step of this recipe, we are creating a `BaseObject` class. This class includes two member variables called `mX` and `mY`, which we can imagine would define the position on the device's display if we are dealing with AndEngine entities. Once we've got our base class set up, we can start creating subtypes of the base class. The `BaseObject` class in this recipe has two inner classes which extend it, one named `LargeObject` and the other, `SmallObject`. The object factory's job is to determine which subtype of the base class that we need to create, as well as define the object's properties, or `mX` and `mY` member variables in this instance.

In the second step, we are taking a look at the `ObjectFactory` code. This class should contain any and all variations for object creation relating to the specific object-types that the factory deals with. In this case, the two separate objects simply require an `mX` and `mY` variable to be defined. In a real-world situation, we may find it helpful to create a `SpriteFactory` class. This class might contain a few different methods for creating ordinary sprites, button sprites, or tiled sprites, via `SpriteFactory.createSprite()`, `SpriteFactory.createButtonSprite()`, and `SpriteFactory.createTiledSprite()`. On top of that, each of these methods would probably require parameters that define the position, scale, texture region, color, and more. The most important aspect to this class is that its methods return a new subtype of an object as this is the whole purpose behind the factory class.

Creating the game manager

The game manager is an important part of most games. A game manager is a class that should contain data relating to gameplay; including, but not limited to keeping track of score, credits/currency, player health, and other general gameplay information. In this topic, we're going to take a look at a game manager class to gain an understanding of how they work into our game structure.

Getting ready

Please refer to the class named `GameManager` in the code bundle.

How to do it...

The game manager we're going to introduce will be following the singleton design pattern. This means that we will only create a single instance of the class throughout the entire application life cycle and we can access its methods across our entire project. Follow these steps:

1. Create the game manager singleton:

    ```
    private static GameManager INSTANCE;

    // The constructor does not do anything for this singleton
    GameManager(){
    }

    public static GameManager getInstance(){
      if(INSTANCE == null){
        INSTANCE = new GameManager();
      }
      return INSTANCE;
    }
    ```

2. Create the member variables with corresponding getters and setters which should keep track of gameplay data:

    ```
    // get the current score
    public int getCurrentScore(){
      return this.mCurrentScore;
    }

    // get the bird count
    public int getBirdCount(){
      return this.mBirdCount;
    }

    // increase the current score, most likely when an enemy is
    destroyed
    public void incrementScore(int pIncrementBy){
      mCurrentScore += pIncrementBy;
    }

    // Any time a bird is launched, we decrement our bird count
    public void decrementBirdCount(){
      mBirdCount -= 1;
    }
    ```

3. Create a reset method that will revert all data back to their initial values:

```
// Resetting the game simply means we must revert back to initial
values.
public void resetGame(){
  this.mCurrentScore = GameManager.INITIAL_SCORE;
  this.mBirdCount = GameManager.INITIAL_BIRD_COUNT;
  this.mEnemyCount = GameManager.INITIAL_ENEMY_COUNT;
}
```

How it works...

Depending on the type of game being created, the game manager is bound to have different tasks. This recipe's `GameManager` class is meant to resemble that of a certain emotional bird franchise. We can see that the tasks involved in this particular `GameManager` class are limited, but as gameplay becomes more complex, the game manager will often grow as it has more info to keep track of.

In the first step for this recipe, we're setting up the `GameManager` class as a singleton. The singleton is a design pattern that is meant to ensure that there is only one static instance of this class that will be instantiated throughout the entire application's life cycle. Being static, this will allow us to make calls to the game manager's methods on a global level, meaning we can reach its methods from any class in our project without having to create a new `GameManager` class. In order to retrieve the `GameManager` class' instance, we can call `GameManager.getInstance()` in any of our project's classes. Doing so will assign a new `GameManager` class to `INSTANCE`, if the `GameManager` class has not yet been referenced. The `INSTANCE` object will then be returned, allowing us to make calls to the `GameManager` class' data-modifying methods, for example, `GameManager.getInstance().getCurrentScore()`.

In step two, we create the getter and setter methods that will be used to modify and obtain the data being stored in the `GameManager` class. The `GameManager` class in this recipe contains three `int` values that are used to keep track of important gameplay data; `mCurrentScore`, `mBirdCount`, and `mEnemyCount`. Each of these variables have their own corresponding getters and setters that allow us to easily make modifications to the game data. During gameplay, if an enemy happened to be destroyed then we could call `GameManager.getInstance().decrementEnemyCount()` along with `GameManager.getInstance().incrementScore(pValue)`, where `pValue` would likely be provided by the enemy object being destroyed.

The final step involved in setting up this game manager is to provide a reset method for game data. Since we are working with a singleton, whether we move from gameplay to the main menu, to the shop, or any other scene, our `GameManager` class' data will not automatically revert back to default values. This means that any time a level is reset, we must reset the game manager's data as well. In the `GameManager` class, we've set up a method called `resetGame()`, whose job is to simply revert data back to original values.

When starting a new level, we can call `GameManager.getInstance().resetGame()` in order to quickly revert all data back to the initial values. However, this is a general `GameManager` class and it is entirely up to the developer which data should be reset pending level reset or level loading. If the `GameManager` class is storing credit/currency data, it might be wise not to reset that particular variable back to default for use in a shop, for example.

Introducing sounds and music

Sound and music plays a big role in gameplay for the user. If used properly, they can give a game the extra edge it needs to allow the player to become fully immersed while playing. On the other hand, they can also cause annoyance and disapproval if used incorrectly. In this recipe, we're going to jump into the subject of `Sound` and `Music` objects in AndEngine, covering the "how-to's" of loading them through to modifying their rates and more.

Getting ready

Complete the *Know the life cycle* recipe given in this chapter, so that we've got a basic AndEngine project set up in our IDE. Additionally, we should create a new subfolder in our project's `assets/` folder. Name this folder as `sfx` and add a sound file named `sound.mp3` and another named `music.mp3`. Once this is done, continue on to the *How to do it...* section.

How to do it...

Perform the following steps to set up a game to use the `Sound` and `Music` objects. Note that `Sound` objects are meant for sound effects, such as explosions, collisions, or other short audio playback events. The `Music` objects are meant for long audio playback events such as looping menu music or game music.

1. The first step involves making sure that our `Engine` object recognizes that we plan to use `Sound` and `Music` objects in our game. Add the following lines in the `onCreateEngineOptions()` method of our activity's life cycle after the `EngineOptions` object has been created:

   ```
   engineOptions.getAudioOptions().setNeedsMusic(true);
   engineOptions.getAudioOptions().setNeedsSound(true);
   ```

2. In step two, we will set our asset paths for the sound and music factories, then load the `Sound` and `Music` objects. `Sound` and `Music` objects are resources, so as you may have guessed, the following code can be dropped into the `onCreateResources()` method of our activity's life cycle:

   ```
   /* Set the base path for our SoundFactory and MusicFactory to
    * define where they will look for audio files.
    */
   SoundFactory.setAssetBasePath("sfx/");
   ```

```
MusicFactory.setAssetBasePath("sfx/");

// Load our "sound.mp3" file into a Sound object
try {
  Sound mSound = SoundFactory.createSoundFromAsset(getSoundManag
er(), this, "sound.mp3");
} catch (IOException e) {
  e.printStackTrace();
}

// Load our "music.mp3" file into a music object
try {
  Music mMusic = MusicFactory.createMusicFromAsset(getMusicManag
er(), this, "music.mp3");
} catch (IOException e) {
  e.printStackTrace();
}
```

3. Once the `Sound` objects are loaded into the `SoundManager` class, we can play them as we see fit by calling `play()` on them, be it during a collision, button click, or otherwise:

```
// Play the mSound object
mSound.play();
```

4. The `Music` objects should be handled in a different manner to `Sound` objects. In cases where our `Music` object should loop continuously throughout the game, which is in most cases, we handle all `play()` and `pause()` methods within the activity life cycle:

```
/* Music objects which loop continuously should be played in
 * onResumeGame() of the activity life cycle
 */
@Override
public synchronized void onResumeGame() {
  if(mMusic != null && !mMusic.isPlaying()){
    mMusic.play();
  }

  super.onResumeGame();
}

/* Music objects which loop continuously should be paused in
 * onPauseGame() of the activity life cycle
 */
@Override
```

```
public synchronized void onPauseGame() {
  if(mMusic != null && mMusic.isPlaying()){
    mMusic.pause();
  }

  super.onPauseGame();
}
```

How it works...

In the first step for this recipe, we are required to let the Engine know whether we will be taking advantage of AndEngine's ability to play `Sound` or `Music` objects. Failing to address this step will cause an error in the application, so before we move forward in implementing audio into our game, make sure this step is done before returning `EngineOptions` in the `onCreateEngineOptions()` method.

In the second step, we are visiting the `onCreateResources()` method of the application's life cycle. Firstly, we are setting the base path of both `SoundFactory` and `MusicFactory`. As mentioned in the *Getting ready* section, we should have a folder for our audio files in the `assets/sfx` folder in our project, which includes all of our audio files. By calling `setAssetBasePath("sfx/")` on each of the two factory classes used for audio, we are now pointing to the proper folder to look for audio files. Once this is done, we can load our `Sound` objects through the use of the `SoundFactory` class and `Music` objects through the use of the `MusicFactory` class. The `Sound` and `Music` objects require us to pass the following parameters: `mEngine.getSoundManager()` or `mEngine.getMusicManager()` depending on the type of audio object we're loading, the `Context` class which is `BaseGameActivity`, or this activity, and the name of the audio file in string format.

In the third step, we can now call the `play()` method on the audio object that we wish to play. However, this method should only be called after the `onCreateResources()` callback has been notified that all resources have been loaded. To be safe, we should simply not play any `Sound` or `Music` objects until after the `onCreateResources()` portion of AndEngine's life cycle.

In the final step, we are setting up our `Music` object to call its `play()` method when our activity starts up and `onResumeGame()` is called from the life cycle. On the other end, during `onPauseGame()`, the `Music` object's `pause()` method is called. It is best practice in most cases to set our `Music` objects up this way, especially due to the eventual inevitability of application interruptions, such as phone calls or accidental pop-up clicking. This approach will allow our `Music` object to automatically be paused when the application leaves focus and start back up once we return from minimization, including execution.

In this recipe, and others relating to resource loading, the names of
the files have been hardcoded in to the code snippets. This is done to
add simplicity, but it is advisable to use the `strings.xml` Android
resource file provided for our project in order to keep strings organized
and easy to manage.

There's more...

AndEngine uses Android native sound classes to provide audio entertainment within our
games. These classes include a few additional methods aside from `play()` and `pause()`
that allow us to have more control over the audio objects during runtime.

Music objects

The following list includes methods provided for the `Music` objects:

*   `seekTo`: The `seekTo(pMilliseconds)` method allows us to define where the
    audio playback of a specific `Music` object should start from. `pMilliseconds` is
    equal to the position of the audio track, in milliseconds, where we'd like to start
    playback upon calling `play()` on the `Music` object. In order to obtain the duration
    of a `Music` object in milliseconds, we can call `mMusic.getMediaPlayer().`
    `getDuration()`.

*   `setLooping`: The `setLooping(pBoolean)` method simply defines whether or
    not the `Music` object should replay from the beginning once it reaches the end of its
    duration. If `setLooping(true)`, the `Music` object will continuously repeat until the
    application is closed or until `setLooping(false)` is called.

*   `setOnCompletionListener`: This method allows us to apply a listener into the
    `Music` object, which gives us the opportunity to execute a function pending track
    completion. This is done by adding `OnCompletionListener` to our `Music` object,
    as follows:

```
mMusic.setOnCompletionListener(new OnCompletionListener(){
   /* In the event that a Music object reaches the end of its
duration,
    * the following method will be called
    */
   @Override
   public void onCompletion(MediaPlayer mp) {
   // Do something pending Music completion
   }
});
```

▶ setVolume: With the setVolume(pLeftVolume, pRightVolume) method, we are able to adjust the left and/or right stereo channels independently. The minimum and maximum range for volume control is equal to 0.0f for no volume and 1.0f for full volume.

Sound objects

The following list includes methods provided for the Sound objects:

▶ setLooping: See the Music object's setLooping method's description above for details. Additionally, Sound objects allow us to set how many times the audio track will loop with mSound.setLoopCount(pLoopCount), where pLoopCount is an int value defining the number of times to loop.

▶ setRate: The setRate(pRate) method allows us to define the rate, or speed, at which the Sound object will play, where pRate is equal to the rate as a floating point value. The default rate is equal to 1.0f, while decreasing the rate will lower the audio pitch and increasing the rate will increase audio pitch. Keep in mind, the Android API documentation states that the rate accepts values between a range of 0.5f through to 2.0f. Exceeding this range on a negative or positive scale may cause errors in playback.

▶ setVolume: See the Music object's setVolume method's description above for details.

For those of us who are not geared toward audio creativity, there are plenty of resources out there which are free to use. There are plenty of free sound databases that can be found online that we can use in public projects, such as http://www.soundjay.com. Keep in mind, most free-to-use databases require attribution for the files used.

Working with different types of textures

Getting to know how to manage textures should be one of the main priorities for every game developer. Of course, it's possible to build a game while only knowing the basics of texturing, but down the road that can very well lead to performance issues, texture bleeding, and other unwanted results. In this recipe, we're going to take a look at how we can build textures into our games in order to provide efficiency, while reducing the possibility of texture padding issues.

Getting ready

Perform the *Know the life cycle* recipe given in this chapter, so that we've get a basic AndEngine project set up in our IDE. Additionally, this recipe will require three images in PNG format. The first rectangle will be named `rectangle_one.png`, at 30 pixels wide by 40 pixels in height. The second rectangle named `rectangle_two.png`, is 40 pixels wide by 30 pixels in height. The final rectangle is named `rectangle_three.png`, at 70 pixels wide by 50 pixels in height. Once these rectangle images have been added to the project's `assets/gfx/` folder, continue on to the *How to do it...* section.

How to do it...

There are two main components involved when building a texture in AndEngine. In the following steps, we will be creating what is known as a texture atlas that will store three texture regions out of the three rectangle PNG images mentioned in the *Getting ready* section.

1. This step is optional. We point the `BitmapTextureAtlasTextureRegionFactory` class to the folder in which our graphical images are located. The factory is pointed to the `assets/` folder by default. By appending `gfx/` to the default base path of the factory, it will now look in `assets/gfx/` for our images:

   ```
   BitmapTextureAtlasTextureRegionFactory.setAssetBasePath("gfx/");
   ```

2. Next, we will create `BitmapTextureAtlas`. The texture atlas can be thought of as a map which contains many different textures. In this case, our "map" or `BitmapTextureAtlas`, will have a size of 120 x 120 pixels:

   ```
   // Create the texture atlas at a size of 120x120 pixels
   BitmapTextureAtlas mBitmapTextureAtlas = new
   BitmapTextureAtlas(mEngine.getTextureManager(), 120, 120);
   ```

3. Once we have `BitmapTextureAtlas` to work with, we can now create our `ITextureRegion` objects and place them onto specific locations within the `BitmapTextureAtlas` texture. We will use the `BitmapTextureAtlasTextureRegionFactory` class, which helps us with binding our PNG images to a specific `ITextureRegion` object as well as define a position to place the `ITextureRegion` object within the `BitmapTextureAtlas` texture atlas we'd created in the previous step:

   ```
   /* Create rectangle one at position (10, 10) on the
   mBitmapTextureAtlas */
   ITextureRegion mRectangleOneTextureRegion =
   BitmapTextureAtlasTextureRegionFactory.createFromAsset(mBitmapText
   ureAtlas, this, "rectangle_one.png", 10, 10);

   /* Create rectangle two at position (50, 10) on the
   mBitmapTextureAtlas */
   ```

```
ITextureRegion mRectangleTwoTextureRegion =
BitmapTextureAtlasTextureRegionFactory.createFromAsset(mBitmapText
ureAtlas, this, "rectangle_two.png", 50, 10);

/* Create rectangle three at position (10, 60) on the
mBitmapTextureAtlas */
ITextureRegion mRectangleThreeTextureRegion =
BitmapTextureAtlasTextureRegionFactory.createFromAsset(mBitmapText
ureAtlas, this, "rectangle_three.png", 10, 60);
```

4. The final step is to load our `ITextureRegion` objects into memory. We can do this in one call to the `BitmapTextureAtlas` atlas which contains the said `ITextureRegion` objects:

```
mBitmapTextureAtlas.load();
```

How it works...

In AndEngine development, there are two main components we will use in order to create textures for our projects. The first component is known as `BitmapTextureAtlas`, which can be thought of as a flat surface with a maximum width and height that can store sub-textures within its width and height boundaries. These sub-textures are called texture regions, or `ITextureRegion` objects in AndEngine to be specific. The purpose of the `ITextureRegion` object is to act solely as a reference to a specific texture in memory, which is located at position x and y within a `BitmapTextureAtlas` atlas. One way to look at these two components is to picture a blank canvas, which will represent a texture atlas, and a handful of stickers, which will represent the texture regions. A canvas would have a maximum size, and within that area we can place the stickers wherever we'd like. With this in mind, we place a handful of stickers on the canvas. We've now got all of our stickers neatly laid out on this canvas and accessible to grab and place wherever we'd like. There is a little bit more to it as well, but that will be covered shortly.

With the basics of `BitmapTextureAtlas` and `ITextureRegion` objects out of the way, the steps involved in creating our textures should now make more sense. As mentioned in the first step, setting the base path of the `BitmapTextureAtlasTextureRegionFactory` class is completely optional. We are simply including this step as it saves us from having to repeat saying which folder our images are in once we move on to creating the `ITextureRegion` objects. For example, if we were not to set the base path, we'd have to reference our images as `gfx/rectangle_one.png`, `gfx/rectangle_two.png`, and so on.

In the second step, we are creating our `BitmapTextureAtlas` object. This step is pretty straightforward as we must simply specify the Engine's `TextureManager` object which will handle the loading of textures, as well as a width and height for the texture atlas, in that order. Since we're only dealing with three small images in these steps, 120 x 120 pixels will be just fine.

One important thing to keep in mind about texture atlases is to never create excessive texture atlases; as in do not create an atlas that is 256 x 256 for holding a single image which is 32 x 32 pixels for example. The other important point is to avoid creating texture atlases which are larger than 1024 x 1024 pixels. Android devices vary in their maximum texture sizes and while some may be able to store textures up to 2048 x 2048 pixels, a large number of devices have a maximum limit of 1024 x 1024. Exceeding the maximum texture size will either cause a force-closure on startup or simply fail to display proper textures depending on the device. If there is no other option and a large image is absolutely necessary, see *Background stitching* in *Chapter 4, Working with Cameras*.

In the third step of this recipe, we are creating our `ITextureRegion` objects. In other words, we are applying a specified image to the `mBitmapTextureAtlas` object as well as defining where, exactly, that image will be placed on the atlas. Using the `BitmapTextureAtlasTextureRegionFactory` class, we can call the `createFromAss et(pBitmapTextureAtlas, pContext, pAssetPath, pTextureX, pTextureY)` method, which makes creating the texture region a piece of cake. In the order the parameters are listed from left to right, the `pBitmapTextureAtlas` parameter specifies the texture atlas which we'd like the `ITextureRegion` object to be stored in. The `pContext` parameter allows the class to open the image from the `gfx/` folder. The `pAssetPath` parameter defines the name of the specific file we're looking for; example, `rectangle_one.png`. And the final two parameters, `pTextureX` and `pTextureY`, define the location on the texture atlas in which to place the `ITextureRegion` object. The following image represents what the three `ITextureRegion` objects would look like as defined in step three. Note that the positions are consistent between the code and image:

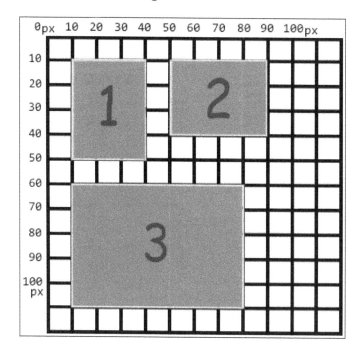

In the previous image, notice that there is a minimum gap of 10 pixels between each of the rectangles and the texture edge. The ITextureRegion objects are not spaced out like this to make things more understandable, although it helps. They are actually spaced out in order to add what is known as **texture atlas source spacing**. What this spacing does is that it prevents the possibility of texture overlapping when a texture is applied to a sprite. This overlapping is called **texture bleeding**. Although creating textures as seen in this recipe does not completely mitigate the chance of texture bleeding, it does reduce the likelihood of this issue when certain texture options are applied to the texture atlas.

See the *Applying texture options* recipe given in this chapter for more information on texture options. Additionally, the *There's more...* section in this topic describes another method of creating texture atlases, which completely solves the texture bleeding issue! It is highly recommended.

There's more...

There is an abundance of different approaches we can take when it comes to adding textures into our game. They all have their own benefits and some even have negative aspects involved.

BuildableBitmapTextureAtlas

The BuildableBitmapTextureAtlas object is a great way to implement ITextureRegion objects into our texture atlases without having to manually define positions. The purpose of the BuildableBitmapTextureAtlas texture atlas is to automatically place its ITextureRegion objects onto the atlas by applying them to the most convenient coordinates. This approach to creating textures is the easiest and most efficient method as it can become time-consuming and sometimes even error-prone when building large games with many texture atlases. In addition to BuildableBitmapTextureAtlas being automated, it also allows for the developer to define transparent padding to the texture atlas sources, removing any occurrence of texture bleeding. This was one of the most prominent visual issues in AndEngine's GLES 1.0 branch as there was no built-in method for supplying padding to the texture atlases.

Using a BuildableBitmapTextureAtlas atlas differs slightly from the BitmapTextureAtlas route. See the following code for this recipe's code using a BuildableBitmapTextureAtlas atlas instead:

```
/* Create a buildable bitmap texture atlas - same parameters required
* as with the original bitmap texture atlas */
BuildableBitmapTextureAtlas mBuildableBitmapTextureAtlas = new Buildab
leBitmapTextureAtlas(mEngine.getTextureManager(), 120, 120);

/* Create the three ITextureRegion objects. Notice that when using
 * the BuildableBitmapTextureAtlas, we do not need to include the
final
```

```
 * two pTextureX and pTextureY parameters. These are handled
automatically! */
ITextureRegion mRectangleOneTextureRegion =
BitmapTextureAtlasTextureRegionFactory.createFromAsset(mBuildableBitma
pTextureAtlas, this, "rectangle_one.png");
ITextureRegion mRectangleTwoTextureRegion =
BitmapTextureAtlasTextureRegionFactory.createFromAsset(mBuildableBitma
pTextureAtlas, this, "rectangle_two.png");
ITextureRegion mRectangleThreeTextureRegion =
BitmapTextureAtlasTextureRegionFactory.createFromAsset(mBuildableBitma
pTextureAtlas, this, "rectangle_three.png");

// Buildable bitmap texture atlases require a try/catch statement
try {
  /* Build the mBuildableBitmapTextureAtlas, supplying a
BlackPawnTextureAtlasBuilder
    * as its only parameter. Within the BlackPawnTextureAtlasBuilder's
parameters, we
    * provide 1 pixel in texture atlas source space and 1 pixel for
texture atlas source
    * padding. This will alleviate the chance of texture bleeding.
    */
  mBuildableBitmapTextureAtlas.build(new BlackPawnTextureAtlasBuilder<
IBitmapTextureAtlasSource, BitmapTextureAtlas>(0, 1, 1));
} catch (TextureAtlasBuilderException e) {
  e.printStackTrace();
}

// Once the atlas has been built, we can now load
mBuildableBitmapTextureAtlas.load();
```

As we can see in this code, there are some minor differences between the
`BuildableBitmapTextureAtlas` and the `BitmapTextureAtlas` atlases. The first
main point to note is that when creating our `ITextureRegion` objects, we no longer have
to specify where the texture region should be placed on the texture atlas. The second minor
change when using the `BuildableBitmapTextureAtlas` alternative is that we must call
the `build(pTextureAtlasBuilder)` method on `mBuildableBitmapTextureAtlas`
before we call the `load()` method. Within the `build(pTextureAtlasBuilder)`
method, we must provide a `BlackPawnTextureAtlasBuilder` class, defining three
parameters. In this order, the parameters are `pTextureAtlasBorderSpacing`,
`pTextureAtlasSourceSpacing`, and `pTextureAtlasSourcePadding`. In the previous
code snippet, we will remove the likelihood of texture bleeding in almost all cases. However, in
extreme cases, if there is texture bleeding, then simply increase the third parameter, this will
help to alleviate any issues.

TiledTextureRegion

A tiled texture region is essentially the same object as a normal texture region. The difference between the two is that a tiled texture region allows us to pass a single image file to it and create a sprite sheet out of it. This is done by specifying the number of columns and rows within our sprite sheet. From there, AndEngine will automatically divide the tiled texture region into evenly distributed segments. This will allow us to navigate through each segment within the `TiledTextureRegion` object. This is how the tiled texture region will appear to create a sprite with animation:

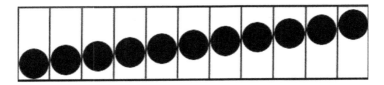

 A real sprite sheet should not have outlines around each column and row. They are in place in the previous image to display how a sprite sheet is divided up into equal segments.

Let's assume that the previous image is 165 pixels wide and 50 pixels high. Since we have 11 individual columns and a single row, we could create the `TiledTextureRegion` object like so:

```
TiledTextureRegion mTiledTextureRegion =
BitmapTextureAtlasTextureRegionFactory.createTiledFromAsset(mBitmapTex
tureAtlas, context,"sprite_sheet.png",11,1);
```

What this code does is it tells AndEngine to divide the `sprite_sheet.png` image into 11 individual segments, each 15 pixels wide (since 165 pixels divided by 11 segments equals 15). We can now use this tiled texture region object to instantiate a sprite with animation.

Compressed textures

In addition to the more common image types (`.bmp`, `.jpeg`, and `.png`), AndEngine also has built-in support for PVR and ETC1 compressed textures. The main benefit in using compressed textures is the impact it has on reducing the load time and possibly increasing frame rates during gameplay. On that note, there are also disadvantages in using compressed textures. ETC1, for example, doesn't allow for an alpha channel to be used in its textures. Compressed textures may also cause a noticeable loss of quality in your textures. The use of these types of textures should be relevant to the significance of the object being represented by the compressed texture. You most likely wouldn't want to base your entire game's texture format on compressed textures, but for large quantities of subtle images, using compressed textures can add noticeable performance to your game.

See also

▸ *Creating the resource manager* in this chapter.

▸ *Applying texture options* in this chapter.

Applying texture options

We've discussed the different types of textures AndEngine provides; now let's go over the options we can supply our textures with. The contents in this topic tend to have noticeable effects on the quality and performance of our games.

Getting ready

Perform the *Working with different types of textures* recipe given in this chapter, so that we've got a basic AndEngine project set up with `BitmapTextureAtlas` or `BuildableBitmapTextureAtlas` loading in place.

How to do it...

In order to modify a texture atlas' option and/or format, we need to add a parameter or two to the `BitmapTextureAtlas` constructor depending on whether we'd like to define either the options, format, or both. See the following code for modifying both, texture format and texture options:

```
BitmapTextureAtlas mBitmapTextureAtlas = new
BitmapTextureAtlas(mEngine.getTextureManager(), 1024, 1024,
BitmapTextureFormat.RGB_565, TextureOptions.BILINEAR);
```

From here on, all texture regions placed on this specific texture atlas will have the defined texture format and option applied to it.

How it works...

AndEngine allows us to apply texture options and formats to our texture atlases. The various combination of options and formats applied to a texture atlas will affect the overall quality and performance impact that sprites have on our game. Of course, that is if the mentioned sprites are using `ITextureRegion` objects, which are related to the modified `BitmapTextureAtlas` atlas.

The base texture options available in AndEngine are as follows:

- **Nearest**: This texture option is applied to texture atlases by default. This is the fastest-performing texture option we can apply to a texture atlas, but also the poorest in quality. This option means that the texture will apply blending of pixels that make up the display by obtaining the nearest texel color to a pixel. Similar to how a pixel represents the smallest element of a digital image, a **texel** represents the smallest element of a texture.

- **Bilinear**: The second main texture filtering option in AndEngine is called bilinear texture filtering. This approach takes a hit performance-wise, but the quality of scaled sprites will increase. Bilinear filtering obtains the four nearest texels per pixel in order to provide smoother blending to an onscreen image.

Take a look at the following figure to see a comparison between bilinear filtering and nearest filtering:

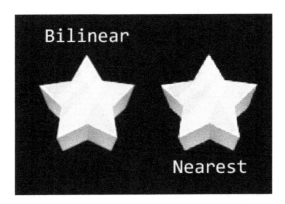

These two images are rendered in the highest bitmap format. The difference between nearest and bilinear filtering is very clear in this case. In the left-hand side of the image, the bilinear star has almost no jagged edges and the colors are very smooth. On the right-hand side, we've got a star rendered with the nearest filtering. The quality level suffers as jagged edges are more apparent and if observed closely, the colors aren't as smooth.

The following are a few additional texture options:

Repeating: The repeating texture option allows the sprite to "repeat" the texture assuming that the `ITextureRegion` object's width and height has been exceeded by the size of the sprite. In most games, the terrain is usually generated by creating a repeating texture and stretching the size of the sprite, rather than creating many separate sprites to cover the ground.

Let's take a look at how to create a repeating texture:

```
    /* Create our repeating texture. Repeating textures require width/
height which are a power of two */
    BuildableBitmapTextureAtlas texture = new BuildableBitmapTexture
Atlas(engine.getTextureManager(), 32, 32, TextureOptions.REPEATING_
BILINEAR);

    // Create our texture region - nothing new here
    mSquareTextureRegion = BitmapTextureAtlasTextureRegionFactory.
createFromAsset(texture, context, "square.png");

    try {
      // Repeating textures should not have padding
      texture.build(new BlackPawnTextureAtlasBuilder<IBitmapTextureAtl
asSource, BitmapTextureAtlas>(0, 0, 0));
      texture.load();

    } catch (TextureAtlasBuilderException e) {
      Debug.e(e);
    }
```

The previous code is based on a square image which is 32 x 32 pixels in dimension. Two things to keep in mind when creating repeating textures are as follows:

▸ Texture atlases using the repeating texture option format require the power of two dimensions (2, 4, 8, 16, and so on)

▸ If you are using a buildable texture atlas, do not apply padding or spacing during the `build()` method, as it will be taken into account in the repeating of the texture, breaking the first rule of repeating textures

Next, we have to create a sprite which uses this repeated texture:

```
/* Increase the texture region's size, allowing repeating textures to
stretch up to 800x480 */
ResourceManager.getInstance().mSquareTextureRegion.setTextureSize(800,
480);
// Create a sprite which stretches across the full screen
Sprite sprite = new Sprite(0, 0, 800, 480, ResourceManager.
getInstance().mSquareTextureRegion, mEngine.
getVertexBufferObjectManager());
```

What we're doing here is increasing the texture region's size to 800 x 480 pixels in dimension. This doesn't alter the size of the image while the repeating option is applied to a texture, rather it allows the image to be repeated up to 800 x 480 pixels. This means that if we create a sprite and supply the repeating texture, we can scale the sprite up to 800 x 480 pixels in dimension, while still displaying a repeat effect. However, if the sprite exceeds the width or height dimensions of the texture region, no texture will be applied to the exceeding area.

Here's the outcome taken from a device screenshot:

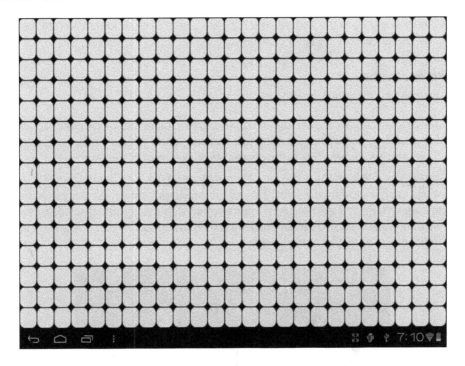

Pre-multiply alpha: Lastly, we have the option to add the pre-multiply alpha texture option to our textures. What this option does is multiply each of the RGB values by the specified alpha channel and then apply the alpha channel in the end. The main purpose of this option is to allow us to modify the opacity of the colors without loss of color. Keep in mind, modifying the alpha value of a sprite directly may introduce unwanted effects when using pre-multiplied alpha values. Sprites will likely not appear fully transparent when this option is applied to sprites with an alpha value of 0.

When applying texture options to our texture atlases, we can choose either nearest or bilinear texture filtering options. On top of these texture filtering options, we can include either the repeating option, the pre-multiply alpha option, or even both.

There's more...

Aside from texture options, AndEngine also allows us to set the texture format of each of our texture atlases. Texture formats, similar to texture options, are often decided upon depending on its purpose. The format of a texture can greatly affect both the performance and quality of an image even more noticeably than the texture options. Texture formats allow us to choose the available color ranges of the RGB values in a texture atlas. Depending on the texture format being used, we may also allow or disallow a sprite from having any alpha value which affects the transparency of the textures.

The texture format naming conventions are not very complicated. All formats have a name similar to **RGBA_8888**, where the left-hand side of the underscore refers to the color or alpha channels available to the texture. The right-hand side of the underscore refers to the bits available to each of the color channels.

Texture formats

The following texture formats are available:

- RGBA_8888: Allows the texture to use red, green, blue, and alpha channels, assigned 8 bits each. Since we have 4 channels each assigned 8 bits (4 x 8), we're left with a 32-bit texture format. This is the slowest texture format of the four.

- RGBA_4444: Allows the texture to use red, green, blue, and alpha channels, assigned 4 bits each. Following the same rule as the previous format, we're left with a 16-bit texture format. You will notice an improvement with this format over RGBA_8888 as we're only saving half as much information as the 32-bit format. The quality will suffer noticeably; see the following image:

In this image, we compare the difference between two texture formats. The stars are both rendered with the default texture option (nearest), which has nothing to do with the RGBA format of the image. What we're more interested here is the color quality of the two stars. The left-hand side star is rendered with full 32-bit color capabilities, the right with 16-bit. The difference between the two stars is rather apparent.

- RGB_565: Another 16-bit texture format, though this one does not include an alpha channel; textures using this texture format will not allow for transparency. Due to the lack of transparency, the need for this format is limited, but it is still valuable. One example of this texture format being used would be to display a fullscreen image such as a background. Backgrounds don't require transparency, so it is wise to keep this format in mind when introducing a background. The performance saved is fairly noticeable.

The `RGB_565` format color quality is more or less the same as you would expect from the `RGBA_4444` star image shown previously.

- ▶ `A_8`: Finally, we have the last texture format, which is an 8-bit alpha channel (does not support colors). Another limited-use format; the A_8 format is generally used as an alpha mask (overlay) for sprites which have colors. One example of a use for this format is a screen fading in or out by simply overlaying a sprite with this texture, then altering the transparency as time passes.

When creating your texture atlases, it is a good idea to think about which types of sprites will use which type of texture regions and pack them into texture atlases accordingly. For more important sprites, we'll most likely want to use the `RGBA_8888` texture format, since these sprites will be the main focus of our games. These objects might include the foreground sprites, main character sprites, or anything on the screen that would be more visually prominent. Backgrounds underlay the entire surface area of the device, so we most likely have no use for transparency. We will use `RGB_565` for these sprites in order to remove the alpha channel, which will help improve performance. Finally, we have objects which might not be very colorful, might be small, or simply may not need as much visual appeal. We can use the texture format `RGBA_4444` for these types of sprites in order to cut the memory needed for these textures in half.

See also

- ▶ *Know the life cycle* in this chapter.
- ▶ *Working with different types of textures* in this chapter.
- ▶ *Bringing a scene to life with sprites* in *Chapter 2, Working with Entities*.

Using AndEngine font resources

AndEngine fonts are simple to set up and include for use in our `Text` objects to be displayed on screen. We can choose from preset fonts or we can add our own via the `assets` folder.

Getting ready

Perform the *Know the life cycle* recipe given in this chapter, so that we've got a basic AndEngine project set up in our IDE, then continue on to the *How to do it...* section.

How to do it...

The following code snippets display the four different options we have for creating preset, custom asset, preset stroke, and custom asset stroke font objects. Font creation should take place in the `onCreateResources()` method of our `BaseGameActivity` class.

- ▶ The `create()` method for preset fonts is as follows:

  ```
  Font mFont = FontFactory.create(mEngine.getFontManager(), mEngine.
  getTextureManager(), 256, 256, Typeface.create(Typeface.DEFAULT,
  Typeface.NORMAL),  32f, true, org.andengine.util.adt.color.Color.
  WHITE_ABGR_PACKED_INT)

  mFont.load();
  ```

- ▶ The `createFromAsset()` method for custom fonts is as follows:

  ```
  Font mFont = FontFactory.createFromAsset(mEngine.getFontManager(),
  mEngine.getTextureManager(), 256, 256, this.getAssets(), "Arial.
  ttf", 32f, true, org.andengine.util.adt.color.Color.WHITE_ABGR_
  PACKED_INT);

  mFont.load();
  ```

- ▶ The `createStroke()` and `createStrokeFromAsset()` methods for outlined fonts are:

  ```
  BitmapTextureAtlas mFontTexture = new BitmapTextureAtlas(mEngine.
  getTextureManager(), 256, 256, TextureOptions.BILINEAR);

  Font mFont = FontFactory.createStroke(mEngine.getFontManager(),
  mFontTexture, Typeface.create(Typeface.DEFAULT, Typeface.BOLD),
  32, true, org.andengine.util.adt.color.Color.WHITE_ABGR_PACKED_
  INT, 3, org.andengine.util.adt.color.Color.BLACK_ABGR_PACKED_INT);

  mFont.load();
  ```

How it works...

As we can see, there are different approaches we can take to create our `Font` objects depending on how we'd like the font to look. However, all fonts share the need for us to define a texture width and texture height, whether it be directly as parameters in the `FontFactory` class' `create` methods or indirectly through the use of a `BitmapTextureAtlas` object. In the previous code snippets, we'd created all three `Font` objects using a texture size of `256` pixels in width by `256` pixels in height. Unfortunately, there is currently no easy way to automatically determine the texture size needed at runtime in order to support different languages, text sizes, stroke value, or font style.

For now, the most common approach is to set the texture width and height to about 256 pixels and make small adjustments upward or downward until the texture is just the right size so as to not cause artifacts in the Text objects. The font size plays the biggest role in determining the final texture size needed for the Font object, so exceedingly large fonts, such as 32 and higher, may need larger texture sizes.

 All Font objects require a method call to load() before they can properly display characters in the Text objects.

Let's take a look at how each of the methods presented in the *How to do it...* section work:

- The create() method: The create() method doesn't allow for too much customization. This method's parameters, starting at the fifth parameter, include supplying a typeface, font size, anti-aliasing option, and a color. We're using the Android native typeface class which only supports a few different fonts and styles.

- The createFromAsset() method: We can use this method in order to introduce custom fonts into our project via our assets folder. Let's assume that we have a true-type font called Arial.ttf located in our project's assets folder. We can see that the general creation is the same. In this method, we must pass the activity's AssetManager class, which can be obtained through our activity's getAssets() method. The parameter following that is the true type font we would like to import.

- The createStroke() and createStrokeFromAsset() methods: Finally, we have our stroke fonts. The stroke font gives us the ability to add outlines to the characters in our Text object. These fonts are useful in situations where we would like our text to "pop". For creating stroke fonts, we'll need to supply a texture atlas as the second parameter rather than passing the engine's texture manager. From this point, we can either create the stroke font via a typeface or through our assets folder. Additionally, we're given the option to define two new color values which have been added as the final two parameters. With these new parameters, we are able to adjust the thickness of the outline as well as the color.

There's more...

The way the Font class is currently set up, it is best to preload the characters that we expect to display via a Text object. Unfortunately, AndEngine currently makes calls to the garbage collector when new letters are still to be drawn, so in order to avoid hiccups when a Text object is first getting "acquainted" with the letters, we can call the method:

```
mFont.prepareLetters("abcdefghijklmnopqrstuvwxyz".toCharArray())
```

This method call would prepare the lowercase letters from a to z. This method should be called during a loading screen at some point within the game in order to avoid any noticeable garbage collection. There's one more important class that we should discuss before moving off the topic of `Font` objects. AndEngine includes a class called `FontUtils` that allows us to retrieve information regarding a `Text` object's width on the screen via the `measureText(pFont, pText)` method. This is important when dealing with dynamically-changing strings as it gives us the option to relocate our `Text` object, assuming that the width or height of the string in pixels has changed.

See also

- ▸ *Know the life cycle* in this chapter.
- ▸ *Working with different types of textures* in this chapter.
- ▸ Applying text to a layer in *Chapter 2, Working with Entities*.

Creating the resource manager

In this topic, we're finally going to look at our resources from a bigger picture. With the resource manager in place, we will easily be able to make a single call to methods such as `loadTextures()`, `loadSounds()`, or `loadFonts()` in order to load the different types of resources needed by our game, all from a single, convenient location.

Getting ready

Please refer to the class named `ResourceManager` in the code bundle.

How to do it...

The `ResourceManager` class is designed with the singleton design pattern in mind. This allows for global access to all of our game's resources through a simple call to `ResourceManager.getInstance()`. The main purpose of the `ResourceManager` class is to store resource objects, load resources, and unload resources. The following steps display how we can use `ResourceManager` to handle textures of one of our game's scenes.

1. Declare all of the resources that will be used throughout the different scenes in our game:

```
/* The variables listed should be kept public, allowing us easy
access
to them when creating new Sprites, Text objects and to play sound
files */
public ITextureRegion mGameBackgroundTextureRegion;
public ITextureRegion mMenuBackgroundTextureRegion;
```

```
public Sound  mSound;

public Font  mFont;
```

2. Provide `load` methods that will handle loading the audio, graphical, and font resources declared in the `ResourceManager` class:

```
public synchronized void loadGameTextures(Engine pEngine, Context
pContext){
// Set our game assets folder in "assets/gfx/game/"
    BitmapTextureAtlasTextureRegionFactory.setAssetBasePath("gfx/
game/");

BuildableBitmapTextureAtlas mBitmapTextureAtlas = new BuildableBit
mapTextureAtlas(pEngine.getTextureManager(), 800, 480);

mGameBackgroundTextureRegion =
BitmapTextureAtlasTextureRegionFactory.createFromAsset(mBitmapText
ureAtlas, pContext, "game_background.png");

try {
  mBitmapTextureAtlas.build(new BlackPawnTextureAtlasBuilder<IBitm
apTextureAtlasSource, BitmapTextureAtlas>(0, 1, 1));
  mBitmapTextureAtlas.load();
} catch (TextureAtlasBuilderException e) {
  Debug.e(e);
}
}
```

3. The third step involves providing a method of unloading all resources corresponding to our `ResourceManager` class' `load` methods:

```
public synchronized void unloadGameTextures(){
  // call unload to remove the corresponding texture atlas from
memory
  BuildableBitmapTextureAtlas mBitmapTextureAtlas =
(BuildableBitmapTextureAtlas) mGameBackgroundTextureRegion.
getTexture();
  mBitmapTextureAtlas.unload();

  // ... Continue to unload all textures related to the 'Game'
scene

  // Once all textures have been unloaded, attempt to invoke the
Garbage Collector
  System.gc();
}
```

How it works...

By implementing a `ResourceManager` class into our project, we can easily load our various scene resources completely indepenently of one another. Because of this, we must make sure that our `public` class methods are synchronized in order to make sure that we're running in a thread-safe environment. This is especially important with the use of singletons, as we've only got one instance of the class, with the potential for multiple threads accessing it. On top of that, we now only require one line of code when it comes to loading our scene resources which helps greatly in keeping our main activity class more organized. Here is what our `onCreateResources()` methods should look like with the use of a resource manager:

```
@Override
public void onCreateResources(
    OnCreateResourcesCallback pOnCreateResourcesCallback) {

    // Load the game texture resources
    ResourceManager.getInstance().loadGameTextures(mEngine, this);

    // Load the font resources
    ResourceManager.getInstance().loadFonts(mEngine);

    // Load the sound resources
    ResourceManager.getInstance().loadSounds(mEngine, this);

    pOnCreateResourcesCallback.onCreateResourcesFinished();
}
```

In the first step, we are declaring all of our resources, including `Font` objects, `ITextureRegion` objects, and `Sound/Music` objects. In this particular recipe, we're only working with a limited number of resources, but in a fully-functional game, this class may include 50, 75, or even more than 100 resources. In order to obtain a resource from our `ResourceManager` class, we can simply include the following line into any class within our project:

`ResourceManager.getInstance().mGameBackgroundTextureRegion.`

In the second step, we create the `loadGameTextures(pEngine, pContext)` method which is used to load the `Game` scene textures. For every additional scene within our game, we should have a separate `load` method in place. This allows for easy loading of resources on the fly.

In the final step, we're creating `unload` methods which handle unloading the resources corresponding to each of the `load` methods. However, if there are any number of resources which happen to be used throughout a number of our game's scenes, it might be necessary to create a `load` method which doesn't come with an accompanying `unload` method.

There's more...

In larger projects, sometimes we may find ourselves passing main objects to classes very frequently. Another use for the resource manager is to store some of the more important game objects such as the `Engine` or `Camera`. This way we no longer have to continuously pass these objects as parameters, rather we can call respective `get` methods in order to get the game's `Camera`, `Engine`, or any other specific object we'll need to reference throughout the classes.

See also

- ▸ *Introducing sounds and music* in this chapter.
- ▸ *Working with different types of textures* in this chapter.
- ▸ *Using AndEngine font resources* in this chapter.

Saving and loading game data

In the final topic for the game structure chapter, we're going to set up a class that can be used in our project to manage data and settings. The more obvious game data we must save should include character stats, high scores, and other various data we may have included in our game. We should also keep track of certain options a game might have, such as whether the user has sounds muted or not, gore effects, and more. In this recipe, we're going to work with a class called `SharedPreferences`, which will allow us to easily store data to a device for retrieval at a later time.

> The `SharedPreferences` class is a great way to quickly store and retrieve primitive datatypes. However, as the data size increases, so will the needs of the method we use to store data. If our games do require a large amount of data to be stored, something to consider is to take a look into SQLite databases for data storage.

Getting ready

Please refer to the class named `UserData` in the code bundle.

How to do it...

In this recipe, we're setting up a `UserData` class that will store a Boolean variable to determine sound muting and an `int` variable that will define the highest, unlocked level a user has reached. Depending on the needs of the game, there may be more or less datatypes to include within the class for different reasons, be it high score, currency, or other game-related data. The following steps describe how to set up a class to contain and store user data on a user's device:

1. The first step involves declaring our constant `String` variables, which will hold references to our preference file, as well as "key" names, which will hold references to data within the preference file, as well as corresponding "value" variables. Additionally, we declare the `SharedPreferences` object as well as an editor:

```
// Include a 'filename' for our shared preferences
private static final String PREFS_NAME = "GAME_USERDATA";

/* These keys will tell the shared preferences editor which
   data we're trying to access */

private static final String UNLOCKED_LEVEL_KEY = "unlockedLevels";
private static final String SOUND_KEY = "soundKey";

/* Create our shared preferences object & editor which will
 be used to save and load data */
private SharedPreferences mSettings;
private SharedPreferences.Editor mEditor;

// keep track of our max unlocked level
private int mUnlockedLevels;

// keep track of whether or not sound is enabled
private boolean mSoundEnabled;
```

2. Create an initialization method for our `SharedPreferences` file. This method will be called when our game is first launched, either creating a new file for our game if one does not already exist, or load existing values from our preference file if it does exist:

```
public synchronized void init(Context pContext) {
  if (mSettings == null) {
    /* Retrieve our shared preference file, or if it's not yet
     * created (first application execution) then create it now
     */
    mSettings = context.getSharedPreferences(PREFS_NAME, Context.
MODE_PRIVATE);
```

```
      /* Define the editor, used to store data to our preference
file
        */
      mEditor = mSettings.edit();

      /* Retrieve our current unlocked levels. if the UNLOCKED_
LEVEL_KEY
        * does not currently exist in our shared preferences, we'll
create
        * the data to unlock level 1 by default
        */
      mUnlockedLevels = mSettings.getInt(UNLOCKED_LEVEL_KEY, 1);

      /* Same idea as above, except we'll set the sound boolean to
true
        * if the setting does not currently exist
        */
      mSoundEnabled = mSettings.getBoolean(SOUND_KEY, true);
   }
}
```

3. Next, we will provide getter methods for each of the values that are meant to be stored in our `SharedPreferences` file, so that we can access the data throughout our game:

```
/* retrieve the max unlocked level value */
public synchronized int getMaxUnlockedLevel() {
  return mUnlockedLevels;
}
```

4. And finally, we must provide setter methods for each of the values that are meant to be stored in our `SharedPreferences` file. The setter methods will be responsible for saving the data to the device:

```
public synchronized void unlockNextLevel() {
  // Increase the max level by 1
  mUnlockedLevels++;

  /* Edit our shared preferences unlockedLevels key, setting its
    * value our new mUnlockedLevels value
    */
  mEditor.putInt(UNLOCKED_LEVEL_KEY, mUnlockedLevels);

  /* commit() must be called by the editor in order to save
    * changes made to the shared preference data
    */
  mEditor.commit();
}
```

How it works...

This class demonstrates just how easily we are able to store and retrieve a game's data and options through the use of the `SharedPreferences` class. The structure of the `UserData` class is fairly straightforward and can be used in this same fashion in order to adapt to various other options we might want to include in our games.

In the first step, we simply start off by declaring all of the necessary constants and member variables that we'll need to handle different types of data within our game. For constants, we have one `String` variable named `PREFS_NAME` that defines the name of our game's preference file, as well as two other `String` variables that will each act as references to a single primitive datatype within the preference file. For each key constant, we should declare a corresponding variable that preference file data will be stored to when it is first loaded.

In the second step, we provide a means of loading the data from our game's preference file. This method only needs to be called once, during the startup process of a game in order to load the `UserData` classes member variables with the data stored in the `SharedPreferences` file. By first calling `context.getSharedPreferences(PREFS_ NAME, Context.MODE_PRIVATE)`, we check to see whether or not a `SharedPreference` file exists for our application under the `PREFS_NAME` string, and if not, then we create a new one a—MODE_PRIVATE, meaning the file is not visible to other applications.

Once that is done, we can call getter methods from the preference file such as `mUnlockedLevels = mSettings.getInt(UNLOCKED_LEVEL_KEY, 1)`. This will pass the data stored in the `UNLOCKED_LEVEL_KEY` key of the preference file to `mUnlockedLevels`. If the game's preference file does not currently hold any value for the defined key, then a default value of `1` is passed to `mUnlockedLevels`. This would continue to be done for each of the datatypes being handled by the `UserData` class. In this case, just the levels and sound.

In the third step, we set up the getter methods that will correspond to each of the datatypes being handled by the `UserData` class. These methods can be used throughout the game; for example, we could call `UserData.getInstance().isSoundMuted()` during level loading to determine whether or not we should call `play()` on the `Music` object.

In the fourth step, we create the methods that save data to the device. These methods are pretty straightforward and should be fairly similar regardless of the data we're working with. We can either take a value from a parameter as seen with `setSoundMuted(pEnableSound)` or simply increment as seen in `unlockNextLevel()`.

When we want to finally save the data to the device, we use the `mEditor` object, using putter methods which are suitable for the primitive datatype we wish to store, specifying the key to store the data as well as the value. For example, for level unlocking, we use the method, `mEditor.putInt(UNLOCKED_LEVEL_KEY, mUnlockedLevels)` as we are storing an `int` variable. For a `boolean` variable, we call `putBoolean(pKey, pValue)`, for a `String` variable, we call `putString(pKey, pValue)`, and so on..

There's more...

Unfortunately, when storing data on a client's device, there's no way of guaranteeing that a user will not have access to the data in order to manipulate it. On the Android platform, most users will not have access to the `SharedPreferences` file that holds our game data, but users with rooted devices on the other hand will be able to see the file and make changes as they see fit. For the sake of explanation, we used obvious key names, such as `soundKey` and `unlockedLevels`. Using some sort of misconstruction can help to make the file look more like gibberish to an average user who had accidentally stumbled upon the game data with their rooted device.

If we feel like going further to protect the game data, then the even more secure approach would be to encrypt the preference file. Java's `javax.crypto.*` package is a good place to start, but keep in mind that encryption and decryption does take time and will likely increase the duration of loading times within the game.

2

Working with Entities

In this chapter, we're going to start getting into displaying objects on the screen and various ways we can work with these objects. The topics include:

- ▶ Understanding AndEngine entities
- ▶ Applying primitives to a layer
- ▶ Bringing a scene to life with sprites
- ▶ Applying text to a layer
- ▶ Using relative rotation
- ▶ Overriding the `onManagedUpdate` method
- ▶ Using modifiers and entity modifiers
- ▶ Working with particle systems

Introduction

In this chapter, we're going to start working with all of the wonderful entities included in AndEngine. Entities provide us with a base foundation that every object displayed within our game world will rely on, be it the score text, the background image, the player's character, buttons, and everything else. One way to think of this is that any object in our game which has the ability to be placed, via AndEngine's coordinate system, is an entity at its most basic level. In this chapter, we're going to start working with `Entity` objects and many of its subtypes in order to allow us to make the most out of them in our own games.

Understanding AndEngine entities

The AndEngine game engine follows the **entity-component** model. The entity-component design is very common in a lot of game engines today, and for a good reason. It's easy to use, it's modular, and it is extremely useful in the sense that all game objects can be traced back to the single, most basic `Entity` object. The entity-component model can be thought of as the "entity" portion referring to the most basic level of the game engine's object system. The `Entity` class handles only the most basic data that our game objects rely on, such as position, rotation, color, attaching and detaching to and from the scene, and more. The "component" portion refers to the modular subtypes of the Entity class, such as the `Scene`, `Sprite`, `Text`, `ParticleSystem`, `Rectangle`, `Mesh`, and every other object which can be placed within our game. The components are meant to handle more specific tasks, while the entity is meant to act as a base foundation that all components will rely on.

How to do it...

To start with the absolute most basic `Entity` method, we will attach an `Entity` object to a `Scene` object:

Creating and attaching an `Entity` object to the `Scene` object requires only the following two lines of code:

```
Entity layer = new Entity();
mScene.attachChild(layer);
```

How it works...

The two lines of code given here allow us to create and attach a basic `Entity` object to our `Scene` object. An `Entity` object that is defined as seen in the *How to do it...* section of this recipe will most commonly be used as a layer. The purpose of a layer will be discussed in the coming paragraphs.

Entities are very important when developing games. In AndEngine, the fact of the matter is that all objects displayed on our scenes are derived from entities (including the `Scene` object itself!). In most cases, we can assume that the entity is either a visually displayed object such as a `Sprite`, `Text`, or `Rectangle` object on the scene, or a layer, such as the `Scene` object. Seeing as how broad the `Entity` class is, we're going to talk about each of the two uses for entities as if they were separate objects.

The first and arguably most important aspect of an entity is the layering capabilities. A layer is a very simple concept in game design; however, due to the amount of entities games tend to support during gameplay, things can quickly become confusing when first getting to know them. We must think of a layer as an object which has one parent and an unlimited amount of children unless otherwise defined. As the name suggests, the purpose of a layer is to apply our various entity objects on our scene in an organized fashion, which fortunately also gives us the ability to perform one action on the layer that will affect all of its children in unison, for example, repositioning and applying certain entity modifiers. We can assume that if we have a background, a mid-ground, and a foreground, that our game will have three separate layers. These three layers would appear in a specific order depending on the order they are attached to the scene, as if stacking pieces of paper on top of each other. The last piece of paper added to the stack will appear in front of the rest if we were to look down on that stack of paper. The same rule applies for `Entity` objects attached to a `Scene` object; this is shown in the following image:

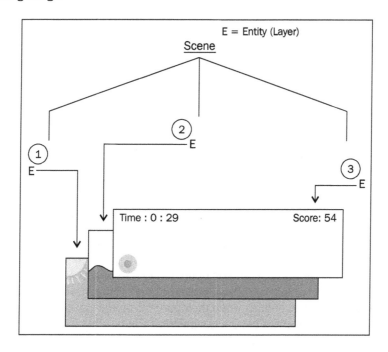

The previous image depicts a basic game scene consisting of three `Entity` object layers. Each of the three layers has a specific purpose, which is to store all relative entities in terms of depth. The first layer applied to the scene is the background layer, including a sprite, which contains a blue sky and a sun. The second layer applied to the scene is the mid-ground layer. On this layer, we would find objects which are relative to the player, including the landscape the player walks on, collectable items, enemies, and more. Lastly, we have the foreground layer, used to display the front-most entities on the device's display. In the figure shown, the foreground layer is used to display the user interface, which includes a button, and two `Text` objects.

Let's take another look at what a scene might look like with layers with child entities attached to it:

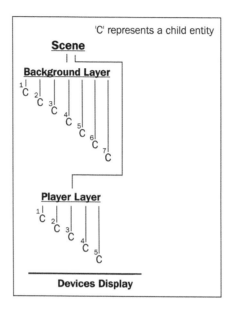

This figure shows how a scene would display entities on the screen in terms of depth/layering. At the bottom of the figure, we've got the device's display. We can see that **Background Layer** is attached to the **Scene** first, then **Player Layer** is attached. This means that the entities attached to the background will be displayed behind the **Player Layer** children. Keeping this in mind, the rule applies to the child entities as well. The first child attached to the layer will appear behind any subsequently attached object as far as depth goes.

Finally, one last vital topic relating to general AndEngine entities is Entity composition. One thing we should go over before moving on is the fact that *children inherit parent values!* This is an area where many new AndEngine developers run into issues when setting up multiple layers in their games. Everything from skew, scale, position, rotation, visibility, and more are all taken into account by child entities when their parent's properties change. Take a look at the following figure, which displays the entity's **position** composition in AndEngine:

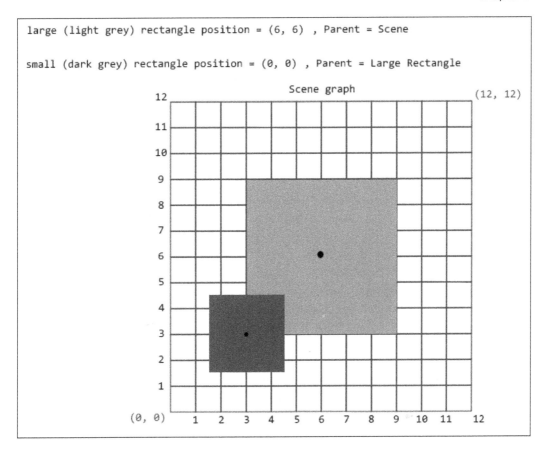

```
large (light grey) rectangle position = (6, 6) , Parent = Scene

small (dark grey) rectangle position = (0, 0) , Parent = Large Rectangle
```

First of all, we should know that in AndEngine's anchor center branch, coordinate systems start in the bottom-left corner of an entity. Increasing the x value will move the entity position to the right, and increasing the y value will move the entity position upward. Decreasing x/y values will have the opposite affect. With this in mind, we can see that the bigger rectangle which is attached to the **Scene** has its position set to coordinates **(6, 6)** on the **Scene**. Since the smaller rectangle is attached to the bigger rectangle, rather than its coordinate system being relative to the **Scene**, it is actually using the large rectangle's coordinate system. This means that the small rectangle's anchor center position will rest directly on position **(0, 0)** of the large rectangle's coordinate system. As we can see in the previous image, the **(0, 0)** position on the large rectangle's coordinate system is its bottom-left corner.

The main difference between the older AndEngine branches and AndEngine's newest anchor center branch is the fact that positioning an entity no longer means we are setting the upper-left corner of an entity to a position on the coordinate system. Rather, the entity's center-point will be placed at the defined position, also seen in the previous figure.

There's more...

The `Entity` object in AndEngine includes many different methods which affect many aspects of the entity. These methods play a vital role in shaping the overall characteristics of `Entity` objects regardless of the entity's subtype. It is a good idea to get to know how to manipulate entities in order to take full control over how the entities appear, react, store information, and much more. Use the following list to familiarize yourself with some of the most important methods of the `Entity` object, paired with their corresponding getter methods. Methods missing from this list will be covered in more detail in this and the following chapters:

- `setVisible(pBoolean)` and `isVisible()`: This method can be used to set whether or not the entity is visible on the scene. Setting these methods to `true` will allow the entity to render, setting them to `false` will disable rendering.

- `setChildrenVisible(pBoolean)` and `isChildrenVisible()`: Similar to the `setVisible(pBoolean)` method, except that it defines the visibility of the calling entity's children and not itself.

- `setCullingEnabled(pBoolean)` and `isCullingEnabled()`: Entity culling can be a very promising performance optimization technique. See *Disabling rendering with entity culling* in Chapter 8, *Maximizing Performance*, for more details.

- `collidesWith(pOtherEntity)`: This method is used to detect when the entity that is calling this method collides, or overlaps, with the `Entity` object supplied as this method's parameter. If the entities are colliding, this method returns `true`.

- `setIgnoreUpdate(pBoolean)` and `isIgnoreUpdate()`: Ignoring entity updates can provide noticeable performance improvements. See *Ignoring entity updates* in Chapter 8, *Maximizing Performance*, for more details.

- `setChildrenIgnoreUpdate(pBoolean)` and `isChildrenIgnoreUpdate()`: Similar to the `setIgnoreUpdate(pBoolean)` method, except that it only affects the calling entity's children and not itself.

- `getRootEntity()`: This method will iterate through the entity's parent until it reaches the root parent. Once the root parent is found, this method will return the root `Entity` object; in most cases, the root being our game's `Scene` object.

- `setTag(pInt)` and `getTag()`: This method can be used for storing an integer value within an entity. Typically used for setting up identification values to entities.

- `setParent(pEntity)` and `hasParent()`: Sets the parent entity to the entity calling this method. The `hasParent()` method returns a `true` or `false` value depending on whether or not the calling entity has a parent.

- `setZIndex(pInt)` and `getZIndex()`: Set the Z index of the calling entity. Entities with a greater value will appear in front of entities with a lesser value. By default, all entities have a Z index of `0`, meaning that they simply appear in the order they are attached. See the following `sortChildren()` method for more details.

- `sortChildren()`: This method must be called on the parent of an entity or group of entities which have had their Z index modified before changes take effect on the screen.

- `setPosition(pX, pY)` or `setPosition(pEntity)`: This method can be used to set the position of an entity to specific x/y values, or it can be used to set to another entity's position. Additionally, we can use the `setX(pX)` and `setY(pY)` methods to make changes to only a single axis position.

- `getX()` and `getY()`: These methods are used to obtain the position of an entity in local coordinates; that is, in relation to its parent.

- `setWidth(pWidth)` and `setHeight(pHeight)` or `setSize(pWidth, pHeight)`: These methods can be used to set the width and height of the calling entity. Additionally, we can use the `getWidth()` and `getHeight()` methods, which return their respective values in as a float datatype.

- `setAnchorCenter(pAnchorCenterX, pAnchorCenterY)`: This method can be used to set the anchor center of the entity. The anchor center is the position within an `Entity` object that it will rotate around, skew from, and scale from. Additionally, modifying the anchor center values will relocate the entity's "positioning" anchor from the default center-point. For example, if we move the anchor center position to the upper-left corner of an entity, calling `setPosition(0,0)` would place the entity's upper-left corner to position `(0,0)`.

- `setColor(pRed, pGreen, pBlue)` and `getColor()`: This method can be used to set the color of an entity, from values ranging from `0.0f` for no color through to `1.0f` for full color.

- `setUserData(pObject)` and `getUserData()`: These two methods are incredibly useful when developing games with AndEngine. They allow us to store an object of our choice within the entity and modify it or retrieve it at any point in time. One possibility for user data storage would be to determine what type of weapon a player's character is holding. Use these methods to the fullest!

Applying primitives to a layer

AndEngine's primitive types include `Line`, `Rectangle`, `Mesh`, and `Gradient` objects. In this topic, we're going to focus on the `Mesh` class. Meshes are useful for creating more complex shapes in our games which can have an unlimited amount of uses. In this recipe, we're going to use `Mesh` objects to build a house as seen in the the following figure:

Getting ready...

Please refer to the class named `ApplyingPrimitives` in the code bundle.

How to do it...

In order to create a `Mesh` object, we need to do a little bit more work than what's required for a typical `Rectangle` or `Line` object. Working with `Mesh` objects is useful for a number of reasons. They allow us to strengthen our skills as far as the OpenGL coordinate system goes, we can create oddly-shaped primitives, and we are able to alter individual vertice positions, which can be useful for certain types of animation.

1. The first step involved in creating `Mesh` objects is to create our buffer data which is used to specify the points that will make up the shape of the mesh:

```
float baseBufferData[] = {
    /* First Triangle */
    0, BASE_HEIGHT, UNUSED, /* first point */
    BASE_WIDTH, BASE_HEIGHT, UNUSED, /* second point */
    BASE_WIDTH, 0, UNUSED,      /* third point */

    /* Second Triangle */
```

```
                BASE_WIDTH, 0, UNUSED, /* first point */
                0, 0, UNUSED, /* second point */
                0, BASE_HEIGHT, UNUSED, /* third point */
        };
```

2. Once the buffer data is configured to our liking, we can go ahead and create the `Mesh` object.

```
Mesh baseMesh = new Mesh((WIDTH * 0.5f) - (BASE_WIDTH * 0.5f),
0, baseBufferData, baseBufferData.length / POINTS_PER_TRIANGLE,
DrawMode.TRIANGLES, mEngine.getVertexBufferObjectManager());
```

How it works...

Let's break down the process a little bit more in order to find out just how we ended up with a house made out of primitive `Mesh` objects.

In step one, we're creating the `baseMesh` object's buffer data. This buffer data is used to store points in 3D space. Every three values stored in the buffer data, separated by line-breaks, make up a single vertice in the 3D world. However, it should be understood that since we are working with a 2D game engine, the third value, which is the z index, is of no use to us. For that reason, we have defined the third value for each vertice as the `UNUSED` constant declared within this recipe's class, which is equal to `0`. The points are represented as `(x, y, z)` for each triangle, as to not get the order confused. See the following figure for a representation of the how the points defined in step one will draw a rectangle onto a mesh:

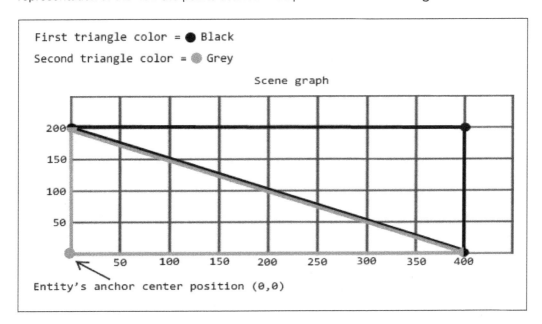

The previous figure represents the `baseMesh` object's buffer data, or plotted points, as seen in the *How to do it...* section's first step. The black lines represent the first set of points:

```
0, BASE_HEIGHT, UNUSED, /* first point */
BASE_WIDTH, BASE_HEIGHT, UNUSED, /* second point */
BASE_WIDTH, 0, UNUSED,  /* third point */
```

The second set of points in the `baseMesh` object's buffer data is represented by the grey lines:

```
BASE_WIDTH, 0, UNUSED, /* first point */
0, 0, UNUSED, /* second point */
0, BASE_HEIGHT, UNUSED, /* third point */
```

Since `BASE_HEIGHT` is equal to `200` and `BASE_WIDTH` is equal to `400`, we can read that the first triangle's first point, which is `(0, BASE_HEIGHT)`, is located in the upper-left corner of the rectangular shape. Moving clockwise, the second point for the first triangle is located at position `(BASE_WIDTH, BASE_HEIGHT)`, which would be the upper-right corner of the rectangular shape. A triangle is obviously made up of three points, so this leaves us with one more vertice to plot. The last vertice of our first triangle is located at position `(BASE_WIDTH, 0)`. As a personal challenge, use the scene graph in the previous figure to find out how the grey triangle's plotted points compare to the buffer data!

In step two, we are taking our `baseMesh` object's buffer data and using it to build the `Mesh` object. The `Mesh` object is a subtype of the `Entity` class, so once we have created the `Mesh` object, we can reposition it, scale it, rotate it, and and make any other adjustments we need. The parameters, in the order they appear in the constructor are as follows; x axis position, y axis position, buffer data, vertex count, draw mode, and vertex buffer object manager. The first two and last parameters are typical for all entities, but the buffer data, vertex count and draw mode are new to us. The buffer data is the array which specifies the plotted vertices, which was covered in step one. The vertex count is simply the number of vertices that the buffer data contains. Every x, y, and z coordinate within our buffer data makes up a single vertice, which is why we are dividing the `baseBufferData.length` value by three for this parameter. And finally, `DrawMode` defines how the `Mesh` object will interpret the buffer data, which can drastically alter the resulting shape of the mesh. The different `DrawMode` types and purposes can be found within the *There's more...* section of this topic.

Before moving on, you may notice that the "door", or rather the blue lines that represent the door are not created in the same manner as the roof and base `Mesh` objects. Instead, we've used lines rather than triangles to draw the outline of the door. Take a look at the following code, which is taken from the `doorBufferData` array, defining the points in which lines connect:

```
0, DOOR_HEIGHT, UNUSED, /* first point */
DOOR_WIDTH, DOOR_HEIGHT, UNUSED, /* second point */
DOOR_WIDTH, 0, UNUSED, /* third point */
0, 0, UNUSED, /* fourth point */
0, DOOR_HEIGHT, UNUSED /* fifth point */
```

Once again, if we draw a scene graph and plot these points similar to the previous figure representing the `baseMesh` object's points, we can actually connect the dots and the lines will result in a rectangular shape. It might seem confusing at first, especially when trying to create the shapes in our heads. The trick to getting started with drawing custom shapes from defined vertices is to keep a blank scene graph saved in a favorite document or image editing software. Create a scene graph similar to the `baseMesh` object's buffer data representation figure and use it to plot points, then simply copy the points to code!

It is very important to remember that the (0,0) position on the previous scene graph figure represents the center of the `Mesh` object. Since we are building the mesh vertices up and to the right, the anchor center position of the mesh will not represent the center of the manually-drawn shapes! This is very important to keep in mind when building `Mesh` objects.

There's more...

Creating meshes can be a pretty daunting subject for beginners, but it's a good idea to get used to them for many reasons. One of the main reasons for AndEngine developers is that it can help us to understand how OpenGL draws shapes to a display on a lower level, which in turn allows us to grasp the higher-level game development functions more easily. The following image contains the various `DrawMode` types that AndEngine has conveniently made available for us in order to create `Mesh` objects in different ways:

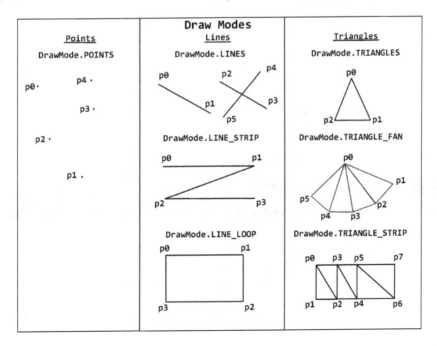

The previous figure shows how vertices within our buffer data will be drawn to the scene by our `Mesh` object depending on the `DrawMode` type selected. Each **p#** in this figure represents a `vertice (x, y, and z value)` within our buffer data array. See the following points for an explanation of the image representations of each `DrawMode` type:

- ▸ `DrawMode.POINTS`: This selection allows us to draw single points for each vertice within the mesh's buffer data. These points will not be connected by any lines; they will simply display a dot on the mesh for each point.

- ▸ `DrawMode.LINES`: This selection allows us to draw individual lines on the mesh. Every two vertices will be connected by a line.

- ▸ `DrawMode.LINE_STRIP`: This selection allows us to draw points on the mesh, with each point after the first point being connected to the previous point. For example, **p1** will be connected to **p0**, **p2** will be connected to **p1**, and so on.

- ▸ `DrawMode.LINE_LOOP`: This selection acts in a similar way to the `DrawMode.LINE_STRIP` type, however, the first point and the final point will also be connected by a line. This allows us to create closed shapes via lines.

- ▸ `DrawMode.TRIANGLES`:– This selection allows us to draw individual triangles on the mesh for each three vertices defined within our buffer data. We are required to keep our vertices at multiples of three for this draw mode.

- ▸ `DrawMode.TRIANGLE_FAN`: This selection allows us to draw coned or pyramidal-shaped meshes. As we can see in the previous figure, we start by specifying a point which defines the top-most point of the cone, then continue on to specify any number of base points for the shape. This draw mode requires three or more vertices to be defined within the buffer data.

- ▸ `DrawMode.TRIANGLE_STRIP`: This selection allows us to easily create customized polygonal meshes. Every vertice defined in the buffer data after the third vertice of the initial triangle will result in a new triangle, creating a new "strip". See the figure representation for an example. This draw mode requires three or more vertices to be defined within the buffer data.

See also

- ▸ *Understanding AndEngine entities* given in this chapter.

Bringing a scene to life with sprites

Here, we come to the topic which might be considered to be the most necessary aspect to creating any 2D game. Sprites allow us to display 2D images on our scene which can be used to display buttons, characters/avatars, environments and themes, backgrounds, and any other entity in our game which may require representation by means of an image file. In this recipe, we'll be covering the various aspects of AndEngine's `Sprite` entities which will give us the information we need to continue to work with `Sprite` objects later on in more complex situations.

Getting ready...

Before we dive into the inner-workings of how sprites are created, we need to understand how to create and manage AndEngine's `BitmapTextureAtlas/BuildableBitmapTextureAtlas` objects as well as the `ITextureRegion` object. For more information, please refer to the recipes, *Working with different types of textures* and *Applying texture options* in *Chapter 1, AndEngine Game Structure*.

Once these recipes have been covered, create a new empty AndEngine project with the `BaseGameActivity` class, provide a PNG formatted image of any size up to 1024 x 1024 pixels in dimension, naming it as `sprite.png` and place it in the `assets/gfx/` folder of the project, then continue to the *How to do it...* section of this recipe.

How to do it...

Sprites can be created and applied to our `Scene` object in just a few quick steps. We must first set up the necessary texture resources that the sprite will use, we must create the `Sprite` object, and then we must attach the `Sprite` object to our `Scene` object. See the following steps for more detail:

1. We will start by creating the texture resources in the `onCreateResources()` method of our `BaseGameActivity` class. Make sure the `mBitmapTextureAtlas` and `mSpriteTextureRegion` objects are global variables, so that they can be reached throughout the various life cycle methods of our activity:

   ```
   BitmapTextureAtlasTextureRegionFactory.setAssetBasePath("gfx/");

   /* Create the bitmap texture atlas for the sprite's texture
   region */
   BuildableBitmapTextureAtlas mBitmapTextureAtlas = new Buil
   dableBitmapTextureAtlas(mEngine.getTextureManager(), 256, 256,
   TextureOptions.BILINEAR);

   /* Create the sprite's texture region via the
   BitmapTextureAtlasTextureRegionFactory */
   mSpriteTextureRegion = BitmapTextureAtlasTextureRegionFactory.
   createFromAsset(mBitmapTextureAtlas, this, "sprite.png");

   /* Build the bitmap texture atlas */
   try {
     mBitmapTextureAtlas.build(new BlackPawnTextureAtlasBuilder<I
   BitmapTextureAtlasSource, BitmapTextureAtlas>(0, 1, 1));
     } catch (TextureAtlasBuilderException e) {
       e.printStackTrace();
     }
   /* Load the bitmap texture atlas into the device's gpu memory
   */
   mBitmapTextureAtlas.load();
   ```

2. Next, we will create the `Sprite` object. We can create and attach the `Sprite` object to the `Scene` object in either the `onCreateScene()` or the `onPopulateScene()` methods of our activity. The parameters to supply in its constructor include, in this order, the sprites initial x coordinate, initial y coordinate, `ITextureRegion` object, and finally the `mEngine` object's vertex buffer object manager:

```
final float positionX = WIDTH * 0.5f;
final float positionY = HEIGHT * 0.5f;

/* Add our marble sprite to the bottom left side of the Scene
initially */
Sprite mSprite = new Sprite(positionX, positionY,
mSpriteTextureRegion, mEngine.getVertexBufferObjectManager());
The last step is to attach our Sprite to the Scene, as is
necessary in order to display any type of Entity on the device's
display:
/* Attach the marble to the Scene */
mScene.attachChild(mSpriteTextureRegion);
```

How it works...

As it might appear in the steps in the previous section, setting up the `mBitmapTextureAtlas` and `mSpriteTextureRegion` objects actually require more work than creating and setting up the `mSprite` object specifically. For this reason, it is encouraged to complete the two recipes mentioned in the *Getting started...* section beforehand.

In the first step, we will create our `mBitmapTextureAtlas` and `mSpriteTextureRegion` objects, suitable to the needs of our `sprite.png` image. Feel free to use any texture options or texture format in this step. It is a very good idea to get to know them well.

Once we've our `ITextureRegion` object created and it's ready for use, we can move to step two where we will create the `Sprite` object. Creating a sprite is a straightforward task. The first two parameters will be used to define the initial position of the sprite, relative to its center point. For the third parameter, we will pass in the `ITextureRegion` object that we created in step one in order to provide the sprite with its appearance as an image on the scene. Finally, we pass in the `mEngine.getVertexBufferObjectManager()` method, which is necessary for most entity subtypes.

Once our `Sprite` object is created, we must attach it to the `Scene` object before it will be displayed on the device, or we can attach it to another `Entity` object which is already attached to the `Scene` object. See the *Understanding AndEngine entities* recipe given in this chapter for more information on entity composition, placement, and other various must-know aspects of `Entity` objects.

There's more...

No game is complete without some sort of sprite animation. After all, a player can only return to a game so many times before getting bored in a game where the characters slide around the screen without moving their feet, don't swing their weapon when attacking an enemy, or even when a grenade simply disappears rather than causing a nice explosion effect. In this day and age, people want to play games which look and feel nice, and nothing says, "Nice!", like buttery smooth animating sprites, right?

In the *Working with different types of textures* recipe in *Chapter 1, AndEngine Game Structure*, we'd covered how to create a `TiledTextureRegion` object which allows us to import useable sprite sheets into our game as a texture. Now let's find out how we can use that `TiledTextureRegion` object with an `AnimatedSprite` object in order to add some animation to our game's sprites. For this demonstration, the code will be working with an image of 300 x 50 pixels in dimension. The sprite sheet can be something as simple as the following figure, just to get an idea of how to create the animation:

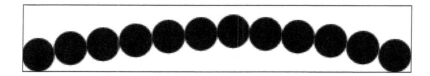

The sprite sheet in the previous figure can be used to create a `TiledTextureRegion` object with 12 columns and 1 row. Creating the `BuildableBitmapTextureAtlas` and `TiledTextureRegion` objects for this sprite sheet can be done with the following code. However, before importing this code, be sure to make a global declaration of the texture region—`TiledTextureRegion mTiledTextureRegion`—in your test project:

```
    /* Create the texture atlas at the same dimensions as the image
    (300x50)*/
    BuildableBitmapTextureAtlas mBitmapTextureAtlas = new BuildableBit
mapTextureAtlas(mEngine.getTextureManager(), 300, 50, TextureOptions.
BILINEAR);

    /* Create the TiledTextureRegion object, passing in the usual
parameters,
     * as well as the number of rows and columns in our sprite sheet
for the
     * final two parameters */
    mTiledTextureRegion = BitmapTextureAtlasTextureRegionFactory.creat
eTiledFromAsset(mBitmapTextureAtlas, this, "gfx/sprite_sheet.png", 12,
1);

    /* Build and load the mBitmapTextureAtlas object */
    try {
```

```
    mBitmapTextureAtlas.build(new BlackPawnTextureAtlasBuilder<IBitm
apTextureAtlasSource, BitmapTextureAtlas>(0, 0, 0));
    } catch (TextureAtlasBuilderException e) {
      e.printStackTrace();
    }
    mBitmapTextureAtlas.load();
```

Now that we've got the `mTiledTextureRegion` sprite sheet to play with in our project, we can create and animate the `AnimatedSprite` object. If you are using a sprite sheet with black circles as seen in the previous figure, don't forget to change the color of the `Scene` object to a non-black color so we can see the `AnimatedSprite` object:

```
    /* Create a new animated sprite in the center of the scene */
    AnimatedSprite animatedSprite = new AnimatedSprite(WIDTH
* 0.5f, HEIGHT * 0.5f, mTiledTextureRegion, mEngine.
getVertexBufferObjectManager());

    /* Length to play each frame before moving to the next */
    long frameDuration[] = {100, 200, 300, 400, 500, 600, 700, 800,
900, 1000, 1100, 1200};

    /* We can define the indices of the animation to play between */
    int firstTileIndex = 0;
    int lastTileIndex = mTiledTextureRegion.getTileCount();

    /* Allow the animation to continuously loop? */
    boolean loopAnimation = true;

    * Animate the sprite with the data as set defined above */
    animatedSprite.animate(frameDuration, firstTileIndex,
lastTileIndex, loopAnimation, new IAnimationListener(){

      @Override
      public void onAnimationStarted(AnimatedSprite pAnimatedSprite,
          int pInitialLoopCount) {
        /* Fired when the animation first begins to run*/
      }

      @Override
      public void onAnimationFrameChanged(AnimatedSprite
pAnimatedSprite,
          int pOldFrameIndex, int pNewFrameIndex) {
        /* Fired every time a new frame is selected to display*/
      }

      @Override
```

```
        public void onAnimationLoopFinished(AnimatedSprite
pAnimatedSprite,
            int pRemainingLoopCount, int pInitialLoopCount) {
          /* Fired when an animation loop ends (from first to last
frame) */
        }

        @Override
        public void onAnimationFinished(AnimatedSprite pAnimatedSprite)
{
          /* Fired when an animation sequence ends */
        }
        );

      mScene.attachChild(animatedSprite);
```

Creating the `AnimatedSprite` object can be done following the steps in this recipe while creating a regular `Sprite` object. Once it's created, we are able to set up its animation data, including individual frame duration, first and last tile indices to animate through, and whether or not to loop the animation continuously. Note that the `frameDuration` array must be equal to the frame count! Failing to follow this rule will result in an `IllegalArgumentException` exception. Once the data has been set up, we can call the `animate()` method on the `AnimatedSprite` object, supplying all of the data and adding an `IAnimationListener` listener if we wish. As the comments in the listener suggest, we gain a large portion of control over the animations with AndEngine's `AnimatedSprite` class.

Using OpenGL's dithering capability

When developing visually appealing games on the mobile platform, it is a likely scenario that we'll want to include some gradients in our images, especially when dealing with 2D graphics. Gradients are great for creating lighting effects, shadows, and many other objects we'd otherwise not be able to apply to a full 2D world. The problem lies in the fact that we're developing for mobile devices, so we unfortunately do not have an unlimited amount of resources at our disposal. Because of this, AndEngine down-samples the surface view color format to `RGB_565` by default. Regardless of the texture format we define within our textures, they will always be down-sampled before being displayed on the device. We could alter the color format applied to AndEngine's surface view, but it's likely that the performance-hit will not be worth it when developing larger games with many sprites.

Here, we have two separate screenshots of a simple sprite with a gradient texture; both textures are using the `RGBA_8888` texture format and `BILINEAR` texture filtering (the highest quality).

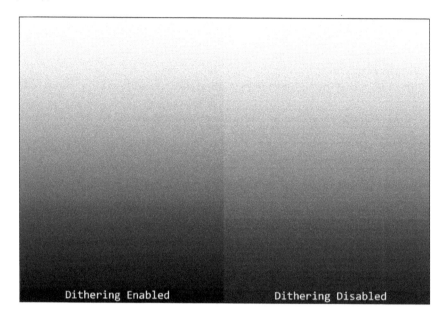

The image on the right-hand side is applied to the `Scene` object without any modifications, while the image on the left-hand side has OpenGL's dithering capability enabled. The difference between the two otherwise identical images is immediately noticeable. Dithering is a great way for us to combat down-sampling applied by the surface view without us having to rely on maximum color quality formats. In short, by dithering low-levels of randomized noise within our image's colors, it results in a smoother finish which is found in the image to the left.

Enabling dithering is simple to apply to our entities in AndEngine, but as with everything, it's wise to pick and choose which textures apply dithering. The algorithm does add a little bit of extra overhead, where if used too often could result in a larger performance loss than simply reverting our surface view to `RGBA_8888`. In the following code, we are enabling dithering in our `preDraw()` method and disabling it in our `postDraw()` method:

```
@Override
protected void preDraw(GLState pGLState, Camera pCamera) {
  // Enable dithering
  pGLState.enableDither();
  super.preDraw(pGLState, pCamera);
}

@Override
protected void postDraw(GLState pGLState, Camera pCamera) {
```

```
    // Disable dithering
    pGLState.disableDither();
    super.postDraw(pGLState, pCamera);
}
```

Dithering can be applied to any subtype of AndEngine's Shape class (Sprites, Text, primitives, and so on.).

 For more information about OpenGL ES 2.0 and how to work with all of the different functions, visit the link at http://www.khronos.org/opengles/sdk/docs/man/.

See also

▶ *Working with different types of textures in Chapter 1, Working with Entities*

▶ *Applying texture options in Chapter 1, Working with Entities.*

▶ *Understanding AndEngine entities in this chapter.*

Applying text to a layer

Text is an important part of game development as it can be used to dynamically display point systems, tutorials, descriptions, and more. AndEngine also allows us to create text styles which suit individual game types better by specifying customized Font objects. In this recipe, we're going to create a Text object, which updates itself with the current system time as well as correct its position every time the length of the string grows or shrinks. This will prepare us for the use of Text objects in cases where we need to display scores, time, and other non-specific dynamic string situations.

Getting ready...

Applying Text objects to our Scene object requires a working knowledge of AndEngine's font resources. Please perform the the recipe, Using AndEngine font resources in *Chapter 1, Working with Entities*, then proceed with the *How to do it...* section of this recipe. Refer to the class named ApplyingText in the code bundle for this recipe's activity in code.

When applying `Text` objects to our `Scene` object, we are required to create a `Font` object which will define the text's style, and create the `Text` object itself. See the following steps for the specific actions we must take in order to properly display a `Text` object on our scene:

1. The first step to creating any `Text` object is to prepare ourselves a `Font` object. The `Font` object will act as the resource which defines the style of the `Text` object. Additionally, we need to prepare the letters that we plan for the `Text` object to display:

```
mFont = FontFactory.create(mEngine.getFontManager(),
    mEngine.getTextureManager(), 256, 256,
        Typeface.create(Typeface.DEFAULT, Typeface.NORMAL), 32f,
true,
        Color.WHITE);
mFont.load();


/*
 * Prepare the mFont object for the most common characters
used. This
 * will eliminate the need for the garbage collector to run
when using a
 * letter/number that's never been used before
 */
 mFont.prepareLetters("Time: 1234567890".toCharArray());
```

Once we've got our Font object created and ready for use, we can create the Text:

```
/* Create the time Text object which will update itself as
time passes */
    Text mTimeText = new Text(0, timeTextHeight, mFont, TIME_
STRING_PREFIX
        + TIME_FORMAT, MAX_CHARACTER_COUNT, mEngine.
getVertexBufferObjectManager()) {

        // Overridden methods as seen in step 3...
    };
```

2. If we're dealing with final strings which may never change, only the first two steps need to be covered. However, in this recipe we will need to override the `onManagedUpdate()` method of the `Text` entity in order to make adjustments to its string over time. In this case, we're updating the time value of the string after every second passed:

```
int lastSecond = 0;

@Override
```

```
protected void onManagedUpdate(float pSecondsElapsed) {

  Calendar c = Calendar.getInstance();

  /*
   * We will only obtain the second for now in order to verify
   * that it's time to update the Text's string
   */
  final int second = c.get(Calendar.SECOND);

  /*
   * If the last update's second value is not equal to the
   * current...
   */
  if (lastSecond != second) {

  /* Obtain the new hour and minute time values */
    final int hour = c.get(Calendar.HOUR);
    final int minute = c.get(Calendar.MINUTE);

    /* also, update the latest second value */
    lastSecond = second;

     /* Build a new string with the current time */
    final String timeTextSuffix = hour + ":" + minute + ":"
      + second;

    /* Set the Text object's string to that of the new time */
    this.setText(TIME_STRING_PREFIX + timeTextSuffix);

    /*
      * Since the width of the Text will change with every
change
      * in second, we should realign the Text position to the
      * edge of the screen minus half the Text's width
    */
    this.setX(WIDTH - this.getWidth() * 0.5f);
  }

  super.onManagedUpdate(pSecondsElapsed);
  }
```

Finally, we can make color adjustments to the Text and then attach it to the Scene or another Entity:

```
  /* Change the color of the Text to blue */
  mTimeText.setColor(0, 0, 1);

  /* Attach the Text object to the Scene */
  mScene.attachChild(mTimeText);
```

How it works...

By this point, we should already have an understanding of how to create the Font object as we had discussed it in the first chapter. If creating Font objects is not yet understood, please visit the recipe, *Using AndEngine font resources* in *Chapter 1, Working with Entities*.

In the first step, we are simply creating a basic Font object which will create a rather generic style for our Text object. Once the Font object has been created, we are preparing only the necessary characters that will be displayed throughout the life of the Text object with the mFont.prepareLetters() method. Doing so allows us to avoid garbage collector invocations within the Font object. The values used in this recipe will obviously range from 0 to 9 as we are dealing with time, as well as the individual characters that make up the string, Time:.

Once step one is completed, we can move onto step two where we create the Text object. The Text object requires that we specify its initial position on the screen in x and y coordinates, the Font object to use as a style, the initial string to display, its maximum character count, and finally the vertex buffer object manager as needed by all Entity objects. However, since we're dealing with a dynamically-updating String value for this Text object, which will require adjustments on the x axis, the parameters including the x coordinate as well as the initial string are not so important as they will be adjusted frequently during updates to the Text object. The most important parameter is the maximum character count. Failing to keep the Text object's maximum character count below that of the value specified within this parameter will result in the application receiving an ArrayIndexOutOfBoundsException exception and will likely require termination. For this reason, we are adding up the length of the largest string as seen in the following code snippet:

```
private static final String TIME_STRING_PREFIX = "Time: ";
private static final String TIME_FORMAT = "00:00:00";

/* Obtain the maximum number of characters that our Text
 * object will need to display*/
private static final int MAX_CHARACTER_COUNT = TIME_STRING_PREFIX.
length() + TIME_FORMAT.length();
```

In the third step, we are overriding the Text object's onManagedUpdate() method in order to apply changes to the Text object's string after every second passed. At first, we simply obtain the device's current second value, using it to compare with the second value in the previous call to the Text object's onManagedUpdate() method. This allows us to avoid updating the Text object with the system time on every single update. If the previous second that the Text object's string was updated with is not the same as the new second value, then we continue on to obtain the current minute and hour values as well via the Calendar.getInstance().get(HOUR) method and MINUTE variation. Now that we've got all of the values, we build a new string containing the updated time, and call setText(pString) on the Text object to change the string it will display on the device.

However, due to the fact that each individual character width might have a different value, we also need to make corrections in the position in order to keep the full `Text` object on the screen. By default, the anchor position is set to the center of an `Entity` object, so by calling `this.setX(WIDTH - this.getWidth() * 0.5f)`, where `this` refers to the `Text` object, we position the entity's center-most point at the maximum screen width to the right, and then subtract half of the entity's width. This will allow the text to sit right along the edge of the screen even after its characters change the width of the `Text` object.

There's more...

Sometimes our games may require a little bit of formatting to the `Text` object's strings. In cases where we need to adjust the `Text` object's horizontal alignment, apply auto-wrapping to the text if its string exceeds a certain width, or a leading space to the text, we can do these with some very easy-to-use methods. The following methods can be called directly on the `Text` object; for example, `mText.setLeading(3)`:

- `setAutoWrap(pAutoWrap)`: This method allows us to define whether or not, and if so, how a `Text` entity will perform auto-wrapping. The options we have for parameters include `AutoWrap.NONE`, `AutoWrap.LETTERS`, `AutoWrap.WORDS`, and `AutoWrap.CJK`. With `LETTERS`, line break won't wait for a whitespace before breaking to a new line while `WORDS` will. The `CJK` variant is an option which allows auto-wrapping for Chinese, Japanese, and Korean characters. This method should be used alongside `setAutoWrapWidth(pWidth)`, where `pWidth` defines the maximum width of any single line within the `Text` object's string, causing line-breaks when necessary.

- `setHorizontalAlign(pHorizontalAlign)`: This method allows us to define the type of alignment the `Text` object's string should follow. The parameters include `HorizontalAlign.LEFT`, `HorizontalAlign.CENTER`, and `HorizontalAlign.RIGHT`. The result is similar to what we'd see when setting alignment within a text editor.

- `setLeading(pLeading)`: This method allows us to set a leading space at the beginning of the `Text` object's string. The parameter required is a float value, which defines the leading width of the string.

See also

- *Using AndEngine font resources* in *Chapter 1, Working with Entities*.
- *Overriding the onManagedUpdate method* in this chapter.

Using relative rotation

Rotating entities relative to the position of other entities in 2D space is a great function to know. The uses for relative rotation are limitless and always seems to be a "hot topic" for newer mobile game developers. One of the more prominent examples of this technique being used is in tower-defense games, which allows a tower's turret to aim towards the direction that an enemy, non-playable character is walking. In this recipe, we're going to introduce a method of rotating our `Entity` objects in order to point them in the direction of a given x/y position. The following image displays how we will create an arrow on the scene, which will automatically point to the position of the circle image, wherever it moves to:

Getting ready...

We'll need to include two images for this recipe; one named `marble.png` at 32 x 32 pixels in dimension and another named `arrow.png` at 31 pixels wide by 59 pixels high. The marble can be any image. We will simply drag this image around the scene as we please. The arrow image should be in the shape of an arrow, with the arrowhead pointing directly upward on the image. See the screenshot in the introduction for an example of the images to include. Include these assets in an empty `BaseGameActivity` test project then please refer to the class named `RelativeRotation` in the code bundle.

How to do it...

Follow these steps:

1. Implement the `IOnSceneTouchListener` listener in the `BaseGameActivity` class:

   ```
   public class RelativeRotation extends BaseGameActivity implements
   IOnSceneTouchListener{
   ```

2. Set the `Scene` object's `onSceneTouchListener` in the activity's `onCreateScene()` method:

```
mScene.setOnSceneTouchListener(this);
```

3. Populate the `Scene` object with the marble and arrow sprites. The arrow sprite is positioned in the center of the scene, while the marble's position is updated to the coordinates of any touch event location:

```
/* Add our marble sprite to the bottom left side of the Scene
initially */
mMarbleSprite = new Sprite(mMarbleTextureRegion.getWidth(),
mMarbleTextureRegion.getHeight(), mMarbleTextureRegion, mEngine.
getVertexBufferObjectManager());

/* Attach the marble to the Scene */
mScene.attachChild(mMarbleSprite);

/* Create the arrow sprite and center it in the Scene */
mArrowSprite = new Sprite(WIDTH * 0.5f, HEIGHT * 0.5f,
mArrowTextureRegion, mEngine.getVertexBufferObjectManager());

/* Attach the arrow to the Scene */
mScene.attachChild(mArrowSprite);
```

4. Step four introduces the `onSceneTouchEvent()` method which handles the movement of the marble sprite via a touch event on the device's display:

```
@Override
public boolean onSceneTouchEvent(Scene pScene, TouchEvent
pSceneTouchEvent) {
    // If a user moves their finger on the device
    if(pSceneTouchEvent.isActionMove()){

        /* Set the marble's position to that of the touch even
coordinates */
        mMarbleSprite.setPosition(pSceneTouchEvent.getX(),
pSceneTouchEvent.getY());

        /* Calculate the difference between the two sprites x and y
coordinates */
        final float dX = mMarbleSprite.getX() - mArrowSprite.getX();
        final float dY = mMarbleSprite.getY() - mArrowSprite.getY();

        /* Calculate the angle of rotation in radians*/
        final float angle = (float) Math.atan2(-dY, dX);
```

```
        /* Convert the angle from radians to degrees, adding the
default image rotation */
        final float rotation = MathUtils.radToDeg(angle) + DEFAULT_
IMAGE_ROTATION;

        /* Set the arrow's new rotation */
        mArrowSprite.setRotation(rotation);

        return true;
    }

    return false;
}
```

How it works...

In this class, we're creating a sprite which is represented by an arrow image and placing it in the direct center of the screen, automatically pointing to a another sprite represented by a marble. The marble is draggable via touch events through the use of an `IOnSceneTouchListener` listener implementation within our `BaseGameActivity` class. We then register the touch listener to the `mScene` object. In situations where an entity rotates according to another entity's position, we'll have to include the rotation functionality in some method that is consistently updated, otherwise our arrow would not continuously react. We can do this through update threads, but in this instance we'll include that functionality in the `onSceneTouchEvent()` overridden method as the "target" will not actually move until we touch the scene anyway.

In the first step, we're allowing our activity to override the `onSceneTouchEvent()` method by implementing the `IOnSceneTouchListener` interface. Once we've implemented the touch listener, we can take care of step two and allow the `Scene` object to receive touch events and respond according to the code situated inside the activity's overridden `onSceneTouchEvent()` method. This is done with the `setOnSceneTouchListener(pSceneTouchListener)` method.

In step four, the `if(pSceneTouchEvent.isActionMove())` conditional statement determines whether a finger is moving over the scene, updating the marble's position, and calculating the new rotation for the arrow sprite if the conditional statement returns `true`.

We first start by updating the marble's position to the location of touch through the use of the `setPosition(pX, pY)` method as seen in the following code snippet:

```
mMarbleSprite.setPosition(pSceneTouchEvent.getX(), pSceneTouchEvent.
getY());
```

Next, we subtract the pointer's x/y coordinates from the target's x/y coordinates. This gives us the difference between each of the sprites' coordinates which will be used to calculate the angle between the two positions. In this case, the pointer is the `mArrowSprite` object and the target is the `mMarbleSprite` object:

```
/* Calculate the difference between the two sprites x and y
coordinates */
final float dX = mMarbleSprite.getX() - mArrowSprite.getX();
final float dY = mMarbleSprite.getY() - mArrowSprite.getY();

/* Calculate the angle of rotation in radians*/
final float angle = (float) Math.atan2(-dY, dX);
```

Lastly, since AndEngine's `setRotation(pRotation)` method uses degrees and the `atan2(pY, pX)` method returns radians, we must perform a simple conversion. We will use AndEngine's `MathUtils` class which includes a `radToDeg(pRadian)` method to convert our angle value from radians to degrees. Once we obtain the correct angle in degrees, we will set the `mArrowSprite` object's rotation:

```
/* Convert the angle from radians to degrees, adding the default image
rotation */
final float rotation = MathUtils.radToDeg(angle) + DEFAULT_IMAGE_
ROTATION;

/* Set the arrow's new rotation */
mArrowSprite.setRotation(rotation);
```

One last thing to note is that the `DEFAULT_IMAGE_ROTATION` value is an `int` value which represents 90 degrees. This value is simply used to offset the rotation of the `mArrowSprite` sprite, otherwise we would be required to properly rotate the image within our image editing software. If the pointer within our custom images is not facing the uppermost point of the image, this value may require adjustments in order to properly align the pointer with the target.

Overriding the onManagedUpdate method

Overriding an `Entity` object's `onManagedUpdate()` method can be extremely useful in all types of situations. By doing so, we can allow our entities to execute code every time the entity is updated through the update thread, occuring many times per second unless the entity is set to ignore updates. There are so many possibilities including animating our entity, checking for collisions, producing timed events, and much more. Using our `Entity` objects's `onManagedUpdate()` method also saves us from having to create and register new timer handlers for time-based events for a single entity.

This recipe requires basic knowledge of the `Entity` object in AndEngine. Please read through the entire recipe, *Understanding AndEngine entities* given in this chapter, then create a new empty AndEngine project with a `BaseGameActivity` class and refer to the class named `OverridingUpdates` in the code bundle.

How to do it...

In this recipe, we are creating two `Rectangle` objects. One rectangle will remain in the center of the scene, rotating consistently. The second rectangle will continuously move from left to right and bottom to top on the scene, resetting back to the left-hand side when it reaches the right, and resetting back to the bottom when it reaches the top of the scene. Additionally, the moving rectangle will turn green anytime it collides with the center rectangle. All of these movements and conditionals will be applied and executed through the use of each object's overridden `onManagedUpdate(pSecondsElapsed)` method.

1. Override the first `Rectangle` object's `onManagedUpdate()` method for continuous rotation:

    ```
    /* Value which defines the rotation speed of this Entity */
    final int rotationIncrementalFactor = 25;

    /* Override the onManagedUpdate() method of this Entity */
    @Override
    protected void onManagedUpdate(float pSecondsElapsed) {

        /* Calculate a rotation offset based on time passed */
        final float rotationOffset = pSecondsElapsed *
    rotationIncrementalFactor;

        /* Apply the rotation offset to this Entity */
        this.setRotation(this.getRotation() + rotationOffset);

        /* Proceed with the rest of this Entity's update process */
        super.onManagedUpdate(pSecondsElapsed);
    }
    ```

2. Override the second `Rectangle` object's `onManagedUpdate()` method for continuous position updates, conditional checking, and collision detection:

    ```
    /* Value to increment this rectangle's position by on each
    update */
    final int incrementXValue = 5;

    /* Obtain half the Entity's width and height values */
    ```

```
final float halfWidth = this.getWidth() * 0.5f;
final float halfHeight = this.getHeight() * 0.5f;


/* Override the onManagedUpdate() method of this Entity */
@Override
protected void onManagedUpdate(float pSecondsElapsed) {

    /* Obtain the current x/y values */
    final float currentX = this.getX();
    final float currentY = this.getY();


    /* obtain the max width and next height, used for condition
checking */
    final float maxWidth = currentX + halfWidth;
    final float nextHeight = currentY + halfHeight;


    // On every update...
    /* Increment the x position if this Entity is within the
camera WIDTH */
        if(maxWidth <= WIDTH){
        /* Increase this Entity's x value by 5 pixels */
        this.setX(currentX + incrementXValue);
    } else {
        /* Reset the Entity back to the bottom left of the Scene
if it exceeds the mCamera's
        * HEIGHT value */
        if(nextHeight >= HEIGHT){
        this.setPosition(halfWidth, halfHeight);
        } else {
            /* if this Entity reaches the WIDTH value of our camera,
move it
            * back to the left side of the Scene and slightly
increment its y position */
            this.setPosition(halfWidth, nextHeight);
        }
    }


    /* If the two rectangle's are colliding, set this
rectangle's color to GREEN */
    if(this.collidesWith(mRectangleOne) && this.getColor() !=
org.andengine.util.adt.color.Color.GREEN){
    this.setColor(org.andengine.util.adt.color.Color.GREEN);


    /* If the rectangle's are no longer colliding, set this
rectangle's color to RED */
```

```
        } else if(this.getColor() != org.andengine.util.adt.color.
Color.RED){
            this.setColor(org.andengine.util.adt.color.Color.RED);
        }

        /* Proceed with the rest of this Entity's update process */
        super.onManagedUpdate(pSecondsElapsed);
    }
```

How it works...

In the first `Rectangle` object that we created, we are overriding its `onManagedUpdate(pSe condsElapsed)` method to continuously update the rotation to a new value. For the second `Rectangle` object, we're moving it from the far left-hand side of the screen to the far right-hand side of the screen continuously. Once the second rectangle reaches the far right-hand side of the screen, it is repositioned back to the left-hand side and we raise the `Rectangle` object on the scene by half of the `Rectangle` object's height. Additionally, when the two rectangles overlap, the moving rectangle will change its color to green until they are no longer touching.

The code in step one allows us to create an event every time the entity is updated. In this specific overridden method, we're calculating a rotation offset for the `Rectangle` object based on the seconds passed since it was last updated. Because the entity is updated many times per second, depending on the number of frames per second the device is able to achieve, we multiply `pSecondsElapsed` by `25` in order to increase the rotation speed a bit. Otherwise, we'd be rotating our entity along the lines of `0.01` degrees every update which would take quite a while for an object to make a full revolution at that rate. We can use the `pSecondsElapsed` update to our advantage when dealing with updates in order to make modifications to events based on time passed since the last update.

Step two is a little bit more robust than the first step. In step two, we are overriding the second rectangle's `onManagedUpdate()` method in order to perform position-checking, collision-checking, and updating the rectangle's position on every update to the entity. To start off, we are declaring variables which will contain values such as the current position of the entity, the half width and half height values of the entity for proper offsetting from the anchor center, and the next update position used for checking the position. Doing so allows us to reduce the number of calculations needed throughout the entity's update. Applying poorly-optimized code in the update thread can lead to lowered frame rate very quickly. It is important to make as method calls and calculations as possible; for example, obtaining the `currentX` value five times throughout the `onManagedUpdate()` method would be more ideal than calling `this.getX()` five times.

Continuing on with the position-checking and updating in step two, we start off by determining whether the `Rectangle` object's anchor center plus half its width, which is represented by the `maxWidth` variable, is less than or equal to the `WIDTH` value that represents the furthest coordinate to the right of the display. If true, we proceed to increment the x coordinate of the `Rectangle` object by `incrementXValue`, which is equal to 5 pixels. On the other hand, we will either reset the `Rectangle` object back to the bottom-left corner of the scene if the `nextHeight` value is greater than or equal to our camera's `HEIGHT` value, or simply increase the `Rectangle` object's height by half its width and return it to the left-hand side of the display if the rectangle has not yet reached the top of the display.

Finally, we've got our collision-checking method within the `onManagedUpdate()` method of our second `Rectangle` object. By calling `this.collidesWith(mRectangleOne)`, we can determine whether or not the `this` object is overlapping with the object specified, or in this case, `mRectangleOne`. We will then make one additional check to determine whether or not the color is not already equal to the color we plan on changing the `Rectangle` object to if collision is detected; setting the `Rectangle` object to green if the conditions return `true`. However, `collidesWith()` can be a rather expensive collision-checking method if it is being performed by multiple `Entity` objects on every update! In this recipe, we're purely using this collision-checking method as an example. One option to look into would be to perform a lightweight distance detection between the two objects prior to performing the collision detection.

There's more...

As briefly mentioned before, *all children receive the update call from their parent*. Child entities in this case also inherit the modified pSecondsElapsed value of the parent. We can even go as far as slowing our entire `Scene` object, including all of its children, by overriding its `onManagedUpdate()` method and reducing the pSecondsElapsed value like so:

```
super.onManagedUpdate(pSecondsElapsed * 0.5f);
```

Returning a value equal to half the pSecondsElapsed value to the `super` method would cause all entities attached to that `Scene` object to slow down by half in all aspects. That's just a little something to keep in mind when considering options for pausing or creating a slow motion effect for our games.

Using modifiers and entity modifiers

AndEngine provides us with what are known as **modifiers** and **entity modifiers**. Through the use of these modifiers we can apply neat effects to our entities with great ease. These modifiers apply specific changes to an `Entity` object over a defined period of time, such as movement, scaling, rotation, and more. On top of that, we can include listeners and ease functions to entity modifiers for full control over how they work, making them some of the most powerful-to-use methods for applying certain types of animation to our `Scene` object in AndEngine.

Before continuing, we should mention that a modifier and an entity modifier in AndEngine are two different objects. A modifier is meant to be applied directly to an entity, causing modifications to an entity's properties over time, such as scaling, movement, and rotation. An entity modifier on the other hand, is meant to act as a container for any number of modifiers, which handle the order in which a group of modifiers are executed. This will be discussed more in depth throughout this recipe.

Getting ready...

This recipe requires basic knowledge of the `Entity` object in AndEngine. Please read through the entire recipe, *Understanding AndEngine entities* given in this chapter, then create a new empty AndEngine project with a `BaseGameActivity` class and then refer to the *How to do it...* section of this recipe.

How to do it...

In this recipe, we're going to cover AndEngine's entity modifiers, including modifier listeners and ease functions to apply smooth transitional effects to the modifiers. If that sounds confusing, have no fear! AndEngine modifiers are actually very simple to work with and can be used to apply different types of animations to our `Entity` objects in as little as a few steps for basic modifiers. The following steps cover setting up an `Entity` object with a movement modifier which will ease us into further discussion of entity modifiers. Import the code in these steps to the `onPopulateScene()` method of the activity:

1. Create and attach any type of entity to the `Scene` object. We will be applying entity modifiers to this entity:

    ```
    /* Define the rectangle's width/height values */
    final int rectangleDimensions = 80;

    /* Define the initial rectangle position in the bottom
     * left corner of the Scene */
    final int initialPosition = (int) (rectangleDimensions * 0.5f);

    /* Create the Entity which we will apply modifiers to */
    Rectangle rectangle = new Rectangle(initialPosition,
    initialPosition, rectangleDimensions, rectangleDimensions,
    mEngine.getVertexBufferObjectManager());

    /* Set the rectangle's color to white so we can see it on the
    Scene */
    rectangle.setColor(org.andengine.util.adt.color.Color.WHITE);

    /* Attach the rectangle to the Scene */
    mScene.attachChild(rectangle);
    ```

2. Once we've got an entity placed on our `Scene` object, we can start to create our modifiers. In this step, we'll be creating a `MoveModifier` object, which allows us to apply a positional change to an entity over time. But first, we will define its values:

```
/* Define the movement modifier values */
final float duration = 3;
final float fromX = initialPosition;
final float toX = WIDTH - rectangleDimension * 0.5f;
final float fromY = initialPosition;
final float toY = HEIGHT - rectangleDimension * 0.5f;

/* Create the MoveModifier with the defined values */
MoveModifier moveModifier = new MoveModifier(duration, fromX,
fromY, toX, toY);
```

3. Now that we've got our `moveModifier` object created and set up as we'd like, we can register this modifier to any entity we wish with the following call, which will start the movement effect:

```
/* Register the moveModifier to our rectangle entity */
rectangle.registerEntityModifier(moveModifier);
```

How it works...

The topic of entity modifiers is quite extensive, so we will start by jumping in to the steps. From there we will use the steps as a base foundation for us to dive deeper into more complex discussions and examples on the use of entity modifiers.

In the first step, we're simply creating our `Entity` object, which is a `Rectangle` in this case, that we'll be using as our test subject for applying modifiers to. Simply add the code in this step to the `onPopulateScene()` method; this code shall remain untouched throughout our upcoming modifier and entity modifier "experiments".

In the second step, we will start to work with one of the most basic modifiers, which is of course the `MoveModifier` modifier. This modifier simply allows us define a start position for the movement, an ending position for the movement, and a duration, in seconds, that it will take to move from the starting point to the ending point. This is very simple stuff as we can see and what's most notable about modifiers is that, for the most part, this is all it really takes to set up most modifiers. All modifiers really require is a "from" value, a "to" value, and a duration defining the time in seconds in which "from-to" occurs. Keep that in mind and working with modifiers will be an absolute breeze for the most part!

Next, in our third step we simply apply our newly created `moveModifier` object to our `rectangle` object via the `registerEntityModifier(pModifier)` method. This will apply the `moveModifier` effect to the rectangle, first positioning it to its "from" coordinate, then move it to the "to" coordinates over a 3 second time span.

We know that to register a modifier or entity modifier to an `Entity` object, we can call `entity.registerEntityModifier(pEntityModifier)`, but we should also know that once we are finished with a modifier we should remove it from the `Entity` object. We can do this by either calling `entity.unregisterEntityModifier(pEntityModifier)` or if we want to remove all entity modifiers attached to an `Entity` object, we can call `entity.clearEntityModifiers()`. On the other hand, if a modifier or entity modifier runs its full duration and we're not quite ready to remove it from the entity, we must call `modifier.reset()` in order to replay the effect. Or if we'd like to make a small adjustment to the modifier before replaying the effect, we can call `modifier.reset(duration, fromValue, toValue)`. Where the parameters in the `reset` method would be relative to the type of modifier we're resetting.

The `moveModifier` object works, but it's dreadfully boring! After all, we're just moving a rectangle from the bottom-left corner of our scene to the upper-right corner. Fortunately, that's only just scratching the surface of modifier application. The following subheading contains a reference, and example where necessary, to all of the modifiers that AndEngine is capable of applying to our `Entity` objects.

AndEngine's modifiers

The following is a collection of all of the AndEngine modifiers that we are able to apply to our entities. The more advanced modifiers will be provided with a quick example code snippet. Feel free to try them out in your test project as we cover them:

  ▶ `AlphaModifier`: Adjust the alpha value of an entity over time with this modifier. The parameters for the constructor include duration, from alpha, and to alpha, in that order.

  ▶ `ColorModifier`: Adjust the color values of an entity over time with this modifier. The parameters for the constructor include duration, from red, to red, from green, to green, from blue, and to blue, in that order.

  ▶ `DelayModifier`: This modifier is meant to be attributed to the entity modifier objects in order to provide a delay between one modifier being executed and another modifier being executed. The parameter includes duration.

  ▶ `FadeInModifier`: Based on the `AlphaModifier` class, the `FadeInModifier` modifier changes an entity's alpha value from `0.0f` to `1.0f` over a defined duration, supplied in the constructor.

  ▶ `FadeOutModifier`: Similar to `FadeOutModifier`, except the alpha values are swapped.

  ▶ `JumpModifier`: This modifier can be used to apply a "jump" motion to an entity. The parameters include duration, from x, to x, from y, to y, and jump height. These values will define the distance and height that the entity appears to jump over the defined duration.

- `MoveByModifier`: This modifier allows us to offset the position of an entity. The parameters include duration, x offset, and y offset, in that order. For example, specifying an offset of `-15` will move the entity to the left by 15 units on the scene.

- `MoveXModifier` and `MoveYModifier`: These modifiers, similar to `MoveModifier`, allow us to provide movement to an entity. However, these methods apply the movement only on a single axis as determined by the method names. The parameters include duration, from coordinate, and to coordinate, in that order.

- `RotationAtModifier`: This modifier allows us to apply a rotation to the entity while offsetting the center of rotation. The parameters include duration, from rotation, to rotation, rotation center x, and rotation center y.

- `RotationByModifier`: This modifier allows us to offset the entity's current rotation value. The parameters include duration and rotation offset value. For example, providing a rotation offset value of `90` will rotate the entity ninety degrees clockwise.

- `RotationModifier`: This modifier allows us to rotate an entity from a specific value, to another specific value. The parameters include duration, from rotation, and to rotation.

- `ScaleAtModifier`: This modifier allows us to scale an entity while offsetting the center of scaling. The parameters include duration, from scale, to scale, scale center x, and scale center y.

- `ScaleModifier`: This modifier allows us to scale an entity from a specific value, to another specific value. The parameters include duration, from scale, and to scale, in that order.

- `SkewModifier`: This modifier allows us to skew an entity's x and y values over time. The parameters include duration, from skew x, to skew x, from skew y, and to skew y, in that specific order.

- `PathModifier`: This modifier is relative to `MoveModifier`, except we are able to add as many "to" coordinates as we please. This allows us to create a path on the `Scene` object for the entity to follow by specifying pairs of x/y coordinates for the `PathModifier` modifier. See the following steps for a walkthrough on the topic of creating a `PathModifier` modifier for our entities:

    1. Define the way-points for the path. The way-point arrays for the x and y coordinates should have the same number of points, as they will be paired up in order to make a single x/y coordinate for `PathModifier`. We must have at least two points set in each of the arrays, as we'll need at least a start and end point:

    ```
    /* Create a list which specifies X coordinates to follow */
    final float pointsListX[] = {
        initialPosition, /* First x position */
        WIDTH - initialPosition, /* Second x position */
        WIDTH - initialPosition, /* Third x position */
        initialPosition, /* Fourth x position */
        initialPosition /* Fifth x position */
    ```

```
    };

    /* Create a list which specifies Y coordinates to follow
*/
    final float pointsListY[] = {
        initialPosition, /* First y position */
        HEIGHT - initialPosition, /* Second y position */
        initialPosition, /* Third y position */
        HEIGHT - initialPosition, /* Fourth y position */
        initialPosition /* Fifth y position */
    };
```

2. Create a `Path` object which we will use to pair the individual points in the separate arrays into way-points. We do this by iterating through the arrays and calling the `to(pX, pY)` method on the `path` object. Note that every time we call this method, we are adding an additional way-point to the `path` object:

```
    /* Obtain the number of control points we have */
    final int controlPointCount = pointsListX.length;


    /* Create our Path object which we will pair our x/y
coordinates into */
    org.andengine.entity.modifier.PathModifier.Path path =
new Path(controlPointCount);


    /* Iterate through our point lists */
    for(int i = 0; i < controlPointCount; i++){
        /* Obtain the coordinates of the control point at the
index */
        final float positionX = pointsListX[i];
        final float positionY = pointsListY[i];


        /* Setup a new way-point by pairing together an x and
y coordinate */
        path.to(positionX, positionY);
    }
```

3. Lastly, once we've defined our way-points, we can create the `PathModifier` object, supplying a duration as well as our `path` object as the parameters:

```
    /* Movement duration */
    final float duration = 3;
```

```
/* Create the PathModifier */
PathModifier pathModifier = new PathModifier(duration,
path);

/* Register the pathModifier object to the rectangle */
rectangle.registerEntityModifier(pathModifier);
```

- ▶ CardinalSplineMoveModifier: This is the final modifier we will be discussing. This modifier is relatively similar to the PathModifier modifier, except we are able to apply tension to the Entity object's movement. This allows for a more fluid and smooth movement when approaching corners, or reversing direction, which looks quite nice actually. See the following steps for a walkthrough on the topic of creating a CardinalSplineMoveModifier modifier for our entities:

    1. The first step, similar to the PathModifier modifier, is to create our point arrays. In this example, we can copy the code from PathModifier example's first step. However, one difference between this modifier and the PathModifier object is that we require a minimum of 4 individual x and y points.

    2. The second step is to determine the number of control points, define the tension, and create a CardinalSplineMoveModifierConfig object. This is the CardinalSplineMoveModifier modifier's equivalent of the PathModifier modifier's Path object. The tension can be between -1 and 1, no more and no less. A tension of -1 will leave the Entity object's movement very loose, making extremely loose corners and changes in direction while a tension of 1 will react very much like the PathModifier modifier in the sense that it is very strict in its movements:

    ```
    /* Obtain the number of control points we have */
    final int controlPointCount = pointsListX.length;

    /* Define the movement tension. Must be between -1 and 1
    */
    final float tension = 0f;

    /* Create the cardinal spline movement modifier
    configuration */
    CardinalSplineMoveModifierConfig config = new CardinalSp
    lineMoveModifierConfig(controlPointCount, tension);
    ```

    3. In step three, again very similar to the PathModifier modifier, we must pair the x/y coordinates within our point arrays, except in this case we're storing them within the config object:

    ```
    /* Iterate through our control point indices */
    for(int index = 0; index < controlPointCount; index++){
    ```

```
            /* Obtain the coordinates of the control point at the
      index */
            final float positionX = pointsListX[index];
            final float positionY = pointsListY[index];

            /* Set position coordinates at the current index in
      the config object */
            config.setControlPoint(index, positionX, positionY);
      }
```

4. Next, we will simply define the duration for the movement, Create the
   `CardinalSplineMoveModifier` modifier, supply the duration and
   `config` object as parameters, and finally register the modifier to the
   `Entity` object:

```
      /* Movement duration */
      final float duration = 3;

      /* Create the cardinal spline move modifier object */
      CardinalSplineMoveModifier cardinalSplineMoveModifier =
new CardinalSplineMoveModifier(duration, config);

      /* Register the cardinalSplineMoveModifier object to the
      rectangle object */
      rectangle.registerEntityModifier(cardinalSplineMoveModi
fier);
```

Now that we've got a solid understanding of the individual modifiers that we are able to apply
to our entities, we will cover the three main entity modifiers in AndEngine and what they're
used for.

AndEngine's entity modifiers

AndEngine includes three entity modifier objects which are used for building complex
animations for our `Entity` objects by combining two or more modifiers into a single event
or sequence. The three different entity modifiers include the `LoopEntityModifier`,
`ParallelEntityModifier`, and `SequenceEntityModifier` objects. Next, we describe
the specifics of these entity modifiers and examples, displaying how they can be used to
combine multiple modifiers into a single animation event.

▶ `LoopEntityModifier`: This entity modifier allows us to loop a specified modifier
  either indefinitely or N number of times if supplied a second `int` parameter. This is
  the simplest of entity modifiers. Once we set up the `LoopEntityModifier` modifier,
  we can apply it directly to the `Entity` object:

```
      /* Define the move modifiers properties */
      final float duration = 3;
      final float fromX = 0;
```

```
final float toX = 100;

/* Create the move modifier */
MoveXModifier moveXModifier = new MoveXModifier(duration,
fromX, toX);

/* Create a loop entity modifier, which will loop the move
modifier
    *   indefinitely, or until unregistered from the rectangle.
    *   If we want to provide a loop count, we can add a second
int parameter
    *   to this constructor */
LoopEntityModifier loopEntityModifier = new LoopEntityModifier
(moveXModifier);

/* register the loopEntityModifier to the rectangle */
rectangle.registerEntityModifier(loopEntityModifier);
```

▶ ParallelEntityModifier: This entity modifier allows us to combine an unlimited number of modifiers into a single animation. The modifiers supplied as parameters of this entity modifier will all run on the Entity object at the same time. This allows us to scale a modifier while rotating it, for example, as seen in the following example. Feel free to add more modifiers to the example for some practice:

```
/* Scale modifier properties */
final float scaleDuration = 2;
final float fromScale = 1;
final float toScale = 2;
/* Create a scale modifier */
ScaleModifier scaleModifier = new ScaleModifier(scaleDuration,
fromScale, toScale);

/* Rotation modifier properties */
final float rotateDuration = 3;
final float fromRotation = 0;
final float toRotation = 360 * 4;
/* Create a rotation modifier */
RotationModifier rotationModifier = new RotationModifier(rotat
eDuration, fromRotation, toRotation);

/* Create a parallel entity modifier */
ParallelEntityModifier parallelEntityModifier = new ParallelEn
tityModifier(scaleModifier, rotationModifier);

/* Register the parallelEntityModifier to the rectangle */
rectangle.registerEntityModifier(parallelEntityModifier);
```

▸ SequenceEntityModifier: This entity modifier allows us to string together modifiers that will be executed sequentially on a single `Entity` object. This modifier is ideally the proper entity modifier to use the `DelayModifier` object as previously mentioned in the modifiers list. The following example displays an `Entity` object which moves from the bottom-left corner to the center of the screen, pauses for 2 seconds, then scales down to a scale factor of 0:

```
/* Move modifier properties */
final float moveDuration = 2;
final float fromX = initialPosition;
final float toX = WIDTH * 0.5f;
final float fromY = initialPosition;
final float toY = HEIGHT * 0.5f;
/* Create a move modifier */
MoveModifier moveModifier = new MoveModifier(moveDuration,
fromX, fromY, toX, toY);

/* Create a delay modifier */
DelayModifier delayModifier = new DelayModifier(2);

/* Scale modifier properties */
final float scaleDuration = 2;
final float fromScale = 1;
final float toScale = 0;
/* Create a scale modifier */
ScaleModifier scaleModifier = new ScaleModifier(scaleDuration,
fromScale, toScale);

/* Create a sequence entity modifier */
SequenceEntityModifier sequenceEntityModifier = new SequenceEn
tityModifier(moveModifier, delayModifier, scaleModifier);

/* Register the sequenceEntityModifier to the rectangle */
rectangle.registerEntityModifier(sequenceEntityModifier);
```

What's even more important to know is that we can add a `SequenceEntityModifier` modifier to a `ParallelEntityModifier` modifier, a `ParallelEntityModifier` modifier to a `LoopEntityModifier` modifier, or any other variation we can think of! This makes the possibilities of modifiers and entity modifiers extremely extensive and allows us to create incredibly complex animations for our entities with a rather significant amount of ease.

There's more...

Before moving on to the next topic, we should take a look at the extra features included for entity modifiers. There are two more parameters that we can pass to our entity modifiers which we haven't discussed yet; those being modifiers listeners and ease functions. These two classes can help to make our modifiers even more customized than we've already seen in the *How it works...* section!

The `IEntityModifierListener` listener can be used in order to fire events when a modifier starts and when a modifier finishes. In the following snippet, we're simply printing logs to logcat which notify us when the modifier has started and finished.

```
IEntityModifierListener entityModifierListener = new
IEntityModifierListener(){

  // When the modifier starts, this method is called
  @Override
  public void onModifierStarted(IModifier<IEntity> pModifier,
      IEntity pItem) {
    Log.i("MODIFIER", "Modifier started!");
  }

  // When the modifier finishes, this method is called
  @Override
  public void onModifierFinished(final IModifier<IEntity> pModifier,
      final IEntity pItem) {
    Log.i("MODIFIER", "Modifier started!");
  }
};

modifier.addModifierListener();
```

The previous code shows the skeleton of a modifier listener with basic log outputs. In a more relative scenario to game development, we could call `pItem.setVisible(false)` once the modifier is finished. For example, this could be useful for handling subtle falling leaves or raindrops in a scene that leaves the camera's view. However, what we decide to use the listener for is completely up to our own discretion.

Finally, we'll quickly discuss the ease functions in AndEngine. Ease functions are a great way to add an extra layer of "awesomeness" to our entity modifiers. After getting used to modifiers, it is likely that ease functions will really grow on you as they give modifiers that extra kick they need to make the perfect effects. The best way to explain an ease function is to think about a game where the menu buttons fall from the top of the screen and "bounce" into place. The bounce in this case would be our ease function taking effect.

```
/* Move modifier properties */
final float duration = 3;
final float fromX = initialPosition;
final float toX = WIDTH - initialPosition;
final float fromY = initialPosition;
final float toY = HEIGHT - initialPosition;

/* Create a move modifier with an ease function */
MoveModifier moveModifier = new MoveModifier(duration, fromX,
fromY, toX, toY, org.andengine.util.modifier.ease.EaseElasticIn.
getInstance());

rectangle.registerEntityModifier(moveModifier);
```

As we can see here, applying an ease function to a modifier is as easy as adding an extra parameter to the modifier's constructor. Often the hardest part is choosing which one to use as the list of ease functions is somewhat large. Take some time to look through the various ease functions provided by locating the `org.andengine.util.modifier.ease` package. Simply replace `EaseElasticIn` from the previous code with the ease function you'd like to test out, and rebuild the project to see it in action!

Ease function reference

Download the **AndEngine – Examples** application from Google Play to your device. Open the application and locate the **Using EaseFunctions** example. While the example application is quite outdated compared to the latest AndEngine branch, the ease function example is still an absolutely effective tool for determining which ease functions best suit our own game's needs!

See also

▶   *Understanding AndEngine entities* in this chapter.

Working with particle systems

Particle systems can provide our games with very attractive effects for many different events in our games, such as explosions, sparks, gore, rain, and much more. In this chapter, we're going to cover AndEngine's `ParticleSystem` classes which will be used to create customized particle effects that will suit our every need.

Getting ready...

This recipe requires basic knowledge of the `Sprite` object in AndEngine. Please read through the entire recipes, *Working with different types of textures* in *Chapter 1, AndEngine Game Structure*, as well as *Understanding AndEngine entities* given in this chapter. Next, create a new empty AndEngine project with a `BaseGameActivity` class and import the code from the `WorkingWithParticles` class in the code bundle.

How to do it...

In order to begin creating particle effects in AndEngine, we require a bare minimum of three objects. These objects include an `ITextureRegion` object which will represent the individual particles spawned, a `ParticleSystem` object, and a `ParticleEmitter` object. Once we have these in place, we can begin to add what are known as particle initializers and particle modifiers to our particle system in order to create our own personalized effects. See the following steps for a walkthrough on how to set up a basic particle system in which we can build on.

1. The first step involves deciding the image we'd like our particle system to spawn. This can be any image, any color, and any size. Feel free to create an image and set up `BuildableBitmapTextureAtlas` and `ITextureRegion` to load the image into the test project's resources. For the sake of keeping things simple, please keep the image under 33 x 33 pixels in dimension for this recipe.

2. Create the `ParticleEmitter` object. For now we'll be using a `PointParticleEmitter` object subtype:

   ```
   /* Define the center point of the particle system spawn
   location */
       final int particleSpawnCenterX = (int) (WIDTH * 0.5f);
       final int particleSpawnCenterY = (int) (HEIGHT * 0.5f);

       /* Create the particle emitter */
       PointParticleEmitter particleEmitter = new PointParticleEmitte
   r(particleSpawnCenterX, particleSpawnCenterY);
   ```

3. Create the `ParticleSystem` object. We'll be using the
   `BatchedSpriteParticleSystem` object implementation as it is the latest and
   greatest `ParticleSystem` object subtype included in AndEngine. It allows us to
   create large amounts of particles while greatly reducing overhead of the typical
   `SpriteParticleSystem` object:

   ```
   /* Define the particle system properties */
   final float minSpawnRate = 25;
   final float maxSpawnRate = 50;
   final int maxParticleCount = 150;

   /* Create the particle system */
   BatchedSpriteParticleSystem particleSystem = new
   BatchedSpriteParticleSystem(
           particleEmitter, minSpawnRate, maxSpawnRate,
   maxParticleCount,
           mTextureRegion,
           mEngine.getVertexBufferObjectManager());
   ```

4. In the final step to creating a particle system, we will add any combination of
   particle emitters and particle modifiers and then attach the particle system
   to the `Scene` object:

   ```
   /* Add an acceleration initializer to the particle system */
   particleSystem.addParticleInitializer(new AccelerationParticle
   Initializer<UncoloredSprite>(25f, -25f, 50f, 100f));

   /* Add an expire initializer to the particle system */
   particleSystem.addParticleInitializer(new ExpireParticleInitia
   lizer<UncoloredSprite>(4));

   /* Add a particle modifier to the particle system */
   particleSystem.addParticleModifier(new ScaleParticleModifier<U
   ncoloredSprite>(0f, 3f, 0.2f, 1f));

   /* Attach the particle system to the Scene */
   mScene.attachChild(particleSystem);
   ```

How it works...

It seems that working with particles for many new AndEngine developers is a rather difficult
subject, but, in fact, it's quite the opposite. Creating particle effects in AndEngine is extremely
simple, but as always, we should learn to walk before we can fly! In this recipe's steps, we're
setting up a rather basic particle system. As the topic progresses, we will discuss and plug in
additional modular components of the particle system in order to broaden our knowledge of
the individual pieces that make up complex particle system effects.

In the first step, we need to set up an `ITextureRegion` object to supply our particle system. The `ITextureRegion` object will visually represent each individual particle that spawns. The texture region can be of any size, but typically they will be between 2 x 2 to 32 x 32 pixels. Remember that the particle system is meant to spawn a large number of objects, so the smaller the `ITextureRegion` object, the better off the performance will be as far as the particle system goes.

In the second step, we create our particle emitter and center it on the `Scene` object. The particle emitter is the component within a particle system that controls where particles will initially spawn. In this recipe, we are using a `PointParticleEmitter` object type, which simply spawns all particles in the exact same coordinates on the scene as defined by the `particleSpawnCenterX` and `particleSpawnCenterY` variables. AndEngine includes four other particle emitter types which will be discussed shortly.

Once we've got our particle emitter created and set up as we see fit, we can move onto the third step and create the `BatchedSpriteParticleSystem` object. The parameters that we are required to pass to the `BatchedSpriteParticleSystem` object include, in this order, the particle emitter, the minimum spawn rate of the particles, the maximum spawn rate, the maximum number of particles that can be simultaneously displayed, the `ITextureRegion` object that the particles should visually represent, and the `mEngine` object's vertex buffer object manager.

Finally, in the fourth step we are adding an `AccelerationParticleInitializer` object, which will provide an accelerating movement to the particles so that they're not simply sitting where they spawn. We are also adding an `ExpireParticleInitializer` object, which is used to destroy particles after a defined amount of time. Without some sort of initializer or modifier removing particles, the `BatchedParticleSystem` object would eventually reach its maximum particle limit and discontinue particle spawning. Lastly, we're adding a `ScaleParticleModifier` object to the particle system which will change each particle's scale over time. These particle initializers and particle modifiers will be explained more in-depth shortly, for now, just know that this is the step where we'd apply them to the particle system. Once we've added our initializers and modifiers of choice, we attach the `particleSystem` object to the `Scene` object.

After completing these four steps, the particle system will begin to spawn particles. However, we may not always want the particles to spawn from a specific particle system. To disable particle spawning, we can make the call, `particleSystem.setParticlesSpawnEnabled(false)`, or `true` to re-enable particle spawning. Aside from this method, the `BatchedSpriteParticleSystem` object contains all of the ordinary functionality and methods of an `Entity` object.

For more information on the individual components of a particle system, see the following subtopics. These topics include particle emitters, particle initializers, and particle modifiers.

Particle emitter selection

AndEngine includes a selection of five ready-to-use particle emitters which can alter the initial placement of particles on the scene, this is not to be confused with defining a particle emitter position. See the list of particle emitters for details on how each of them work. Please feel free to substitute the particle emitter in step two of the recipe with a particle emitter given in the following list:

- `PointParticleEmitter`: The most basic particle emitter of the bunch; this particle emitter causes all spawning particles to be initially spawned in the same defined position on the scene. There will be no variance in the position that particles spawn. However, general particle emitter position can change via a call to the `pointParticleEmitter.setCenter(pX, pY)` method, where `pX` and `pY` define the new coordinates to spawn particles.

- `CircleOutlineParticleEmitter`: This particle emitter subtype will cause particles to spawn in positions outlining the shape of a circle. The parameters to include in this emitter's constructor include the x coordinate, the y coordinate, and a radius which defines the overall size of the circle outline. See the following example:

```
/* Define the center point of the particle system spawn
location */
    final int particleSpawnCenterX = (int) (WIDTH * 0.5f);
    final int particleSpawnCenterY = (int) (HEIGHT * 0.5f);

    /* Define the radius of the circle for the particle emitter */
    final float particleEmitterRadius = 50;

    /* Create the particle emitter */
    CircleOutlineParticleEmitter particleEmitter = new CircleOut
lineParticleEmitter(particleSpawnCenterX, particleSpawnCenterY,
particleEmitterRadius);
```

- `CircleParticleEmitter`: This particle emitter subtype will allow particles to spawn within any area of a circle opposed to just the outlining edge in the `CircleOutlineParticleEmitter` object. The `CircleParticleEmitter` object requires the same parameters in its constructor as the `CircleOutlineParticleEmitter` object. To test this particle emitter subtype, simply refactor the object in the `CircleOutlineParticleEmitter` example to use the `CircleParticleEmitter` object instead.

- `RectangleOutlineParticleEmitter`: This particle emitter subtype will cause the particles to spawn from four corners of a rectangle whose size is defined by the constructor parameters. Unlike the `CircleOutlineParticleEmitter` object, this particle emitter doesn't allow particles to spawn around the full parameter of the rectangle. See the following example:

```
    /* Define the center point of the particle system spawn
location */
```

```
final int particleSpawnCenterX = (int) (WIDTH * 0.5f);
final int particleSpawnCenterY = (int) (HEIGHT * 0.5f);

/* Define the width and height of the rectangle particle
emitter */
final float particleEmitterWidth = 50;
final float particleEmitterHeight = 100;

/* Create the particle emitter */
RectangleOutlineParticleEmitter particleEmitter
= new RectangleOutlineParticleEmitter(particleSpawnC
enterX, particleSpawnCenterY, particleEmitterWidth,
particleEmitterHeight);
```

▸ `RectangleParticleEmitter`: This particle emitter subtype allows for particles to spawn anywhere within the bounding area of a rectangle shape as defined by the constructor parameters. To test this particle emitter subtype, simply refactor the object in the `RectangleOutlineParticleEmitter` example to use the `RectangleParticleEmitter` object instead.

Particle initializer selection

Particle initializers are of vital importance to particle systems. They provide us with the possibility to perform actions on each individual particle that is initially spawned. The greatest thing about these particle initializers is that they allow us to provide min/max values, giving us the opportunity to randomize the properties of spawned particles. Here, find a list of all of the particle initializers that AndEngine has to offer as well as examples of their use. Feel free to substitute the particle initializers in the recipe with those found in this list.

The following particle initializers can be added with a simple call to `particleSystem.addParticleInitializer(pInitializer)`. Additionally, they can be removed via `particleSystem.removeParticl eInitializer(pInitializer)`.

▸ `ExpireParticleInitializer`: We will start off with the most necessary particle initializer in the list. The `ExpireParticleInitializer` object provides a means of removing particles which have been alive for too long. If we were not to include some form of particle expiration, our particle would quickly run out of particles to spawn as all particle systems have a limit to the number of particles that can be active at any given time. The following example creates an `ExpireParticleModifier` object which causes individual particles to expire between 2 and 4 seconds:

```
/* Define min/max particle expiration time */
final float minExpireTime = 2;
final float maxExpireTime = 4;
```

```
ExpireParticleInitializer<UncoloredSprite>
expireParticleInitializer = new ExpireParticleInitializer<Uncolore
dSprite>(minExpireTime, maxExpireTime);
```

▶ AccelerationParticleInitializer: This initializer allows us to apply movement in the form of acceleration, causing the spawned particles to pick up speed before reaching the defined velocity. A positive value on the x or y axis will cause the particle to move up and to the right, while negative values will move the particle down and to the left. In the following example, the particles will be given min/max values which will cause particle movement direction to be random:

```
/* Define the acceleration values */
final float minAccelerationX = -25;
final float maxAccelerationX = 25;
final float minAccelerationY = 25;
final float maxAccelerationY = 50;

AccelerationParticleInitializer<UncoloredSprite>
accelerationParticleInitializer = new AccelerationParticleIni
tializer<UncoloredSprite>(minAccelerationX, maxAccelerationX,
minAccelerationY, maxAccelerationY);
```

▶ AlphaInitializer: The AlphaInitializer object is pretty basic. It simply allows us to initialize particles with an undetermined alpha value. The following example will cause individual particles to spawn with an alpha value of between 0.5f and 1f:

```
/* Define the alpha values */
final float minAlpha = 0.5f;
final float maxAlpha = 1;

AlphaParticleInitializer<UncoloredSprite>
alphaParticleInitializer = new AlphaParticleInitializer<UncoloredS
prite>(minAlpha, maxAlpha);
```

▶ BlendFunctionParticleInitializer: This particle initializer allows us to spawn particles with specific OpenGL blend functions applied to them. For more information on blend functions and results, there are many resources that can be found online. The following is an example using the BlendFunctionParticleInitializer object:

```
BlendFunctionParticleInitializer<UncoloredSprite>
blendFunctionParticleInitializer = new BlendFunctionParticleInit
ializer<UncoloredSprite>(GLES20.GL_ONE, GLES20.GL_ONE_MINUS_SRC_
ALPHA);
```

- ColorParticleInitializer: The ColorParticleInitializer object allows us to provide our sprites with colors between min/max values. This allows us to randomize the color of each particle spawned. The following example will generate particles, each with a completely different random color:

```
/* Define min/max values for particle colors */
final float minRed = 0f;
final float maxRed = 1f;
final float minGreen = 0f;
final float maxGreen = 1f;
final float minBlue = 0f;
final float maxBlue = 1f;


ColorParticleInitializer<UncoloredSprite>
colorParticleInitializer = new ColorParticleInitializer<UncoloredS
prite>(minRed, maxRed, minGreen, maxGreen, minBlue, maxBlue);
```

- GravityParticleInitializer: This particle initializer allows us to spawn particles which will act as though they follow the rules of the earth's gravity. The GravityParticleInitializer object requires no parameters in its constructor:

```
GravityParticleInitializer<UncoloredSprite>
gravityParticleInitializer = new GravityParticleInitializer<Uncolo
redSprite>();
```

- RotationParticleInitializer: The RotationParticleInitializer object allows us to define the min/max values for the particle's rotation when spawned. The following example will cause individual particles to spawn anywhere between 0 and 359 degrees:

```
/* Define min/max values for the particle's rotation */
final float minRotation = 0;
final float maxRotation = 359;


RotationParticleInitializer<UncoloredSprite>
rotationParticleInitializer = new RotationParticleInitializer<Unco
loredSprite>(minRotation, maxRotation);
```

- ScaleParticleInitializer: The ScaleParticleInitializer object allows us to define the min/max values for the particle's scale when spawned. The following example will allow particles to spawn with a scale factor of anywhere between 0.5f and 1.5f:

```
/* Define min/max values for the particle's scale */
final float minScale = 0.5f;
final float maxScale = 1.5f;
```

```
ScaleParticleInitializer<UncoloredSprite>
scaleParticleInitializer = new ScaleParticleInitializer<UncoloredS
prite>(minScale, maxScale);
```

▸ VelocityParticleInitializer: This final particle initializer, similar to the
  AccelerationParticleInitializer object, allows us to provide movement to
  individual particles when spawned. However, this initializer causes the particles to
  move at a constant speed, and will not increase or decrease velocity over time unless
  manually configured to do so:

```
/* Define min/max velocity values of the particles */
final float minVelocityX = -25;
final float maxVelocityX = 25;
final float minVelocityY = 25;
final float maxVelocityY = 50;

VelocityParticleInitializer<UncoloredSprite>
velocityParticleInitializer = new VelocityParticleInitialize
r<UncoloredSprite>(minVelocityX, maxVelocityX, minVelocityY,
maxVelocityY);
```

See the following section for a list of AndEngine's particle modifiers.

Particle modifier selection

AndEngine's particle modifiers are useful in the development of complex particle systems.
They allow us to provide changes to individual particles depending on how long they've been
alive for. Similar to entity modifiers, particle modifiers are of the "from time-to time, from
value-to value" format. Once again, feel free to add any of the particle modifiers in the list to
your current test project.

> The following particle modifiers can be added with a simple call to
> particleSystem.addParticleModifier(pModifier). Additionally,
> they can be removed via particleSystem.removeParticleModifier
> (pModifier).

▸ AlphaParticleModifier: This modifier allows a particle to shift in alpha values
  between two points in time during a particle's lifetime. In the following example, the
  modifier will transition from an alpha value of 1 to 0 over a duration of 1 second.
  The modifier will take effect 1 second after the particle has spawned:

```
/* Define the alpha modifier's properties */
final float fromTime = 1;
final float toTime = 2;
final float fromAlpha = 1;
final float toAlpha = 0;
```

```
AlphaParticleModifier<UncoloredSprite> alphaParticleModifier
= new AlphaParticleModifier<UncoloredSprite>(fromTime, toTime,
fromAlpha, toAlpha);
```

- ► `ColorParticleModifier`: This modifier will allow a particle to change in color between two points in time during a particle's lifetime. The following modifier will cause particles to change from green to red over two seconds, with a from time of `0`. This means the transition will begin as soon as a particle is spawned:

```
/* Define the color modifier's properties */
final float fromTime = 0;
final float toTime = 2;
final float fromRed = 0;
final float toRed = 1;
final float fromGreen = 1;
final float toGreen = 0;
final float fromBlue 0;
final float toBlue = 0;

ColorParticleModifier<UncoloredSprite> colorParticleModifier
= new ColorParticleModifier<UncoloredSprite>(fromTime, toTime,
fromRed, toRed, fromGreen, toGreen, fromBlue, toBlue);
```

- ► `OffCameraExpireParticleModifier`: By adding this modifier to the particle system, particles that leave the view of our `Camera` object will be destroyed. We can use this as an alternative to the `ExpireParticleInitializer` object, but at least one of the two should be active on any particle system. The only parameter to supply to this modifier is our `Camera` object:

```
OffCameraExpireParticleModifier<UncoloredSprite>
offCameraExpireParticleModifier = new OffCameraExpireParticleModif
ier<UncoloredSprite>(mCamera);
```

- ► `RotationParticleModifier`: This modifier allows us to change the rotation of particles between two points in time during a particle's lifetime. The following example will cause particles to rotate `180` degrees between `1` and `4` seconds of a particle's lifetime:

```
/* Define the rotation modifier's properties */
final float fromTime = 1;
final float toTime = 4;
final float fromRotation = 0;
final float toRotation = 180;

RotationParticleModifier<UncoloredSprite>
rotationParticleModifier = new RotationParticleModifier<UncoloredS
prite>(fromTime, toTime, fromRotation, toRotation);
```

- ► ScaleParticleModifier: The ScaleParticleModifier object allows us to change the scale of a particle between two points in time during a particle's lifetime. The following example will cause particles to grow from a scale of 0.5f to 1.5f between 1 and 3 seconds of a particle's lifetime:

```
/* Define the scale modifier's properties */
final float fromTime = 1;
final float toTime = 3;
final float fromScale = 0.5f;
final float toScale = 1.5f;

ScaleParticleModifier<UncoloredSprite> scaleParticleModifier
= new ScaleParticleModifier<UncoloredSprite>(fromTime, toTime,
fromScale, toScale);
```

- ► IParticleModifier: Finally, we have the particle modifier interface which allows us to create our own modifications to individual particles in the event of particle initialization or on every update to a particle via the update thread. The following example displays how we can simulate a particle landing on the ground by disabling movement on the y axis once a particle reaches less than a value of 20 on the Scene object's coordinate system. We can use this interface to virtually make any changes we'd like to particles as we see fit:

```
IParticleModifier<UncoloredSprite> customParticleModifier =
new IParticleModifier<UncoloredSprite>(){

    /* Fired only once when a particle is first spawned */
    @Override
    public void onInitializeParticle(Particle<UncoloredSprite>
pParticle) {
        * Make customized modifications to a particle on
initialization */
    }

    /* Fired on every update to a particle in the particle
system */
    @Override
    public void onUpdateParticle(Particle<UncoloredSprite>
pParticle) {
        * Make customized modifications to a particle on every
update to the particle */
            Entity entity = pParticle.getEntity();
```

```
                * Obtain the particle's position and movement properties
      */
            final float currentY = entity.getY();
            final float currentVelocityY = pParticle.
      getPhysicsHandler().getVelocityY();
            final float currentAccelerationY = pParticle.
      getPhysicsHandler().getAccelerationY();

            /* If the particle is close to the bottom of the Scene and
      is moving... */
            if(entity.getY() < 20 && currentVelocityY != 0 ||
      currentAccelerationY != 0){

            /* Restrict movement on the Y axis. Simulates landing on
      the ground */
                pParticle.getPhysicsHandler().setVelocityY(0);
                pParticle.getPhysicsHandler().setAccelerationY(0);
            }
            }

        };
```

Now that we've covered all of the particle emitters, particle initializers, and particle modifiers, practice making more complex particle systems by combining any number of initializers and modifiers you'd like to your own systems!

See also

▸ *Working with different types of textures* in Chapter 1, *AndEngine Game Structure*.

▸ *Understanding AndEngine entities* in this chapter.

3
Designing Your Menu

In this chapter, we will begin to take a look at how to create a manageable menu system with AndEngine. The topics include:

- Adding buttons to the menu
- Adding music to the menu
- Applying a background
- Using parallax backgrounds to create perspective
- Creating our level selection system
- Hiding and retrieving layers

Introduction

Menu systems in games are essentially a map of the scenes or activities a game provides. In a game, a menu should look attractive and give a subtle hint of what to expect during gameplay. The menu should be organized and easy for a player to understand. In this chapter, we're going to take a look at various options we have which we can apply to our own games in order to create functional and appealing menus for any type of game.

Adding buttons to the menu

In AndEngine, we can create touch-responsive buttons out of any `Entity` object or `Entity` object subtype. However, AndEngine includes a class called `ButtonSprite` whose texture representation depends on whether the `Entity` object is pressed or unpressed. In this recipe, we're going to take advantage of AndEngine's `ButtonSprite` class and override its `onAreaTouched()` method in order to add touch-responsive buttons to our menu and/or game's `Scene` object. Additionally, the code within this recipe regarding touch events can be applied to any other `Entity` object within our game.

Getting ready...

This recipe requires basic knowledge of the `Sprite` object in AndEngine. Please read through the entire recipe, *Working with different types of textures* in *Chapter 1, AndEngine Game Structure*, specifically the section regarding tiled texture regions. Next, visit the recipe, *Bringing a scene to life with sprites* in *Chapter 2, Working with Entities*.

Once the recipes regarding textures and sprites have been covered, create a new AndEngine project with an empty `BaseGameActivity` class. Finally, we will need to create a sprite sheet named `button_tiles.png` with two images and place it in the `assets/gfx/` folder of the project; one for the "unpressed" button representation and one for the "pressed" button representation. See the following image for an idea of what the image should look like. The following image is 300 x 50 pixels, or 150 x 50 pixels per tile:

Refer to the class named `CreatingButtons` in the code bundle and import the code into your project.

How to do it...

The `ButtonSprite` class is convenient as it handles the tiled texture region versus button state changes for us. The following steps outline the tasks involved in setting up a `ButtonSprite` object:

1. Declare a global `ITiledTextureRegion` object, naming it `mButtonTextureRegion`, then in the `onCreateResources()` method of the `BaseGameActivity` class, create a new `BuildableBitmapTextureAtlas` object suitable for your `button_tiles.png` image. Build and load the texture region and texture atlas objects so that we can use them later to create the `ButtonSprite` object.

2. In order for the `ButtonSprite` object to work as intended, we should set up proper touch area binding on the `mScene` object. Copy the following code into the `onCreateScene()` method of the activity:

   ```
   mScene.setTouchAreaBindingOnActionDownEnabled(true);
   ```

3. Create the `ButtonSprite` object, supplying it the `mButtonTextureRegion` object and overriding its `onAreaTouched()` method:

   ```
   /* Create the buttonSprite object in the center of the Scene */
   ButtonSprite buttonSprite = new ButtonSprite(WIDTH * 0.5f,
       HEIGHT * 0.5f, mButtonTextureRegion,
   ```

```
        mEngine.getVertexBufferObjectManager()) {
    /* Override the onAreaTouched() event method */
    @Override
    public boolean onAreaTouched(TouchEvent pSceneTouchEvent,
        float pTouchAreaLocalX, float pTouchAreaLocalY) {
      /* If buttonSprite is touched with the finger */
      if(pSceneTouchEvent.isActionDown()){
        /* When the button is pressed, we can create an event
         * In this case, we're simply displaying a quick toast */
        CreatingButtons.this.runOnUiThread(new Runnable(){
          @Override
          public void run() {
            Toast.makeText(getApplicationContext(), "Button
Pressed!", Toast.LENGTH_SHORT).show();
          }
        });
      }
      /* In order to allow the ButtonSprite to swap tiled texture
region
       * index on our buttonSprite object, we must return the super
method */
      return super.onAreaTouched(pSceneTouchEvent, pTouchAreaLocalX,
pTouchAreaLocalY);
    }
  };
```

4. The final step is to register the touch area and attach the `buttonSprite` object to the `mScene` object:

```
/* Register the buttonSprite as a 'touchable' Entity */
mScene.registerTouchArea(buttonSprite);
/* Attach the buttonSprite to the Scene */
mScene.attachChild(buttonSprite);
```

How it works...

This recipe makes use of a `ButtonSprite` object with an `ITiledTextureRegion` object to display two separate button states. One tile will act as the button's unpressed texture, the other will act as the button's pressed texture when a finger is touching the `Entity` object on the display.

In the first step, we are creating our texture resources to be applied to the `ButtonSprite` object, which will be implemented in the coming steps. The `ButtonSprite` class will need an `ITiledTextureRegion` object with two indices, or two tiles as seen in the figure in the *Getting started...* section of this recipe. The first index of the `ITiledTextureRegion` object should contain the unpressed representation of the button, which will be applied to the `ButtonSprite` object by default. The second `ITiledTextureRegion` index should represent a pressed state of the `ButtonSprite` object. The `ButtonSprite` class will automatically alternate between these two `ITiledTextureRegion` indices depending on which state the `ButtonSprite` object is currently in; being either `ButtonSprite.State.NORMAL` for unpressed, setting the `ButtonSprite` object's current tile index to `0`, and `ButtonSprite.State.PRESSED` for, you guessed it, the pressed state which sets the `ButtonSprite` object's current tile index to `1`.

In the second step, in order for the `ButtonSprite` object to work as intended, we need to enable touch area binding on the down action within the `mScene` object. We enable this within the `onCreateScene()` method of our activity's life cycle, just after the `mScene` object is created. What this does is, it allows our `ButtonSprite` object to register as unpressed when we drag our finger off of the `ButtonSprite` touch area. Disregarding this step will cause the `ButtonSprite` object to remain in a pressed state in the event that we press and drag our finger off the `Entity` object's touch area, which may very well be considered "buggy" if left for players to deal with. In the third step, we create the `ButtonSprite` object, centering it in within the scene. Ideally, we can create the `ButtonSprite` object and place it on the scene and it will work as it should. However, `ButtonSprite` is a button, after all, and therefore it should prompt an event to occur when pressed. We can do this by overriding the `onAreaTouched()` super method and creating events based on whether the `ButtonSprite` object's touch area is pressed down on, if a finger is dragged over it, or if a finger is released from the display while inside the touch area. In this recipe, we're simply displaying a `Toast` message in the event that the `ButtonSprite` object's `pSceneTouchEvent` registers the `isActionDown()` method. In a more realistic scenario during the development of a game, this button may just as well allow/disallow sound muting, start a new game, or any other action we choose for it. The other two methods used for touch event state-checking are `pSceneTouchEvent.isActionMove()` and `pSceneTouchEvent.isActionUp()`.

Finally, once the `buttonSprite` object has been created we will need to register the touch area and attach the `Entity` object to the `mScene` object. By now, we should be well aware that in order to display an entity on the scene we must first attach it. Just as well, in order for the `buttonSprite` object's `onAreaTouched()` super method to execute, we must remember to call `mScene.registerTouchArea(buttonSprite)`. The same goes for any other `Entity` object for which we wish to provide touch events.

See also

▸ *Working with different types of textures* in *Chapter 1, AndEngine Game Structure*.

▸ *Understanding AndEngine entities* in *Chapter 2, Working with Entities*.

▸ *Bringing a scene to life with sprites* in *Chapter 2, Working with Entities*.

Adding music to the menu

In this topic, we're going to create a mute button which will control our menu's theme music. Pressing the mute button will cause the music to either play if currently paused, or pause if currently playing. This method for muting music and sounds can also be applied to in-game options and other areas of a game which allow sound and music playback. The difference between this recipe and the previous, is that we're going to be using a `TiledSprite` object which will allow us to set the `Sprite` object's tile index depending on whether the sound is playing or paused. Keep in mind that this recipe is useful for more than just enabling and disabling menu music. We can also follow the same approach for many other toggle-able options and states during gameplay.

Getting ready...

This recipe requires basic knowledge of the `Sprite` object in AndEngine as well as using touch events to perform actions. Additionally, since we'll be incorporating the `Music` object into this recipe, we should understand how to load `Sound` and `Music` objects into our game's resources. Please read through the entire recipe, *Working with different types of textures* in *Chapter 1, AndEngine Game Structure*, specifically the section regarding tiled texture regions. Next, check into the recipe, *Introducing sounds and music* in *Chapter 1, AndEngine Game Structure*. Finally, we will be working with sprites, so we should take a quick peak into the recipe, *Bringing a scene to life with sprites*, in *Chapter 2, Working with Entities*.

Once the topics regarding textures, sounds, and sprites have been covered, create a new AndEngine project with an empty `BaseGameActivity` class. We will need to create a sprite sheet named `sound_button_tiles.png` with two images and place it in the `assets/gfx/` folder of the project; one for the "non-muted" button representation and one for the "muted" button representation. See the following image for an idea of what the image should look like. The following image is 100 x 50 pixels, or 50 x 50 pixels per tile:

We will also need to include a sound file that is in the MP3 format in the `assets/sfx/` folder of our project. The sound file can be any preferred music track of your choice for the purpose of executing this recipe.

Refer to the class named `MenuMusic` in the code bundle and import the code into your project.

How to do it...

This recipe introduces a combination of AndEngine features. We are combining music, textures, sprites, tiled texture regions, and touch events all into one convenient little package. The result—a toggle button that will control the playback of a `Music` object. Follow these steps to see how we create the toggle button.

1. In the first step, we will be working with two global objects; mMenuMusic which is a `Music` object and mButtonTextureRegion which is an `ITiledTextureRegion` object. In the `onCreateResources()` method of the activity, we create these objects with their respective resources in the `assets/*` folder. Refer to the recipes mentioned in the *Getting started...* section for more information on creating these resources if needed.

2. Next, we can skip directly to the `onPopulateScene()` method of the activity where we will create our mMuteButton object using the `TiledSprite` class. We will need to override the `onAreaTouched()` method of the mMuteButton object in order to either pause or play the music when the button is pressed:

```
/* Create the music mute/unmute button */
TiledSprite mMuteButton = new TiledSprite(buttonX, buttonY,
    mButtonTextureRegion, mEngine.getVertexBufferObjectManager())
{

  /* Override the onAreaTouched() method allowing us to define
custom
  * actions */
  @Override
  public boolean onAreaTouched(TouchEvent pSceneTouchEvent,
      float pTouchAreaLocalX, float pTouchAreaLocalY) {
    /* In the event the mute button is pressed down on... */
    if (pSceneTouchEvent.isActionDown()) {
      if (mMenuMusic.isPlaying()) {
        /* If music is playing, pause it and set tile index to
MUTE */
        this.setCurrentTileIndex(MUTE);
        mMenuMusic.pause();
      } else {
        /* If music is paused, play it and set tile index to
UNMUTE */
```

```
        this.setCurrentTileIndex(UNMUTE);
        mMenuMusic.play();
      }
      return true;
    }
    return super.onAreaTouched(pSceneTouchEvent, pTouchAreaLocalX,
      pTouchAreaLocalY);
  }
};
```

3. Once the button has been created, we need to initialize the mMuteButton and mMenuMusic objects' initial states. This step involved setting the mMuteButton object's tile index to that of the UNMUTE constant value which equals 1, registering and attaching the mMuteButton object to the mScene object, setting mMenuMusic to loop, and then finally calling play() on the mMenuMusic object:

```
/* Set the current tile index to unmuted on application startup */
mMuteButton.setCurrentTileIndex(UNMUTE);

/* Register and attach the mMuteButton to the Scene */
mScene.registerTouchArea(mMuteButton);
mScene.attachChild(mMuteButton);

/* Set the mMenuMusic object to loop once it reaches the track's
end */
mMenuMusic.setLooping(true);
/* Play the mMenuMusic object */
mMenuMusic.play();
```

4. The final step to include when dealing with any Music object is to make sure we pause it upon app minimization, otherwise it will continue to play in the background. In this recipe, we are pausing the mMenuMusic object on minimization. However, in the event a user returns to the application, the music will play only if the mMuteButton object's tile index was equal to the UNMUTE constant value when the app was minimized:

```
@Override
public synchronized void onResumeGame() {
  super.onResumeGame();

  /* If the music and button have been created */
  if (mMenuMusic != null && mMuteButton != null) {
    /* If the mMuteButton is set to unmuted on resume... */
    if(mMuteButton.getCurrentTileIndex() == UNMUTE){
      /* Play the menu music */
      mMenuMusic.play();
```

```
      }
    }
  }

  @Override
  public synchronized void onPauseGame() {
    super.onPauseGame();

    /* Always pause the music on pause */
    if(mMenuMusic != null && mMenuMusic.isPlaying()){
      mMenuMusic.pause();
    }
  }
```

How it works...

This particular recipe is very useful in game development; not only for sound and music muting, but for all sorts of toggle buttons. While this recipe is dealing specifically with `Music` object playback, it contains all of the necessary code in order to start working with various other toggle buttons which might suit the more specific needs of our games.

In the first step, we must set up the necessary resources for use within the `mMenuMusic` object and the `mMuteButton` object. The `mMenuMusic` object will load a sound file named `menu_music.mp3`, which can be any MP3 file, preferably a music track. The `mMuteButton` object will load a sprite sheet called `sound_button_tiles.png` with two separate tiles. These objects are both taken care of within the `onCreateResourceS()` method of the `BaseGameActivity` object's life cycle. More information on the creation of these resources can be found within the recipes mentioned in the *Getting started...* section of this recipe.

In step two, we are setting up the `mMuteButton` object, which is of the `TiledSprite` type. The `TiledSprite` class allows us to use an `ITiledTextureRegion` object which gives us the ability to set the current tile index that the `mMuteButton` object will display on our scene. In the overridden `onAreaTouched()` method, we check to see whether or not the `mMuteButton` object has been pressed down on with the `if (pSceneTouchEvent.isActionDown())` statement. We then proceed to determine whether or not the `mMenuMusic` object is currently playing with the `isPlaying()` method of the `Music` object. If the music is playing, then pressing a finger down on the `mMuteButton` button will cause the `mMenuMusic` object to call `pause()` and revert the `mMuteButton` object's current tile index to that of the `MUTE` constant value, which is equal to `0`. If the music is not playing, then we do the exact opposite, calling `play()` on the `mMenuMusic` object and reverting the `mMuteButton` object's tile index back to `UNMUTE`, which is equal to `1`.

In step three, we are setting up the `mMenuMusic` and `mMuteButton` objects' default state, which is equal to playing the music and setting the current tile index to UNMUTE. This will cause the music to play anytime the application initially starts up. Once we've set up the default button and music states, we continue on to register the `mMuteButton` object's touch area and attach the `Entity` object to the `Scene` object. This step can be taken further in order to save the state of the `mMuteButton` object to the device, allowing us to load the default state of music muting based on a user's past preference. For more information on saving/loading data and states, see the recipe, *Saving and loading game data* in *Chapter 1, AndEngine Game Structure*.

The final step is very important and should always be included when dealing with `Music` objects. The purpose of this step is explained in more detail in the recipe, *Introducing sounds and music* in *Chapter 1, AndEngine Game Structure*. However, there is a slight variation to the code in the `onResumeGame()` method for this recipe. In the event of application minimization, a user is likely expecting their game state to be waiting as it was left when they finally return it to focus. For this reason, rather than playing the `mMenuMusic` object when `onResumeGame()` is fired on app maximization, we determine whether or not the `mMuteButton` button's tile index was set to UNMUTE just prior to our game's window minimization. If so, then we can call the `play()` method on the `mMenuMusic` object, otherwise we can ignore it until a user decides to play the music by pressing the `mMuteButton` again.

See also

- *Working with different types of textures* in *Chapter 1, AndEngine Game Structure*.
- *Introducing sounds and music* in *Chapter 1, AndEngine Game Structure*.
- *Understanding AndEngine entities* in *Chapter 2, Working with Entities*.
- *Bringing a scene to life with sprites* in *Chapter 2, Working with Entities*.

Applying a background

AndEngine's `Scene` object allows us to apply a static background to it. The background can be used to display a solid color, an entity, a sprite, or a repeating sprite which are not affected by changes to the `Camera` object's position or zoom factor. In this recipe, we're going to take a look at how to apply the different types of backgrounds to our `Scene` object.

How to do it..

The `Background` object is the most basic type of background for our `Scene` object in AndEngine. This object allows the scene to visually represent a solid color. We will start this recipe off by setting up the `Scene` object to display a `Background` object in order to become familiar with how applying backgrounds to a scene works. Later on in this recipe we'll be introducing the majority of the remaining `Background` object's subtypes in order to cover all options as far as applying backgrounds to our scene goes. Setting the `Scene` object up with a background involves just two steps as follows:

1. Define the properties of and create the `Background` object:

    ```
    /* Define background color values */
    final float red = 0;
    final float green = 1;
    final float blue = 1;
    final float alpha = 1;

    /* Create a new background with the specified color values */
    Background background = new Background(red, green, blue, alpha);
    ```

2. Set the `Background` object to the `Scene` object and enable the background feature:

    ```
    /* Set the mScene object's background */
    mScene.setBackground(background);

    /* Set the background to be enabled */
    mScene.setBackgroundEnabled(true);
    ```

How it works...

Before deciding to use one of AndEngine's default backgrounds, we must figure out whether or not our background should take camera movement into consideration. We can think of these backgrounds as being "stuck" to the camera view. This means that any movements made to the camera will have absolutely no effect on the position of the background. The same rule applies for any other form of camera repositioning, including zooming. For this reason, we should not include any objects on our background which we need to scroll with camera movement. This is the difference between a `Background` object applied to the `Scene` object and an `Entity` object attached to the `Scene` object. Any "backgrounds" which should appear to move in response to the camera movement should be attached to the `Scene` object as an `Entity` object instead. This is most conveniently accomplished by applying an `Entity` object to the `Scene` object to act as a "background layer", which all sprites representing the background image would be attached to.

Now that we've covered the difference between a `Background` object and an `Entity` object, we'll continue on to the steps for this recipe. As we can see in this recipe's steps, setting up a boring, old colored background is a straightforward task. However, it still happens to be useful to know. In the first step, we will define the properties of the `Background` object and create the `Background` object supplying said properties as the parameters. For the basic `Background` object, these parameters simply include the three color values and the alpha value of the `Background` object's color. However, as we will soon discuss, the different types of backgrounds will require different parameters depending on the type. The differences will be outlined for convenience when we get to that point.

The second step for setting up a `Background` object on the `Scene` object will be the same two method calls no matter what type of background we are applying. We must set the scene's background with `setBackground(pBackground)` and make sure the scene's background is enabled by calling `setBackgroundEnabled(true)`. On the other hand, we can also disable the background by supplying the latter method with a `false` parameter.

That's all it takes when setting up a background on our `Scene` object. However, in our own games it is rather unlikely that we'll be satisfied with a basic colored background. See the *There's more...* section of this recipe for a list and examples of the various `Background` object subtypes.

There's more...

In the following sections we will cover the different types of static backgrounds which we can use in our games. All of the `Background` object subtypes allow us to specify a background color for portions of the background which are not covered by a `Sprite` entity, `Rectangle` entity, or otherwise. These backgrounds all share the same "static" rule as mentioned in the *How it works...* section, that they will not move pending camera movement.

The EntityBackground class

The `EntityBackground` class allows us to apply a single `Entity` object, or an entire Entity object's layer as our scene's background. This can be useful for combining multiple `Entity` objects into a single `Background` object to be displayed on the scene. In the following code, we're attaching two rectangles to an `Entity` object's layer, then using the `Entity` object as a background:

```
/* Create a rectangle in the bottom left corner of the Scene */
Rectangle rectangleLeft = new Rectangle(100, 100, 200, 200,
    mEngine.getVertexBufferObjectManager());

/* Create a rectangle in the top right corner of the Scene */
Rectangle rectangleRight = new Rectangle(WIDTH - 100, HEIGHT -
100, 200, 200,
    mEngine.getVertexBufferObjectManager());
```

```
    /* Create the entity to be used as a background */
    Entity backgroundEntity = new Entity();

    /* Attach the rectangles to the entity which will be applied as a
background */
    backgroundEntity.attachChild(rectangleLeft);
    backgroundEntity.attachChild(rectangleRight);

    /* Define the background color properties */
    final float red = 0;
    final float green = 0;
    final float blue = 0;

    /* Create the EntityBackground, specifying its background color &
entity to represent the background image */
    EntityBackground background = new EntityBackground(red, green,
blue, backgroundEntity);

    /* Set & enable the background */
    mScene.setBackground(background);
    mScene.setBackgroundEnabled(true);
```

The `EntityBackground` object's parameters include `red`, `green`, and `blue` color values and finally the `Entity` object or layer to display as the background. Once the `EntityBackground` object has been created, we simply follow step two in this recipe's *How to do it...* section and our `EntityBackground` object will be ready to display whatever we choose to attach to the `backgroundEntity` object!

The SpriteBackground class

The `SpriteBackground` class allows us to attach a single `Sprite` object to our scene as a background image. Keep in mind, the sprite will not be stretched or distorted in any way to accommodate for the size of the display. In order to have a sprite stretch across the full width and height of the camera's view, we must create the `Sprite` object while taking into consideration the camera's width and height. With the following code, we can apply a single `Sprite` object as our background image on the scene. Assume the `mBackgroundTextureRegion` object's dimensions are the same as the `WIDTH` and `HEIGHT` values in the following code, which represent the camera's width and height values:

```
    /* Create the Sprite object */
    Sprite sprite = new Sprite(WIDTH * 0.5f, HEIGHT * 0.5f,
    mBackgroundTextureRegion,
        mEngine.getVertexBufferObjectManager());

    /* Define the background color values */
    final float red = 0;
```

```
final float green = 0;
final float blue = 0;

/* Create the SpriteBackground object, specifying
 * the color values & Sprite object to display*/
SpriteBackground background = new SpriteBackground(red, green, blue,
sprite);

/* Set & Enable the background */
mScene.setBackground(background);
mScene.setBackgroundEnabled(true);
```

We can create the `Sprite` object as we would any other. When creating the `SpriteBackground` object, we pass the usual color parameters along with the `Sprite` object we wish to display on the background.

It is a good idea, when using `SpriteBackground` and `RepeatingSpriteBackground`, to apply `BitmapTextureFormat.RGB_565` to the texture atlas. Since the background will likely stretch across the full display, we usually do not require an alpha channel which can improve the performance of our game on low-end devices.

The RepeatingSpriteBackground class

The `RepeatingSpriteBackground` class is useful for creating textured maps for terrain or simply filling empty space on the scene with a texture. We can easily turn the following 128 x 128 pixel texture into a background which repeats the texture across the full length of the display:

The resulting background after creating a `RepeatingSpriteBackground` object out of the preceding texture would look like the following image at 1280 x 752 pixels in dimension:

Creating a `RepeatingSpriteBackground` object requires a little bit more work than the previous `Background` object subtypes. We will be loading our repeating image file into an `AssetBitmapTexture` object which will then be extracted into an `ITextureRegion` object for use by the background. Since we're using the texture for the purpose of repeating it across `RepeatingSpriteBackground`, we must provide the `TextureOptions.` `REPEATING_BILINEAR` or `TextureOptions.REPEATING_NEAREST` texture options within the `AssetBitmapTexture` constructor. On top of that, when dealing with repeating textures, we must keep our image file bound to the power of two dimensions. Texture dimensions with a power of two are required by OpenGL's wrap modes in order to properly repeat a texture. Failure to follow this rule will cause repeating sprites to appear as a black shape instead. Place the following code into the `onCreateResources()` method of your test activity. The `mRepeatingTextureRegion` object must be declared as a global `ITextureRegion` object:

```
AssetBitmapTexture mBitmapTexture = null;

try {
  /* Create the AssetBitmapTexture with the REPEATING_* texture option
*/
  mBitmapTexture = new AssetBitmapTexture(mEngine.getTextureManager(),
this.getAssets(), "gfx/grass.png", BitmapTextureFormat.
RGB_565,TextureOptions.REPEATING_BILINEAR);
} catch (IOException e) {
```

```
      e.printStackTrace();
   }
   /* Load the bitmap texture */
   mBitmapTexture.load();

   /* Extract the bitmap texture into an ITextureRegion */
   mRepeatingTextureRegion = TextureRegionFactory.extractFromTexture(mBi
   tmapTexture);
```

Next step is to create the `RepeatingSpriteBackground` object. We will include this code in the `onCreateScene()` method of our activity's life cycle:

```
   /* Define the RepeatingSpriteBackground sizing parameters */
   final float cameraWidth = WIDTH;
   final float cameraHeight = HEIGHT;
   final float repeatingScale = 1f;

   /* Create the RepeatingSpriteBackground */
   RepeatingSpriteBackground background = new RepeatingSpriteBackground(c
   ameraWidth, cameraHeight, mRepeatingTextureRegion, repeatingScale,
       mEngine.getVertexBufferObjectManager());

   /* Set & Enable the background */
   mScene.setBackground(background);
   mScene.setBackgroundEnabled(true);
```

The first two parameters for the `RepeatingSpriteBackground` object define the maximum area that the repeating texture will cover, extending from the bottom-left corner of the display. In this case, we're covering the entire display. The third texture we pass is the `ITextureRegion` object to be used as the repeating texture. As previously mentioned, this texture region must be following the power-of-two dimension rule. The fourth parameter is the scale factor of the repeating texture. The default scale is `1`; increasing the scale will cause the repeating texture to enlarge which can make it easier to see the repeating pattern. Reducing the scale factor will shrink each repeated texture which can sometimes help to hide the pattern or obvious flaws in the repeating textures. Keep in mind, adjusting the scale of the repeating texture does not affect the overall size of the `RepeatingSpriteBackground` object as defined in the first two parameters, so feel free to adjust them until the texture looks right.

See also

- ▶ *Working with different types of textures* in *Chapter 1, AndEngine Game Structure*.
- ▶ *Bringing a scene to life with sprites* in *Chapter 2, Working with Entities*.

Using parallax backgrounds to create perspective

Applying a **parallax** background to a game can result in a visually-pleasing perspective effect. Even though we're working with a 2D engine, we can create a background which will gives off an illusion of depth through the use of parallax values which determine the movement speed of sprites based on the camera movement. This topic is going to introduce parallax backgrounds and how we can use them to add a sense of depth to an otherwise fully 2D world. The classes we will be using are the `ParallaxBackground` and the `AutoParallaxBackground` classes.

Getting ready...

This recipe requires basic knowledge of the `Sprite` object in AndEngine. Please read through the entire recipe, *Working with different types of textures* in *Chapter 1, AndEngine Game Structure*. Next, please visit the recipe, *Bringing a scene to life with sprites* in *Chapter 2, Working with Entities*.

Once the recipes regarding textures and sprites have been covered, create a new AndEngine project with an empty `BaseGameActivity` class. Finally, we will need to create an image named `hill.png` and place it in the `assets/gfx/` folder of the project. This image should be 800 x 150 pixels in dimension. The image can resemble the following figure:

Refer to the class named `UsingParallaxBackgrounds` in the code bundle and import the code into your project.

How to do it...

The `ParallaxBackground` object is the most advanced `Background` object subtype in AndEngine. It requires the most setting up out of all of the `Background` object subtypes, but if broken down into small steps, it is really not that difficult. Perform the following steps for a walkthrough on how to set up a `ParallaxBackground` object to work in relation to the camera's movement. For the sake of brevity, we're going to omit the automatic camera movement code which can be found in the `onCreateEngineOptions()` method of the activity's life cycle:

1. The first step is typical when creating an `ITextureRegion` object for `Sprite` objects and is to create our `BuildableBitmapTextureAtlas`. The texture atlas should be just big enough to contain the `hill.png` image, which is 800 pixels wide by 150 pixels high. Once the texture atlas has been created, continue on to create the `ITextureRegion` object, then build and load the texture atlas as usual. This should all take place within the `onCreateResources()` method of the activity's life cycle.

2. The remaining steps will take place within the `onCreateScene()` method of the activity's life cycle. First, we need to create all of the `Sprite` objects which will appear on the background. In this recipe, we're applying three `Sprite` objects which will be placed conveniently on the background in order to enhance the illusion of distance between the different sprites:

```
final float textureHeight = mHillTextureRegion.getHeight();

/* Create the hill which will appear to be the furthest
 * into the distance. This Sprite will be placed higher than the
 * rest in order to retain visibility of it */
Sprite hillFurthest = new Sprite(WIDTH * 0.5f, textureHeight *
0.5f + 50, mHillTextureRegion,
    mEngine.getVertexBufferObjectManager());

/* Create the hill which will appear between the furthest and
closest
 * hills. This Sprite will be placed higher than the closest hill,
but
 * lower than the furthest hill in order to retain visibility */
Sprite hillMid = new Sprite(WIDTH * 0.5f, textureHeight * 0.5f +
25, mHillTextureRegion,
    mEngine.getVertexBufferObjectManager());

/* Create the closest hill which will not be obstructed by any
other hill
 * Sprites. This Sprite will be placed at the bottom of the Scene
since
 * nothing will be covering its view */
Sprite hillClosest = new Sprite(WIDTH * 0.5f, textureHeight *
0.5f, mHillTextureRegion,
    mEngine.getVertexBufferObjectManager());
```

3. Next, we will create the `ParallaxBackground` object. The three parameters for the constructor define the background color as usual. More importantly, we must override the `onUpdate()` method of the `ParallaxBackground` object in order to handle movement of the `Sprite` objects on the background pending any camera movement:

```
/* Create the ParallaxBackground, setting the color values to
represent
 * a blue sky */
```

```
ParallaxBackground background = new ParallaxBackground(0.3f, 0.3f,
0.9f) {

    /* We'll use these values to calculate the parallax value of the
background */
    float cameraPreviousX = 0;
    float parallaxValueOffset = 0;

    /* onUpdates to the background, we need to calculate new
     * parallax values in order to apply movement to the background
     * objects (the hills in this case) */
    @Override
    public void onUpdate(float pSecondsElapsed) {
        /* Obtain the camera's current center X value */
        final float cameraCurrentX = mCamera.getCenterX();

        /* If the camera's position has changed since last
         * update... */
        if (cameraPreviousX != cameraCurrentX) {

            /* Calculate the new parallax value offset by
             * subtracting the previous update's camera x coordinate
             * from the current update's camera x coordinate */
            parallaxValueOffset +=  cameraCurrentX - cameraPreviousX;

            /* Apply the parallax value offset to the background, which
             * will in-turn offset the positions of entities attached
             * to the background */
            this.setParallaxValue(parallaxValueOffset);

            /* Update the previous camera X since we're finished with
this
             * update */
            cameraPreviousX = cameraCurrentX;
        }
        super.onUpdate(pSecondsElapsed);
    }
};
```

4. Once the `ParallaxBackground` object has been created, we must now attach `ParallaxEntity` objects to the `ParallaxBackground` object. The `ParallaxEntity` object requires that we define a parallax factor for the entity as well as a `Sprite` object for visual representation, which would be the hills in this case:

```
background.attachParallaxEntity(new ParallaxEntity(5,
hillFurthest));
background.attachParallaxEntity(new ParallaxEntity(10, hillMid));
background.attachParallaxEntity(new ParallaxEntity(15,
hillClosest));
```

5. Lastly, as with all `Background` objects we must apply it to the `Scene` object and enable it:

```
/* Set & Enabled the background */
mScene.setBackground(background);
mScene.setBackgroundEnabled(true);
```

How it works...

In this recipe, we're setting up a `ParallaxBackground` object which will contain three separate `ParallaxEntity` objects. Each of these three `ParallaxEntity` objects will represent a hill within the background of our scene. Through the use of parallax factors and parallax values, the `ParallaxBackground` object allows each of the `ParallaxEntity` objects to offset their position at different speeds in the event that the `Camera` object changes its position. This allows the `ParallaxEntity` objects to give off the perspective effect. As we all know, objects which are closer to us will appear to move much faster than objects which are in the distance.

The first step in the *How to do it...* section is a basic and necessary task for creating our `Sprite` objects. In this recipe, we're using a single texture region/image to represent all three sprites which will be attached to the background. However, feel free to modify this recipe in order to allow each of the three `Sprite` objects to use their own customized images. Practice will help to further understand how a `ParallaxBackground` object can be manipulated to create neat scenes within a game.

In the second step, we set up our three `Sprite` objects which will be attached to the background as `ParallaxEntity` objects. We're placing them all in the center of the scene as far as the x coordinate goes. The `ParallaxBackground` class is only meant for applying perspective to the x coordinate movement, therefore the position of sprites on the background will move out of the initial x coordinate as the camera moves. With that being said, it is important to know that the `ParallaxBackground` object will continuously stitch together copies of each `ParallaxEntity` object attached to the background in order to compensate for background objects which may leave the camera's view. See the following figure for a visual representation of how the `ParallaxBackground` object stitches background objects end-to-end:

Due to the way `ParallaxEntity` object stitching works on the `ParallaxBackground` object, in order to create objects which may not appear so often on the background, we must include transparent padding within the image file itself.

As for defining a sprite's y coordinate, it is best to spread the sprites out in order to be able to differentiate between the closest and the furthest hills on the background. In order to create the best perspective effect, the most distant objects should appear to be higher up on the scene as they will be hiding behind the closer objects as far as layering goes.

In the third step, we create the `ParallaxBackground` object. The constructor, similar to all other `Background` object subtypes, defines the background color. The real magic takes place within the overridden `onUpdate()` method of the `ParallaxBackground` object. We have two variables; `cameraPreviousX` and `cameraCurrentX` which will be tested against initially to make sure there is a difference between the two in order to reduce any unnecessary execution of code. If the two values are not equal to each other, we accumulate the difference between the previous and current camera position into a `parallaxValueOffset` variable. By calling `setParallaxValue(parallaxValueOffset)` on the `ParallaxBackground` object, we are basically just telling the background that the camera has changed positions and it's time to update all of the `ParallaxEntity` object positions to compensate. Increasing the parallax value will cause `ParallaxEntity` objects to pan to the left, while decreasing it causes them to pan to the right.

In the fourth step, we finally create the `ParallaxEntity` objects, supplying each of them with a parallax factor and a `Sprite` object. The parallax factor will define exactly how fast or how slow the `Sprite` object will move based on the camera's movement. In order to create a more realistic scenery, the objects furthest away should have a lesser value than closer objects. Additionally, the `attachParallaxEntity(pParallaxEntity)` method is similar to attaching `Entity` objects to a `Scene` object in the sense that the second object attached will appear in front of the first, the third will appear in front of the second, and so on. For this reason, we attach `ParallaxEntity` objects to `ParallaxBackground` from furthest first, then work our way up to the closest object.

Once all of the previous steps have been done, we can simply apply `ParallaxBackground` to the `Scene` object and enable it. From here on out, any and all camera movement will determine the position of the objects within the background scenery!

There's more...

AndEngine also includes an `AutoParallaxBackground` class which is similar to the `ParallaxBackground` class in terms of setting up a visual effect. The difference between the two is that the `AutoParallaxBackground` class allows us to specify a constant rate in which the `ParallaxEntity` objects will move across the screen regardless of the camera's movement. This type of background is useful for games which should appear to be constantly moving such as a racing game or any type of fast-paced side-scroller. On the other hand, the `AutoParallaxBackground` class can also be used to create simple effects such as clouds scrolling consistently across the screen during gameplay, even in games which may appear to remain static in terms of `Camera` and `Scene` object position.

We can create an `AutoParallaxBackground` object by making a simple adjustment to this recipe's activity. Replace the current `ParallaxBackground` object creation with the following code snippet. Note that the `autoParallaxSpeed` variable defines how fast the `ParallaxEntity` objects will move on the background, since they're no longer based on the camera's movement:

```
/* Define the speed that the parallax entities will move at.
 *
 * Set to a negative value for movement in the opposite direction */
final float autoParallaxSpeed = 3;

/* Create an AutoParallaxBackground */
AutoParallaxBackground background = new AutoParallaxBackground(0.3f,
0.3f, 0.9f, autoParallaxSpeed);
```

Additionally, remove all code associated with the `mCamera` object's `onUpdate()` method as it will no longer affect the position of the `ParallaxEntity` objects.

The following figure displays the outcome of attaching three hill layers to the `ParallaxBackground` or `AutoParallaxBackground` objects at different heights, minus the movement, of course:

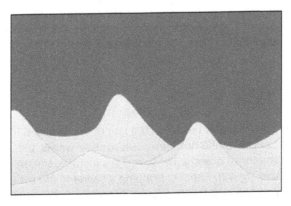

See also

- ▸ *Working with different types of textures* in *Chapter 1, AndEngine Game Structure*.
- ▸ *Bringing a scene to life with sprites* in *Chapter 2, Working with Entities*.
- ▸ *Applying a background* given in this chapter.

Creating our level selection system

Chances are, if you've ever played a mobile game with multiple levels then you already have an idea of what we'll be working with in this chapter. We're going to be creating a class which provides our game with a grid containing level tiles that we can use in order to allow a user to select a level to play. This class can be very easily managed and is highly customizable, from button texture, column count, row count, and more, with ease. The end result will look something like this:

 This implementation of the `LevelSelector` class extends AndEngine's `Entity` object. This makes applying transitional effects with entity modifiers and allowing scrolling based on touch events a rather trivial task.

Getting ready...

The `LevelSelector` class is highly based on the use of AndEngine's `Entity`, `Sprite`, and `Text` objects. In order to understand how `LevelSelector` works, please take the time to go over the recipes regarding these objects. These recipes include, *Understanding AndEngine entities* in *Chapter 2, Working with Entities*, *Bringing a scene to life with sprites* in *Chapter 2, Working with Entities*, and *Applying text to a layer* in *Chapter 2, Working with Entities*.

The `LevelSelector` object requires an `ITextureRegion` object with a reference to an image file. Feel free to create an image which will represent a square button at 50 x 50 pixels in dimension, such as those seen in the figure in this recipe's introduction. While this `ITextureRegion` object is not needed internally within the `LevelSelector` class, it is needed in order to test out the `LevelSelector` class in an empty `BaseGameActivity` test project at the end of this recipe.

Refer to the class named `LevelSelector` in the code bundle for the working code for this recipe. Feel free to use this class and modify it as you see fit in order to fit the needs of your own games!

How to do it...

The `LevelSelector` class is actually quite simple to work with even though its size might be quite large. In this recipe, we're actually going to be introducing two classes; the first is the `LevelSelector` class which handles how the level tiles, or buttons, come to form a grid on the scene. The second is an inner class of `LevelSelector`, called `LevelTile`. The `LevelTile` class allows us to easily add or remove additional data that may be necessary for our own games. For the sake of keeping things simple, we're going to discuss each of the two classes in their own steps starting with the `LevelSelector` class.

The following steps explain how the `LevelSelector` class works in order to arrange `LevelTile` objects on the scene in a grid format:

1. Create the `LevelSelector` constructor, initializing all variables. This constructor is straightforward until we come to the point where we must specify the very first `LevelTile` object's position via the `mInitialX` and `mInitialY` variables:

```
final float halfLevelSelectorWidth = ((TILE_DIMENSION * COLUMNS) +
TILE_PADDING
    * (COLUMNS - 1)) * 0.5f;
this.mInitialX = (this.mCameraWidth * 0.5f) -
halfLevelSelectorWidth;

/* Same math as above applies to the Y coordinate */
final float halfLevelSelectorHeight = ((TILE_DIMENSION * ROWS) +
TILE_PADDING
    * (ROWS - 1)) * 0.5f;
this.mInitialY = (this.mCameraHeight * 0.5f) +
halfLevelSelectorHeight;
```

2. Next, we must create the method which will be used to build the
   `LevelSelector` object's tile grid. We are creating a method called
   `createTiles(pTextureRegion, pFont)` which makes creating the
   level tile grid completely automated by looping through a set number of
   ROWS and COLUMNS values, placing tiles in predetermined coordinates:

```
public void createTiles(final ITextureRegion pTextureRegion,
    final Font pFont) {

  /* Temp coordinates for placing level tiles */
  float tempX = this.mInitialX + TILE_DIMENSION * 0.5f;
  float tempY = this.mInitialY - TILE_DIMENSION * 0.5f;

  /* Current level of the tile to be placed */
  int currentTileLevel = 1;

  /* Loop through the Rows, adjusting tempY coordinate after each
   * iteration */
  for (int i = 0; i < ROWS; i++) {

    /* Loop through the column positions, placing a LevelTile in
each
      * column */
    for (int o = 0; o < COLUMNS; o++) {

      final boolean locked;

      /* Determine whether the current tile is locked or not */
      if (currentTileLevel <= mMaxLevel) {
        locked = false;
      } else {
        locked = true;
      }

      /* Create a level tile */
      LevelTile levelTile = new LevelTile(tempX, tempY, locked,
          currentTileLevel, pTextureRegion, pFont);

      /* Attach the level tile's text based on the locked and
       * currentTileLevel variables pass to its constructor */
      levelTile.attachText();

      /* Register & Attach the levelTile object to the
LevelSelector */
      mScene.registerTouchArea(levelTile);
      this.attachChild(levelTile);

      /* Increment the tempX coordinate to the next column */
```

```
        tempX = tempX + TILE_DIMENSION + TILE_PADDING;

        /* Increment the level tile count */
        currentTileLevel++;
      }

    /* Reposition the tempX coordinate back to the first row (far
left) */
      tempX = mInitialX + TILE_DIMENSION * 0.5f;

    /* Reposition the tempY coordinate for the next row to apply
tiles */
      tempY = tempY - TILE_DIMENSION - TILE_PADDING;
    }
  }
```

3. The third and final step for the LevelSelector class is to include two methods; one for displaying the LevelSelector class' grid and another for hiding the LevelSelector class' grid. For simplicity, we'll call these methods show() and hide() with no parameters:

```
/* Display the LevelSelector on the Scene. */
public void show() {

  /* Register as non-hidden, allowing touch events */
  mHidden = false;

  /* Attach the LevelSelector the the Scene if it currently has no
parent */
  if (!this.hasParent()) {
    mScene.attachChild(this);
  }

  /* Set the LevelSelector to visible */
  this.setVisible(true);
}

/* Hide the LevelSelector on the Scene. */
public void hide() {

  /* Register as hidden, disallowing touch events */
  mHidden = true;

  /* Remove the LevelSelector from view */
  this.setVisible(false);
}
```

Now we move on to the `LevelTile` class' steps. The `LevelTile` inner class is an extension of AndEngine's `Sprite` object. The reason we implement our own `LevelTile` class is to allow each tile to store its own data, such as whether the level the tile represents is locked or not, `Font` and `Text` objects used to display the tile's level number, the tile's level number itself, and more. This class can easily be modified to store even more information such as a user's high-score for a specific level, level color themes, or whatever else we'd like to include. The following steps walk us through the creation of the `LevelTile` inner class:

1. Create the `LevelTile` constructor:

```
public LevelTile(float pX, float pY, boolean pIsLocked,
    int pLevelNumber, ITextureRegion pTextureRegion, Font pFont) {
  super(pX, pY, LevelSelector.this.TILE_DIMENSION,
    LevelSelector.this.TILE_DIMENSION, pTextureRegion,
    LevelSelector.this.mEngine.getVertexBufferObjectManager());

  /* Initialize the necessary variables for the LevelTile */
  this.mFont = pFont;
  this.mIsLocked = pIsLocked;
  this.mLevelNumber = pLevelNumber;
}
```

2. Create the necessary getters for the `LevelTile` class. For a basic `LevelTile` class such as this, all we'll need access to is data regarding the locked state of the level number the tile represents as well as the level number the tile represents:

```
/* Method used to obtain whether or not this level tile represents a
 * level which is currently locked */
public boolean isLocked() {
  return this.mIsLocked;
}

/* Method used to obtain this specific level tiles level number */
public int getLevelNumber() {
  return this.mLevelNumber;
}
```

3. In order to display the level number on each `LevelTile` object, we'll create an `attachText()` method to handle applying a `Text` object to each `LevelTile` object after it is created:

```
public void attachText() {
  String tileTextString = null;

  /* If the tile's text is currently null... */
  if (this.mTileText == null) {
```

```
    /* Determine the tile's string based on whether it's locked or
    * not */
    if (this.mIsLocked) {
      tileTextString = "Locked";
    } else {
      tileTextString = String.valueOf(this.mLevelNumber);
    }
    /* Setup the text position to be placed in the center of the
tile */
    final float textPositionX = LevelSelector.this.TILE_DIMENSION
* 0.5f;
    final float textPositionY = textPositionX;

    /* Create the tile's text in the center of the tile */
    this.mTileText = new Text( textPositionX,
        textPositionY, this.mFont,
        tileTextString, tileTextString.length(),
        LevelSelector.this.mEngine.
getVertexBufferObjectManager());

    /* Attach the Text to the LevelTile */
    this.attachChild(mTileText);
  }
}
```

4. Last but certainly not the least, we'll override the onAreaTouched() method of the LevelTile class in order to provide a default action in the event a tile is pressed down on. The event executed should differ depending on the mIsLocked Boolean value:

```
@Override
public boolean onAreaTouched(TouchEvent pSceneTouchEvent,
    float pTouchAreaLocalX, float pTouchAreaLocalY) {
  /* If the LevelSelector is not hidden, proceed to execute the
touch
    * event */
  if (!LevelSelector.this.mHidden) {
    /* If a level tile is initially pressed down on */
    if (pSceneTouchEvent.isActionDown()) {
      /* If this level tile is locked... */
      if (this.mIsLocked) {
        /* Tile Locked event... */
    LevelSelector.this.mScene.getBackground().setColor(
        org.andengine.util.adt.color.Color.RED);
      } else {
```

```
                    /* Tile unlocked event... This event would likely prompt
                     * level loading but without getting too complicated we
                     * will simply set the Scene's background color to green
        */
            LevelSelector.this.mScene.getBackground().setColor(
                    org.andengine.util.adt.color.Color.GREEN);


            /**
             * Example level loading:
             *      LevelSelector.this.hide();
             * SceneManager.loadLevel(this.mLevelNumber);
             */
        }
        return true;
        }
    }
    return super.onAreaTouched(pSceneTouchEvent, pTouchAreaLocalX,
        pTouchAreaLocalY);
}
```

How it works...

This implementation of a `LevelSelector` class allows us to create a grid of selectable level tiles by adding a minimal amount of code in our activity. Before we go over the implementation of the `LevelSelector` class into our activity, let's take a look at how this class works in order to give us an idea of how we might modify this class to better suit the specific needs of a range of different games. Just as the *How to do it...* section divides the steps into two segments based on each of the two classes used in this recipe, we will also explain how each class works in two segments. We will start with the `LevelSelector` class once again.

Explaining the LevelSelector class

First and foremost, the `LevelSelector` class includes a number of member variables, which we should get to know in order to take full advantage of this object. The following is a list of the variables used in this class along with a description for each:

  ▶ COLUMNS: The number of `LevelTile` objects to be displayed on the horizontal axis of the `LevelSelector` class' grid.

  ▶ ROWS: The number of `LevelTile` objects to be displayed on the vertical axis of the `LevelSelector` class' grid.

  ▶ TILE_DIMENSION: The width and height values of each individual `LevelTile` object.

- ▶ TILE_PADDING: The spacing, in pixels, between each LevelTile object on the LevelSelector class' grid.

- ▶ mChapter: This value defines the LevelSelector class' chapter value. This variable can allow us to create a number of LevelSelector objects which represent different chapters/worlds/zones within our game by specifying different chapter values for each LevelSelector object.

- ▶ mMaxLevel: This value defines the maximum unlocked level that a user has currently reached within our game. This variable would be tested against the level number of each LevelTile object that is touched. Users should not be allowed entry into levels which are greater than this variable.

- ▶ mCameraWidth/mCameraHeight: These values are simply used to help properly align the LevelSelector and LevelTile objects in the center of the scene.

- ▶ mInitialX: This variable is in place to hold a reference to the initial x coordinate of each of the LevelSelector class' grid rows. Each time an entire row of the grid is laid out, the first LevelTile object of the next row reverts back to this x coordinate.

- ▶ mInitialY: This variable is used only once to define the very first LevelTile object's y coordinate. Since we're building the LevelSelector class' grid from left to right and from the top to bottom, we will never have to revert back to the initial y coordinate for subsequent tile placement.

- ▶ mHidden: The boolean statement of this variable determines whether or not the LevelTile objects will respond to touch events. This variable is set true if the LevelSelector object is not visible on the scene, false otherwise.

With all of the member variables out of the way, understanding how the LevelSelector class works will be a breeze! In the first step, we're creating the LevelSelector constructor to initialize all of the class variables. The constructor should be easy to follow up until the point where we define the mInitialX and mInitialY variables. All we are doing is calculating half of the overall width and height of the LevelSelector class' grid based on the number of columns, the number of rows, the tile dimension, and the tile padding. To calculate the overall width, we need to multiply the number of COLUMNS values by the width of each LevelTile object. Since we're including padding between each tile, we must also calculate how much space the padding will consume. However, padding will only occur in between tiles, meaning there will be no padding to calculate for the final column, so we can subtract a column from the padding calculation. We then divide this value by half in order to come up with half the width of the entire grid. Finally, subtracting half the width of the entire grid from the center position of the Camera object will give us the first LevelTile object's x coordinate! The same math applies to calculate the initial y coordinate, except the y axis deals with rows instead of columns, so we need to make that adjustment in the mInitiaY variable calculation in order to obtain the proper y coordinate.

The second step for the `LevelSelector` class introduces the method of `LevelTile` object creation and placement. This is where the grid-making magic begins. Before we begin the iteration, we declare and define temporary coordinates which will be used to place each `LevelTile` object on the grid, incrementing their value accordingly after each tile is placed. The `TILE_DIMENSION * 0.5f` calculations are simply in place to accommodate for AndEngine's `Entity` object's anchor, or placement coordinate relying on the center of the `Entity` object. Additionally, we are initializing a temporary level number called `currentTileLevel` which is initialized to 1, which signifies the level 1 tile. This variable is incremented by a value of 1 each time a level tile is placed on the grid. Once the initial level tile's values have been defined, we proceed to create the `for` loops which will loop through each position of the rows and columns which make up the grid. Starting with the first row, we will then loop N number of columns, incrementing the `tempX` variable by adding `TILE_DIMENSION` and `TILE_PADDING` after each tile is placed which will give us the next position. Once we reach the maximum number of columns, we decrease the `tempY` variable by adding `TILE_DIMENSION` and `TILE_PADDING` in order to drop us to the next row to populate. This process continues on until there are no rows left to populate.

The final step included in the `LevelSelector` class includes the code which calls `setVisible(pBoolean)` on the `LevelSelector` object, enabling visibility if the `show()` method is called and disabling visibility if the `hide()` method is called. The first time a `LevelSelector` object calls `show()`, it will be attached to the `Scene` object. Additionally, the `mHidden` variable will be adjusted according to the visibility of the `LevelSelector` object.

Explaining the LevelTile class

As with the `LevelSelector` class, we will begin by outlining the purpose of the different `LevelTile` class member variables. The following is a list of the variables used in this class along with a description for each:

- `mIsLocked`: The `mIsLocked` Boolean variable is defined by a parameter in the `LevelTile` constructor. This variable defines whether or not this `LevelTile` object's touch event should produce a positive event, such as proceeding to load a level, or a negative event, such as notification that the level is locked.

- `mLevelNumber`: This variable simply holds the value of the `LevelTile` object's level number representation. This value is determined according to its position on the grid; for example, the first tile placed on a grid will represent level 1, the second tile will represent level 2, and so on.

- `mFont` and `mTileText`: The `mFont` and `mTileText` objects are used to display a `Text` object on each `LevelTile`. If the `LevelTile` object is considered to be locked, a string displaying the word, **locked** will be displayed on the tile, otherwise the level number of the tile is displayed.

In the `LevelTile` class' first step, we're simply introducing the constructor. There's nothing out of the ordinary here. However, one thing to note is that the constructor does rely on the constant `TILE_DIMENSION` value to specify the tile's width/height dimensions without specifying a parameter. This is in place to keep a level of conformity between the `LevelSelector` and `LevelTile` classes.

In the second step, we had introduced two getter methods which can be used to obtain the more important values of the `LevelTile` class. Even though we aren't currently using these methods within either class, they can be important later on when the `LevelSelector`/`LevelTile` objects are implemented into a full-featured game which requires data such as level numbers to be passed around within the game.

The third step introduces a method which is used to attach a `Text` object to `LevelTile` called `attachText()`. This method will place the `mTileText` object in the direct center of the `LevelTile` object with a string dependent on the `LevelTile` object's locked state. As stated in the `mFont` and `mTileText` variable explanation, the `mTileText` object's `String` variable will display either **locked** or the tile's level number.

The final step requires us to override the `onAreaTouched()` method of the `LevelTile` object. Before we even consider responding to a touch event on any tile, we first determine whether or not the `LevelSelector` object containing the `LevelTile` object is visible. If not, there is no point in proceeding with any touch events, but if the `LevelSelector` object is visible then we proceed to check whether the tile was pressed down on. If a `LevelTile` object is pressed down on, we then continue to check whether or not the tile is locked or unlocked. In the class' current state, we are simply setting the color of the scene's background in order to signify whether or not the pressed tile is locked or not. However, in a real-world application, the current locked event can be replaced with a basic notification stating that the selected tile is locked. In the event that a tile is not locked, then the touch event should take the user to the selected level based on the `LevelTile` object's `mLevelNumber` variable. If the game contains multiple chapters/worlds/zones, then we could even go as far as the following pseudo-code implementation, depending on the game's method of loading levels:

```
LevelSelector.this.hide();
SceneManager.loadLevel(this.mLevelNumber, LevelSelector.this.
mChapter);
```

There's more...

Once we've included the `LevelSelector` class into any project we choose, we can easily implement a working-level selection grid into our `BaseGameActivity`. In order to properly create the `LevelSelector` object and display it on our scene, we'll need to make sure we've created an `ITextureRegion` object and `Font` object to be used when creating the `LevelTile` objects for the `LevelSelector` class. We're going to omit the resource creation code in order to keep the `LevelSelector` class' example brief. If need be, please visit the recipes, *Working with different types of textures* in *Chapter 1, AndEngine Game Structure*, and *Using AndEngine font resources* in *Chapter 1, AndEngine Game Structure*, for more information on how to set up the necessary resources for this class.

The following code displaying how to create the `LevelSelector` object can be copied into the `onCreateScene()` method of any activity prior to creating the necessary `ITextureRegion` and `Font` objects:

```
/* Define the level selector properties */
final int maxUnlockedLevel = 7;
final int levelSelectorChapter = 1;
final int cameraWidth = WIDTH;
final int cameraHeight = HEIGHT

/* Create a new level selector */
LevelSelector levelSelector = new LevelSelector(maxUnlockedLevel,
levelSelectorChapter, cameraWidth, cameraHeight, mScene, mEngine);

/* Generate the level tiles for the levelSelector object */
levelSelector.createTiles(mTextureRegion, mFont);

/* Display the levelSelector object on the scene */
levelSelector.show();
```

A great feature of this `LevelSelector` class is the fact that it is an `Entity` object subtype. If we wish to apply fancy transition effects for it to move in and out of the camera's view as needed, we can simply call `levelSelector.registerEntityModifier(pEntityModifier)`. Since the `LevelTile` objects are attached to the `LevelSelector` object upon calling the `createTiles()` method, any change in the `LevelSelector` object's position will also affect all `LevelTile` objects, in sync. This also makes creating scrollable level selector implementation very easy to add if dealing with multiple chapters.

See also

- ▶ *Understanding AndEngine entities* in *Chapter 2, Working with Entities*.
- ▶ *Bringing a scene to life with sprites* in *Chapter 2, Working with Entities*
- ▶ *Applying text to a layer* in *Chapter 2, Working with Entities*.

Hiding and retrieving layers

There are a few different options we have for screen management in our games; a screen being a menu screen, loading screen, gameplay screen, and more. We can use multiple activities to act as each screen, we can use the more obvious `Scene` object to act as each screen in our game, or we can use `Entity` objects to act as each screen. While the majority of developers tend to follow the multiple activities or multiple `Scene` objects to act as different game screens, we're going to be taking a quick look into using `Entity` objects to act as the different screens in our games.

Using `Entity` objects to act as the various screens of our game has many benefits over the other two approaches mentioned. The entity approach allows us to apply many different screens, or layers to our game at the same time. Unlike with using multiple activities or `Scene` objects to act as different screens in our game, we can visually display a number of screens on the device using `Entity` objects. This is extremely useful as we can apply transitional effects when entering or leaving gameplay and easily load and unload resources as we see fit.

The following image displays this recipe's code in action. What we're seeing is two `Entity` object layers with a number of `Rectangle` children objects alternating between being transitioned in and transitioned out of the camera's view. This represents how we can use `Entity` objects to handle transitional effects among a small or large group of children:

Getting ready...

This recipe requires an understanding of `Entity` objects and how they can be used as layers to contain a set of children. Additionally, we're incorporating transitional effects to these layers through the use of entity modifiers. Before continuing on with this recipe, please make sure to read through the entire recipes, *Understanding AndEngine entities* in *Chapter 2, Working with Entities*, *Overriding the onManagedUpdate() method* in *Chapter 2, Working with Entities*, and *Using modifiers and entity modifiers* in *Chapter 2, Working with Entities*.

Refer to the class named `HidingAndRetrievingLayers` in the code bundle for the working code for this recipe and import it into an empty AndEngine `BaseGameActivity` class.

How to do it...

The following steps outline how we can use entity modifiers to handle transitional effects between different screens/layers within our game. This recipe includes a simple method which handles the transitioning of layers, however in a real-world application this task is generally performed with the use of a screen/layer manager class. The layers are swapped based on the time passed solely for the purpose of automated demonstration.

1. Create and define the layers/screens as `Entity` objects and the transitional effects with `ParallelEntityModifier` objects. These objects should be global:

```
/* These three Entity objects will represent different screens */
private final Entity mScreenOne = new Entity();
private final Entity mScreenTwo = new Entity();
private final Entity mScreenThree = new Entity();

/* This entity modifier is defined as the 'transition-in' modifier
 * which will move an Entity/screen into the camera-view */
private final ParallelEntityModifier mMoveInModifier = new
ParallelEntityModifier(
  new MoveXModifier(3, WIDTH, 0),
  new RotationModifier(3, 0, 360),
  new ScaleModifier(3, 0, 1));

/* This entity modifier is defined as the 'transition-out'
modifier
 * which will move an Entity/screen out of the camera-view */
private final ParallelEntityModifier mMoveOutModifier = new
ParallelEntityModifier(
  new MoveXModifier(3, 0, -WIDTH),
  new RotationModifier(3, 360, 0),
  new ScaleModifier(3, 1, 0));
```

2. Create the `mScene` object, overriding its `onManagedUpdate()` method in order to handle calling the `setLayer(pLayerIn, pLayerOut)` method introduced in the next step. Additionally, we will attach our `Entity` object layers once the `mScene` object has been created:

```
mScene = new Scene() {
  /* Variable which will accumulate time passed to
   * determine when to switch screens */
  float timeCounter = 0;

  /* Define the first screen indices to be transitioned in and out */
  int layerInIndex = 0;
  int layerOutIndex = SCREEN_COUNT - 1;

  /* Execute the code below on every update to the mScene object */
  @Override
  protected void onManagedUpdate(float pSecondsElapsed) {

    /* If accumulated time is equal to or greater than 4 seconds */
    if (timeCounter >= 4) {

      /* Set screens to be transitioned in and out */
      setLayer(mScene.getChildByIndex(layerInIndex),
          mScene.getChildByIndex(layerOutIndex));

      /* Reset the time counter */
      timeCounter = 0;

      /* Setup the next screens to be swapped in and out */
      if (layerInIndex >= SCREEN_COUNT - 1) {
        layerInIndex = 0;
        layerOutIndex = SCREEN_COUNT - 1;
      } else {
        layerInIndex++;
        layerOutIndex = layerInIndex - 1;
      }

    }
    /* Accumulate seconds passed since last update */
    timeCounter += pSecondsElapsed;
    super.onManagedUpdate(pSecondsElapsed);
  }
```

```
    };

    /* Attach the layers to the scene.
     * Their layer index (according to mScene) is relevant to the
     * order in which they are attached */
    mScene.attachChild(mScreenOne); // layer index == 0
    mScene.attachChild(mScreenTwo); // layer index == 1
    mScene.attachChild(mScreenThree); // layer index == 2
```

3. Lastly, we will create a `setLayer(pLayerIn, pLayerOut)` method which we can use to handle registering the entity modifiers to the appropriate `Entity` object, depending on if it should be entering or leaving the camera's view:

```
    /* This method is used to swap screens in and out of the camera-
    view */
    private void setLayer(IEntity pLayerIn, IEntity pLayerOut) {

      /* If the layer being transitioned into the camera-view is
    invisible,
       * set it to visibile */
      if (!pLayerIn.isVisible()) {
       pLayerIn.setVisible(true);
      }

      /* Global modifiers must be reset after each use */
      mMoveInModifier.reset();
      mMoveOutModifier.reset();

      /* Register the transitional effects to the screens */
      pLayerIn.registerEntityModifier(mMoveInModifier);
      pLayerOut.registerEntityModifier(mMoveOutModifier);
    }
```

How it works...

This recipe covers a simple, yet useful system relating to working with `Entity` layer transitioning. Larger games will likely involve more variables to take into account when handling layer swapping, but the concept is relevant across all project sizes as far as entity/screen indexing and creating the method of transitioning screens goes.

In the first step we are creating our global objects. The three `Entity` objects will represent the different screens within our game. In this recipe, all three of the `Entity` objects contain four `Rectangle` children objects,which allow us to visualize the screen transitions, however we can interpret each of the three `Entity` objects as a different screen such as the menu screen, the loading screen, and the gameplay screen. We are also creating two global `ParallelEntityModifier` entity modifiers to handle the positional changes of the screens. The `mMoveInModifier` modifier will move the registered screen from outside the right-hand side of the camera's view into the center of the camera's view. The `mMoveOutModifier` modifier will move the registered screen from the center of the camera's view to outside the left-hand side of the camera's view. Both modifiers include a simple rotation and scaling effect to produce a "rolling" transitional effect.

In the next step, we are creating our `mScene` object and attaching the globally-declared `Entity` objects to it. In this recipe, we are setting up the `mScene` object to handle screen swapping based on the time passed, however before discussing how the `onManagedUpdate()` method of the `mScene` object works to handle screen swapping, let's take a look at how we're obtaining our `Entity` object indices as they will be used to determine which screens will be transitioned:

```
mScene.attachChild(mScreenOne); // layer index == 0
mScene.attachChild(mScreenTwo); // layer index == 1
mScene.attachChild(mScreenThree); // layer index == 2
```

As we can see in this code snippet, we are attaching the screens in numerical order according to their name. Once an `Entity` object has been attached to the `Scene` object, we can then call the method, `getChildByIndex(pIndex)` on a parent in order to obtain an `Entity` object by its index. A child's index is determined by the order they are attached to another object. We use these indices within the `mScene` object's `onManagedUpdate()` method in order to determine which entity/screen to swap in and which to swap out of the camera's view every four seconds.

During the initialization of the `mScene` object, we are instantiating two `int` variables which will be used to determine which screens to transition in and out of the camera's view. Initially, we are defining `layerInIndex` to a value of `0`, which is equal to the `mScreenOne` object's index and `layerOutIndex` to a value of `SCREEN_COUNT - 1`, which is equal to the `mScreenThree` object's index based on the order they were attached to the `Scene` object. After every four seconds within the `onManagedUpdate()` method of the `mScene` object, we are calling the `setLayer(pLayerIn, pLayerOut)` method to begin the screen transitioning, resetting the `timeCounter` variable to accumulate the next four seconds, and determining the next `Entity` objects to be transitioned in and out of the camera's view. While this example is not exactly relative to most games, it is meant to give us an understanding of how we can use child indices to make transition calls with a method such as `setLayer(pLayerIn,pLayerOut)`.

In the final step, we introduce the `setLayer(pLayerIn, pLayerOut)` method which handles the application of entity modifiers to the `Entity` objects passed in via parameters. This method has three goals; first it sets the layer being transitioned into the view to be visible if it's currently non-visible, it resets our `mMoveInModifier` and `mMoveOutModifier` objects, so that they can provide the `Entity` objects with full transitional effects, and lastly it calls `registerEntityModifier(pEntityModifier)` on both the `pLayerIn` and `pLayerOut` parameters, initiating the transitional effects on the `Entity` objects.

There's more...

This recipe is only relevant for game structures which use multiple `Entity` objects to act as different screens within our games. However, the choice between how to handle transitioning between screens is entirely up to the developer. Before making a decision, it is wise to know what the pros and cons are to the different options we have for handling multiple screens within a game. Please take a look at the following list which covers the good and the bad of the different approaches:

▸ **Activity/screen**:
  ❏ Pro: The Android OS will handle resource unloading for us with a simple call to the activity's `finish()` method, making resource management very simple.
  ❏ Con: Each screen transition will prompt a brief black screen to be displayed upon launching a new activity/screen.
  ❏ Con: Multiple activities must each load their own resources. This means that preloading resources is not an option, which can increase the overall loading time, especially considering resources that may be used on all screens, such as font, or music playback resources.
  ❏ Con: Due to Android's memory management features, activities which are considered background processes may be killed at any time assuming the device is running low on memory. This can cause issues when we leave an activity which should remain in a paused state until a user returns. There is a possibility any activity transitioned from may not be returned to in the same state when needed.

▸ **Scene/screen**:
  ❏ Pro: Possibility of preloading necessary resources which may be used across multiple screens. This can drastically help reduce loading times depending on the number of preloadable resources.
  ❏ Pro: We are able to introduce a loading screen within our game, rather than displaying a blank screen while the resources load.

- ❏ Pro/con: A screen and resource management system must be developed in order to handle the loading/unloading of resources and screens. Depending on the size and needs of the specific game, this can be a rather large task. However, this approach can allow for seamless transition times when moving between screens as we are able to load/unload resources at more convenient times, rather than as soon as a user decides to switch between screens.

- ❏ Con: Typically only one `Scene` object can be applied to our Engine object at a time, meaning that screen transitions will be lacking in terms of animation/fluidity. The screen being set will simply replace the previous screen.

▸ **Entity/screen**:

- ❏ Pro: When dealing with `Entity` objects as screens, we are able to attach as many as we'd like to a `Scene` object. This gives us all of the pro's of the scene/screen approach, as well as the added benefit of being able to add time-based transitional effects, such as "sliding" between the menu screen, to the loading screen, to the gameplay screen. This is the demonstration being made by this recipe's code.

- ❏ Pro/con: As with the scene/screen route, we are required to handle all screen and resource cleanup ourselves. The positive outweighs the negative, but when comparing with the activity/screen approach, the need for a screen/resource management system may be considered a con by some, depending on the size of the project.

Before we wrap up this recipe, there's one more important topic that was not discussed in this recipe. Take a look at the following figure which displays what this recipe's displayed results on a device might resemble:

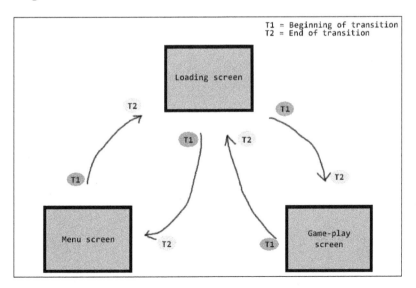

The preceding figure displays the typical transitional events when a user navigates around the different screens within a game. We covered how this navigation works in terms of bringing a new screen into the camera's view. Even more importantly, these transitional events should also handle the loading and unloading of resources. After all, there's no reason to have the **Menu screen** taking up the device's precious resources while it's not being displayed to the user. In an ideal situation if we are moving from the **Menu screen** to the **Game-play screen** as seen in the previous figure, during the **T1** phase the **Game-play** screen will begin to load its resources. Once the **T2** phase is reached, meaning the **Loading screen** is the game's current main screen, the **Menu screen** will be unloaded of all necessary resources and detached from the `Scene` object in order to remove the unnecessary overhead.

This is just a brief overview of how transitioning between screens within a game is best handled in order to allow smooth transitions, and reduce the load-time involved between transitions. For a more in-depth information on the inner-workings of screen management, please see *Chapter 5, Scene and layer management*.

See also

- ▶ *Understanding AndEngine entities* in *Chapter 2, Working with Entities*.
- ▶ *Overriding the onManagedUpdate() method* in *Chapter 2, Working with Entities*.
- ▶ *Using modifiers and entity modifiers* in *Chapter 2, Working with Entities*.

4

Working with Cameras

This chapter will cover AndEngine's various camera objects and advanced camera control. The topics include:

- ▶ Introducing the camera object
- ▶ Limiting the camera area with the bound camera
- ▶ Taking a closer look with zoom cameras
- ▶ Creating smooth moves with a smooth camera
- ▶ Pinch-zoom camera functionality
- ▶ Stitching a background together
- ▶ Applying a HUD to the camera
- ▶ Attaching a controller to the display
- ▶ Coordinate conversion
- ▶ Creating a split screen game

Introduction

AndEngine includes three types of cameras, not including the base `Camera` object, which allow us to control (more specifically) how the camera behaves. Cameras can play many different roles in a game, and in some cases, we may find ourselves in need of more than one camera. This chapter is going to cover some of the different purposes and ways we can use AndEngine's `Camera` objects in order to apply more advanced camera functionality into our own games.

Introducing the camera object

Cameras can have many purposes when it comes to designing a large-scale game, but its main objective is to display a particular area of the game world on the device's display. This topic is going to introduce the base `Camera` class, covering the general aspects of the camera in order to provide a reference for future camera use.

How to do it...

Cameras are important in game development as they control what we see on the device. Creating our camera is as easy as the following code:

```
final int WIDTH = 800;
final int HEIGHT = 480;

// Create the camera
Camera mCamera = new Camera(0, 0, WIDTH, HEIGHT);
```

The `WIDTH` and `HEIGHT` values will define the area of the game's scene that will be displayed on the device.

How it works...

It's important to get to know the main functions of a camera in order to make the most of it in our projects. All of the different cameras inherit the methods found in this topic. Let's take a look at some of the most necessary camera methods needed for AndEngine development:

Positioning the camera:

The `Camera` object follows the same coordinate system as entities. Setting the camera's coordinates to `(0,0)`, for example, will set the center point of the camera to the defined coordinates. Additionally, increasing the x value moves the camera to the right-hand side and increasing the y value moves the camera upward. Decreasing the values will have the opposite effect. In order to relocate the camera to center on a defined location, we can call the following method:

```
// We can position the camera anywhere in the game world
mCamera.setCenter(WIDTH / 2, HEIGHT / 2);
```

The preceding code would not have any effect on the default camera position (assuming that the `WIDTH` and `HEIGHT` values were used to define the camera's width and height). This would set the camera's center to the "center" of our scene, which is naturally equal to half the camera `WIDTH` and `HEIGHT` values when the `Camera` object is created. The preceding method call could be used in a situation where we'd like to reset the camera back to its initial position, which is useful in cases where a camera moves during gameplay, but should return to its initial position when a user returns to the menu.

Moving the camera without setting specific coordinates can be achieved through the `offsetCenter(x,y)` method, where the `x` and `y` values define the distance to offset the camera in scene coordinates. This method adds the specified parameter values to the camera's current position:

```
// Move the camera up and to the right by 5 pixels
mCamera.offsetCenter(5, 5);
// Move the camera down and to the left by 5 pixels
mCamera.offsetCenter(-5, -5);
```

Additionally, we can obtain the camera's center x and y coordinates through the use of the following methods:

```
mCamera.getCenterX();
mCamera.getCenterY();
```

Adjusting the camera's width and height:

The camera's initial width and height can be adjusted via the camera's `set()` method. We can also set the camera's minimum/maximum x and y values by calling methods such as `setXMin()`/`setXMax()` and `setYMin()`/`setYMax()`. The following code will cause the camera width to shrink by half, while sustaining the initial camera height:

```
// Shrink the camera by half its width
mCamera.set(0, 0, mCamera.getWidth() / 2, mCamera.getHeight());
```

Keep in mind that while shrinking the camera width, we lose visibility on the pixels and any entities outside of the defined area. Additionally, shrinking or extending the camera's width and height may cause entities to appear stretched or squeezed. Generally, modifying the camera's width and height are not necessary in the development of a typical game.

The `Camera` object also allows us to obtain the camera's current min/max width and height values by calling `getXMin()`/`getXMax()` and `getYMin()`/`getYMax()`.

Visibility checking:

The `Camera` class allows us to check if specific `Entity` objects are visible within the camera's view. `Entity` object subtypes include, but are not limited to, the `Line` and `Rectangle` primitives, `Sprite`, and `Text` objects, as well as all of their subtypes such as `TiledSprite` and `ButtonSprite` objects and more. Visibility checking can be called through the use of the following method:

```
// Check if entity is visible. true if so, false otherwise
mCamera.isEntityVisible(entityObject);
```

Visibility checks can be very useful for many games in order to re-use objects which might leave the camera's view, to name one scenario. This can allow us to limit the overall number of objects created in situations where we may have many objects being spawned, which eventually leave the camera view. Instead, we can re-use objects which leave the camera view.

The chase entity functionality:

Often times, games require the camera to follow an `Entity` object as it moves around the screen, such as in a side-scroller. We can easily set up our camera to follow entities wherever they move in the game world by calling a single method:

```
mCamera.setChaseEntity(entityObject);
```

The preceding code will apply the camera position to the specified entity's position on every update to the camera. This ensures that the entity stays in the center of the camera at all times.

> In the majority of recipes in this book, we are specifying a camera width of 800 pixels and a camera height of 480 pixels. However, these values are entirely up to the developer and should be defined by the needs of the game. These specific values are chosen for this book's recipes due to the fact that they are relatively suitable for both small and large screen devices.

Limiting the camera area with the bound camera

The `BoundCamera` object allows us to define specific bounds on the camera's area, limiting the distance the camera can travel on both the x and y axis. This camera is useful in situations where the camera may follow a player, but still not exceed the level bounds if the user travels close to a wall.

How to do it...

The `BoundCamera` object creation requires the same parameters as a regular `Camera` object:

```
BoundCamera mCamera = new BoundCamera(0, 0, WIDTH, HEIGHT);
```

How it works...

The `BoundCamera` object extends the ordinary `Camera` object, giving us all of the original functionality of a camera as described in the *Introducing the camera object* recipe, which is given in this chapter. In fact, unless we configure a bounded area on the `BoundCamera` object, we are ideally working with a basic `Camera` object.

Before our camera will apply restrictions to its available movement area, we must define the available area in which the camera is free to move:

```
// WIDTH = 800;
// HEIGHT = 480;
// WIDTH and HEIGHT are equal to the camera's width and height
mCamera.setBounds(0, 0, WIDTH * 4, HEIGHT);

// We must call this method in order to apply camera bounds
mCamera.setBoundsEnabled(true);
```

The preceding code will set up the camera bounds starting from position (0,0) in scene coordinates through to (3200,480) since we are multiplying the camera's width by four times for the maximum x area, allowing the camera to scroll four times the camera's width. The camera will not respond to changes on the y axis as the bound height is set to the same value as the camera's height.

See also

▶   *Introducing the camera object* given in this chapter.

Taking a closer look with zoom cameras

AndEngine's `BoundCamera` and `Camera` objects do not support zooming in and out by default. If we would like to allow zooming of the camera, we can create a `ZoomCamera` object which extends the `BoundCamera` class. This object includes all of the functionality of its inherited classes, including creating camera bounds.

How to do it...

The `ZoomCamera` object, similar to `BoundCamera`, requires no additional parameters to be defined while creating the camera:

```
ZoomCamera mCamera = new ZoomCamera(0, 0, WIDTH, HEIGHT);
```

How it works...

In order to apply zoom effects to the camera, we can call the `setZoomFactor(factor)` method, where `factor` is the magnification we would like to apply to our `Scene` object. Zooming in and out can be achieved with the following code:

```
// Divide the camera width/height by 1.5x (Zoom in)
mCamera.setZoomFactor(1.5f);

// Divide the camera width and height by 0.5x (Zoom out)
mCamera.setZoomFactor(0.5f);
```

When handling the camera's zoom factor, we must know that a factor of `1` is equal to the default factor of the `Camera` class. A zoom factor greater than `1` will zoom the camera into the scene, while any value less than `1` will zoom the camera out.

The math involved for handling the zoom factor is very basic. The camera will simply divide the zoom factor by our camera's `WIDTH` and `HEIGHT` values, effectively causing the camera to "zoom". If our camera's width is `800`, then a zoom factor of `1.5f` will zoom the camera inward, ultimately setting the camera's width to `533.3333` which will limit the amount of area of the scene that is displayed.

The `getMinX()`, `getMaxX()`, `getMinY()`, `getMaxY()`, `getWidth()`, and `getHeight()` values returned by the `ZoomCamera` object in a situation where a zoom factor (not equal to 1) is applied, will automatically have had their values divided by the zoom factor.

There's more...

Enabling bounds on a zoom camera with a factor not equal to 1 will have an effect on the total available area the camera is able to pan. Assuming that the bounds are set from 0 to 800 for the bounds' minimum and maximum x values, if the camera width is equal to 800 there will not be any movement allowed on the x axis. In the event we zoom the camera in, the camera's width will decrease, allowing for slack in the movement of the camera.

In the event that a zoom factor is defined which would cause the camera's width or height to exceed the camera bounds, the zoom factor would be applied to the camera, but there would be no movement allowed on the exceeded axis.

See also

▸ *Introducing the camera object* given in this chapter.
▸ *Limiting camera area with the bound camera* given in this chapter.

Creating smooth moves with a smooth camera

The `SmoothCamera` object is the most advanced of the four cameras to choose from. This camera allows for all of the different types of camera functionality (bounds, zooming, and so on) with an additional option to apply a defined velocity to the camera's movement speed upon setting a new position for the camera. The result may appear as if the camera "eases" in and out of movement, allowing for rather subtle camera movements.

How to do it...

This camera type is the only one of the four which requires additional parameters to be defined in the constructor. These extra parameters include the maximum x and y velocities in which the camera can travel and the maximum zoom factor change which handles the speed that the camera will zoom in and out. Let's take a look at what this camera creation will look like:

```
// Camera movement speeds
final float maxVelocityX = 10;
final float maxVelocityY = 5;
// Camera zoom speed
final float maxZoomFactorChange = 5;

// Create smooth camera
mCamera = new SmoothCamera(0, 0, WIDTH, HEIGHT, maxVelocityX,
maxVelocityY, maxZoomFactorChange);
```

How it works...

In this recipe, we're creating a camera that applies a smooth transitional affect to camera movement and zooming. Unlike the other three camera types, rather than directly setting the camera center to the defined position with `setCenter(x,y)`, the camera uses the `maxVelocityX`, `maxVelocityY`, and `maxZoomFactorChange` variables to define how fast the camera will move from point A to point B. Increasing the velocities will cause the camera to make faster movements.

There are two options, both for camera movement and camera zooming for the `SmoothCamera` class. We can allow the camera to move or zoom smoothly by calling the default camera methods for these tasks (`camera.setCenter()` and `camera.setZoomFactor()`). On the other hand, sometimes we need to reposition our camera immediately. This can be done by calling the `camera.setCenterDirect()` and `camera.setZoomFactorDirect()` methods respectively. These methods are most commonly used in order to reset the position of a smooth camera.

See also

- ▸ *Introducing the camera object* given in this chapter.
- ▸ *Limiting camera area with the bound camera* given in this chapter.
- ▸ *Taking a closer look with zoom cameras* given in this chapter.

Pinch-zoom camera functionality

AndEngine includes a small list of "detector" classes which can be used in combination with scene touch events. This topic is going to cover the use of the `PinchZoomDetector` class in order to allow zooming of the camera by pressing two fingers on the display, moving them closer or further apart to adjust the zoom factor.

Getting started..

Please refer to the class named `ApplyingPinchToZoom` in the code bundle.

How to do it...

Follow these steps for a walkthrough on setting up the pinch-to-zoom functionality.

1. The first thing we must do is implement the appropriate listeners into our class. Since we'll be working with touch events, we'll need to include the `IOnSceneTouchListener` interface. Additionally, we'll need to implement the `IPinchZoomDetectorListener` interface to handle changes in the camera's zoom factor pending touch events:

   ```
   public class ApplyingPinchToZoom extends BaseGameActivity
   implements
        IOnSceneTouchListener, IPinchZoomDetectorListener {
   ```

2. In the `onCreateScene()` method of the `BaseGameActivity` class, set the `Scene` object's touch listener to the `this` activity since we are letting the `BaseGameActivity` class implement the touch listener classes. We will also create and enable the `mPinchZoomDetector` object within this method:

   ```
   /* Set the scene to listen for touch events using
   * this activity's listener */
   mScene.setOnSceneTouchListener(this);

   /* Create and set the zoom detector to listen for
    * touch events using this activity's listener */
   mPinchZoomDetector = new PinchZoomDetector(this);

   // Enable the zoom detector
   mPinchZoomDetector.setEnabled(true);
   ```

3. In the implemented `onSceneTouchEvent()` method of the `BaseGameActivity` class, we must pass the touch events to the `mPinchZoomDetector` object:

   ```
   @Override
   public boolean onSceneTouchEvent(Scene pScene, TouchEvent
   pSceneTouchEvent) {
   ```

```
    // Pass scene touch events to the pinch zoom detector
    mPinchZoomDetector.onTouchEvent(pSceneTouchEvent);
    return true;
}
```

4. Next, we will obtain the initial zoom factor of the `ZoomCamera` object when the `mPinchZoomDetector` object registers that a user is applying two fingers to the display. We will use the `onPinchZoomStarted()` method, which is implemented via the `IPinchZoomDetectorListener` interface:

```
/* This method is fired when two fingers press down
* on the display */
@Override
public void onPinchZoomStarted(PinchZoomDetector
pPinchZoomDetector,
    TouchEvent pSceneTouchEvent) {
    // On first detection of pinch zooming, obtain the initial zoom
factor
    mInitialTouchZoomFactor = mCamera.getZoomFactor();
}
```

5. Lastly, we will make changes to the `ZoomCamera` object's zoom factor in the event that a pinching motion is detected on the display. This code will be placed in both the `onPinchZoom()` and `onPinchZoomFinished()` methods:

```
@Override
public void onPinchZoom(PinchZoomDetector pPinchZoomDetector,
    TouchEvent pTouchEvent, float pZoomFactor) {

    /* On every sub-sequent touch event (after the initial touch) we
offset
    * the initial camera zoom factor by the zoom factor calculated
by
    * pinch-zooming */
    final float newZoomFactor = mInitialTouchZoomFactor *
pZoomFactor;

    // If the camera is within zooming bounds
    if(newZoomFactor < MAX_ZOOM_FACTOR && newZoomFactor > MIN_ZOOM_
FACTOR){
        // Set the new zoom factor
        mCamera.setZoomFactor(newZoomFactor);
    }
}
```

How it works...

In this recipe, we are overriding the scene touch events which take place on our scene, passing the touch events to the `PinchZoomDetector` object, which will handle the zoom functionality of the `ZoomCamera` object. The following steps will guide us through the process of how pinch-zooming works. Because we're working with zoom factors in this activity, we'll need to use either a `ZoomCamera` class or a `SmoothCamera` class implementation.

In the first two steps for this recipe, we're implementing the required listeners and registering them to the `mScene` object and the `mPinchZoomDetector` object. Since the `ApplyingPinchToZoom` activity is implementing the listeners, we can pass `this`, which represents our `BaseGameActivity` class, to the `mScene` object as the touch listener. We can also pass this activity as the pinch detection listener. Once the pinch detector is created, we can enable or disable it by calling the `setEnabled(pSetEnabled)` method.

In step three, we are passing the `pSceneTouchEvent` object to the `onTouchEvent()` method of the pinch detector. Doing so will allow the pinch detector to obtain specific touch coordinates which will be used internally to calculate zoom factors based on finger positions.

Upon pressing two fingers on the screen, the pinch detector will fire the code snippet displayed in step four. We must obtain the initial zoom factor of the camera at this point in order to properly offset the zoom factor when the touch coordinates change.

The final step involves calculating the offset zoom factor and applying it to the `ZoomCamera` object. By multiplying the initial zoom factor by the zoom factor change calculated by the `PinchZoomDetector` object, we can successfully offset the zoom factor of the camera. Once we've calculated the value for our `newZoomFactor` object, we call `setZoomFactor(newZoomFactor)` in order to change the zoom level of our camera.

Containing the zoom factor within a specific range is as simple as adding an `if` statement, specifying the minimum and/or maximum zoom factors required for our needs. In this case, our camera cannot zoom out further than `0.5f` or zoom in closer than `1.5f`.

See also

▶ *Taking a closer look with zoom cameras* given in this chapter.

Stitching a background together

Although AndEngine's `Scene` object allows us to set a background for the scene, this is not always a viable solution for our projects. In order to allow panning and zooming of the background, we can stitch together multiple texture regions and apply them directly to the scene as sprites. This topic is going to cover stitching two 800 x 480 texture regions together in order to create a larger pan-able and zoom-able background. The idea behind background stitching is to allow for portions of a scene to be displayed in smaller chunks. This gives us the opportunity to create smaller texture sizes as to not exceed the 1024 x 1024 maximum texture size for most devices. Additionally, we can enable culling so that segments of the scene are not drawn when they aren't displayed onscreen in order to improve performance. See the following figure for a look at the results:

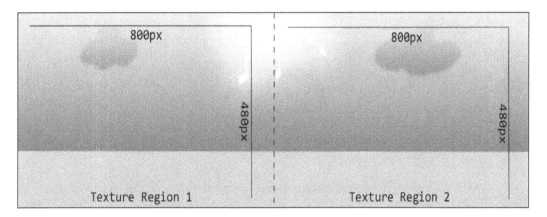

Getting started...

Perform the recipe, *Pinch-zoom camera functionality*, which is given in this chapter for an understanding of how pinch-to-zoom works. Additionally, we must prepare two separate 800 x 480 images, similar to the previous figure in this recipe's introduction, in PNG format, then refer to the class named `StitchedBackground` in the code bundle.

How to do it...

Background stitching is a simple concept which involves placing two or more sprites directly beside each other, on top of each other, or below each other in order to appear to have one single, large sprite. In this recipe, we're going to cover how to do this in order to avoid the dreaded texture bleeding effect. Follow these steps:

1. First of all, we need to create our `BuildableBitmapTextureAtlas` and `ITextureRegion` objects. It is very important that the texture atlas is the exact same size as our image files in order to avoid texture bleeding. Also, we must not include any padding or spacing during the build process of the texture atlas. The following code will create the left-hand side texture atlas and texture region, however the same code will apply for the right-hand side:

```
/* Create the background left texture atlas */
BuildableBitmapTextureAtlas backgroundTextureLeft = new
BuildableBitmapTextureAtlas(
    mEngine.getTextureManager(), 800, 480);

/* Create the background left texture region */
mBackgroundLeftTextureRegion =
BitmapTextureAtlasTextureRegionFactory
    .createFromAsset(backgroundTextureLeft, getAssets(),
        "background_left.png");

/* Build and load the background left texture atlas */
try {
  backgroundTextureLeft
      .build(new BlackPawnTextureAtlasBuilder<IBitmapTextureAtlasS
ource, BitmapTextureAtlas>(
          0, 0, 0));
  backgroundTextureLeft.load();
} catch (TextureAtlasBuilderException e) {
  e.printStackTrace();
}
```

2. Once the texture resources are in place, we can move to the `onPopulateScene()` method of the activity where we will create and apply the sprites to the `Scene` object:

```
final int halfTextureWidth = (int) (mBackgroundLeftTextureRegion.
getWidth() * 0.5f);
final int halfTextureHeight = (int) (mBackgroundLeftTextureRegion.
getHeight() * 0.5f);

// Create left background sprite
mBackgroundLeftSprite = new Sprite(halfTextureWidth,
halfTextureHeight, mBackgroundLeftTextureRegion,
```

```
            mEngine.getVertexBufferObjectManager())
    ;
    // Attach left background sprite to the background scene
    mScene.attachChild(mBackgroundLeftSprite);

    // Create the right background sprite, positioned directly to the
    right of the first segment
    mBackgroundRightSprite = new Sprite(mBackgroundLeftSprite.getX() +
    mBackgroundLeftTextureRegion.getWidth(),
        halfTextureHeight, mBackgroundRightTextureRegion,
        mEngine.getVertexBufferObjectManager());

    // Attach right background sprite to the background scene
    mScene.attachChild(mBackgroundRightSprite);
```

How it works...

Background stitching can be used in many different scenarios in order to avoid certain problems. These problems range from excessive texture sizes which lead to incompatibility on certain devices, static backgrounds which do not respond to changes in camera position or zoom factor, and performance issues to name a few. In this recipe, we're creating a large background which is created by stitching together two Sprite objects side-by-side, each representing a different TextureRegion object. The result is a large background which is double the size of the camera's width at 1600 x 480 pixels.

In most cases when dealing with stitched backgrounds which allow scrolling of the scene, we'll need to enable some camera bounds in order to stop updating camera position if it attempts to exceed the background's area. We can use a ZoomCamera object to do this, setting the bounds to the predetermined size of the background. Since we're working with two PNG images, each 800 x 480 pixels stitched side-by-side, it's safe to say coordinates (0,0) to (1600 x 480) will suffice for the camera bounds.

As stated in step one, there are a few rules we must follow when creating large-scale backgrounds with this approach. The image size must be exactly the same as the BuildableBitmapTextureAtlas texture atlas size! Failing to follow this rule will likely cause artifacts to occur between the sprites periodically, which is very distracting to the player. This also means that we should not include more than one ITextureRegion object in a BuildableBitmapTextureAtlas object that is meant for background stitching. Padding and spacing is also one of the features we should avoid in this case. However, following these rules, we are still able to apply the TextureOptions.BILINEAR texture filtering to the texture atlas and it will not cause issues.

In step two, we continue on to create the `Sprite` objects. There's nothing special here; we simply create one `Sprite` object in a given position, then set up the next sprite directly beside the first. For backgrounds which are extremely large and diverse, this method of stitching textures together can help to dramatically reduce the performance cost of an application by allowing us to stop rendering smaller segments of a background which are no longer visible. This feature is called **culling**. See *Disabling rendering with entity culling* in *Chapter 8, Maximizing Performance*, for more information on how to achieve this.

See also

- *Bringing a scene to life with sprites* in Chapter 2, *Designing Your Menu*.
- *Taking a closer look with zoom cameras* given in this chapter.
- *Pinch-zoom camera functionality* in this chapter.
- *Disabling rendering with entity culling* in Chapter 8, *Maximizing Performance*.

Applying a HUD to the camera

A **HUD** (**Heads-Up Display**) can be a very useful component for even the simplest of games. The purpose of the HUD is to contain a set of buttons, text, or any other `Entity` object in order to supply the user with an interface. The HUD has two key points; the first being that the HUD's children will always be visible onscreen, regardless of whether or not the camera changes position. The second point is the fact that the HUD's children will always be shown in front of the scene's children. In this chapter, we're going to be applying a HUD to the camera in order to supply users with an interface during gameplay.

How to do it...

Import the following code into the `onCreateEngineOptions()` method of any `BaseGameActivity` of your choice, substituting the camera type in this code snippet if necessary:

```
@Override
public EngineOptions onCreateEngineOptions() {

  // Create the camera
  Camera mCamera = new Camera(0, 0, WIDTH, HEIGHT);

  // Create the HUD
  HUD mHud = new HUD();

  // Attach the HUD to the camera
  mCamera.setHUD(mHud);

  EngineOptions engineOptions = new EngineOptions(true,
```

```
        ScreenOrientation.LANDSCAPE_FIXED, new FillResolutionPolicy(),
        mCamera);

    return engineOptions;
}
```

How it works...

Working with a HUD class is generally a very easy task. The usefulness of a HUD class can range drastically depending on the type of game being created, but in any case, there are a few things we must know before deciding to use this class:

- ▸ The HUD entities will not change positions upon camera movement. Once their position is defined, the entity will remain in that position onscreen unless otherwise set via setPosition().

- ▸ The HUD entities will always appear on top of any Scene entity, regardless of z-index, order of application, or any other scenario.

- ▸ Culling should _not_ be applied to entities which are to be attached to the HUD class in any circumstance. Culling affects an Entity object on the HUD class the same way it would affect the Entity object on the Scene object, even though the Entity object does not appear to move off-screen. This will cause what seems like randomly disappearing HUD entities. Just don't do it!

In the code found in the _How to do it..._ section, we can see that it's very easy to set up the HUD class. Creating and applying the HUD object to the camera can be done in as little as the following two lines of code:

```
// Create the HUD
HUD mHud = new HUD();

// Attach the HUD to the camera
mCamera.setHUD(mHud);
```

From this point, we can treat the HUD object as if it were any other layer in our game in terms of applying entities.

Applying a controller to the display

Depending on the type of game we are creating, there are many possible solutions for player interactivity. AndEngine includes two separate classes, one of which simulates a directional control pad called a DigitalOnScreenControl, the other which simulates a joystick called an AnalogOnScreenControl. This topic is going to introduce AndEngine's AnalogOnScreenControl class, but working with this class will give us enough info to use either controller.

Getting started..

This recipe requires two separate assets which will act as the base of the controller and the knob of the controller. Before moving on to the *How to do it...* section, please include an image called `controller_base.png` and `controller_knob.png` to the `assets/gfx` folder in a project of your choice. The images may look something like the following figure, with the base being 128 x 128 pixels and the knob being 64 x 64 pixels:

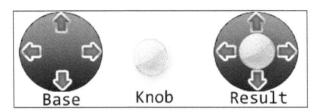

How to do it...

Once we've got the two necessary assets in place for our controller, we can start coding it. First of all, we can start by creating the `ITextureRegion` and `BuildableBitmapTextureAtlas` objects that will hold each of the controller's assets. No special steps are required for the controller texture atlas or texture regions; simply create them as we would for an ordinary sprite. As usual, do this in the `onCreateResources()` method of an activity of your choice.

Once the `ITextureRegion` objects have been coded and are ready for use within the activity, we can create the `AnalogOnScreenControl` class in the `onCreateScene()` method of our activity object as follows:

```
// Position the controller in the bottom left corner of the screen
final float controllerX = mControllerBaseTextureRegion.getWidth();
final float controllerY = mControllerBaseTextureRegion.getHeight();

// Create the controller
mController = new AnalogOnScreenControl(controllerX, controllerY,
mCamera, mControllerBaseTextureRegion, mControllerKnobTextureRegion,
0.1f, mEngine.getVertexBufferObjectManager(), new
IAnalogOnScreenControlListener(){
    /* The following method is called every X amount of seconds,
     * where the seconds are determined by the pTimeBetweenUpdates
     * parameter in the controller's constructor   */
    @Override
    public void onControlChange(
        BaseOnScreenControl pBaseOnScreenControl, float pValueX,
```

```
        float pValueY) {
    mCamera.setCenter(mCamera.getCenterX() + (pValueX * 10), mCamera.
getCenterY() + (pValueY * 10));
    Log.d("Camera", String.valueOf(mCamera.getCenterX()));
  }

  // Fired when the knob is simply pressed
  @Override
  public void onControlClick(
      AnalogOnScreenControl pAnalogOnScreenControl) {
    // Do nothing
  }

});

// Initialize the knob to its center position
mController.refreshControlKnobPosition();

// Set the controller as a child scene
mScene.setChildScene(mController);
```

How it works...

As we can see, a few of the parameters are no different from what we would define while creating a `Sprite` object. The first five parameters are self-explanatory. The sixth parameter (`0.1f`) is the "time between updates" parameter. This value controls how often the events within the `onControlChange()` method are fired. More CPU-intensive code may benefit from increased time between updates, while less complex code may have no problem with a very low update time.

The last parameter we have to include in the controller's constructor is `IanalogOnScreenControlListener`, which handles events based on whether the controller was simply clicked or whether the controller is pressed and held in an offset position.

As we can see in the `onControlChange()` event, we can obtain the current position of the controllers knob via the `pValueX` and `pValueY` variables. These values contain the x and y offsets of the controller. In this recipe, we are using the x and y offsets of the knob to move the camera's position, also giving us an idea of how we can put these variables to use in order to move other entities such as a player's sprite.

Coordinate conversion

Coordinate conversion can be very useful in situations where a `Scene` object relies on a number of entities to act as base layers for a game's sprites. It's not uncommon for games which contain many parents, each with their own set of children, to need to obtain a child's position relative to the `Scene` object at one point or another. This isn't a problem in situations where each of the layers remain at the same (0, 0) coordinates on the scene throughout the entire game. On the other hand, when our layers start to move around, child positions will move with the parent but their coordinates on the layer will remain the same. This topic is going to cover converting scene coordinates to local coordinates in order to allow nested entities to be properly positioned on the scene.

How to do it...

Import the following code to the `onCreateScene()` method of any `BaseGameActivity` of your choice.

1. The first step in this recipe is to create and apply a `Rectangle` object to the `Scene` object. This `Rectangle` object will act as the parent entity to another `Rectangle` object. We set its color to blue in order to differentiate between the two rectangles when they overlap since the parent `Rectangle` object will constantly be moving:

```
/* Create a rectangle on the Scene that will act as a layer */
final Rectangle rectangleLayer = new Rectangle(0, HEIGHT * 0.5f,
200, 200, mEngine.getVertexBufferObjectManager()){

  /* Obtain the half width of this rectangle */
  int halfWidth = (int) (this.getWidth() * 0.5f);

  /* Boolean value to determine whether to pan left or right */
  boolean incrementX = true;

  @Override
  protected void onManagedUpdate(float pSecondsElapsed) {

    float currentX = this.getX();

    /* Determine whether or not the layer should pan left or right
*/
    if(currentX + halfWidth > WIDTH){
      incrementX = false;
    }
    else if (currentX - halfWidth < 0){
      incrementX = true;
    }
```

```
    /* Increment or decrement the layer's position based on
incrementX */
        if(incrementX){
          this.setX(currentX + 5f);
        } else {
          this.setX(currentX - 5f);
        }

        super.onManagedUpdate(pSecondsElapsed);
    }
};

rectangleLayer.setColor(0, 0, 1);

// Attach the layer to the scene
mScene.attachChild(rectangleLayer);
```

2. Next, we will add the child `Rectangle` object to the first `Rectangle` object we had created. This `Rectangle` object will not move; instead, it will remain in the center of the screen while its parent continues to move around. This `Rectangle` object will be making use of coordinate conversion in order to hold its position:

```
/* Create a smaller, second rectangle and attach it to the first
*/
Rectangle rectangle = new Rectangle(0, 0, 50, 50, mEngine.
getVertexBufferObjectManager()){

  /* Obtain the coordinates in the middle of the Scene that we
will
    * convert to everytime the parent rectangle moves */
  final float convertToMidSceneX = WIDTH * 0.5f;
  final float convertToMidSceneY = HEIGHT * 0.5f;

  @Override
  protected void onManagedUpdate(float pSecondsElapsed) {

    /* Convert the specified x/y coordinates into Scene
coordinates,
      * passing the resulting coordinates into the
convertedCoordinates array */
    final float convertedCoordinates[] = rectangleLayer.co
nvertSceneCoordinatesToLocalCoordinates(convertToMidSceneX,
convertToMidSceneY);

    /* Since the parent is moving constantly, we must adjust this
rectangle's
```

```
        * position on every update as well. This will keep in in the
center of the
        * display at all times */
     this.setPosition(convertedCoordinates[0],
convertedCoordinates[1]);

        super.onManagedUpdate(pSecondsElapsed);
   }

};

     /* Attach the second rectangle to the first rectangle */
     rectangleLayer.attachChild(rectangle);
```

How it works...

The `onCreateScene()` method above creates a `Scene` object which contains two separate `Rectangle` entities. The first `Rectangle` entity will be attached directly to the `Scene` object. The second `Rectangle` entity will be attached to the first `Rectangle` entity. The first `Rectangle` entity, named `rectangleLayer`, will constantly be moving from left to right and right to left. Typically, this would cause its child's position to follow the same movement pattern, but in this recipe we're using coordinate conversion in order to allow the child `Rectangle` entity to remain still as its parent moves.

The `rectangle` object in this recipe includes two variables named `convertToMidSceneX` and `convertToMidSceneY`. These variables simply hold the position in `Scene` coordinates that we would like to convert the local coordinates to. As we can see, their coordinates are defined to the middle of the scene. Within the `onManagedUpdate()` method of the `rectangle` object, we then use the `rectangleLayer.convertSceneCoordinatesToLocalCoordinates(convertToMidSceneX, convertToMidSceneY)` method, passing the resulting coordinates to a float array. What this does is basically asks the `rectangleLayer` object, "Where is position x/y on the scene in your opinion?" Since the `rectangleLayer` object is attached directly to the `Scene` object, it can easily determine where specific `Scene` coordinates are as it relies on the native `Scene` coordinate system.

When attempting to access the returned coordinates, we can access `convertedCoordinates[0]` to obtain the converted x coordinate and use `convertedCoordinates[1]` to obtain the converted y coordinate.

On top of converting `Scene` to local `Entity` coordinates, we can also convert local `Entity` to `Scene` coordinates, touch event coordinates, camera coordinates, and a whole slew of other options. However, once we obtain a basic understanding of coordinate conversion, starting with this recipe, the rest of the conversion methods will seem very similar to one another.

Creating a split screen game

This recipe will introduce the `DoubleSceneSplitScreenEngine` class, most commonly used in games which allow multiple players to play their own instance of a game on each half of the display. The `DoubleSceneSplitScreenEngine` class allows us to provide each half of the device's display with its own `Scene` and `Camera` objects, giving us full control over what each half of the display will see.

Getting started..

Please refer to the class named `SplitScreenExample` in the code bundle.

How to do it...

Setting up our game to allow two separate `Scene` objects requires us to take a slightly different approach when initially setting up the `BaseGameActivity` class. However, once we have set up the separate `Scene` objects, managing them is actually very similar to if we were dealing with only one scene, aside from the fact that we've only got half of the original display space per scene. Perform the following steps to gain an understanding of how to set up the `DoubleSceneSplitScreenEngine` class.

1. The first thing we must take care of is decreasing the `WIDTH` value by half, since each camera will require half of the device's display. Attempting to fit 800 pixels in width onto each camera will cause noticeable skewing of objects on each scene. While we are declaring variables, we will also set up two `Scene` objects and two `Camera` objects which will be needed for the `DoubleSceneSplitScreenEngine` implementation:

   ```
   public static final int WIDTH = 400;
   public static final int HEIGHT = 480;


   /* We'll need two Scene's for the DoubleSceneSplitScreenEngine */
   private Scene mSceneOne;
   private Scene mSceneTwo;

   /* We'll also need two Camera's for the
   DoubleSceneSplitScreenEngine */
   private SmoothCamera mCameraOne;
   private SmoothCamera mCameraTwo;
   ```

2. Next, we will create two separate `SmoothCamera` objects in the `onCreateEngineOptions()` method of the `BaseGameActivity` class. These cameras will be used for displaying separate views for each half of the display. In this recipe, we're applying automatic zooming in order to show the results of `DoubleSceneSplitScreenEngine`:

```
/* Create the first camera (Left half of the display) */
mCameraOne = new SmoothCamera(0, 0, WIDTH, HEIGHT, 0, 0, 0.4f){
  /* During each update to the camera, we will determine whether
   * or not to set a new zoom factor for this camera */
  @Override
  public void onUpdate(float pSecondsElapsed) {
    final float currentZoomFactor = this.getZoomFactor();
    if(currentZoomFactor >= MAX_ZOOM_FACTOR){
      this.setZoomFactor(MIN_ZOOM_FACTOR);
    }
    else if(currentZoomFactor <= MIN_ZOOM_FACTOR){
      this.setZoomFactor(MAX_ZOOM_FACTOR);
    }
    super.onUpdate(pSecondsElapsed);
  }
};
/* Set the initial zoom factor for camera one*/
mCameraOne.setZoomFactor(MAX_ZOOM_FACTOR);

/* Create the second camera (Right half of the display) */
mCameraTwo = new SmoothCamera(0, 0, WIDTH, HEIGHT, 0, 0, 1.2f){
  /* During each update to the camera, we will determine whether
   * or not to set a new zoom factor for this camera */
  @Override
  public void onUpdate(float pSecondsElapsed) {
    final float currentZoomFactor = this.getZoomFactor();
    if(currentZoomFactor >= MAX_ZOOM_FACTOR){
      this.setZoomFactor(MIN_ZOOM_FACTOR);
    }
    else if(currentZoomFactor <= MIN_ZOOM_FACTOR){
      this.setZoomFactor(MAX_ZOOM_FACTOR);
    }
    super.onUpdate(pSecondsElapsed);
  }
};
/* Set the initial zoom factor for camera two */
mCameraTwo.setZoomFactor(MIN_ZOOM_FACTOR);
```

3. One more task to take care of in the `onCreateEngineOptions()` method of our `BaseGameActivity` class is to create the `EngineOptions` object, passing the `mCameraOne` object as the main camera. Additionally, chances are the scenes might require simultaneous touch events, so we will enable multitouch as well:

```
/* The first camera is set via the EngineOptions creation, as
usual */
EngineOptions engineOptions = new EngineOptions(true,
    ScreenOrientation.LANDSCAPE_FIXED, new FillResolutionPolicy(),
    mCameraOne);

/* If users should be able to control each have of the display
 *    simultaneously with touch events, we'll need to enable
 *    multi-touch in the engine options */
engineOptions.getTouchOptions().setNeedsMultiTouch(true);
```

4. In the fourth step, we will override the `BaseGameActivity` class' `onCreateEngine()` method in order to create a `DoubleSceneSplitScreenEngine` object rather than the default `Engine` object:

```
@Override
public Engine onCreateEngine(EngineOptions pEngineOptions) {

    /* Return the DoubleSceneSplitScreenEngine, passing the
pEngineOptions
    * as well as the second camera object. Remember, the first
camera has
    * already been applied to the engineOptions which in-turn
applies the
    * camera to the engine. */
    return new DoubleSceneSplitScreenEngine(pEngineOptions,
mCameraTwo);
}
```

5. Moving onto the `onCreateScene()` method, we will create the two `Scene` objects, set them up how we choose, and finally set each `Scene` object to the `DoubleSceneSplitScreenEngine` object:

```
@Override
public void onCreateScene(OnCreateSceneCallback
pOnCreateSceneCallback) {

    /* Create and setup the first scene */
    mSceneOne = new Scene();
    mSceneOne.setBackground(new Background(0.5f, 0, 0));

    /* In order to keep our camera's and scenes organized, we can
     * set the Scene's user data to store its own camera */
```

```
mSceneOne.setUserData(mCameraOne);

/* Create and setup the second scene */
mSceneTwo = new Scene();
mSceneTwo.setBackground(new Background(0,0,0.5f));

/* Same as the first Scene, we set the second scene's user data
 * to hold its own camera */
mSceneTwo.setUserData(mCameraTwo);

/* We must set the second scene within mEngine object manually.
 * This does NOT need to be done with the first scene as we will
 * be passing it to the onCreateSceneCallback, which passes it
 * to the Engine object for us at the end of onCreateScene()*/
((DoubleSceneSplitScreenEngine) mEngine).
setSecondScene(mSceneTwo);

/* Pass the first Scene to the engine */
pOnCreateSceneCallback.onCreateSceneFinished(mSceneOne);
}
```

6. Now that both of our `Camera` objects are set up and both of our `Scene` objects are set up and attached to the engine, we can start attaching `Entity` objects to each `Scene` object as we see fit, simply by specifying which `Scene` object to attach to as usual. This code should be placed within the `onPopulateScene()` method of the `BaseGameActivity` class:

```
/* Apply a rectangle to the center of the first scene */
Rectangle rectangleOne = new Rectangle(WIDTH * 0.5f, HEIGHT
* 0.5f, rectangleDimensions, rectangleDimensions, mEngine.
getVertexBufferObjectManager());
rectangleOne.setColor(org.andengine.util.adt.color.Color.
BLUE);
mSceneOne.attachChild(rectangleOne);

/* Apply a rectangle to the center of the second scene */
Rectangle rectangleTwo = new Rectangle(WIDTH * 0.5f, HEIGHT
* 0.5f, rectangleDimensions, rectangleDimensions, mEngine.
getVertexBufferObjectManager());
rectangleTwo.setColor(org.andengine.util.adt.color.Color.RED);
mSceneTwo.attachChild(rectangleTwo);
```

How it works...

When working with the `DoubleSceneSplitScreenEngine` class, we can assume that our project will need two of everything if we are setting up for a multiplayer game. More specifically, we need two `Scene` objects for each half of the screen as well as two `Camera` objects. Due to the fact that we are splitting the viewing area of each `Camera` object in half, we shall reduce the `WIDTH` value of our cameras by half. Camera dimensions of 400 pixels in width by 480 pixels in height are reasonable in most cases, which allow us to keep a proper perspective on entities as well.

In the second step, we are setting up two `SmoothCamera` objects which will automatically zoom in and out of their respective scenes in order to supply a visual result to this recipe. However, the `DoubleSceneSplitScreenEngine` class can use any variation of the `Camera` object, including the most basic type without causing any issue.

In the third step, we're continuing on to create the `EngineOptions` object. We supply the `mCameraOne` object as the `pCamera` parameter in the `EngineOptions` constructor, just as we would in any ordinary instance. Additionally, we are enabling multitouch in the `EngineOptions` object in order to allow simultaneous touch events to register for each `Scene` object. Ignoring the multitouch setup will result in each scene having to wait until the other scene is not being pressed down on before it can register touch events.

In step four, we create the `DoubleSceneSplitScreenEngine` object, passing in the `pEngineOptions` parameter created in the previous step as well as the second `Camera` object—`mCameraTwo`. At this point in code, we've now got both of our cameras registered to the engine; the first was registered within the `EngineOptions` object, and the second passed as a parameter to the `DoubleSceneSplitScreenEngine` class.

Step five includes the `onCreateScene()` method of the `BaseGameActivity` class, where we will create and set up each of the two `Scene` objects how we would like. At the most basic level, this involves creating the `Scene` objects, enabling and setting up or disabling the scene's background, setting the scene's user data to store its respective camera, and finally passing the `Scene` object to our `mEngine` object. While the second `Scene` object requires us to call the `setSecondScene(mSceneTwo)` method on our `mEngine` object, the `mSceneOne` object is passed to the `Engine` object as in any `BaseGameActivity`; in the `pOnCreateSceneCallback.onCreateSceneFinished(mSceneOne)` method.

In the sixth step, we are now "out of the woods", so to speak. At this point, we are finished setting up the engine, scenes, and cameras and we can now start to populate each scene however we'd like. The possibilities are quite extensive in terms of what we can do at this point, including using the second scene as a mini-map, a view for a multiplayer game, an alternative perspective on the first scene, and much more. Selecting which `Scene` object to attach an `Entity` object to at this point would be as simple as calling either `mSceneOne.attachChild(pEntity)` or `mSceneTwo.attachChild(pEntity)`.

5
Scene and Layer Management

Managing scenes and layers is a necessity for a game that utilizes menus and multiple game levels. This chapter will cover the creation and use of a scene manager with the following topics:

- ▶ Creating the scene manager
- ▶ Setting up the resource manager for scene resources
- ▶ Customizing managed scenes and layers
- ▶ Setting up an activity to use the scene manager

Introduction

Creating a process to manage and handle menus and scenes for a game is one of the quickest ways to improve a framework. A well-designed game usually relies on a robust and customized scene manager to handle menus and in-game levels. There are various approaches to customize a scene manager, but the foundation usually consists of:

- ▶ Switching between scenes
- ▶ Automatic loading and unloading of scene resources and elements
- ▶ Showing a loading screen while handling scene resources and scene construction

In addition to the core functions of a scene manager, we are going to create a method of showing layers on top of our scenes so that we can add another level of usability to our games.

Creating the scene manager

Creating a scene manager that just swaps the engine's current scene for another scene is quite simple, but not graphically appealing to players. Showing a loading screen while resources load and the scene is constructed has become a well-accepted practice in game design because it lets the player know that the game is doing more than just idling.

Getting ready...

Open the `SceneManager.java` class in this chapter's code bundle. Also, open the `ManagedScene.java` and `ManagedLayer.java` classes. We will be referencing all three of these classes throughout this recipe. The inline comments within the classes provide additional information to what is discussed throughout this recipe.

How to do it...

Follow these steps to understand how a `SceneManager` class functions so that we can create a custom-tailored one for future projects:

1. First, notice that the `SceneManager` class is created as a singleton so that we can access it from anywhere in our project. Furthermore, it uses the `getEngine()` reference provided by our `ResourceManager` class to store a local reference to the engine object, but this reference could be set at the creation of the `SceneManager` class if we opted to not use a resource manager.

2. Second, note the variables created after the `getInstance()` method. The first two variables, `mCurrentScene` and `mNextScene`, hold references to the currently loaded scene and next scene to be loaded. The `mEngine` variable holds a reference to the engine. We will use the engine reference to set our managed scenes and for registering/unregistering the `mLoadingScreenHandler` update handler. The `mNumFramesPassed` integer counts the number of rendered frames within the update handler to ensure that the loading screen has been shown for at least one frame. The functionality of showing a loading screen is achieved by the next variable, `mLoadingScreenHandler`, at which we will take a closer look in the next step. The remaining variables are used for the management of layers and either keep track of the state of the layering process or hold references to entities related to the layering process.

3. Third, look at the `onUpdate()` method within the `mLoadingScreenHandler` `IUpdateHandler` update handler. Take note that there are two conditional blocks—the first waits one frame before it unloads the previous scene and subsequently loads the next, while the second waits until the loading screen for the next scene has been shown for the minimum amount of time before it hides the loading screen and resets the variables used by the update handler. This entire process within the update handler enables the use of a loading screen while `ManagedScene` loads and constructs itself.

4. The next method in the class is the `showScene()` method, which we will call when we want to navigate away from the current scene to a following scene. It first resets the position and size of the engine's camera to its starting location and size to prevent any prior adjustments to the camera from ruining the presentation of a new scene. Next, we check if the new scene will show a loading screen via the `hasLoadingScreen` property of the `ManagedScene` class.

   If the new `ManagedScene` class' will be showing a loading screen, we set its child scene to the scene returned by the `onLoadingScreenLoadAndShown()` method and pause all of the `ManagedScene` class' renderings, updates, and touch events. The following `if` block ensures that a new scene can load if one is already in the loading stage. This case should be rare, but can happen if a new scene is called to be shown from the UI thread. The `mNextScene` variable is then set to the new `ManagedScene` class' to be used by the `mLoadingScreenHandler` update handler and the engine's scene is set to the new `ManagedScene` class.

   If the new `ManagedScene` class will not be showing a loading screen, we set the `mNextScene` variable to the new `ManagedScene` class, set the new `ManagedScene` class as the engine's scene, unload the previously shown scene, and load the new scene. If no loading screen is shown, the `showScene()` method simply acts to swap the new scene for the previously shown one.

5. Next, take a look at the `showLayer()` method. Because our layers are shown on top of everything else in the game, we attach them as the camera `HUD` object's child scene. This method starts by first determining if the camera has a `HUD` object to attach a child scene. If so, it sets the `mCameraHadHud` Boolean value to `true`. If not, we create a placeholder HUD object and set it as the camera's `HUD` object. Next, if the `showLayer()` method is called to suspend rendering, updates, or touch events of the underlying `ManagedScene`, we set a placeholder scene as the `ManagedScene` scene's child scene with the modal properties passed to the `showLayer()` method. Finally, we set the layer's camera to the engine's camera, scale the layer to match the camera's screen-dependent scale, and set the local layer-related variables to be used by the `hideLayer()` method referenced in the next step.

6. The `hideLayer()` method first checks whether a layer is currently being shown. If it is, the camera `HUD` object's child scene is cleared, the placeholder child scene is cleared from the `ManagedScene` class, and the layer-showing system is reset.

Follow these steps to understand how the `ManagedScene` and `MangedLayer` classes are constructed:

1. Looking at the `ManagedScene` class, take note of the variables listed at the beginning of the class. The `hasLoadingScreen` Boolean, `minLoadingScreenTime` float, and `elapsedLoadingScreenTime` float variables are used by the `SceneManager` class when it is handling the `ManagedScene` class' loading screen. The `isLoaded` Boolean value reflects the completion state of the `ManagedScene` class' construction. The first constructor is a convenient constructor in the event that no loading screen is needed. The second constructor sets the loading screen variables according to the passed value, which determines the minimum length of time that the loading screen should be shown. The public methods following the constructor are called by the `SceneManager` class and call the appropriate abstract methods, listed at the bottom of the class.

2. The `ManagedLayer` class is very similar to the `ManagedScene` class, but its inherent function and lack of a loading screen make it easier to create. The constructors set whether the layer should be unloaded after it is hidden according to the passed `pUnloadOnHidden` Boolean variable. The public methods following the constructors call the appropriate abstract methods below them.

How it works...

The scene manager stores a reference to the engine's current scene. When the scene manager is told to show a new scene, it hides and unloads the current scene before setting the new scene as the current scene. Then, it loads and shows the new scene's loading screen if the scene has one. To show the loading screen before loading the rest of the scene, we have to allow the engine to render one frame. The `mNumFramesPassed` integer value keeps track of how many updates, and thus scene renderings, have occurred since the start of the process.

After the loading screen is shown, or if no loading screen will be used, the scene manager calls the scene to load itself by calling `onLoadManagedScene()`. Upon completion of the load, and after the loading screen—if present—has been shown for a minimum amount of time, the loading screen is hidden and the scene is shown. In case the loading screen has not been shown for the minimum amount of time, we pause the scene's updates so that the scene will keep from starting until the loading screen is hidden. Refer to the inline comments of the supplemental code in `SceneManager.java` to learn even more about how this scene manager handles the switching of scenes.

To facilitate the use of layers, the scene manager utilizes the camera's HUD to ensure that the layer is drawn on top of everything else. If the camera has a HUD already, we store it before applying the layer so that we can restore the original HUD after the layer is hidden. Furthermore, we have the option of pausing the underlying scene's updates, renderings, and touch-areas via the use of a placeholder scene. The placeholder scene is attached as a child to the underlying scene, so we must store any child scene that the underlying scene already has attached. The loading and showing of layers is handled by the same method call from the scene manager to let the layer's subclasses determine if reloading is necessary or if the layer should be loaded only once to reduce performance-heavy loading.

See also...

▶ *Customizing managed scenes and layers* given in this chapter.

▶ *Setting up an activity to use the scene manager* given in this chapter.

▶ *Applying a HUD to the camera* in *Chapter 4, Working with Cameras*.

Setting up the resource manager for scene resources

In order to facilitate the loading of resources by the menu and game scenes, the resource manager must be first set up to handle the resources. Our resource manager will automatically load the respective resources when we call its `loadMenuResources()` or `loadGameResources()` methods. Likewise, unloading resources for menus or game scenes that use a large amount of memory will simply be a call to the resource manager using `unloadMenuResources()`, `unloadGameResources()`, or `unloadSharedResources()`.

Getting ready...

Open the `ResourceManager.java` class in this chapter's code bundle, as we will be referencing it for this recipe. Also, refer to the inline comments of the class for more information on specific portions of code.

How to do it...

Follow these steps to understand how the `ResourceManager` class is set up to be used with our managed scenes:

1. Take note of the public, non-static variables defined in the `ResourceManager` class. The engine and context variables are used in the class when loading textures, but they also give us a way to access those important objects throughout our project. The `cameraWidth`, `cameraHeight`, `cameraScaleFactorX`, and `cameraScaleFactorY` variables are not used in this class, but will be used throughout the project for placing and scaling entities relative to the screen.

2. Find the `setup()` method. This method sets the non-static variables referenced in the previous step and will be called from the overridden `onCreateResources()` method in our activity class. It is important that `setup()` is called prior to any other calls to the `ResourceManager` class as every other method and variable relies on the engine and context variables.

3. Next, take a look at the static resource variables. These will be used by our scenes for entities or sounds and must be set before they are called. Also note that the static variables with a game or menu prefix will be respectively used by our game or menu scenes while the static variables without a prefix will be shared between the two types.

4. Now find the `loadGameResources()` and `loadMenuResources()` methods. Our managed game and menu scenes will call these methods when they first start. These methods have the important duty of calling the subsequent `ResourceManager` methods that set the static variables referenced in the previous step. Conversely, `unloadGameResources()` and `unloadMenuResources()` unload the resources for their respective scenes and should be called when the application's flow is finished with the resources.

How it works...

The resource manager, at its most basic level, provides a means of loading and unloading resources. In addition to this, we define a set of variables, including the engine and context objects, that gives us easy access to some common elements of the game when creating entities in our scenes. These variables can be placed within a game manager or object factory as well, but we will include it in our resource manager since most calls to the resource manager will be near code used to create entities.

See also...

- *Creating the resource manager* in Chapter 1, *AndEngine Game Structure*.
- *Creating the game manager* in Chapter 1, *AndEngine Game Structure*.
- *Creating object factories* in Chapter 1, *AndEngine Game Structure*.

Customizing managed scenes and layers

The main purpose of the scene manager is to handle the managed scenes in our game. The managed scenes are highly customizable, but we want to avoid rewriting as much of our code as possible. To achieve that task, we will use two classes that extend the `ManagedScene` class, `ManagedGameScene` and `ManagedMenuScene`. By structuring our scene classes in this way, we will have menus and game scenes that share a common, respective foundation.

Getting ready...

Open the following classes from this chapter's code bundle: `ManagedMenuScene.java`, `ManagedGameScene.java`, `MainMenu.java`, `GameLevel.java`, and `OptionsLayer.java`. We will be referencing these classes throughout this recipe.

How to do it...

Follow these steps to understand how the `ManagedMenuScene` and `ManagedGameScene` classes build upon the `ManagedScene` class to create customized, extendable scenes that can be passed to the `SceneManager` class:

1. Look at the `ManagedMenuScene` class. It holds only two simple constructors and the overridden `onUnloadManagedScene()` method. The overridden method keeps the `isLoaded` Boolean value from being set because we will not be taking advantage of the scene manager's automatic unloading of menu scenes.

2. Now, we turn our attention to the `ManagedGameScene` class. The class starts off by creating an in-game `HUD` object, a loading screen `Text` object, and a loading screen `Scene` object. The main constructor of the `ManagedGameScene` class starts by setting the touch-event-binding settings of the scene to true. Next, the scene's scale is set to mirror the camera's screen-dependent scaling and the scene's position is set to the bottom-center of the camera. Finally, the constructor sets the HUD's scale to match the camera's scale.

   The `ManagedGameScene` class overrides the `onLoadingScreenLoadAndShown()` and `onLoadingScreenUnloadAndHidden()` methods of the `ManagedScene` class to show and hide a simple loading screen that displays a single `Text` object.

   The `onLoadScene()` method from the `ManagedScene` class is overridden to construct a scene that represents the in-game portion of a game with a background and two buttons that allow the player to return to the `MainMenu` or show the `OptionsLayer`.

Follow these steps to understand how the `ManagedMenuScene` and `ManagedGameScene` classes can be extended to create the `MainMenu` and `GameLevel` scenes:

1. The `MainMenu` class is created as a singleton to prevent more than one instance of the class from being created and taking up valuable memory. It also foregoes a loading screen because it is loaded and created almost instantly. All of the entities that make up the `MainMenu` class are defined as class level variables and include the background, buttons, text, and moving entities. The scene-flow methods inherited from the `ManagedScene` class by the `MainMenu` class are the `onLoadScene()`, `onShowScene()`, `onHideScene()`, and `onUnloadScene()` methods, of which only the `onLoadScene()` method contains any code. The `onLoadScene()` method loads and constructs a scene consisting of a background, 20 horizontally-moving clouds, a title, and two buttons. Notice that each of the buttons makes a call to the scene manager—the play button shows the `GameLevel` scene and the options button shows `OptionsLayer`.

2. The `GameLevel` class extends the `ManagedGameScene` class and only overrides the `onLoadScene()` method to create and randomly position a square rectangle on the scene. This shows that the `ManagedGameScene` class creates the bulk of the `GameLevel` class and that elements that differ between levels can still use the same foundation created by the `ManagedGameScene` class.

Follow these steps to understand how the `OptionsLayer` class extends the layer-functionality of the `ManagedLayer` class:

1. Concerning the `OptionsLayer` class, first notice that it is defined as a singleton, so that it will remain in memory after it is first created. Next, note the two update handlers, `SlideIn` and `SlideOut`. These animate the layer when it is shown or hidden and give an extra layer of graphical interest to the game. The update handlers simply move the layer to a specific position at a speed that is proportional to the `pSecondsElapsed` parameter of the `onUpdate()` method to make the movement smooth.

2. The `onLoadLayer()` method inherited from the `ManagedLayer` class is overridden to create a black rectangle, which acts as a background for the layer, and two `Text` objects that show a title and the way to exit the layer. The `onShowLayer()` and `onHideLayer()` methods register the appropriate update handler with the engine. Upon sliding the layer offscreen, notice that the `SlideOut` update handler calls the scene manager to hide the layer—this is how an ending animation is implemented using this particular scene manager's framework.

How it works...

The single purpose of the `ManagedMenuScene` class is to override the `onUnloadManagedScene()` method inherited from the `ManagedScene` class to prevent the recreation of entities within the scene. Take note of the overridden `onUnloadScene()` method within the `MainMenu` class, which extends `ManagedMenuScene`. We leave it empty to ensure that the `MainMenu` class is kept in memory so that we can quickly switch back to it from the game scenes and other menus.

> When running this project, if there are any animations in the main menu, take note that the animations pause while another scene is being displayed, but resume as soon as the main menu is shown again. This is because the main menu is not updated as the engine's current scene even though it is still loaded in memory.

The `ManagedGameScene` class uses a `HUD` object to allow the game levels a set of controls that move with the engine's camera. Even though we add buttons to the `GameHud` object in this example, any control may be used on the HUD. The constructors that we use for the `ManagedGameScene` class set the loading screen duration, touch options, and the scales of the game scene and `GameHud` to improve the visual appeal of the game across devices. For the game scenes, we take advantage of the loading screens enabled by the scene manager. For the loading screen, we create a simple scene that shows the text, **Loading...**, but any arrangement of non-animated entities can be used. While the loading screen is shown, we load the game resources and create the game scene. In this case, a simple background is constructed from a single sprite, and the onscreen controls are added to the `GameHud` object. Notice that the controls added to the `GameHud` object are scaled to the inverse of the camera's scale factor. This is necessary because we want to create them to be the same physical size across all devices. The last method that we define in the `ManagedGameScene` class, `onUnloadScene()`, unloads the scene.

> Notice that we do all of the unloading on the update thread. This keeps the engine from trying to process an entity if it was removed earlier in the thread and prevents an `ArrayIndexOutOfBoundsException` exception from being thrown.

For the main menu we do not need a loading screen so we simply return `null` in the `onLoadingScreenLoadAndShown()` method. When creating the simple sprite background for the main menu, we must scale it to fill the screen. Notice how the main menu utilizes the menu assets from the `ResourceManager` class when creating sprites and buttons. Also, notice that by clicking the buttons, we call the `SceneManager` class to load the next scene or show a layer. The following two screenshots show the main menu on two different devices to demonstrate how the camera scaling functions with the scene's composition. The first screenshot is on a 10.1 inch Motorola Xoom:

And, the second is on a 5.3 inch Samsung Galaxy Note:

Our `GameLevel` class is relatively small compared to its super class, `ManagedGameScene`. This is because we want the levels to include only the information needed for each individual level. The following screenshot shows the `GameLevel` class in action:

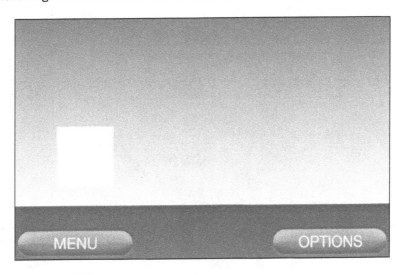

The `OptionsLayer` class can be shown from any scene, as seen in the following two screenshots. The first is at the main menu:

While the second is in-game with the `GameLevel` class loaded:

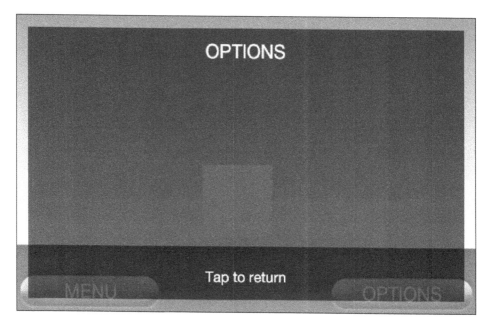

See also...

- ▸ *Creating the scene manager* in this chapter.
- ▸ *Attaching a controller to the display* in *Chapter 4, Working with Cameras.*

Setting up an activity to use the scene manager

Because of the way that our scene manager works, setting it up for use by an `Activity` class that extends AndEngine's `BaseGameActivity` class requires little effort. We are also going to implement an accurate screen-resolution scaling approach to ensure a consistent appearance across all devices. The `SceneManager` class and `ManagedScenes` class rely on the variables defined in the `ResourceManager` class to register update handlers and create entities. As we go through the recipe, take note that we set up the `ResourceManager` class prior to using any functions of the `SceneManager` class.

Getting ready...

Create a new activity that extends AndEngine's `BaseGameActivity` class, or load one that you have already created. Adapting an existing activity to use the scene manager requires the same steps as a new one would require, so do not worry about starting over on a project just to implement the scene manager.

How to do it...

Follow these steps to prepare an activity to use our scene manager:

1. Define the following variables in your activity to handle accurate screen-resolution scaling. Doing so will make onscreen elements almost physically identical across all Android devices:

```
static float DESIGN_SCREEN_WIDTH_PIXELS = 800f;
static float DESIGN_SCREEN_HEIGHT_PIXELS = 480f;
static float DESIGN_SCREEN_WIDTH_INCHES = 4.472441f;
static float DESIGN_SCREEN_HEIGHT_INCHES = 2.805118f;
static float MIN_WIDTH_PIXELS = 320f, MIN_HEIGHT_PIXELS = 240f;
static float MAX_WIDTH_PIXELS = 1600f, MAX_HEIGHT_PIXELS = 960f;
public float cameraWidth;
public float cameraHeight;
public float actualScreenWidthInches;
public float actualScreenHeightInches;
```

2. Place the following method in the activity's class to handle the **Back** button:

```
public boolean onKeyDown(final int keyCode, final KeyEvent event)
{
  if (keyCode == KeyEvent.KEYCODE_BACK
    && event.getAction() == KeyEvent.ACTION_DOWN) {
    if(ResourceManager.getInstance().engine!=null){
      if(SceneManager.getInstance().isLayerShown)
        SceneManager.getInstance().
          currentLayer.onHideLayer();
      else if ( SceneManager.getInstance().
          mCurrentScene.getClass().
          getGenericSuperclass().
          equals(ManagedGameScene.class) ||
          (SceneManager.getInstance().
          mCurrentScene.getClass().
          getGenericSuperclass().
          equals(ManagedMenuScene.class) &!
          SceneManager.getInstance().
          mCurrentScene.getClass().
```

```
        equals(MainMenu.class)))
        SceneManager.getInstance().
        showMainMenu();
      else
        System.exit(0);
    }
    return true;
  } else {
    return super.onKeyDown(keyCode, event);
  }
}
```

3. Next, fill the onCreateEngineOptions() method with the following code:

```
actualScreenWidthInches = getResources().
  getDisplayMetrics().widthPixels /
  getResources().getDisplayMetrics().xdpi;
actualScreenHeightInches = getResources().
  getDisplayMetrics().heightPixels /
  getResources().getDisplayMetrics().ydpi;
cameraWidth = Math.round(
  Math.max(
    Math.min(
      DESIGN_SCREEN_WIDTH_PIXELS *
      (actualScreenWidthInches /
        DESIGN_SCREEN_WIDTH_INCHES),
    MAX_WIDTH_PIXELS),
  MIN_WIDTH_PIXELS));
cameraHeight = Math.round(
  Math.max(
    Math.min(
      DESIGN_SCREEN_HEIGHT_PIXELS *
      (actualScreenHeightInches /
        DESIGN_SCREEN_HEIGHT_INCHES),
    MAX_HEIGHT_PIXELS),
  MIN_HEIGHT_PIXELS));
EngineOptions engineOptions = new EngineOptions(true,
  ScreenOrientation.LANDSCAPE_SENSOR,
  new FillResolutionPolicy(),
  new Camera(0, 0, cameraWidth, cameraHeight));
engineOptions.getAudioOptions().setNeedsSound(true);
engineOptions.getAudioOptions().setNeedsMusic(true);
engineOptions.getRenderOptions().setDithering(true);
```

```
engineOptions.getRenderOptions().
    getConfigChooserOptions().setRequestedMultiSampling(true);
engineOptions.setWakeLockOptions(WakeLockOptions.SCREEN_ON);
return engineOptions;
```

4. Place the following line in the `onCreateResources()` method:

```
ResourceManager.getInstance().setup(this.getEngine(),
    this.getApplicationContext(),
    cameraWidth, cameraHeight,
    cameraWidth/DESIGN_SCREEN_WIDTH_PIXELS,
    cameraHeight/DESIGN_SCREEN_HEIGHT_PIXELS);
```

5. Finally, add the following code to the `onCreateScene()` method:

```
SceneManager.getInstance().showMainMenu();
pOnCreateSceneCallback.onCreateSceneFinished(
    MainMenu.getInstance());
```

How it works...

The first thing that we do is to define the attributes of our development device's screen so that we can make the calculations to ensure that all players see our game as close to the way that we see it as possible. The calculations are actually handled in the `onCreateEngineOptions()` method as shown in the third step. For the engine options, we enable sounds, music, dithering for smooth gradients, multisampling for smooth edges, and wake-lock to keep our game's resources from being destroyed if the player briefly switches away from our game.

In step 4, we set up the `ResourceManager` class by passing it the `Engine` object, `Context`, the current camera width and height, and the ratio of the current camera's size to the design device's screen size. Lastly, we tell the `SceneManager` class to show the main menu, and we pass the `MainMenu` class as the engine's scene via the `pOnCreateSceneCallback` parameter.

See also...

▶ *Creating the scene manager* in this chapter.
▶ *Know the life cycle* in *Chapter 1, AndEngine Game Structure.*

6

Applications of Physics

Physics-based games provide players with a unique type of experience not encountered in many other genres. This chapter covers the use of AndEngine's **Box2D physics extension**. Our recipes include:

- ▶ Introduction to the Box2D physics extension
- ▶ Understanding different body types
- ▶ Creating category-filtered bodies
- ▶ Creating multiple-fixture bodies
- ▶ Creating unique bodies by specifying vertices
- ▶ Using forces, velocities, and torque
- ▶ Applying anti-gravity to a specific body
- ▶ Working with joints
- ▶ Creating a rag doll
- ▶ Creating a rope
- ▶ Working with collisions
- ▶ Using preSolve and postSolve
- ▶ Creating destructible objects
- ▶ Raycasting

Introduction to the Box2D physics extension

Physics-based games are one of the most popular types of games available for mobile devices. AndEngine allows the creation of physics-based games with the Box2D extension. With this extension, we can construct any type of physically realistic 2D environment from small, simple simulations to complex games. In this recipe, we will create an activity that demonstrates a simple setup for utilizing the Box2D physics engine extension. Furthermore, we will use this activity for the remaining recipes in this chapter.

Getting ready...

First, create a new activity class named `PhysicsApplication` that extends `BaseGameActivity` and implements `IAccelerationListener` and `IOnSceneTouchListener`.

How to do it...

Follow these steps to build our `PhysicsApplication` activity class:

1. Create the following variables in the class:

```
public static int cameraWidth = 800;
public static int cameraHeight = 480;
public Scene mScene;
public FixedStepPhysicsWorld mPhysicsWorld;
public Body groundWallBody;
public Body roofWallBody;
public Body leftWallBody;
public Body rightWallBody;
```

2. We need to set up the foundation of our activity. To start doing so, place these four, common overridden methods in the class to set up the engine, resources, and the main scene:

```
@Override
public Engine onCreateEngine(final EngineOptions
    pEngineOptions) {
  return new FixedStepEngine(pEngineOptions, 60);
}

@Override
public EngineOptions onCreateEngineOptions() {
  EngineOptions engineOptions = new EngineOptions(true,
    ScreenOrientation.LANDSCAPE_SENSOR, new
      FillResolutionPolicy(), new Camera(0,
```

```
              0, cameraWidth, cameraHeight));
    engineOptions.getRenderOptions().setDithering(true);
    engineOptions.getRenderOptions().
      getConfigChooserOptions()
        .setRequestedMultiSampling(true);
    engineOptions.setWakeLockOptions(
      WakeLockOptions.SCREEN_ON);
    return engineOptions;
}

@Override
public void onCreateResources(OnCreateResourcesCallback
    pOnCreateResourcesCallback) {
  pOnCreateResourcesCallback.
    onCreateResourcesFinished();
}

@Override
public void onCreateScene(OnCreateSceneCallback
    pOnCreateSceneCallback) {
  mScene = new Scene();
  mScene.setBackground(new Background(0.9f,0.9f,0.9f));
  pOnCreateSceneCallback.onCreateSceneFinished(mScene);
}
```

3. Continue setting up the activity by adding the following overridden method, which will be used to populate our scene:

```
@Override
public void onPopulateScene(Scene pScene,
  OnPopulateSceneCallback pOnPopulateSceneCallback) {
}
```

4. Next, we will fill the previous method with the following code to create our `PhysicsWorld` object and `Scene` object:

```
mPhysicsWorld = new FixedStepPhysicsWorld(60, new
  Vector2(0f,-SensorManager.GRAVITY_EARTH*2),
    false, 8, 3);
mScene.registerUpdateHandler(mPhysicsWorld);
final FixtureDef WALL_FIXTURE_DEF =
  PhysicsFactory.createFixtureDef(0, 0.1f,
    0.5f);
final Rectangle ground =
  new Rectangle(cameraWidth / 2f, 6f,
    cameraWidth - 4f, 8f,
```

```
                this.getVertexBufferObjectManager());
        final Rectangle roof =
          new Rectangle(cameraWidth / 2f, cameraHeight -
            6f, cameraWidth - 4f, 8f,
            this.getVertexBufferObjectManager());
        final Rectangle left =
          new Rectangle(6f, cameraHeight / 2f, 8f,
            cameraHeight - 4f,
            this.getVertexBufferObjectManager());
        final Rectangle right =
            new Rectangle(cameraWidth - 6f,
            cameraHeight / 2f, 8f,
            cameraHeight - 4f,
            this.getVertexBufferObjectManager());
        ground.setColor(0f, 0f, 0f);
        roof.setColor(0f, 0f, 0f);
        left.setColor(0f, 0f, 0f);
        right.setColor(0f, 0f, 0f);
        groundWallBody =
          PhysicsFactory.createBoxBody(
          this.mPhysicsWorld, ground,
          BodyType.StaticBody, WALL_FIXTURE_DEF);
        roofWallBody =
          PhysicsFactory.createBoxBody(
          this.mPhysicsWorld, roof,
          BodyType.StaticBody, WALL_FIXTURE_DEF);
        leftWallBody =
          PhysicsFactory.createBoxBody(
          this.mPhysicsWorld, left,
          BodyType.StaticBody, WALL_FIXTURE_DEF);
        rightWallBody =
          PhysicsFactory.createBoxBody(
          this.mPhysicsWorld, right,
          BodyType.StaticBody, WALL_FIXTURE_DEF);
        this.mScene.attachChild(ground);
        this.mScene.attachChild(roof);
        this.mScene.attachChild(left);
        this.mScene.attachChild(right);
        // Further recipes in this chapter will require us
          to place code here.
        mScene.setOnSceneTouchListener(this);
        pOnPopulateSceneCallback.onPopulateSceneFinished();
```

5. The following overridden activities handle the scene touch events, the accelerometer input, and the two engine life cycle events—`onResumeGame` and `onPauseGame`. Place them at the end of the class to finish this recipe:

```
@Override
public boolean onSceneTouchEvent(Scene pScene, TouchEvent
    pSceneTouchEvent) {
  // Further recipes in this chapter will require us
    to place code here.
  return true;
}

@Override
public void onAccelerationAccuracyChanged(
    AccelerationData pAccelerationData) {}

@Override
public void onAccelerationChanged(
    AccelerationData pAccelerationData) {
  final Vector2 gravity = Vector2Pool.obtain(
    pAccelerationData.getX(),
    pAccelerationData.getY());
  this.mPhysicsWorld.setGravity(gravity);
  Vector2Pool.recycle(gravity);
}

@Override
public void onResumeGame() {
  super.onResumeGame();
  this.enableAccelerationSensor(this);
}

@Override
public void onPauseGame() {
  super.onPauseGame();
  this.disableAccelerationSensor();
}
```

How it works...

The first thing that we do is define a camera width and height. Then, we define a `Scene` object and a `FixedStepPhysicsWorld` object in which the physics simulations will take place. The last set of variables defines what will act as the borders for our physics-based scenes.

In the second step, we override the `onCreateEngine()` method to return a `FixedStepEngine` object that will process `60` updates per second. The reason that we do this, while also using a `FixedStepPhysicsWorld` object, is to create a simulation that will be consistent across all devices, regardless of how efficiently a device can process the physics simulation. We then create the `EngineOptions` object with standard preferences, create the `onCreateResources()` method with only a simple callback, and set the main scene with a light-gray background.

In the `onPopulateScene()` method, we create our `FixedStepPhysicsWorld` object that has double the gravity of the Earth, passed as an `(x, y)` coordinate `Vector2` object, and will update `60` times per second. The gravity can be set to other values to make our simulations more realistic or `0` to create a zero gravity simulation. A gravity setting of `0` is useful for space simulations or for games that use a top-down camera view instead of a profile. The `false` Boolean parameter sets the `AllowSleep` property of the `PhysicsWorld` object, which tells `PhysicsWorld` to not let any bodies deactivate themselves after coming to a stop. The last two parameters of the `FixedStepPhysicsWorld` object tell the physics engine how many times to calculate velocity and position movements. Higher iterations will create simulations that are more accurate, but can cause lag or jitteriness because of the extra load on the processor. After creating the `FixedStepPhysicsWorld` object, we register it with the main scene as an update handler. The physics world will not run a simulation without being registered.

The variable `WALL_FIXTURE_DEF` is a **fixture definition**. Fixture definitions hold the shape and material properties of entities that will be created within the physics world as fixtures. The shape of a fixture can be either circular or polygonal. The material of a fixture is defined by its density, elasticity, and friction, all of which are required when creating a fixture definition. Following the creation of the `WALL_FIXTURE_DEF` variable, we create four rectangles that will represent the locations of the wall bodies. A body in the Box2D physics world is made of fixtures. While only one fixture is necessary to create a body, multiple fixtures can create complex bodies with varying properties.

Further along in the `onPopulateScene()` method, we create the box bodies that will act as our walls in the physics world. The rectangles that were previously created are passed to the bodies to define their position and shape. We then define the bodies as static, which means that they will not react to any forces in the physics simulation. Lastly, we pass the wall fixture definition to the bodies to complete their creation.

After creating the bodies, we attach the rectangles to the main scene and set the scene's touch listener to our activity, which will be accessed by the `onSceneTouchEvent()` method. The final line of the `onPopulateScene()` method tells the engine that the scene is ready to be shown.

The overridden `onSceneTouchEvent()` method will handle all touch interactions for our scene. The `onAccelerationAccuracyChanged()` and `onAccelerationChanged()` methods are inherited from the `IAccelerationListener` interface and allow us to change the gravity of our physics world when the device is tilted, rotated, or panned. We override `onResumeGame()` and `onPauseGame()` to keep the accelerometer from using unnecessary battery power when our game activity is not in the foreground.

There's more...

In the overridden `onAccelerationChanged()` method, we make two calls to the `Vector2Pool` class. The `Vector2Pool` class simply gives us a way of re-using our `Vector2` objects that might otherwise require garbage collection by the system. On newer devices, the Android Garbage Collector has been streamlined to reduce noticeable hiccups, but older devices might still experience lag depending on how much memory the variables being garbage collected occupy.

 Visit `http://www.box2d.org/manual.html` to see the **Box2D User Manual**. The AndEngine Box2D extension is based on a Java port of the official Box2D C++ physics engine, so some variations in procedure exist, but the general concepts still apply.

See also

▶ *Understanding different body types* in this chapter.

Understanding different body types

The Box2D physics world gives us the means to create different body types that allow us to control the physics simulation. We can generate **dynamic bodies** that react to forces and other bodies, **static bodies** that do not move, and **kinematic bodies** that move but are not affected by forces or other bodies. Choosing which type each body will be is vital to producing an accurate physics simulation. In this recipe, we will see how three bodies react to each other during collision, depending on their body types.

Getting ready...

Follow the recipe in the *Introduction to the Box2D physics extension* section given at the beginning of this chapter to create a new activity that will facilitate the creation of our bodies with varying body types.

How to do it...

Complete the following steps to see how specifying a body type for bodies affects them:

1. First, insert the following fixture definition into the `onPopulateScene()` method:

```
FixtureDef BoxBodyFixtureDef =
    PhysicsFactory.createFixtureDef(20f, 0f, 0.5f);
```

2. Next, place the following code that creates three rectangles and their corresponding bodies after the fixture definition from the previous step:

```
Rectangle staticRectangle = new Rectangle(cameraWidth /
    2f,75f,400f,40f,this.getVertexBufferObjectManager());
staticRectangle.setColor(0.8f, 0f, 0f);
mScene.attachChild(staticRectangle);
PhysicsFactory.createBoxBody(mPhysicsWorld, staticRectangle,
    BodyType.StaticBody, BoxBodyFixtureDef);

Rectangle dynamicRectangle = new Rectangle(400f, 120f, 40f, 40f,
    this.getVertexBufferObjectManager());
dynamicRectangle.setColor(0f, 0.8f, 0f);
mScene.attachChild(dynamicRectangle);
Body dynamicBody = PhysicsFactory.createBoxBody(mPhysicsWorld,
    dynamicRectangle, BodyType.DynamicBody, BoxBodyFixtureDef);
mPhysicsWorld.registerPhysicsConnector(new PhysicsConnector(
    dynamicRectangle, dynamicBody);

Rectangle kinematicRectangle = new Rectangle(600f, 100f,
    40f, 40f, this.getVertexBufferObjectManager());
kinematicRectangle.setColor(0.8f, 0.8f, 0f);
mScene.attachChild(kinematicRectangle);
Body kinematicBody = PhysicsFactory.createBoxBody(mPhysicsWorld,
    kinematicRectangle, BodyType.KinematicBody, BoxBodyFixtureDef);
mPhysicsWorld.registerPhysicsConnector(new PhysicsConnector(
    kinematicRectangle, kinematicBody);
```

3. Lastly, add the following code after the definitions from the previous step to set the linear and angular velocities for our kinematic body:

```
kinematicBody.setLinearVelocity(-2f, 0f);
kinematicBody.setAngularVelocity((float) (-Math.PI));
```

How it works...

In the first step, we create the `BoxBodyFixtureDef` fixture definition that we will use when creating our bodies in the second step. For more information on fixture definitions, see the *Introduction to the Box2D physics extension* recipe in this chapter.

In step two, we first define the `staticRectangle` rectangle by calling the `Rectangle` constructor. We place `staticRectangle` at the position of `cameraWidth / 2f, 75f`, which is near the lower-center of the scene, and we set the rectangle to have a width of `400f` and a height of `40f`, which makes the rectangle into a long, flat bar. Then, we set the `staticRectangle` rectangle's color to be red by calling `staticRectangle.setColor(0.8f, 0f, 0f)`. Lastly, for the `staticRectangle` rectangle, we attach it to the scene by calling the `mScene.attachChild()` method with `staticRectangle` as the parameter. Next, we create a body in the physics world that matches our `staticRectangle`. To do this, we call the `PhysicsFactory.createBoxBody()` method with the parameters of `mPhysicsWorld`, which is our physics world, `staticRectangle` to tell the box to be created with the same position and size as the `staticRectangle` rectangle, `BodyType.StaticBody` to define the body as static, and our `BoxBodyFixtureDef` fixture definition.

Our next rectangle, `dynamicRectangle`, is created at the location of `400f` and `120f`, which is the middle of the scene slightly above the `staticRectangle` rectangle. Our `dynamicRectangle` rectangle's width and height are set to `40f` to make it a small square. Then, we set its color to green by calling `dynamicRectangle.setColor(0f, 0.8f, 0f)` and attach it to our scene using `mScene.attachChild(dynamicRectangle)`. Next, we create the `dynamicBody` variable using the `PhysicsFactory.createBoxBody()` method in the same way that we did for our `staticRectangle` rectangle. Notice that we set the `dynamicBody` variable to have `BodyType` of `DynamicBody`. This sets the body to be dynamic. Now, we register `PhysicsConnector` with the physics world to link `dynamicRectangle` and `dynamicBody`. A `PhysicsConnecter` class links an entity within our scene to a body in the physics world, representing the body's realtime position and rotation in our scene.

Our last rectangle, `kinematicRectangle`, is created at the location of `600f` and `100f`, which places it on top of our `staticRectangle` rectangle toward the right-hand side of the scene. It is set to have a height and width of `40f`, which makes it a small square like our `dynamicRectangle` rectangle. We then set the `kinematicRectangle` rectangle's color to yellow and attach it to our scene. Similar to the previous two bodies that we created, we call the `PhysicsFactory.createBoxBody()` method to create our `kinematicBody` variable. Take note that we create our `kinematicBody` variable with a `BodyType` type of `KinematicBody`. This sets it to be kinematic and thus moved only by the setting of its velocities. Lastly, we register a `PhysicsConnector` class between our `kinematicRectangle` rectangle and our `kinematicBody` body type.

In the last step, we set our `kinematicBody` body's linear velocity by calling the `setLinearVelocity()` method with a vector of `-2f` on the x axis, which makes it move to the left. Finally, we set our `kinematicBody` body's angular velocity to negative `pi` by calling `kinematicBody.setAngularVelocity((float) (-Math.PI))`. For more information on setting a body's velocities, see the *Using forces, velocities, and torque* recipe in this chapter.

There's more...

Static bodies cannot move from applied or set forces, but can be relocated using the `setTransform()` method. However, we should avoid using the `setTransform()` method while a simulation is running, because it makes the simulation unstable and can cause some strange behaviors. Instead, if we want to change the position of a static body, we can do so whenever creating the simulation or, if we need to change the position at runtime, simply check that the new position will not cause the static body to overlap existing dynamic bodies or kinematic bodies.

Kinematic bodies cannot have forces applied, but we can set their velocities via the `setLinearVelocity()` and `setAngularVelocity()` methods.

See also

▸ *Introduction to the Box2D physics extension* in this chapter.

▸ *Using forces, velocities, and torque* in this chapter.

Creating category-filtered bodies

Depending on the type of physics simulation that we want to achieve, controlling which bodies are capable of colliding can be very beneficial. In Box2D, we can assign a category, and category-filter to fixtures to control which fixtures can interact. This recipe will cover the defining of two category-filtered fixtures that will be applied to bodies created by touching the scene to demonstrate category-filtering.

Getting ready...

Create an activity by following the steps in the *Introduction to the Box2D physics extension* section given at the beginning of the chapter. This activity will facilitate the creation of the category-filtered bodies used in this section.

How to do it...

Follow these steps to build our category-filtering demonstration activity:

1. Define the following class-level variables within the activity:

```
private int mBodyCount = 0;
public static final short CATEGORYBIT_DEFAULT = 1;
public static final short CATEGORYBIT_RED_BOX = 2;
public static final short CATEGORYBIT_GREEN_BOX = 4;
public static final short MASKBITS_RED_BOX =
  CATEGORYBIT_DEFAULT + CATEGORYBIT_RED_BOX;
public static final short MASKBITS_GREEN_BOX =
  CATEGORYBIT_DEFAULT + CATEGORYBIT_GREEN_BOX;
public static final FixtureDef RED_BOX_FIXTURE_DEF =
  PhysicsFactory.createFixtureDef(1, 0.5f, 0.5f, false,
    CATEGORYBIT_RED_BOX, MASKBITS_RED_BOX, (short)0);
public static final FixtureDef GREEN_BOX_FIXTURE_DEF =
  PhysicsFactory.createFixtureDef(1, 0.5f, 0.5f, false,
    CATEGORYBIT_GREEN_BOX, MASKBITS_GREEN_BOX, (short)0);
```

2. Next, create this method within the class that generates new category-filtered bodies at a given location:

```
private void addBody(final float pX, final float pY) {
  this.mBodyCount++;
  final Rectangle rectangle = new Rectangle(pX, pY, 50f, 50f,
    this.getVertexBufferObjectManager());
  rectangle.setAlpha(0.5f);
  final Body body;
  if(this.mBodyCount % 2 == 0) {
    rectangle.setColor(1f, 0f, 0f);
    body = PhysicsFactory.createBoxBody(this.mPhysicsWorld,
      rectangle, BodyType.DynamicBody, RED_FIXTURE_DEF);
  } else {
    rectangle.setColor(0f, 1f, 0f);
    body = PhysicsFactory.createBoxBody(this.mPhysicsWorld,
      rectangle, BodyType.DynamicBody, GREEN_FIXTURE_DEF);
  }
  this.mScene.attachChild(rectangle);
  this.mPhysicsWorld.registerPhysicsConnector(new
PhysicsConnector(
    rectangle, body, true, true));
}
```

3. Lastly, fill the body of the `onSceneTouchEvent()` method with the following code that calls the `addBody()` method by passing the touched location:

```
if(this.mPhysicsWorld != null)
  if(pSceneTouchEvent.isActionDown())
    this.addBody(pSceneTouchEvent.getX(),
      pSceneTouchEvent.getY());
```

How it works...

In the first step, we create an integer, `mBodyCount`, which counts how many bodies we have added to the physics world. The `mBodyCount` integer is used in the second step to determine which color, and thus which category, should be assigned to the new body.

We also create the `CATEGORYBIT_DEFAULT`, `CATEGORYBIT_RED_BOX`, and `CATEGORYBIT_GREEN_BOX` category bits by defining them with unique power-of-two short integers and the `MASKBITS_RED_BOX` and `MASKBITS_GREEN_BOX` mask bits by adding their associated category bits together. The category bits are used to assign a category to a fixture, while the mask bits combine the different category bits to determine which categories a fixture can collide with. We then pass the category bits and mask bits to the fixture definitions to create fixtures that have category collision rules.

The second step is a simple method that creates a rectangle and its corresponding body. The method takes the `X` and `Y` location parameters that we want to use to create a new body and passes them to a `Rectangle` object's constructor, to which we also pass a height and width of `50f` and the activity's `VertexBufferObjectManager`. Then, we set the rectangle to be 50 percent transparent using the `rectangle.setAlpha()` method. After that, we define a body and modulate the `mBodyCount` variable by `2` to determine the color and fixture of every other created body. After determining the color and fixture, we assign them by setting the rectangle's color and creating a body by passing our `mPhysicsWorld` physics world, the rectangle, a dynamic body type, and the previously-determined fixture to use. Finally, we attach the rectangle to our scene and register a `PhysicsConnector` class to connect the rectangle to our body.

The third step calls the `addBody()` method from step two only if the physics world has been created and only if the scene's `TouchEvent` is `ActionDown`. The parameters that are passed, `pSceneTouchEvent.getX()` and `pSceneTouchEvent.getY()`, represent the location on the scene that received a touch input, which is also the location where we want to create a new category-filtered body.

There's more...

The default category of all fixtures has a value of one. When creating mask bits for specific fixtures, remember that any combination that includes the default category will cause the fixture to collide with all other fixtures that are not masked to avoid collision with the fixture.

See also

- ▸ *Introduction to the Box2D physics extension* in this chapter.
- ▸ *Understanding different body types* in this chapter.

Creating multiple-fixture bodies

We sometimes need a body that has varying physics attributes on certain parts of it. For instance, a car with a bumper should react differently if it hits a wall to a car without a bumper. The creation of such a multifixture body in Box2D is fairly simple and straightforward. In this recipe, we will see how to create a multifixture body by creating two fixtures and adding them to an empty body.

Getting ready...

Follow the steps in the *Introduction to the Box2D physics extension* section at the beginning of the chapter to create a new activity that will facilitate the creation of our multifixture body.

How to do it...

Follow these steps to see how we can create multifixture bodies:

1. Place the following code in the onPopulateScene() method to create two rectangles that have a modified AnchorCenter value which allows for precise placement when linked to a body:

```
Rectangle nonbouncyBoxRect = new Rectangle(0f, 0f, 100f, 100f,
   this.getEngine().getVertexBufferObjectManager());
nonbouncyBoxRect.setColor(0f, 0f, 0f);
nonbouncyBoxRect.setAnchorCenter(((nonbouncyBoxRect.getWidth() /
2) -
   nonbouncyBoxRect.getX()) / nonbouncyBoxRect.getWidth(),
     ((nonbouncyBoxRect.getHeight() / 2) -
       nonbouncyBoxRect.getY()) /
         nonbouncyBoxRect.getHeight());
mScene.attachChild(nonbouncyBoxRect);
Rectangle bouncyBoxRect = new Rectangle(0f, -55f, 90f, 10f,
   this.getEngine().getVertexBufferObjectManager());
bouncyBoxRect.setColor(0f, 0.75f, 0f);
bouncyBoxRect.setAnchorCenter(((bouncyBoxRect.getWidth() / 2) -
   bouncyBoxRect.getX()) / bouncyBoxRect.getWidth(),
     ((bouncyBoxRect.getHeight() / 2) -
       bouncyBoxRect.getY()) /
         bouncyBoxRect.getHeight());
mScene.attachChild(bouncyBoxRect);
```

2. The following code creates a `Body` object and two fixtures, one that is perfectly elastic and another that is perfectly inelastic. Add it after the creation of the rectangles in the preceding step:

```
Body multiFixtureBody = mPhysicsWorld.createBody(new BodyDef());
multiFixtureBody.setType(BodyType.DynamicBody);

FixtureDef nonbouncyBoxFixtureDef =    PhysicsFactory.
createFixtureDef(20, 0.0f, 0.5f);
final PolygonShape nonbouncyBoxShape = new PolygonShape();
nonbouncyBoxShape.setAsBox((nonbouncyBoxRect.getWidth() / 2f) /
  PhysicsConstants.PIXEL_TO_METER_RATIO_DEFAULT,
    (nonbouncyBoxRect.getHeight() / 2f) /
      PhysicsConstants.PIXEL_TO_METER_RATIO_DEFAULT,
        new Vector2(nonbouncyBoxRect.getX() /
      PhysicsConstants.PIXEL_TO_METER_RATIO_DEFAULT,
          nonbouncyBoxRect.getY() /
      PhysicsConstants.PIXEL_TO_METER_RATIO_DEFAULT), 0f);
nonbouncyBoxFixtureDef.shape = nonbouncyBoxShape;
multiFixtureBody.createFixture(nonbouncyBoxFixtureDef);
mPhysicsWorld.registerPhysicsConnector(new PhysicsConnector(
  nonbouncyBoxRect, multiFixtureBody));

FixtureDef bouncyBoxFixtureDef =
  PhysicsFactory.createFixtureDef(20,    1f, 0.5f);
final PolygonShape bouncyBoxShape = new PolygonShape();
bouncyBoxShape.setAsBox((bouncyBoxRect.getWidth() / 2f) /
  PhysicsConstants.PIXEL_TO_METER_RATIO_DEFAULT,
    (bouncyBoxRect.getHeight() / 2f) /
      PhysicsConstants.PIXEL_TO_METER_RATIO_DEFAULT,
        new Vector2(bouncyBoxRect.getX() /
      PhysicsConstants.PIXEL_TO_METER_RATIO_DEFAULT,
          bouncyBoxRect.getY() /
      PhysicsConstants.PIXEL_TO_METER_RATIO_DEFAULT), 0f);
bouncyBoxFixtureDef.shape = bouncyBoxShape;
multiFixtureBody.createFixture(bouncyBoxFixtureDef);
mPhysicsWorld.registerPhysicsConnector(new PhysicsConnector(
  bouncyBoxRect, multiFixtureBody));
```

3. Lastly, we need to set the location of our multifixture body now that it has been created. Place the following call to `setTransform()` after the creation of the bodies in the previous step:

```
multiFixtureBody.setTransform(400f /
  PhysicsConstants.PIXEL_TO_METER_RATIO_DEFAULT, 240f /
    PhysicsConstants.PIXEL_TO_METER_RATIO_DEFAULT, 0f);
```

How it works...

The first step that we take is to define a rectangle that will represent a non-bouncy fixture by using the `Rectangle` constructor and passing `0f` on the x axis and `0f` on the y axis, representing the origin of the world. We then pass a height and width of `100f`, which makes the rectangle a large square, and the activity's `VertexBufferObjectManager`.

Then, we set the color of the non-bouncy rectangle to black, `0f, 0f, 0f`, and set its anchor-center using the `nonbouncyBoxRect.setAnchorCenter()` method to represent the location on the body, created in the second step, at which the non-bouncy rectangle will be attached. The anchor-center location of `(((nonbouncyBoxRect.getWidth() / 2) - nonbouncyBoxRect.getX()) / nonbouncyBoxRect.getWidth(), ((nonbouncyBoxRect.getHeight() / 2) - nonbouncyBoxRect.getY()) / nonbouncyBoxRect.getHeight()` converts the rectangle's location and size to the location that the rectangle rests on the origin. In the case of our non-bouncy rectangle, the anchor-center remains at the default `0.5f, 0.5f`, but the formula is necessary for any fixture that will be created from a rectangle that is not centered on the origin. Next, we attach our non-bouncy rectangle to the scene. Then, we create a rectangle that will represent a bouncy fixture using the same method that we used to create the non-bouncy rectangle, but we place the rectangle at `-55f` on the y axis to put it directly below the non-bouncy rectangle. We also set the width of the rectangle to `90f`, making it slightly smaller than the previous rectangle, and the height to `10f` to make it a slim bar that will act as a bouncy portion directly below the non-bouncy rectangle. After setting the bouncy rectangle's anchor-center using the same formula used for the non-bouncy rectangle, we attach it to the scene. Take note that we have modified the `AnchorCenter` values of each of the rectangles, so that the `PhysicsConnectors` class that we register in the second step can place the rectangles in the proper location when we run the simulation. Also, note that we create our rectangles and multifixture body at the world's origin to make calculations simple and fast. After our body has been created, we move it to the position that it should be in for the simulation, as can be seen in the third step, when we call the `multiFixtureBody.setTransform()` method with the parameters `400f / PhysicsConstants.PIXEL_TO_METER_RATIO_DEFAULT` and `240f / PhysicsConstants.PIXEL_TO_METER_RATIO_DEFAULT`, which represent the center of the screen in the physics world, and `0f`, which represents the zero-rotation that the body will have.

In the second step, we create an empty body, `multiFixtureBody`, by calling `mPhysicsWorld.createBody(new BodyDef())` and set it to be dynamic by calling its `setType()` method with the parameter `BodyType.DynamicBody`. Then, we define a fixture definition, `nonbouncyBoxFixtureDef`, for the non-bouncy fixture.

Next, we create a `PolygonShape` shape named `nonbouncyBoxShape` and set it as a box that mimics our `nonbouncyBoxRect` by calling `nonbouncyBoxShape` shape's `setAsBox()` method with the first two parameters as `nonbouncyBoxRect.getWidth() / 2f` and `nonbouncyBoxRect.getHeight() / 2f` to set the `nonbouncyBoxShape` object to have the same width and height as our `nonbouncyBoxRect` rectangle. Both of the parameters are divided by `PhysicsConstants.PIXEL_TO_METER_RATIO_DEFAULT` to scale the values to the physics world. Furthermore, the `setAsBox()` method's first two parameters are half sizes. This means that a normal width of `10f` will be passed to the `setAsBox()` method as `5f`. The next parameter of the `setAsBox()` method is a `Vector2` parameter that will identify the location of our `nonbouncyBoxShape` shape in the physics world. We set it to the location of our `nonbouncyBoxRect` rectangle, converting the location to physics world coordinates by scaling with the `PhysicsConstants.PIXEL_TO_METER_RATIO_DEFAULT` variable. The last parameter of the `setAsBox()` method is the rotation that `nonbouncyBoxShape` should have. Because our `nonbouncyBoxRect` rectangle is not rotated, we use `0f`.

Then, we set the `shape` property of our `nonbouncyBoxFixtureDef` fixture definition to `nonbouncyBoxShape`, which applies the shape to our fixture definition. Next, we attach the fixture to our multifixture body by calling the body's `createFixture()` method with the `nonbouncyBoxFixtureDef` fixture definition as the parameter. Then, we register a `PhysicsConnector` class to link the `nonbouncyBoxRect` rectangle in our scene to the `multiFixtureBody` body in the physics world. Finally, we follow the same procedures that we used when creating the non-bouncy fixture to create our bouncy fixture. The result should be a black square with one bouncy, green side.

 By setting the `isSensor` property of a fixture definition to `true`, a fixture can be created as a sensor, which allows it to contact other fixtures without a physical interaction occurring. For more information on sensors, see the **Fixtures** section of the Box2D manual at `http://www.box2d.org/manual.html`.

See also

▶ *Introduction to the Box2D physics extension* in this chapter.

▶ *Understanding different body types* in this chapter.

Creating unique bodies by specifying vertices

Not everything in our physics simulations must be made of rectangles or circles. We can also create polygonal bodies by creating a list of the polygonal points. This approach is useful for creating certain types of terrain, vehicles, and characters. In this recipe, we will demonstrate how to create a unique body from a list of vertices.

Getting ready...

Create an activity by following the steps in the *Introduction to the Box2D physics extension* section given at the beginning of the chapter. This activity will easily allow the creation of a uniquely constructed body with vertices.

How to do it...

Complete the following steps to define and create our unique, polygonal body:

1. Our unique body's vertices will be defined by a list of `Vector2` objects. Add the following list to the `onPopulateScene()` method:

```
List<Vector2> UniqueBodyVertices = new ArrayList<Vector2>();
UniqueBodyVertices.addAll((List<Vector2>) ListUtils.toList(
  new Vector2[] {
    new Vector2(-53f,-75f),
    new Vector2(-107f,-14f),
    new Vector2(-101f,41f),
    new Vector2(-71f,74f),
    new Vector2(69f,74f),
    new Vector2(98f,41f),
    new Vector2(104f,-14f),
    new Vector2(51f,-75f),
    new Vector2(79f,9f),
    new Vector2(43f,34f),
    new Vector2(-46f,34f),
    new Vector2(-80f,9f)
  }));
```

2. To use the preceding list of vertices, we must run them through the `EarClippingTriangulator` class to turn the vertices list into a list of triangles that the physics engine will use to create multiple fixtures that are joined into a single body. Place this code after the creation of the initial `Vector2` list:

```
List<Vector2> UniqueBodyVerticesTriangulated =
  new EarClippingTriangulator().
    computeTriangles(UniqueBodyVertices);
```

3. To create a mesh that will represent our unique body, as well as adapt the triangulated vertices for use in the physics world, add the following code snippet:

```
float[] MeshTriangles =
  new float[UniqueBodyVerticesTriangulated.size() * 3];
for(int i = 0; i < UniqueBodyVerticesTriangulated.size(); i++) {
  MeshTriangles[i*3] = UniqueBodyVerticesTriangulated.get(i).x;
  MeshTriangles[i*3+1] = UniqueBodyVerticesTriangulated.get(i).y;
  UniqueBodyVerticesTriangulated.get(i).
    mul(1/PhysicsConstants.PIXEL_TO_METER_RATIO_DEFAULT);
}
Mesh UniqueBodyMesh = new Mesh(400f, 260f, MeshTriangles,
  UniqueBodyVerticesTriangulated.size(), DrawMode.TRIANGLES,
    this.getVertexBufferObjectManager());
UniqueBodyMesh.setColor(1f, 0f, 0f);
mScene.attachChild(UniqueBodyMesh);
```

4. Now that we have adapted the vertices to be used in the physics world, we can create the body:

```
FixtureDef uniqueBodyFixtureDef =
  PhysicsFactory.createFixtureDef(20f, 0.5f, 0.5f);
Body uniqueBody = PhysicsFactory.createTrianglulatedBody(
  mPhysicsWorld, UniqueBodyMesh, UniqueBodyVerticesTriangulated,
    BodyType.DynamicBody, uniqueBodyFixtureDef);
mPhysicsWorld.registerPhysicsConnector(
  new PhysicsConnector(UniqueBodyMesh, uniqueBody));
```

5. Lastly, we want the unique body to have something to collide with. Add the following body definitions to create two static bodies that will act as small pegs in our physics world:

```
FixtureDef BoxBodyFixtureDef =
  PhysicsFactory.createFixtureDef(20f, 0.6f, 0.5f);
Rectangle Box1 = new Rectangle(340f, 160f, 20f, 20f,
  this.getVertexBufferObjectManager());
mScene.attachChild(Box1);
PhysicsFactory.createBoxBody(mPhysicsWorld, Box1,
  BodyType.StaticBody, BoxBodyFixtureDef);
```

```
Rectangle Box2 = new Rectangle(600f, 160f, 20f, 20f,
    this.getVertexBufferObjectManager());
mScene.attachChild(Box2);
PhysicsFactory.createBoxBody(mPhysicsWorld, Box2,
    BodyType.StaticBody, BoxBodyFixtureDef);
```

How it works...

The list of vertices that we first create represents the shape that our unique body will be, relative to the center of the body. In the second step, we create another list of vertices using the `EarClippingTriangulator` class. This list that is returned from the `computeTriangles()` method of the `EarClippingTriangulator` class contains all of the points of the triangles that make up our unique body. The following figure shows what our polygonal body looks like before and after running its vertices through the `EarClippingTriangulator` class. Notice that our body will be made from several triangular shapes that represent the original shape:

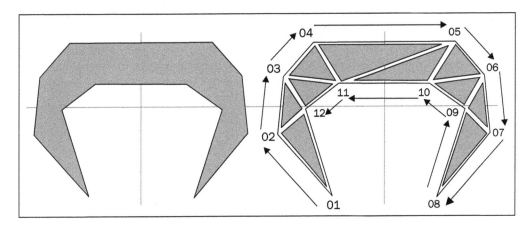

In step three, after adding each vertex to the `MeshTriangles` array for use in creating a mesh to represent our body, we multiply each vertex by `1/PhysicsConstants.PIXEL_TO_METER_RATIO_DEFAULT`, which is the same as dividing the vertex's coordinates by the default pixel-to-meter ratio. This division process is a common practice used to convert the scene coordinates to the physics world coordinates. The physics world measures distance in meters, so a conversion from pixels is necessary. Any consistent, reasonable value can be used as the conversion constant, but the default pixel-to-meter-ratio is 32 pixels per meter and has been proven to work in almost every simulation.

Step four creates the unique body by calling `PhysicsFactory.createTrianglulatedBody`. It is important to note that while it is possible to create polygonal bodies from a non-triangulated list of vertices, the only benefit to doing so would be if we were using a list with less than seven vertexes. Even with such a small list, triangulating the body does not have a noticeable negative impact on the simulation.

Several physics-body editors are available to simplify body creation. The following are all usable with AndEngine:

 ▶ **Physics Body Editor** (free): http://code.google.com/p/box2d-editor

 ▶ **PhysicsEditor** (paid): http://www.codeandweb.com/physicseditor

 ▶ **Inkscape** (free, plugins required): http://inkscape.org/

See also

 ▶ *Introduction to the Box2D physics extension* in this chapter.

 ▶ *Understanding different body types* in this chapter.

Using forces, velocities, and torque

No matter what kind of simulation we are creating, we will more than likely want to control at least one body. To move bodies in Box2D, we can apply linear or angular forces, set linear or angular velocities, and apply an angular force in the form of torque. In this recipe, we will see how we can apply these forces and velocities on multiple bodies.

Getting ready...

Follow the steps in the *Introduction to the Box2D physics extension* section at the beginning of the chapter to create a new activity that will facilitate the creation of bodies that will react to forces, velocities, and torque. Then, update the activity to include the additional code from the `ForcesVelocitiesTorqueActivity` class found in the code bundle.

How to do it...

Refer to the supplemental `ForcesVelocitiesTorqueActivity` class for the complete example of this recipe. We will cover only the basics of the recipe in this section:

1. We will first work with the methods that handle the linear motion of our bodies. Place the following code snippet in the overridden `onAreaTouched()` method of the `LinearForceRect` rectangle:

```
LinearForceBody.applyForce(0f, 2000f,
  LinearForceBody.getWorldCenter().x,
  LinearForceBody.getWorldCenter().y);
```

2. Next, insert this code in the `onAreaTouched()` method of the `LinearImpulseRect` rectangle:

```
LinearImpulseBody.applyLinearImpulse(0f, 200f,
   LinearImpulseBody.getWorldCenter().x,
   LinearImpulseBody.getWorldCenter().y);
```

3. Then, add this code to the `onAreaTouched()` method of the `LinearVelocityRect` rectangle:

```
LinearVelocityBody.setLinearVelocity(0f, 20f);
```

4. Now, we will work with the `Body` methods that affect the angular motion of our bodies. Place this code in the `onAreaTouched()` method of the `AngularTorqueRect` rectangle:

```
AngularTorqueBody.applyTorque(2000f);
```

5. Insert the following code in the `onAreaTouched()` method of the `AngularImpulseRect` rectangle:

```
AngularImpulseBody.applyAngularImpulse(20f);
```

6. Finally, add this code to the `onAreaTouched()` method of the `AngularVelocityRect` rectangle:

```
AngularVelocityBody.setAngularVelocity(10f);
```

How it works...

In step one, we apply a linear force on `LinearForceBody` by calling its `applyForce()` method with the force parameters of `0f` on the x axis and `2000f` on the y axis to apply a strong, positive vertical force and the force location in world coordinates of `LinearForceBody.getWorldCenter().x` and `LinearForceBody.getWorldCenter().y` to apply the force at the center of the `LinearForceBody` body.

Step two applies a linear impulse on the `LinearImpulseBody` body via its `applyLinearImpulse()` method. The `applyLinearImpulse()` method's first two parameters are the impulse amount with respect to the world axis. We use the values of `0f` and `200f` to apply the moderate impulse pointing straight up. The remaining two parameters of the `applyLinearImpulse()` method are the x and y location that the impulse will be applied to the body in world coordinates. We pass `LinearImpulseBody.getWorldCenter().x` and `LinearImpulseBody.getWorldCenter().y` to apply the impulse at the center of the `LinearImpulseBody` body.

In step three, we set the linear velocity of `LinearVelocityBody` by calling its `setLinearVelocity()` method with the parameters `0f` and `20f`. The parameter of `0f` signifies that the body will not be moving on the x axis, and the parameter of `20f` sets the y axis motion immediately to be 20 meters per second. When using the `setLinearVelocity()` method, the velocity is automatically set at the body's center of mass.

Step four applies a torque to `AngularTorqueBody`. We call the `AngularTorqueBody.applyTorque()` method with a value of `2000f` to apply a very strong torque to the `AngularTorqueBody` body at the body's center of mass.

In the fifth step, we apply an angular impulse to the `AngularImpulseBody` body by calling the `AngularImpulseBody.applyAngularImpulse()` method with a value of `20f`. This small, angular impulse will be applied to the `AngularImpulseBody` body's center of mass.

For the final step, we set the angular velocity of the `AngularVelocityBody` body. We call the `AngularVelocityBody.setAngularVelocity()` method with the value of `10f` to make the body immediately rotate at 10 radians per second.

There's more...

Impulses differ from *forces* in that they function independently of the timestep. An impulse actually equals *force* multiplied by *time*. Likewise, *forces* equal the *impulse* divided by *time*.

Setting the velocity of bodies and applying an impulse are similar, but there is an important distinction to make—applying impulses directly adds to or subtracts from the velocity, while setting a velocity does not incrementally increase or decrease the velocity.

See also

- ▸ *Introduction to the Box2D physics extension* in this chapter.
- ▸ *Understanding different body types* in this chapter.

Applying anti-gravity to a specific body

In the previous recipe, we looked at how forces affect bodies. Using a constant force that opposes gravity, we can release a body from the gravity of the physics world. If the force that opposes gravity is great enough, the body will even float away! In this recipe, we will create a body that counteracts the force of gravity.

Getting ready...

Create an activity by following the steps in the *Introduction to the Box2D physics extension* section at the beginning of the chapter. This activity will facilitate the creation of a body that has a constant force applied that opposes gravity.

How to do it...

For this recipe, follow these steps to create a body that opposes gravity:

1. Place the following definitions in the activity:

```
Body gravityBody;
Body antigravityBody;
final FixtureDef boxFixtureDef = PhysicsFactory.
createFixtureDef(2f, 0.5f, 0.9f);
```

2. Next, create a rectangle and body that will demonstrate the normal effects of gravity on a body. Place the following code snippet in the onPopulateScene() method:

```
Rectangle GravityRect = new Rectangle(300f, 240f, 100f, 100f,
this.getEngine().getVertexBufferObjectManager());
GravityRect.setColor(0f, 0.7f, 0f);
mScene.attachChild(GravityRect);
mScene.registerTouchArea(GravityRect);
gravityBody = PhysicsFactory.createBoxBody(mPhysicsWorld,
  GravityRect, BodyType.DynamicBody, boxFixtureDef);
gravityBody.setLinearDamping(0.4f);
gravityBody.setAngularDamping(0.6f);
mPhysicsWorld.registerPhysicsConnector(new PhysicsConnector(
  GravityRect, gravityBody));
```

3. Finally, create a rectangle and body that show how a body can ignore gravity by applying an anti-gravity force during every update:

```
Rectangle AntiGravityRect = new Rectangle(500f, 240f, 100f, 100f,
  this.getEngine().getVertexBufferObjectManager()) {
  @Override
  protected void onManagedUpdate(final float pSecondsElapsed) {
    super.onManagedUpdate(pSecondsElapsed);
    antigravityBody.applyForce(
      -mPhysicsWorld.getGravity().x *
        antigravityBody.getMass(),
      -mPhysicsWorld.getGravity().y *
        antigravityBody.getMass(),
      antigravityBody.getWorldCenter().x,
      antigravityBody.getWorldCenter().y);
  }
};
AntiGravityRect.setColor(0f, 0f, 0.7f);
```

```
mScene.attachChild(AntiGravityRect);
mScene.registerTouchArea(AntiGravityRect);
antigravityBody = PhysicsFactory.createBoxBody(mPhysicsWorld,
    AntiGravityRect, BodyType.DynamicBody, boxFixtureDef);
antigravityBody.setLinearDamping(0.4f);
antigravityBody.setAngularDamping(0.6f);
mPhysicsWorld.registerPhysicsConnector(new PhysicsConnector(
    AntiGravityRect, antigravityBody));
```

How it works...

The first step that we take is to define a body affected by gravity, a body that opposes gravity, and a fixture definition used when creating the bodies.

Next, we create a rectangle and its corresponding body that is affected by gravity. For more information on creating rectangles, refer to the *Applying primitives to a layer* recipe in *Chapter 2*, *Working with Entities*, or for more information on creating bodies, refer to the *Understanding different body types* recipe in this chapter.

Then, we create the anti-gravity body and its connected rectangle. By overriding the anti-gravity rectangle's onManagedUpdate() method, we can place code in it that will run after every engine update. In the case of our AntiGravityRect rectangle, we fill the onManagedUpdate() method with the antigravityBody.applyForce() method, passing the negated mPhysicsWorld.getGravity() method's x and y values multiplied by antigravityBody body's mass and finally set the force to be applied at the world center of antigravityBody. By using this force that is the exact opposite of the physics-world's gravity within the onManagedUpdate() method, the anti-gravity body is corrected against the physics-world's gravity after every update. Furthermore, the force that we apply must be multiplied by the body's mass to fully compensate for the effects of gravity. Refer to the following diagram to better understand how anti-gravity bodies function:

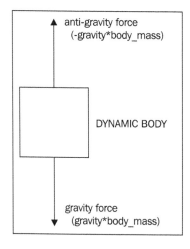

See also

- ▶ *Introduction to the Box2D physics extension* in this chapter.
- ▶ *Using forces, velocities, and torque* in this chapter.

Working with joints

In Box2d, **joints** are used to connect two bodies so that each body is in some way attached to the other. The various types of joints make it possible to customize our characters, vehicles, and the world. Furthermore, joints can be created and destroyed during a simulation, which gives us endless possibilities for our games. In this recipe, we will create a line joint to demonstrate how joints are set up and used in the physics world.

Getting ready...

Create an activity following the steps in the *Introduction to the Box2D physics extension* section given at the beginning of the chapter. This activity will facilitate the creation of two bodies and a connecting line joint that we will use for this recipe. Refer to the JointsActivity class in the supplemental code for examples of more types of joints.

How to do it...

Follow these steps to create a line joint:

1. Define the following variables within our activity:

```
Body LineJointBodyA;
Body LineJointBodyB;
final FixtureDef boxFixtureDef =
   PhysicsFactory.createFixtureDef(20f, 0.2f, 0.9f);
```

2. Add the following code in the onPopulateScene() method to create two rectangles and their associated bodies:

```
Rectangle LineJointRectA = new Rectangle(228f, 240f, 30f, 30f,
this.getEngine().getVertexBufferObjectManager());
LineJointRectA.setColor(0.5f, 0.25f, 0f);
mScene.attachChild(LineJointRectA);
LineJointBodyA = PhysicsFactory.createBoxBody(mPhysicsWorld,
   LineJointRectA, BodyType.KinematicBody, boxFixtureDef);
Rectangle LineJointRectB = new Rectangle(228f, 200f, 30f, 30f,
    this.getEngine().getVertexBufferObjectManager()) {
@Override
protected void onManagedUpdate(final float pSecondsElapsed)
{
```

```
        super.onManagedUpdate(pSecondsElapsed);
        LineJointBodyB.applyTorque(1000f);
        LineJointBodyB.setAngularVelocity( Math.min(
          LineJointBodyB.getAngularVelocity(),0.2f));
      }
    };
    LineJointRectB.setColor(0.75f, 0.375f, 0f);
    mScene.attachChild(LineJointRectB);
    LineJointBodyB = PhysicsFactory.createBoxBody(mPhysicsWorld,
      LineJointRectB, BodyType.DynamicBody, boxFixtureDef);
    mPhysicsWorld.registerPhysicsConnector(new PhysicsConnector(
      LineJointRectB, LineJointBodyB));
```

3. Place the following code after the code shown in the previous step to create a line joint that connects the bodies from the previous step:

```
final LineJointDef lineJointDef = new LineJointDef();
lineJointDef.initialize(LineJointBodyA, LineJointBodyB,
      LineJointBodyB.getWorldCenter(), new Vector2(0f,1f));
lineJointDef.collideConnected = true;
lineJointDef.enableLimit = true;
lineJointDef.lowerTranslation = -220f /
  PhysicsConstants.PIXEL_TO_METER_RATIO_DEFAULT;
lineJointDef.upperTranslation = 0f;
lineJointDef.enableMotor = true;
lineJointDef.motorSpeed = -200f;
lineJointDef.maxMotorForce = 420f;
mPhysicsWorld.createJoint(lineJointDef);
```

How it works...

We first define the two bodies, `LineJointBodyA` and `LineJointBodyB`, that will be connected to our line joint and the `boxFixtureDef` fixture definition that will be applied to the bodies. For more information about creating fixture definitions, refer to the *Introduction to the Box2D physics extension* recipe given at the beginning of this chapter.

In step two, we create the `LineJointRectA` rectangle using the `Rectangle()` constructor with a position of `228f` and `240f`, which places it in the middle of the left-half of our scene, and a height and width of `30f` to make it a small square. We then set its color to dark orange by calling the `LineJointRectA.setColor()` method with the parameters `0.5f`, `0.25f` and `0f`. Next, we create `LineJointRectA` rectangle's associated `LineJointBodyA` body by calling the `PhysicsFactory.createBoxBody()` constructor with the parameters `mPhysicsWorld`, which is our physics world, `LineJointRectA`, which is used to define the shape and position of the body, `BodyType` of `BodyType.KinematicBody`, and the `boxFixtureDef` fixture definition.

Next, we handle the creation of `LineJointRectB` and `LineJointBodyB` in the same way that we created `LineJointRectA` and `LineJointBodyA`, but with the addition of the overridden `onManagedUpdate()` method in the creation of `LineJointRectB` and a `PhysicsConnector` class to connect `LineJointRectB` and `LineJointBodyB`. The overridden `onManagedUpdate()` method of `LineJointRectB` applies a large torque to `LineJointBodyB` by calling the `LineJointBodyB.applyTorque()` method with a value of `1000f`. After we apply the torque, we make sure that LineJointBodyB body's angular velocity does not exceed `0.2f` by passing `Math.min(LineJointBodyB.getAngularVelocity(), 0.2f)` to the `LineJointBodyB.setAngularVelocity()` method. Finally, the `PhysicsConnector` class created and registered at the end of step two links `LineJointRectB` in our scene to `LineJointBodyB` in the physics world.

In step three, we create our line joint. To initialize the line joint, we use the `lineJointDef.initialize()` method to which we pass the associated bodies, `LineJointBodyA` and `LineJointBodyB`. Then, we pass the world-based center of `LineJointBodyB` as the anchor point of the joint and `Vector2`, that contains the unit vector world axis of our joint. The world axis for our joint is set at `0f` and `1f`, which means zero movement on the x axis and a movement with a scale of `1f` on the y axis. We then tell the joint to allow collisions between the joint's bodies by setting the `lineJointDef.collideConnected` variable to `true` and enable the limit of the joint by setting the `lineJointDef.enableLimit` variable to `true`, which limits `LineJointBodyB` body's distance from the first. To set the lower distance limit of our joint, which represents how far from the joint that `LineJointBodyB` body can travel in the negative, we set the `lineJointDef.lowerTranslation` variable to `-220f / PhysicsConstants.PIXEL_TO_METER_RATIO_DEFAULT`. For the upper distance limit, we set the `lineJointDef.upperTranslation` variable to `0f` to keep `LineJointBodyB` from being forced above `LineJointBodyA`. Next, we enable the joint's motor by setting the `lineJointDef.enableMotor` variable to `true`, which will either pull or push `LineJointBodyB` toward or away from `LineJointBodyA` depending on the motor's speed. Lastly, we give the joint's motor a fast, negative speed by setting the `lineJointDef.motorSpeed` variable to `-200f` to move `LineJointBodyB` toward the `lowerTranslation` limit and give the motor a strong maximum force by setting the `lineJointDef.maxMotorForce` variable to `420f`.

The line joint acts similarly to the suspension-and-wheel part of a car. It allows for constrained movement on an axis, usually vertical for vehicles, and allows the second body to rotate or act as a powered wheel if necessary. The following diagram illustrates the various components of the line joint:

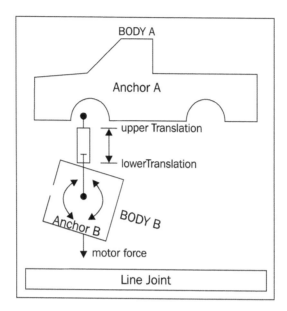

There's more...

All joints have two bodies and give us the option of allowing collision between those connected bodies. We enable the collision whenever we need it, but the default value of every joint's `collideConnected` variable is `false`. Furthermore, the second body of all joints should always be one with a `BodyType` type of `BodyType.DynamicBody`.

For any joints that have a frequency, which determines how elastically the joint behaves, never set the frequency to exceed more than half of the physics world timestep. If the timestep of the physics world is 40, the maximum value that we should assign as the frequency of our joints would be `20f`.

If either body connected to a joint is destroyed while the joint is active, the joint is also destroyed. This means that when we dispose of a physics world, we do not need to dispose of the joints within it as long as we destroy all of the bodies.

More joint types

The line joint is only one of several types of joints available for use in our physics simulations. The other types of joints are the distance, mouse, prismatic, pulley, revolute, and weld joints. Continue reading to learn more about each type. Refer to the supplemental `JointsActivity` class for a more in-depth example of each of the joint types.

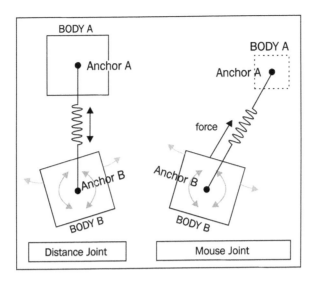

The distance joint

The **distance joint** simply attempts to keep its connected bodies a certain distance from each other. If we do not set the length of the distance joint, it assumes the length to be the initial distance between its bodies. The following code creates a distance joint:

```
final DistanceJointDef distanceJointDef = new DistanceJointDef();
distanceJointDef.initialize(DistanceJointBodyA,
   DistanceJointBodyB, DistanceJointBodyA.getWorldCenter(),
     DistanceJointBodyB.getWorldCenter());
distanceJointDef.length = 3.0f;
distanceJointDef.frequencyHz = 1f;
distanceJointDef.dampingRatio = 0.001f;
```

Notice that we initialize the distance joint by passing the two bodies to be connected, `DistanceJointBodyA` and `DistanceJointBodyB`, and the centers of the bodies, `DistanceJointBodyA.getWorldCenter()` and `DistanceJointBodyB. getWorldCenter()`, as the anchor points for the joint. Next, we set the length of the joint by setting the `distanceJointDef.length` variable to `3.0f`, which tells the joint that the two bodies should be 3 meters apart in the physics world. Finally, we set the `distanceJointDef.frequencyHz` variable to `1f` to force a small frequency for the spring of the joint and the `distanceJointDef.dampingRatio` variable to `0.001f` to produce a very small dampening effect for the connected bodies. For an easier understanding of what the distance joint looks like, refer to the preceding diagram.

The mouse joint

The **mouse joint** attempts to pull a body to a specific location, usually the location of a touch, using a set maximum force. It is a great joint for testing purposes, but for the release version of most games, we should opt for using a kinematic body with the appropriate code to move it to where a touch is registered. To understand how the mouse joint acts, reference the preceding diagram. The following code defines a mouse joint:

```
final MouseJointDef mouseJointDef = new MouseJointDef();
mouseJointDef.bodyA = MouseJointBodyA;
mouseJointDef.bodyB = MouseJointBodyB;
mouseJointDef.dampingRatio = 0.0f;
mouseJointDef.frequencyHz = 1f;
mouseJointDef.maxForce = (100.0f * MouseJointBodyB.getMass());
```

Unlike other joints, the mouse joint does not have an `initialize()` method to help set up the joint. We first create the `mouseJointDef` mouse joint definition and set the `mouseJointDef.bodyA` variable to `MouseJointBodyA` and the `mouseJointDef.bodyB` variable to `MouseJointBodyB` in order to tell the joint which bodies it will be linking. In all of our simulations, `MouseJointBodyA` should be an immobile body that does not move while the mouse joint is active.

Next, we set the `mouseJointDef.dampingRatio` variable to `0.0f` to cause the joint to have absolutely no damping. We then set the `mouseJointDef.frequencyHz` variable to `1f` to force a slight frequency response whenever `MouseJointBodyB` has reached the mouse joint's target, which we can see being set in the following code. Finally, we set the `maxForce` variable of our `mouseJointDef to (100.0f * MouseJointBodyB.getMass())` method. The strong force of `100.0f` is multiplied by `MouseJointBodyB` body's mass to account for any changes in the mass of `MouseJointBodyB`.

In this code, we initialized the mouse joint, but it should only be active after the simulation has started. To activate the mouse joint from within the `onSceneTouchEvent()` method of a class while the simulation is running, see the following code. Note that the `mouseJoint` variable, which is a mouse joint, is created at the class level:

```
if (pSceneTouchEvent.isActionDown()) {
  mouseJointDef.target.set(MouseJointBodyB.getWorldCenter());
  mouseJoint = (MouseJoint)mPhysicsWorld.createJoint(
    mouseJointDef);
  final Vector2 vec = Vector2Pool.obtain(
    pSceneTouchEvent.getX() /
    PhysicsConstants.PIXEL_TO_METER_RATIO_DEFAULT,
    pSceneTouchEvent.getY() /
```

```
    PhysicsConstants.PIXEL_TO_METER_RATIO_DEFAULT);
  mouseJoint.setTarget(vec);
  Vector2Pool.recycle(vec);
} else if(pSceneTouchEvent.isActionMove()) {
  final Vector2 vec = Vector2Pool.obtain(
    pSceneTouchEvent.getX() /
    PhysicsConstants.PIXEL_TO_METER_RATIO_DEFAULT,
    pSceneTouchEvent.getY() /
    PhysicsConstants.PIXEL_TO_METER_RATIO_DEFAULT);
  mouseJoint.setTarget(vec);
  Vector2Pool.recycle(vec);
} else if(pSceneTouchEvent.isActionCancel() ||
    pSceneTouchEvent.isActionOutside() ||
      pSceneTouchEvent.isActionUp()) {
  mPhysicsWorld.destroyJoint(mouseJoint);
}
```

When the screen is first touched, which is determined by checking `pSceneTouchEvent.`
`isActionDown()`, we set the initial mouse joint target using the `mouseJointDef.target.`
`set()` method to the world center of `MouseJointBodyB` via the `MouseJointBodyB.`
`getWorldCenter()` method. Then, we set the `mouseJoint` variable by creating the mouse
joint definition in the physics world using the `MouseJoint` joint-casted `mPhysicsWorld.`
`createJoint()` method with the `mouseJointDef` variable as the parameter. After the joint
is created, we create `Vector2` from `Vector2Pool`, that holds the location of the scene's
touch location, `pSceneTouchEvent.getX()` and `pSceneTouchEvent.getY()`, converted
to physics-world coordinated by dividing the location by `PhysicsConstants.PIXEL_TO_`
`METER_RATIO_DEFAULT`.

We then change the `mouseJoint` joint's target variable to the previously created `Vector2` and recycle `Vector2` to `Vector2Pool`. While the touch is still active, determined by checking `pSceneTouchEvent.isActionMove()`, we update the target of the mouse joint using the same procedure that we used immediately after creating the mouse joint in the physics world. We call for `Vector2` from `Vector2Pool`, that is set to the physics world-converted touch location, set the target of the mouse joint to that `Vector2`, and then recycle `Vector2`. As soon as the touch is released, which is determined by checking `pSceneTouchEvent.isActionCancel()`, `pSceneTouchEvent.isActionOutside()`, or `pSceneTouchEvent.isActionUp()`, we destroy the mouse joint in the world by calling the `mPhysicsWorld.destroyJoint()` method with our `mouseJoint` variable as the parameter.

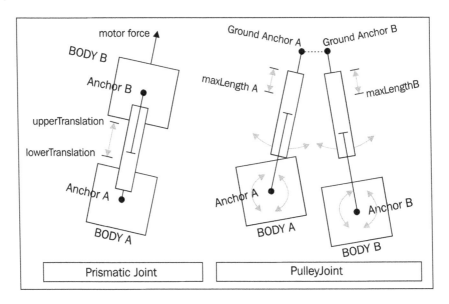

The prismatic joint

The **prismatic joint** allows its connected bodies to slide apart or together on a single axis, powered by a motor if necessary. The bodies have a locked rotation, so we must keep that in mind when designing a simulation that uses a prismatic joint. Consider the preceding diagram to grasp how this joint functions. The following code creates a prismatic joint:

```
final PrismaticJointDef prismaticJointDef =
  new PrismaticJointDef();
prismaticJointDef.initialize(PrismaticJointBodyA,
  PrismaticJointBodyB, PrismaticJointBodyA.getWorldCenter(),
    new Vector2(0f,1f));
prismaticJointDef.collideConnected = false;
prismaticJointDef.enableLimit = true;
```

```
prismaticJointDef.lowerTranslation = -80f /
   PhysicsConstants.PIXEL_TO_METER_RATIO_DEFAULT;
prismaticJointDef.upperTranslation = 80f /
   PhysicsConstants.PIXEL_TO_METER_RATIO_DEFAULT;
prismaticJointDef.enableMotor = true;
prismaticJointDef.maxMotorForce = 400f;
prismaticJointDef.motorSpeed = 500f;
mPhysicsWorld.createJoint(prismaticJointDef);
```

After defining our `prismaticJointDef` variable, we initialize it using the
`prismaticJointDef.initialize()` method and passing to it our connected bodies,
`PrismaticJointBodyA` and `PrismaticJointBodyB`, the anchor point, which we
declare to be the center of `PrismaticJointBodyA` in world coordinates, and the unit
vector world axis of the joint in terms of a `Vector2` object, `Vector2(0f,1f)`. We disable
collision between the bodies by setting the `prismaticJointDef.collideConnected`
variable to `false` and then enable limits for the range of sliding of the joint by setting the
`prismaticJointDef.enableLimit` variable to `true`.

To set the limits of the joint, we set the `lowerTranslation` and `upperTranslation`
properties to `-80f` and `80f` pixels, respectively, divided by `PhysicsConstants.PIXEL_
TO_METER_RATIO_DEFAULT` to convert the pixel limits to meters in the physics world. Finally,
we enable the motor by setting the `prismaticJointDef.enableMotor` property to `true`,
set its max force to `400f` via the `prismaticJointDef.maxMotorForce` property, and set
its speed to a positive `500f` via the `prismaticJointDef.motorSpeed` property to drive
`PrismaticJointBodyB` toward the upper-limit of the joint.

The pulley joint

The **pulley joint** acts much like a realistic pulley—when one side descends, the other ascends.
The length of the pulley joint is determined at initialization and should not be changed after
creation. Refer to the preceding diagram to see what a pulley joint looks like. The following
code creates a pulley joint:

```
final PulleyJointDef pulleyJointDef = new PulleyJointDef();
pulleyJointDef.initialize(
    PulleyJointBodyA,
    PulleyJointBodyB,
    PulleyJointBodyA.getWorldPoint(
      new Vector2(0f, 2.5f)),
    PulleyJointBodyB.getWorldPoint(
      new Vector2(0f, 2.5f)),
    PulleyJointBodyA.getWorldCenter(),
    PulleyJointBodyB.getWorldCenter(),
    1f);
mPhysicsWorld.createJoint(pulleyJointDef);
```

After creating the `pulleyJointDef` variable, we initialize it via the `pulleyJointDef.initialize()` method. The first two parameters of the `pulleyJointDef.initialize()` method are the two connected bodies, `PulleyJointBodyA` and `PulleyJointBodyB`. The next two parameters are the ground anchors for the pulley, which in this case are `2.5f` meters above each body. To get the relative point above each body in world coordinates, we use the `getWorldPoint()` method of each of the bodies with an x parameter of `0` and a y parameter of `2.5` meters above each body. The fifth and sixth parameters of the `pulleyJointDef.initialize()` method are the anchor points of each body in world coordinates. We use the center in this simulation, so we pass the `getWorldCenter()` method of each of the connected bodies.

The final parameter of the method is the ratio of the pulley, `1f` in this case. A ratio of `2` would cause `PulleyJointBodyA` to move twice the distance from its ground anchor for every distance change of `PulleyJointBodyB` from its ground anchor. Furthermore, because the work required by `PulleyJointBodyA` to move in relation to its ground anchor would be half of the work that `PulleyJointBodyB` would take to move, `PulleyJointBodyA` would have more leverage than `PulleyJointBodyB`, causing `PulleyJointBodyA` to be more easily affected by gravity and thus acting to lift `PulleyJointBodyB` in a normal simulation. The last step in creating a pulley joint is to call the `mPhysicsWorld.createJoint()` method by passing to it our `pulleyJointDef` variable.

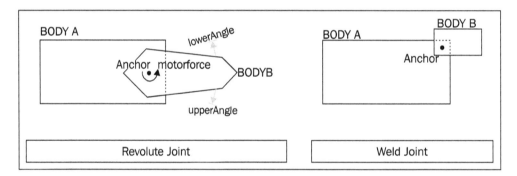

The revolute joint

The **revolute joint** is the most popular joint in Box2D simulations. It is essentially a pivot point between its two connected bodies with an optional motor and limits. See the previous diagram to help clarify how the revolute joint functions. The following code creates a revolute joint:

```
final RevoluteJointDef revoluteJointDef = new RevoluteJointDef();
revoluteJointDef.initialize(
    RevoluteJointBodyA,
```

```
    RevoluteJointBodyB,
    RevoluteJointBodyA.getWorldCenter());
revoluteJointDef.enableMotor = true;
revoluteJointDef.maxMotorTorque = 5000f;
revoluteJointDef.motorSpeed = -1f;
mPhysicsWorld.createJoint(revoluteJointDef);
```

We first define the `revoluteJointDef` definition as a new `RevoluteJointDef()` method. Then, we initialize it using the `revoluteJointDef.initialize()` method with the parameters of `RevoluteJointBodyA` and `RevoluteJointBodyB` to connect the bodies and the `getWorldCenter()` method of `RevoluteJointBodyA` to define where the joint will rotate. Then, we enable our revolute joint's motor by setting the `revoluteJointDef.enableMotor` property to `true`. Next, we set the `maxMotorTorque` property to `5000f` to make the motor very strong and the `motorSpeed` property to `-1f` to make the motor spin clockwise at a very slow rate. Finally, we create the revolute joint in the physics world by calling `mPhysicsWorld.createJoint(revoluteJointDef)` to make the physics world create a revolute joint using our `revoluteJointDef` variable.

The weld joint

The **weld joint** bonds two bodies together and disables rotation between them. It is a useful joint for destructible objects, but larger destructible objects will occasionally fail due to jittering from Box2D's iterative position solver. In such a case, we would create the object from multiple fixtures, and recreate each piece of the object, when detached, in the form of a new body. Refer to the previous diagram of the weld joint to better understand how it works. The following code creates a weld joint:

```
final WeldJointDef weldJointDef = new WeldJointDef();
weldJointDef.initialize(WeldJointBodyA, WeldJointBodyB,
    WeldJointBodyA.getWorldCenter());
mPhysicsWorld.createJoint(weldJointDef);
```

To create our weld joint, we first create a `WeldJointDef` definition named `weldJointDef`. Then, we initialize it by calling the `weldJointDef.initialize()` method with the body parameters of `WeldJointBodyA` and `WeldJointBodyB` to connect our bodies and the anchor point of the joint at the center of `WeldJointBodyA` body in world coordinates. The anchor point of a weld joint may seem like it could be placed anywhere, but because of how Box2D handles the anchor of weld joints during collision, we want to put it at the center location of one of the connected bodies. Doing otherwise can cause shearing or displacement of the joint when colliding with a body that has a large mass.

See also

▶ *Introduction to the Box2D physics extension* in this chapter.

▶ *Understanding different body types* in this chapter.

Creating a rag doll

One of the most popular depictions of characters in physics simulations is the rag doll. The visual look of such characters differs according to detail, but the underlying system is always the same—we just attach several physics bodies to a larger physics body via joints. In this recipe, we will create a rag doll.

Getting ready...

Review the creation of a physics-based activity in the *Introduction to the Box2D physics extension* recipe, the creation of bodies in the *Understanding different body types* recipe, and the use of revolute joints and mouse joints in the *Working with joints* recipe, all found in this chapter.

How to do it...

Refer to the supplemental `RagdollActivity` class for the code that we use in this recipe.

How it works...

The first step is to define the variables that represent the multiple bodies that make up our rag doll. Our bodies are the `headBody`, which represents the head, the `torsoBody`, which represents the torso, the `leftUpperarmBody` and `leftForearmBody`, representing the left arm, the `rightUpperarmBody` and `rightForearmBody`, representing the right arm, the `leftThighBody` and `leftCalfBody`, which represent the left leg, and finally the `rightThighBody` and `rightCalfBody`, which represent the right leg. The following diagram shows how all of our bodies will be linked together using revolute joints:

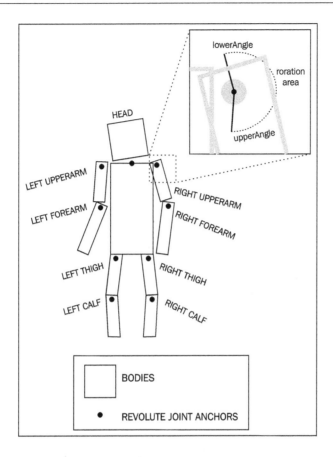

Next, we define the necessary variables used by our mouse joint to throw the rag doll when the screen is touched, the `Vector2 localMouseJointTarget` target for the mouse joint, the `mouseJointDef` mouse joint definition, the `mouseJoint` joint, and the ground body for the mouse joint, `MouseJointGround`. We then create the fixture definitions that we will apply to the various parts of our ragdoll—`headFixtureDef` for the head, `torsoFixtureDef` for the torso, `armsFixtureDef` for the arms, and `legsFixtureDef` for the legs. For more information on creating fixture definitions, refer to the *Introduction to the Box2D physics extension* recipe in this chapter.

Then, in the `onPopulateScene()` method, we create individual rectangles and their linked bodies, which are defined in the activity, for each body part of the rag doll. Each rectangle matches the exact location and size in which its corresponding body part is located As we create the bodies to be linked to the rectangles, we assign the appropriate fixture definition defined in the activity via the final parameter of the `PhysicsFactory.createBoxBody()` method. Finally, for each rectangle body group, we register a `PhysicsConnector` object with the physics world. For more information on creating bodies and `PhysicsConnector` objects, refer to the *Understanding different body types* recipe in this chapter.

Next, we create the many revolute joints that connect the body parts of our rag doll. The locations of the anchor points of each joint are where we want that body part to rotate, in world coordinates, passed via the final parameter of the `initialize()` method of each of the joint definitions. We make sure that each joint's connected bodies do not collide by setting the joint's `collideConnected` property to `false`. This does not keep the bodies from colliding with other portions of the rag doll, but it does allow the joint's bodies to overlap when rotating. Next, notice that we apply limits to the joint definitions to keep the body parts from moving beyond a set range of motion, much like the limits that humans have when moving their limbs. Not setting limits for the joints would create a rag doll that would allow complete rotation of its limbs, which is an unrealistic representation but necessary for some simulations. For more information on revolute joints, refer to the *Working with joints* recipe in this chapter.

After creating the revolute joints that represent the joints of our rag doll, we create the `mouseJointDef` mouse joint definition that will allow us to fling the rag doll around the scene. We attach the `headBody` body of our rag doll as the mouse joint's second body, but any of the bodies attached to the rag doll could be used depending on the simulation. Our final step in creating our rag doll is to set up the mouse joint for use at runtime via touch interactions passed by the `onSceneTouchEvent()` method of our activity. For more information on using mouse joints, refer to the *Working with joints* recipe in this chapter.

See also

- *Introduction to the Box2D physics extension* in this chapter.
- *Understanding different body types* in this chapter.
- *Working with joints* in this chapter.

Creating a rope

Though it is performance-intensive to simulate a realistic rope using Box2D, a simple rope is not only fast, but also very customizable. A rope, from a construction standpoint, is similar to a rag doll and can add an extra layer of playability to a game. If a physics simulation seems to be too bland to attract players, the addition of rope will be sure to give players another reason to like a game. In this recipe, we will create a physics-enabled rope for use in our simulations.

Getting ready...

Review the creation of a physics-based activity in the *Introduction to the Box2D physics extension* recipe, the creation of bodies in the *Understanding different body types* recipe, and the use of revolute joints and mouse joints in the *Working with joints* recipe, all found in this chapter.

How to do it...

Refer to the supplemental `Rope` and `RopeActivity` classes for the code that we use in this recipe.

How it works...

A rope created in Box2D can be thought of as a chain of similar bodies linked together by joints. We can use either rectangular or circular bodies to define each section of a rope, but circular bodies will have less chance of catching onto and stretching from collision with other bodies. See the following diagram to get an idea of how we design a rope for a physics simulation:

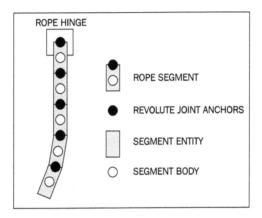

First, refer to the `Rope` class, which will make it easier for us to create multiple ropes and fine-tune all of the ropes at once for our simulation. The initial code in the `Rope` class is a set of variables that reflect the specific properties of each rope. The `numRopeSegments` variable holds the number of segments that our rope will have. The `ropeSegmentsLength` and `ropeSegmentsWidth` variables hold the length and width that each segment of rope will have. Next, the `ropeSegmentsOverlap` variable represents how much each rope segment will overlap the previous rope segment, which prevents gaps during slight stretches. The `RopeSegments` array and `RopeSegmentsBodies` array define the rectangles and bodies for each segment of our rope. Finally, the `RopeSegmentFixtureDef` fixture definition will hold the fixture data that we will apply to each segment of the rope.

Next, we create a constructor, named `Rope`, to handle the placement, detail, length, width, weight, and general creation of the rope. Then, we assign values to the variables created in the previous step. Notice that the `RopeSegmentFixtureDef` fixture definition starts with the maximum density. As each segment of the rope is created via the `for` loop later in the constructor, the density, and thus mass, of the fixture decrements to the minimum density. This prevents stretching by giving the highest body segments the most strength to hold the lower body segments.

At the beginning of the `Rope` constructor's `for` loop, we define the revolute joint for each rope segment. For more information on revolute joints, see the *Working with joints* recipe in this chapter. Then, we create the rectangle, `RopeSegments[i]`, that will represent the segment, checking to make sure that the first segment, when `i` is less than `1`, is placed according to the `pAttachTo` hinge passed in the constructor while the remaining segments are placed relative to their previous segment, `RopeSegments[i-1]`. The creation of the rectangles includes an overlap value, `ropeSegmentsOverlap`, to remove spacing in the rope caused by the iterative process of Box2D.

After we have created the segment's rectangle and set its color to brown by calling `RopeSegments[i].setColor(0.97f, 0.75f, 0.54f)`, we apply the density calculation to the `RopeSegmentFixtureDef` fixture definition and create a circular body based on the segment's rectangle using the `PhysicsFactory.createCircleBody()` method. For more information on creating bodies, refer to the *Understanding different body types* recipe in this chapter. We then set a moderate angular damping of each rope segment body via the `setAngularDamping(4f)` method and a slight linear damping via the `setLinearDamping(0.5f)` method to remove unpredictability in the rope's behavior.

After that, we enable the rope segment to act as a bullet by setting the `RopeSegmentsBodies[i].setBullet` property to `true`, which reduces the chances of our segments slipping through colliding bodies. Finally, we create the revolute joint for the current rope segment in relation to the previous segment, or the hinge if the current segment is the first in the rope. For more information on revolute joints, refer to the *Working with joints* recipe in this chapter.

For our activity class, we first create the variables necessary for our mouse joint, which will move the rope's hinge body to the touched location, and define our `RopeHingeBody` body that will act as the anchor point of the rope. Then, in the `onPopulateScene()` method, we create our `RopeHingeBody` body and, subsequently, our `rope` object, passing the rope-hinge body as the first parameter to the `Rope` constructor. For more information on creating bodies, refer to the *Understanding different body types* recipe in this chapter. The next parameters of the `Rope` constructor tell our rope to be `10` segments long, make each segment `25f` pixels long and `10f` pixels wide with an overlap of `2f` pixels, have a minimum density of `5f` and a maximum density of `50f`, and our `mScene` scene to which we attach the rope segment rectangles. The final two parameters of the `Rope` constructor tell the rope to create the segment bodies in our `mPhysicsWorld` physics world and to set each segment's rectangle to be managed by the activity's `VertexBufferObjectManager` class.

Next, we define and set up the variables used for our mouse joint. Take note that we set the `RopeHingeBody` body as the mouse joint's second body. Finally, we set up the `onSceneTouchEvent()` method to handle our mouse joint. For more information on mouse joints, refer to the *Working with joints* recipe in this chapter.

See also

▸ *Introduction to the Box2D physics extension* in this chapter.

▸ *Understanding different body types* in this chapter.

▸ *Working with joints* in this chapter.

Working with collisions

Causing an effect to occur from the collisions between bodies, whether it is the playing of sound or the disposal of a body, is often a necessary part of a game based on a physics simulation. Handling collisions seems like an intimidating task at first, but it will become second nature after we learn how each part of the `ContactListener` interface functions. In this recipe, we will demonstrate how to handle collisions between fixtures.

Getting ready...

Follow the steps in the *Introduction to the Box2D physics extension* section at the beginning of the chapter to create a new activity that will facilitate the creation of our simulation in which we will control collision behavior.

How to do it...

Follow these steps to demonstrate our control of collisions:

1. Place the following definitions at the beginning of the activity class:

```
public Rectangle dynamicRect;
public Rectangle staticRect;
public Body dynamicBody;
public Body staticBody;
public boolean setFullAlphaForDynamicBody = false;
public boolean setHalfAlphaForDynamicBody = false;
public boolean setFullAlphaForStaticBody = false;
public boolean setHalfAlphaForStaticBody = false;
final FixtureDef boxFixtureDef = PhysicsFactory.
createFixtureDef(2f,
  0f, 0.9f);
```

2. To determine whether a specific body is contacted in the `ContactListener` interface, insert the following method in the activity:

```
public boolean isBodyContacted(Body pBody, Contact pContact)
{
  if(pContact.getFixtureA().getBody().equals(pBody) ||
    pContact.getFixtureB().getBody().equals(pBody))
    return true;
  return false;
}
```

3. The following method is similar to the previous method, but tests another body in addition to the first. Add it to the class after the previous method:

```
public boolean areBodiesContacted(Body pBody1, Body pBody2,
Contact pContact)
{
  if(pContact.getFixtureA().getBody().equals(pBody1) ||
      pContact.getFixtureB().getBody().equals(pBody1))
    if(pContact.getFixtureA().getBody().equals(pBody2) ||
      pContact.getFixtureB().getBody().equals(pBody2))
      return true;
  return false;
}
```

4. Next, we are going to create a dynamic body and a static body to test collisions. Place the following in the `onPopulateScene()` method:

```
dynamicRect = new Rectangle(300f, 240f, 100f, 100f,
  this.getEngine().getVertexBufferObjectManager());
dynamicRect.setColor(0f, 0.7f, 0f);
dynamicRect.setAlpha(0.5f);
mScene.attachChild(dynamicRect);
dynamicBody = PhysicsFactory.createBoxBody(mPhysicsWorld,
  dynamicRect, BodyType.DynamicBody, boxFixtureDef);
dynamicBody.setLinearDamping(0.4f);
dynamicBody.setAngularDamping(0.6f);
mPhysicsWorld.registerPhysicsConnector(new PhysicsConnector(
  dynamicRect, dynamicBody));

staticRect = new Rectangle(500f, 240f, 100f, 100f,
  this.getEngine().getVertexBufferObjectManager());
staticRect.setColor(0f, 0f, 0.7f);
staticRect.setAlpha(0.5f);
mScene.attachChild(staticRect);
staticBody = PhysicsFactory.createBoxBody(mPhysicsWorld,
staticRect,
  BodyType.StaticBody, boxFixtureDef);
```

5. Now we need to set the `ContactListener` property of the physics world. Add the following to the `onPopulateScene()` method:

```
mPhysicsWorld.setContactListener(new ContactListener(){
  @Override
  public void beginContact(Contact contact) {
    if(contact.isTouching())
    if(areBodiesContacted(staticBody,dynamicBody,contact))
      setFullAlphaForStaticBody = true;
    if(isBodyContacted(dynamicBody,contact))
      setFullAlphaForDynamicBody = true;
  }
  @Override
  public void endContact(Contact contact) {
    if(areBodiesContacted(staticBody,dynamicBody,contact))
      setHalfAlphaForStaticBody = true;
    if(isBodyContacted(dynamicBody,contact))
      setHalfAlphaForDynamicBody = true;
  }
  @Override
  public void preSolve(Contact contact, Manifold oldManifold) {}
  @Override
  public void postSolve(Contact contact, ContactImpulse impulse)
{}
});
```

6. Because the physics world may call the `ContactListener` interface multiple times per contact, we want to move all logic from the `ContactListener` interface to an update handler called once per engine update. Place the following in the `onPopulateScene()` method to complete our activity:

```
mScene.registerUpdateHandler(new IUpdateHandler() {
  @Override
  public void onUpdate(float pSecondsElapsed) {
    if(setFullAlphaForDynamicBody) {
      dynamicRect.setAlpha(1f);
      setFullAlphaForDynamicBody = false;
    } else if(setHalfAlphaForDynamicBody) {
      dynamicRect.setAlpha(0.5f);
      setHalfAlphaForDynamicBody = false;
    }
    if(setFullAlphaForStaticBody) {
      staticRect.setAlpha(1f);
      setFullAlphaForStaticBody = false;
    } else if(setHalfAlphaForStaticBody) {
      staticRect.setAlpha(0.5f);
```

```
        setHalfAlphaForStaticBody = false;
      }
    }
    @Override public void reset() {}
  });
```

How it works...

First, we define the rectangles and bodies that we will be using to visualize collisions. We also define several Boolean variables that will be changed depending on the results of the `ContactListener` interface. The final variable is the fixture definition used to create the collision-enabled bodies.

In steps two and three, we create two convenience methods, `isBodyContacted()` and `areBodiesContacted()`, that will make determining the presence of bodies in the `ContactListener` interface easier. Notice that the `if` statements in each of the methods check both of the fixtures against each body. Because of the way that the contact listener passes the `Contact` object, we cannot be certain which fixture will correlate with a certain body, so we must check both.

Step four creates the rectangles and bodies—one static and one dynamic—used in this simulation. We set the alpha of the rectangles using their `setAlpha()` method with a value of `0.5f` to demonstrate that contact is not currently occurring. The alpha of the rectangles is restored to opaque upon collision and set back to transparent after the collision has ended.

In step five, we set the physics world's contact listener by overriding the inherited methods. The first method, `beginContact()`, is called when a collision has occurred within the physics world. In that method, we first test that the collision actually involves the touching of two bodies by checking the `isTouching()` property of the `contact` parameter. Box2D considers a collision to start whenever the **AABB**, or bounding box, of two bodies overlap, not when the actual bodies touch. Refer to the next diagram to see how collisions and touching differ. After that, we check to see if both, or just one, of our bodies are involved in the collision. If so, we set our full-alpha Boolean variables to `true`. The next method, `endContact()`, is called when bodies are no longer colliding. If our bodies are involved in the collision that is ending, we set the half-alpha Boolean variables to `true`. The remaining methods in the contact listener are called either before or after the collision-correcting calculations have occurred. Because we simply want to test which bodies have collided, we do not need to use those two methods.

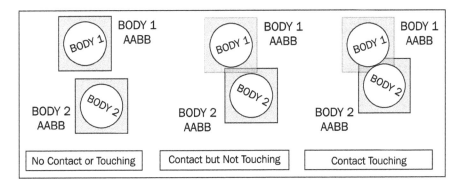

In step six, we create an update handler to remove the effective code from the `ContactListener` interface. It simply checks the Boolean values set within the `ContactListener` interface to determine which actions need to be taken after every engine update. After the correct actions have been taken, we reset the Boolean variables. The reason that we need to remove effectual code from the contact listener is that the contact listener can, and often is, called multiple times per collision. If we were to change the score of a game from inside the contact listener, the score would often change at a much greater magnitude than we intended. We could have a variable that checks whether a contact has already been handled, but the flow of such code becomes messy and eventually counter productive.

See also

▸ *Introduction to the Box2D physics extension* in this chapter.

▸ *Understanding different body types* in this chapter.

▸ Pre-solve and Post-solve in this chapter.

Using preSolve and postSolve

Making use of the available data for a collision inside the contact listener's `presolve` method, which is called before the Box2D iterator causes a reaction, allows us to have unique control over how our collisions occur. The `preSolve()` method is most commonly used to create "one-way" platforms that a character can jump through from below while still being able to walk on them from above. The `postSolve()` method, which is called after a reaction has been set in motion, gives us the corrective data, also known as the **impact force**, for the collision. This data can then be used to destroy or break apart objects. In this recipe, we will demonstrate how to properly use the `preSolve()` and `postSolve()` methods of a `ContactListener` interface.

Getting ready...

Create a new activity by following the steps in the *Introduction to the Box2D physics extension* section given at the beginning of the chapter. This new activity will facilitate our use of the `preSolve()` and `postSolve()` methods called within the contact listener.

How to do it...

Follow these steps to complete the activity that demonstrates the use of these methods:

1. Place the following definitions at the beginning of the activity:

    ```
    Body dynamicBody;
    Body staticBody;
    FixtureDef boxFixtureDef = PhysicsFactory.createFixtureDef(20f,
    0.5f,
       0.9f);
    Vector2 localMouseJointTarget = new Vector2();
    MouseJointDef mouseJointDef;
    MouseJoint mouseJoint;
    Body groundBody;
    ```

2. To determine which body or bodies are contacted, insert these methods into the class:

    ```
    public boolean isBodyContacted(Body pBody, Contact pContact)
    {
      if(pContact.getFixtureA().getBody().equals(pBody) ||
          pContact.getFixtureB().getBody().equals(pBody))
        return true;
      return false;
    }


    public boolean areBodiesContacted(Body pBody1, Body pBody2,
    Contact pContact)
    {
      if(pContact.getFixtureA().getBody().equals(pBody1) ||
          pContact.getFixtureB().getBody().equals(pBody1))
        if(pContact.getFixtureA().getBody().equals(pBody2) ||
            pContact.getFixtureB().getBody().equals(pBody2))
          return true;
      return false;
    }
    ```

3. We are going to test the collisions between a small, dynamic body and a larger, static body. Place the following code in the `onPopulateScene()` method to create such bodies:

```
Rectangle dynamicRect = new Rectangle(400f, 60f, 40f, 40f,
  this.getEngine().getVertexBufferObjectManager());
dynamicRect.setColor(0f, 0.6f, 0f);
mScene.attachChild(dynamicRect);
dynamicBody = PhysicsFactory.createBoxBody(mPhysicsWorld,
  dynamicRect, BodyType.DynamicBody, boxFixtureDef);
mPhysicsWorld.registerPhysicsConnector(new PhysicsConnector(
  dynamicRect, dynamicBody));

Rectangle staticRect = new Rectangle(400f, 240f, 200f, 10f,
  this.getEngine().getVertexBufferObjectManager());
staticRect.setColor(0f, 0f, 0f);
mScene.attachChild(staticRect);
staticBody = PhysicsFactory.createBoxBody(mPhysicsWorld,
staticRect,
  BodyType.StaticBody, boxFixtureDef);
mPhysicsWorld.registerPhysicsConnector(new PhysicsConnector(
  staticRect, staticBody));
```

4. Next, we need to set the contact listener for our physics world. Insert the following into the `onPopulateScene()` method:

```
mPhysicsWorld.setContactListener(new ContactListener(){
  float maxImpulse;
  @Override
  public void beginContact(Contact contact) {}

  @Override
  public void endContact(Contact contact) {}

  @Override
  public void preSolve(Contact contact, Manifold oldManifold) {
    if(areBodiesContacted(dynamicBody, staticBody, contact))
      if(dynamicBody.getWorldCenter().y <
          staticBody.getWorldCenter().y)
        contact.setEnabled(false);
  }

  @Override
  public void postSolve(Contact contact, ContactImpulse impulse) {
    if(areBodiesContacted(dynamicBody, staticBody, contact)) {
      maxImpulse = impulse.getNormalImpulses()[0];
```

```
        for(int i = 1; i <
            impulse.getNormalImpulses().length;
            i++)
          maxImpulse = Math.max(
            impulse.getNormalImpulses()[i],
            maxImpulse);
        if(maxImpulse>400f)
          dynamicBody.setAngularVelocity(30f);
      }
    }
  }
});
```

5. We want to be able to move the smaller body by touching where we want it to move to. Add the following code to set up a mouse joint which will allow us to do so:

```
groundBody = mPhysicsWorld.createBody(new BodyDef());
mouseJointDef = new MouseJointDef();
mouseJointDef.bodyA = groundBody;
mouseJointDef.bodyB = dynamicBody;
mouseJointDef.dampingRatio = 0.5f;
mouseJointDef.frequencyHz = 1f;
mouseJointDef.maxForce = (40.0f * dynamicBody.getMass());
mouseJointDef.collideConnected = false;
```

6. Finally, insert the following in the `onSceneTouchEvent()` method to control the mouse joint created in the previous step:

```
if(pSceneTouchEvent.isActionDown()) {
  mouseJointDef.target.set(dynamicBody.getWorldCenter());
  mouseJoint = (MouseJoint)mPhysicsWorld.
createJoint(mouseJointDef);
  final Vector2 vec = Vector2Pool.obtain(pSceneTouchEvent.getX() /
    PhysicsConstants.PIXEL_TO_METER_RATIO_DEFAULT,
      pSceneTouchEvent.getY() /
      PhysicsConstants.PIXEL_TO_METER_RATIO_DEFAULT);
  mouseJoint.setTarget(vec);
  Vector2Pool.recycle(vec);
} else if(pSceneTouchEvent.isActionMove()) {
  final Vector2 vec = Vector2Pool.obtain(pSceneTouchEvent.getX() /
    PhysicsConstants.PIXEL_TO_METER_RATIO_DEFAULT,
      pSceneTouchEvent.getY() /
      PhysicsConstants.PIXEL_TO_METER_RATIO_DEFAULT);
  mouseJoint.setTarget(vec);
  Vector2Pool.recycle(vec);
  return true;
```

```
    } else if(pSceneTouchEvent.isActionCancel() ||
        pSceneTouchEvent.isActionOutside() ||
        pSceneTouchEvent.isActionUp()) {
      mPhysicsWorld.destroyJoint(mouseJoint);
    }
```

How it works...

We first define a static body, a dynamic body, and a fixture definition that will be used to create the two bodies. Then, we create two methods that make managing collisions using the contact listener much easier. Next, we create the bodies using their associated rectangles.

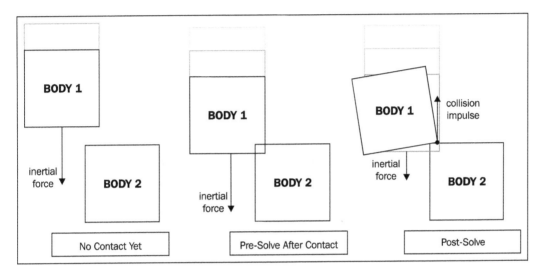

In step four, we set the physics world's contact listener. Notice that we create a variable, `maxImpulse`, at the beginning of the contact listener for use in the `postSolve()` method at the end of the contact listener. For this simulation we have no use for the `beginContact()` and `endContact()` methods so we leave them empty. In the `preSolve()` method, we first test to determine if the contact is between our two bodies, `dynamicBody` and `staticBody`. If it is, we test if the `dynamicBody` body is below our `staticBody` body by checking if the `dynamicBody.getWorldCenter().y` property is less than the `staticBody.getWorldCenter().y` property, and if so, we cancel the collision. This allows the dynamic body to pass through the static body from below while still colliding with the static body from above.

In the `postSolve()` method, we test to ensure that we are only handling the dynamic and static bodies that we had defined previously. If so, we set the `maxImpulse` variable to the first impulse in the `impulse.getNormalImpulses()` array. This list holds the corrective impulses of all contacted points between the two colliding fixtures. Next, we step through the list of impulses and set the `maxImpulse` variable to either the current `maxImpulse` value or the current impulse value from the list, whichever is greater. This gives us the greatest corrective impulse in the collision, which we then use to spin the dynamic body if the impulsive force is great enough, an impulse of `400f` in this simulation.

Step five initializes the mouse joint for dragging our dynamic body around the screen, and step six controls the mouse joint using the `onSceneTouchEvent()` method. Refer to *Working with joints* for more information on the mouse joint.

See also

- ▸ *Introduction to the Box2D physics extension* in this chapter.
- ▸ *Understanding different body types* in this chapter.
- ▸ *Working with joints* in this chapter.
- ▸ *Working with collisions* in this chapter.

Creating destructible objects

Using the impulse data from the `postSolve()` method in the physics world's contact listener gives us a force of impact for each collision. Extending that data to cause a multiple-body object to break apart simply involves determining which body collided and if the force was great enough to break the body from the multiple-body object. In this recipe, we will demonstrate the creation of a destructible object made from bodies.

Getting ready...

Create an activity by following the steps in the *Introduction to the Box2D physics extension* section at the beginning of the chapter. This activity will facilitate the creation of the destructible body groups that we will use in this section.

How to do it...

Follow these steps to create a destructible object that breaks apart when it collides with a large force:

1. Add the following definitions to the activity class:

```
public Body box1Body;
public Body box2Body;
```

```
public Body box3Body;
public boolean breakOffBox1 = false;
public boolean breakOffBox2 = false;
public boolean breakOffBox3 = false;
public Joint box1And2Joint;
public Joint box2And3Joint;
public Joint box3And1Joint;
public boolean box1And2JointActive = true;
public boolean box2And3JointActive = true;
public boolean box3And1JointActive = true;
public final FixtureDef boxFixtureDef =
   PhysicsFactory.createFixtureDef(20f, 0.0f, 0.9f);
```

2. To determine which body is contacted easier, insert this method into the class:

```
public boolean isBodyContacted(Body pBody, Contact pContact)
{
  if(pContact.getFixtureA().getBody().equals(pBody) ||
      pContact.getFixtureB().getBody().equals(pBody))
    return true;
  return false;
}
```

3. We are going to create a physics object comprised of three boxes that are held together by weld joints. Define the following boxes in the `onPopulateScene()` method:

```
Rectangle box1Rect = new Rectangle(400f, 260f, 40f, 40f,
   this.getEngine().getVertexBufferObjectManager());
box1Rect.setColor(0.75f, 0f, 0f);
mScene.attachChild(box1Rect);
box1Body = PhysicsFactory.createBoxBody(mPhysicsWorld, box1Rect,
   BodyType.DynamicBody, boxFixtureDef);
mPhysicsWorld.registerPhysicsConnector(new PhysicsConnector(
   box1Rect, box1Body));

Rectangle box2Rect = new Rectangle(380f, 220f, 40f, 40f,
   this.getEngine().getVertexBufferObjectManager());
box2Rect.setColor(0f, 0.75f, 0f);
mScene.attachChild(box2Rect);
box2Body = PhysicsFactory.createBoxBody(mPhysicsWorld, box2Rect,
   BodyType.DynamicBody, boxFixtureDef);
mPhysicsWorld.registerPhysicsConnector(new PhysicsConnector(
   box2Rect, box2Body));
```

```
Rectangle box3Rect = new Rectangle(420f, 220f, 40f, 40f,
  this.getEngine().getVertexBufferObjectManager());
box3Rect.setColor(0f, 0f, 0.75f);
mScene.attachChild(box3Rect);
box3Body = PhysicsFactory.createBoxBody(mPhysicsWorld, box3Rect,
  BodyType.DynamicBody, boxFixtureDef);
mPhysicsWorld.registerPhysicsConnector(new PhysicsConnector(
  box3Rect, box3Body));
```

4. Next, place the following weld joint definitions in the `onPopulateScene()` method after the box definitions defined in the previous step:

```
final WeldJointDef box1and2JointDef = new WeldJointDef();
box1and2JointDef.initialize(box1Body, box2Body,
  box1Body.getWorldCenter());
box1And2Joint = mPhysicsWorld.createJoint(box1and2JointDef);

final WeldJointDef box2and3JointDef = new WeldJointDef();
box2and3JointDef.initialize(box2Body, box3Body,
  box2Body.getWorldCenter());
box2And3Joint = mPhysicsWorld.createJoint(box2and3JointDef);

final WeldJointDef box3and1JointDef = new WeldJointDef();
box3and1JointDef.initialize(box3Body, box1Body,
  box3Body.getWorldCenter());
box3And1Joint = mPhysicsWorld.createJoint(box3and1JointDef);
```

5. We now need to set our physics world's contact listener. Add the following code to the `onPopulateScene()` method:

```
mPhysicsWorld.setContactListener(new ContactListener(){
  float maxImpulse;
  @Override
  public void beginContact(Contact contact) {}
  @Override
  public void endContact(Contact contact) {}
  @Override
  public void preSolve(Contact contact, Manifold oldManifold) {}
@Override
  public void postSolve(Contact contact, ContactImpulse impulse) {
    maxImpulse = impulse.getNormalImpulses()[0];
    for(int i = 1; i < impulse.getNormalImpulses().length; i++)
    {
      maxImpulse = Math.max(impulse.getNormalImpulses()[i],
        maxImpulse);
    }
    if(maxImpulse>800f) {
```

```
          if(isBodyContacted(box1Body,contact))
            breakOffBox1 = true;
          else if(isBodyContacted(box2Body,contact))
            breakOffBox2 = true;
          else if(isBodyContacted(box3Body,contact))
            breakOffBox3 = true;
      }
    }
});
```

6. Lastly, to remove the logic from the contact listener, place the following update handler in the onPopulateScene() method:

```
mScene.registerUpdateHandler(new IUpdateHandler() {
  @Override
  public void onUpdate(float pSecondsElapsed) {
    if(breakOffBox1) {
      if(box1And2JointActive)
        mPhysicsWorld.destroyJoint(box1And2Joint);
      if(box3And1JointActive)
        mPhysicsWorld.destroyJoint(box3And1Joint);
      box1And2JointActive = false;
      box3And1JointActive = false;
      breakOffBox1 = false;
    }
    if(breakOffBox2) {
      if(box1And2JointActive)
        mPhysicsWorld.destroyJoint(box1And2Joint);
      if(box2And3JointActive)
        mPhysicsWorld.destroyJoint(box2And3Joint);
      box1And2JointActive = false;
      box2And3JointActive = false;
      breakOffBox1 = false;
    }
    if(breakOffBox3) {
      if(box2And3JointActive)
        mPhysicsWorld.destroyJoint(box2And3Joint);
      if(box3And1JointActive)
        mPhysicsWorld.destroyJoint(box3And1Joint);
      box2And3JointActive = false;
      box3And1JointActive = false;
      breakOffBox1 = false;
    }
  }
  @Override public void reset() {}
});
```

How it works...

Step one initially defines three bodies that we will link together with weld joints. Next, we define three Boolean variables that represent which body, if any, should be released from the group of bodies. Then, we define three weld joints that hold our bodies together and their respective Boolean values that represent whether the joint exists. Finally, we define a fixture definition from which we will create our three box bodies.

Step two creates a method that allows us to determine if a particular body is involved in a collision, as also seen in the *Working with collisions* recipe. Step three creates our bodies, and step four creates the weld joints that attach them. Refer to the *Understanding different body types* recipe for more information about creating bodies, or the *Working with joints* recipe for more information on using joints.

In step five, we set the physics world's contact listener, creating only the `maxImpulse` variable and filling only the `postSolve()` method. In the `postSolve()` method, we determine if the force of the collision impulse is great enough to break the joints connected to a body. If it is, we determine which of the bodies should be broken off from the group and set the associated Boolean value for that body. After the `ContactListener` interface is set, we register an update handler to destroy the appropriate joints according to which bodies are flagged to be broken off. Because each of the three bodies is connected to the other two bodies, there are two joints to destroy for each body in the group. As we destroy the joints, we flag each destroyed joint as inactive so that we do not attempt to destroy an already destroyed joint.

See also

▶ *Introduction to the Box2D physics extension* in this chapter.

▶ *Understanding different body types* in this chapter.

▶ *Working with joints* in this chapter.

▶ *Using preSolve and postSolve* in this chapter.

Raycasting

Raycasting via the physics world is a calculation that shoots an imaginary line from one point to another, and reports back with the distance, each encountered fixture, and the normal vector of each surface hit. Raycasts can be used for anything from lasers and vision cones to determining what an imaginary bullet hit. In this recipe, we will demonstrate raycasting within our physics world.

Getting ready...

Follow the steps in the *Introduction to the Box2D physics extension* section at the beginning of the chapter to create a new activity that will facilitate our use of raycasting in the physics world.

How to do it...

Follow these steps to create a raycasting demonstration:

1. Place the following definitions at the beginning of the activity:

```
Body BoxBody;
Line RayCastLine;
Line RayCastLineHitNormal;
Line RayCastLineHitBounce;
float[] RayCastStart = {cameraWidth/2f,15f};
float RayCastAngle = 0f;
float RayCastNormalAngle = 0f;
float RayCastBounceAngle = 0f;
float RaycastBounceLineLength = 200f;
final FixtureDef boxFixtureDef =
  PhysicsFactory.createFixtureDef(1f, 0.5f, 0.9f);
```

2. When we tell the physics world to perform a raycast, it will use a provided `callback` interface to allow us to make use of the information gathered by the raycast. Place the following `RayCastCallback` definition in the activity:

```
RayCastCallback rayCastCallBack = new RayCastCallback() {
  @Override
  public float reportRayFixture(Fixture fixture, Vector2 point,
    Vector2 normal, float fraction)
  {
    float[] linePos = {
      point.x *
      PhysicsConstants.PIXEL_TO_METER_RATIO_DEFAULT,
      point.y *
      PhysicsConstants.PIXEL_TO_METER_RATIO_DEFAULT,
      (point.x + (normal.x)) *
      PhysicsConstants.PIXEL_TO_METER_RATIO_DEFAULT,
      (point.y + (normal.y)) *
      PhysicsConstants.PIXEL_TO_METER_RATIO_DEFAULT};
  RayCastLineHitNormal.setPosition(
    linePos[0],linePos[1],
    linePos[2],linePos[3]);
  RayCastLineHitNormal.setVisible(true);
```

```
        RayCastNormalAngle = MathUtils.radToDeg(
          (float) Math.atan2(
            linePos[3]-linePos[1],
            linePos[2]-linePos[0]));
        RayCastBounceAngle = (2*RayCastNormalAngle)-RayCastAngle;
        RayCastLineHitBounce.setPosition(
          linePos[0], linePos[1],
          (linePos[0] + FloatMath.cos((RayCastBounceAngle + 180f) *
            MathConstants.DEG_TO_RAD) * RaycastBounceLineLength),
          (linePos[1] + FloatMath.sin((RayCastBounceAngle + 180f) *
            MathConstants.DEG_TO_RAD)*RaycastBounceLineLength));
        RayCastLineHitBounce.setVisible(true);
        return 0f;
        }
    };
```

3. To give our raycast something to impact, we will create a box in the physics world. Insert the following code snippet in the `onPopulateScene()` method:

```
Rectangle Box1 = new Rectangle(400f, 350f, 200f, 200f,
  this.getEngine().getVertexBufferObjectManager());
Box1.setColor(0.3f, 0.3f, 0.3f);
BoxBody = PhysicsFactory.createBoxBody(mPhysicsWorld, Box1,
  BodyType.StaticBody, boxFixtureDef);
BoxBody.setTransform(BoxBody.getWorldCenter(), MathUtils.
random(0.349f, 1.222f));
mScene.attachChild(Box1);
mPhysicsWorld.registerPhysicsConnector(
  new PhysicsConnector(Box1, BoxBody));
```

4. Next, we will define the `Line` object that represents some of the information gathered from the raycast. Add the following to the `onPopulateScne()` method:

```
RayCastLine = new Line(0f, 0f, 0f, 0f,
  mEngine.getVertexBufferObjectManager());
RayCastLine.setColor(0f, 1f, 0f);
RayCastLine.setLineWidth(8f);
mScene.attachChild(RayCastLine);

RayCastLineHitNormal = new Line(0f, 0f, 0f, 0f,
  mEngine.getVertexBufferObjectManager());
RayCastLineHitNormal.setColor(1f, 0f, 0f);
RayCastLineHitNormal.setLineWidth(8f);
mScene.attachChild(RayCastLineHitNormal);

RayCastLineHitBounce = new Line(0f, 0f, 0f, 0f,
```

```
    mEngine.getVertexBufferObjectManager());
RayCastLineHitBounce.setColor(0f, 0f, 1f);
RayCastLineHitBounce.setLineWidth(8f);
mScene.attachChild(RayCastLineHitBounce);
```

5. Lastly, we want the raycast to occur wherever we touch the scene. Place the following in the `onSceneTouchEvent()` method:

```
if(pSceneTouchEvent.isActionMove()||pSceneTouchEvent.
isActionDown()){
  RayCastAngle = MathUtils.radToDeg((float)
    Math.atan2(pSceneTouchEvent.getY() - RayCastStart[1],
      pSceneTouchEvent.getX() - RayCastStart[0]));
  RayCastLine.setPosition(
    RayCastStart[0], RayCastStart[1],
    pSceneTouchEvent.getX(), pSceneTouchEvent.getY());
  RayCastLine.setVisible(true);
  RayCastLineHitNormal.setVisible(false);
  RayCastLineHitBounce.setVisible(false);
  mPhysicsWorld.rayCast(rayCastCallBack,
    new Vector2(
      RayCastStart[0] /
      PhysicsConstants.PIXEL_TO_METER_RATIO_DEFAULT,
      RayCastStart[1] /
      PhysicsConstants.PIXEL_TO_METER_RATIO_DEFAULT),
    new Vector2(
      pSceneTouchEvent.getX() /
      PhysicsConstants.PIXEL_TO_METER_RATIO_DEFAULT,
      pSceneTouchEvent.getY() /
      PhysicsConstants.PIXEL_TO_METER_RATIO_DEFAULT));
}
if(pSceneTouchEvent.isActionUp() ||
  pSceneTouchEvent.isActionOutside() ||
  pSceneTouchEvent.isActionCancel())
{
  RayCastLine.setVisible(false);
}
```

How it works...

We first define a body, `BoxBody`, against which we will use the raycast. Then, we define several lines that will visually represent the raycast. Lastly, we define a series of variables that help us to determine the positioning and results of the raycast.

In step two, we define a `RayCastCallback` interface, which we will pass to the physics world whenever we request it to calculate a raycast. In the callback, we use the overridden `reportRayFixture()` method. This method is called every time that a requested raycast encounters a new fixture. In the method, we use the raycast-returned point and normal variables to modify the position of our line that represents the normal line of the reported fixture's hit surface. After setting the normal line to be visible, we determine the normal angle and then the bounce angle. We then position the bounce line to represent the bounce of the raycast and set the bounce line to be visible. Finally, we return `0` for the method to tell the raycast to terminate after hitting the first fixture. For a better understanding of the various parameters returned in a raycast callback, consider the following diagram:

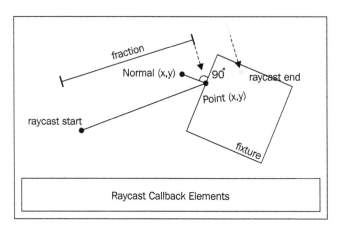

Raycast Callback Elements

Step three creates the body defined in step one and sets it to have a semi-random rotation by calling the `BoxBody.setTransform()` method with the last parameter of `MathUtils.random(0.349f, 1.222f)`, which orients the body to a rotation between `0.349` radians and `1.222` radians. Step four creates the visual lines that represent the various parts of the raycast. For more information on creating bodies, see the *Understanding different body types* recipe in this chapter, and for more information on lines, see *Chapter 2, Working with Entities*.

In step five, we assign the `onSceneTouchEvent()` method to handle our raycasting. When a touch occurs, we first set the `RayCastAngle` variable for use in the raycast's callback. Then, we position the main raycast line and set it to be visible while also setting the other lines associated with the raycast to be invisible. Lastly, we request a raycast from the physics world by passing our callback, the start position of the raycast, and the end position of the raycast. When the touch event has ended, we set the main raycast line to be invisible.

See also

▸   *Introduction to the Box2D physics extension* in this chapter.

7
Working with Update Handlers

Update handlers give us a way to run specific portions of code every time that the engine updates. Some game engines have one built in as a main loop, but with AndEngine we can create as many of these loops as necessary with ease. This chapter will cover the following recipes:

- ▶ Getting started with update handlers
- ▶ Attaching an update handler to an entity
- ▶ Using update handlers with conditionals
- ▶ Handling the removal of an entity from the game
- ▶ Adding game timers
- ▶ Setting entity properties based on the time passed

Getting started with update handlers

Update handlers are essentially portions of code that we register with either entities or the engine, that are run whenever the engine updates the scene. In most situations, this updating occurs every time a frame is drawn, regardless of whether entities or the scene have been altered. Update handlers can be a powerful means of running a game, but overusing them or performing heavy calculations in them will lead to poor performance. This recipe will cover the basics of adding a simple update handler to an activity.

Create a new class named `UpdateHandlersActivity` that extends `BaseGameActivity`. We will use this class to create a basic update handler.

Follow these steps to create an update handler that displays how many updates have occurred:

1. Place the following definitions within our `UpdateHandlersActivity` class:

```
public static int cameraWidth = 800;
public static int cameraHeight = 480;
public Scene mScene;public Font fontDefault32Bold;
public Text countingText;
public int countingInt = 0;
```

2. Next, add the following overridden methods to the class.

```
@Override
public EngineOptions onCreateEngineOptions() {
  return new EngineOptions(true,
    ScreenOrientation.LANDSCAPE_SENSOR,
    new FillResolutionPolicy(), new Camera(0, 0,
    cameraWidth, cameraHeight)).setWakeLockOptions(
    WakeLockOptions.SCREEN_ON);
}
@Override
public void onCreateResources(OnCreateResourcesCallback
    pOnCreateResourcesCallback) {
  fontDefault32Bold = FontFactory.create(
    mEngine.getFontManager(),
    mEngine.getTextureManager(), 256, 256,
    Typeface.create(Typeface.DEFAULT, Typeface.BOLD),
    32f, true, Color.BLACK_ARGB_PACKED_INT);
  fontDefault32Bold.load();
  pOnCreateResourcesCallback.onCreateResourcesFinished();
}
@Override
public void onCreateScene(OnCreateSceneCallback
    pOnCreateSceneCallback) {
  mScene = new Scene();
  mScene.setBackground(new Background(0.9f,0.9f,0.9f));
  pOnCreateSceneCallback.onCreateSceneFinished(mScene);
}
```

3. Finally, insert this last method into our class:

```
@Override
public void onPopulateScene(Scene pScene,
    OnPopulateSceneCallback pOnPopulateSceneCallback) {
  countingText = new Text(400f, 240f,
    fontDefault32Bold, "0", 10,
    this.getVertexBufferObjectManager());
  mScene.attachChild(countingText);
  mScene.registerUpdateHandler(new IUpdateHandler() {
    @Override
    public void onUpdate(float pSecondsElapsed) {
      countingInt++;
      countingText.setText(
        String.valueOf(countingInt));
    }
    @Override public void reset() {}
  });
  pOnPopulateSceneCallback.onPopulateSceneFinished();
}
```

How it works...

The first and the second step cover the creation of a simple `BaseGameActivity` class. For more information on creating a `BaseGameActivity` class, see the *Know the life cycle* recipe in *Chapter 1, AndEngine Game Structure*. Notice, however, that we create and load a `Font` object in the `onCreateResources()` method. For more information on fonts and the `Text` entities that use them, see the *Applying text to a layer* recipe in *Chapter 2, Working with Entities*.

In step three, we create a `Text` entity, `countingText`, by passing the `fontDefault32Bold` font, created in the `onCreateResources()` method of the activity, to the `Text` constructor, with location parameters to center it on the screen and a maximum string length parameter of `10` characters. After attaching the `countingText` entity to the scene, we register our update handler. In the `onUpdate()` method of our update handler, we increment the `countingInt` integer and set the `countingText` entity's text to the integer. This gives us a direct textual display in our game of how many updates have occurred, and thus how many frames have been drawn.

See also

▶ *Know the life cycle* in *Chapter 1, AndEngine Game Structure*.

▶ *Applying text to a layer* in *Chapter 2, Working with Entities*.

Attaching an update handler to an entity

In addition to being able to register an update handler with a `Scene` object, we can register update handlers with specific entities. By registering an update handler with an entity, the handler is only called whenever the entity is attached to the engine's scene. This recipe demonstrates this process by creating an update handler, which is registered with an initially unattached entity, that increments the onscreen text.

Getting ready...

Create a new class named `AttachUpdateHandlerToEntityActivity` that extends `BaseGameActivity` and implements `IOnSceneTouchListener`. We will use this class to attach an update handler to an `Entity` object that will wait to be attached to the scene until the scene is touched.

How to do it...

Follow these steps to create an activity that demonstrates how update handlers depend on their parent entity to run:

1. Insert the following definitions into our new activity class:

```
public static int cameraWidth = 800;
public static int cameraHeight = 480;
public Scene mScene;
public Font fontDefault32Bold;
public Text countingText;
public int countingInt = 0;
public Entity blankEntity;
```

2. Then, place the following overridden methods within the class:

```
@Override
public EngineOptions onCreateEngineOptions() {
  return new EngineOptions(true,
    ScreenOrientation.LANDSCAPE_SENSOR,
    new FillResolutionPolicy(), new Camera(0, 0,
    cameraWidth, cameraHeight)).setWakeLockOptions(
    WakeLockOptions.SCREEN_ON);
}
@Override
public void onCreateResources(OnCreateResourcesCallback
    pOnCreateResourcesCallback) {
  fontDefault32Bold = FontFactory.create(
    mEngine.getFontManager(),
```

```
      mEngine.getTextureManager(), 256, 256,
      Typeface.create(Typeface.DEFAULT, Typeface.BOLD),
      32f, true, Color.BLACK_ARGB_PACKED_INT);
   fontDefault32Bold.load();
   pOnCreateResourcesCallback.onCreateResourcesFinished();
}
@Override
public void onCreateScene(OnCreateSceneCallback
   pOnCreateSceneCallback) {
   mScene = new Scene();
   mScene.setBackground(new Background(0.9f,0.9f,0.9f));
   pOnCreateSceneCallback.onCreateSceneFinished(mScene);
}
```

3. Next, add this overridden `onPopulateScene()` method to our activity class:

```
@Override
public void onPopulateScene(Scene pScene,
   OnPopulateSceneCallback pOnPopulateSceneCallback) {
   countingText = new Text(400f, 240f,
      fontDefault32Bold, "0", 10,
      this.getVertexBufferObjectManager());
   mScene.attachChild(countingText);
   blankEntity = new Entity();
   blankEntity.registerUpdateHandler(new IUpdateHandler() {
      @Override
      public void onUpdate(float pSecondsElapsed) {
         countingInt++;
         countingText.setText(
            String.valueOf(countingInt));
      }
      @Override public void reset() {}
   });
   mScene.setOnSceneTouchListener(this);
   pOnPopulateSceneCallback.onPopulateSceneFinished();
}
```

4. Lastly, insert the following overridden method in our `AttachUpdateHandlerToEntityActivity` class to complete it:

```
@Override
public boolean onSceneTouchEvent(Scene pScene,
   TouchEvent pSceneTouchEvent) {
   if (pSceneTouchEvent.isActionDown() &&
       !blankEntity.hasParent())
      mScene.attachChild(blankEntity);
   return true;
}
```

How it works...

The first and the second step cover the creation of a simple `BaseGameActivity` class. For more information on creating a BaseGameActivity class, see the *Know the life cycle* recipe in *Chapter 1, AndEngine Game Structure*. Notice, however, that we create and load a `Font` object in the `onCreateResources()` method. For more information on fonts and the `Text` entities that use them, see the *Applying text to a layer* recipe in *Chapter 2, Working with Entities*.

Step three creates a text entity, `countingText`, and attaches it to the center of our scene. Then, our blank entity, `blankEntity`, is created by calling the `Entity()` constructor and our update handler is registered with it. Note that the blank entity is not attached to the scene until a touch occurs within the `onSceneTouchEvent()` method in step four. The `onUpdate()` method of the update handler simply increments the `countingText` entity's text to show that the update handler it is running.

Step four creates the `onSceneTouchEvent()` method that gets called when the scene is touched. We check to make sure that the touch event is a down action and that our blank entity does not already have a parent before attaching `blankEntity` to the scene.

There's more...

When running this recipe, we can see that the update handler is not called until the blank entity is attached to the scene. This effect is similar to overriding the `onManagedUpdate()` method of entities. The process of registering an update handler with an entity can be useful for creating enemies that have their own logic, or portions of the scene that should not be animated until shown. Update handlers registered with a child `Entity` object of another `Entity` object that is attached to the `Scene` object will still be active. Furthermore, the visibility of entities does not affect whether or not their registered update handlers will run.

See also

- ▶ *Getting started with update handlers* in this chapter.
- ▶ *Know the life cycle* in *Chapter 1, AndEngine Game Structure*.
- ▶ *Understanding AndEngine entities* in *Chapter 2, Working with Entities*.
- ▶ *Applying text to a layer* in *Chapter 2, Working with Entities*.
- ▶ *Overriding onManagedUpdate* in *Chapter 2, Working with Entities*.

Using update handlers with conditionals

To reduce the performance cost of running an update handler with heavy calculations, we can include a conditional statement that tells the update handler to run a specific set of instructions over another. For instance, if we have enemies that check to see if the player is within their sight, we can choose to let the vision calculations run only once every three updates. In this recipe, we will demonstrate a simple conditional statement that switches between a performance-intensive calculation and a very simple calculation by touching the screen.

Getting ready...

Create a new class named `UpdateHandlersAndConditionalsActivity` that extends `BaseGameActivity` and implements `IOnSceneTouchListener`. We will use this class to demonstrate how to use conditional statements with an update handler.

How to do it...

Follow these steps to create an update handler that uses a conditional block to determine which code to run:

1. Place the following definitions in the new class:

```
public static int cameraWidth = 800;
public static int cameraHeight = 480;
public Scene mScene;
public Font fontDefault32Bold;
public Text countingText;
public int countingInt = 0;
public boolean performanceIntensiveLoop = true;
public double performanceHeavyVariable;
```

2. Then, add the following overridden methods:

```
@Override
public EngineOptions onCreateEngineOptions() {
  return new EngineOptions(true,
    ScreenOrientation.LANDSCAPE_SENSOR,
    new FillResolutionPolicy(), new Camera(0, 0,
    cameraWidth, cameraHeight)).setWakeLockOptions(
    WakeLockOptions.SCREEN_ON);
}
@Override
public void onCreateResources(OnCreateResourcesCallback
    pOnCreateResourcesCallback) {
```

```
      fontDefault32Bold = FontFactory.create(
        mEngine.getFontManager(),
        mEngine.getTextureManager(), 256, 256,
        Typeface.create(Typeface.DEFAULT, Typeface.BOLD),
        32f, true, Color.BLACK_ARGB_PACKED_INT);
      fontDefault32Bold.load();
      pOnCreateResourcesCallback.onCreateResourcesFinished();
    }
    @Override
    public void onCreateScene(OnCreateSceneCallback
        pOnCreateSceneCallback) {
      mScene = new Scene();
      mScene.setBackground(new Background(0.9f,0.9f,0.9f));
      pOnCreateSceneCallback.onCreateSceneFinished(mScene);
    }
```

3. Next, insert the following overridden `onPopulateScene()` method:

```
    @Override
    public void onPopulateScene(Scene pScene,
        OnPopulateSceneCallback pOnPopulateSceneCallback) {
      countingText = new Text(400f, 240f,
        fontDefault32Bold, "0", 10,
        this.getVertexBufferObjectManager());
      mScene.attachChild(countingText);
      mScene.registerUpdateHandler(new IUpdateHandler() {
        @Override
        public void onUpdate(float pSecondsElapsed) {
          if(performanceIntensiveLoop) {
            countingInt++;
            for(int i = 3; i < 1000000; i++)
            performanceHeavyVariable =
              Math.sqrt(i);
          } else {
            countingInt--;
          }
          countingText.setText(
            String.valueOf(countingInt));
        }
        @Override public void reset() {}
      });
      mScene.setOnSceneTouchListener(this);
      pOnPopulateSceneCallback.onPopulateSceneFinished();
    }
```

4. Finally, create this `onSceneTouchEvent()` method to complete our activity:

```
@Override
public boolean onSceneTouchEvent(Scene pScene, TouchEvent
    pSceneTouchEvent) {
  if(pSceneTouchEvent.isActionDown())
    performanceIntensiveLoop = !performanceIntensiveLoop;
  return true;
}
```

How it works...

In step one, we define variables that are common to our test bed as well as a Boolean `performanceIntensiveLoop` variable, that tells our update handler which action to take and a double variable, `performanceHeavyVariable`, that we will use in our performance-intensive calculation. Step two creates the standard methods for our activity. For more information on creating `BaseGameActivity` classes, see the *Know the life cycle* recipe in *Chapter 1, AndEngine Game Structure*.

In step three, we create `countingText` before registering our update handler with the scene. On every update, it checks the `performanceIntensiveLoop` Boolean variable to determine whether it should perform a heavy task, calling the `Math` class' `sqrt()` method almost one million times, or a simple task, decrementing the `countingInt` variable's text.

Step four is the `onSceneTouchEvent()` method that switches the `performanceIntensiveLoop` Boolean variable every time the screen is touched.

See also

- ▶ *Getting started with update handlers* in this chapter.
- ▶ *Know the life cycle* in *Chapter 1, AndEngine Game Structure*.
- ▶ *Applying text to a layer* in *Chapter 2, Working with Entities*.

Handling the removal of an entity from the game

Detaching entities within an update handler can occasionally throw an `IndexOutOfBoundsException` exception, because the entity is removed in the middle of an engine update. To avoid that exception, we create a `Runnable` parameter that is run last on the update thread, after all other updating has occurred. In this recipe, we will safely remove an entity from the game by using the BaseGameActivity class' `runOnUpdateThread()` method.

Getting ready...

Create a new class named `HandlingRemovalOfEntityActivity` that extends `BaseGameActivity`. We will use this class to learn how to safely remove an entity from an update handler.

How to do it...

Follow these steps to see how we can remove an entity from its parent without throwing an exception:

1. Insert the following definitions into the `HandlingRemovalOfEntityActivity` class:

   ```
   public static int cameraWidth = 800;
   public static int cameraHeight = 480;
   public Scene mScene;
   public Rectangle spinningRect;
   public float totalElapsedSeconds = 0f;
   ```

2. Next, add these overridden methods to the class:

   ```
   @Override
   public EngineOptions onCreateEngineOptions() {
     return new EngineOptions(true,
       ScreenOrientation.LANDSCAPE_SENSOR,
       new FillResolutionPolicy(), new Camera(0, 0,
       cameraWidth, cameraHeight)).setWakeLockOptions(
       WakeLockOptions.SCREEN_ON);
   }
   @Override
   public void onCreateResources(OnCreateResourcesCallback
       pOnCreateResourcesCallback) {
     pOnCreateResourcesCallback.onCreateResourcesFinished();
   }
   @Override
   public void onCreateScene(OnCreateSceneCallback
       pOnCreateSceneCallback) {
     mScene = new Scene();
     mScene.setBackground(new Background(0.9f,0.9f,0.9f));
     pOnCreateSceneCallback.onCreateSceneFinished(mScene);
   }
   ```

3. Lastly, place the following `onPopulateScene()` method in the activity to finish it:

```java
@Override
public void onPopulateScene(Scene pScene,
    OnPopulateSceneCallback pOnPopulateSceneCallback) {
  spinningRect = new Rectangle(400f, 240f, 100f, 20f,
    this.getVertexBufferObjectManager());
  spinningRect.setColor(Color.BLACK);
  spinningRect.registerUpdateHandler(new IUpdateHandler() {
    @Override
    public void onUpdate(float pSecondsElapsed) {
      spinningRect.setRotation(
        spinningRect.getRotation()+0.4f);
      totalElapsedSeconds += pSecondsElapsed;
      if(totalElapsedSeconds > 5f) {
        runOnUpdateThread(new Runnable() {
          @Override
          public void run() {
            spinningRect.detachSelf();
          }});
      }
    }
    @Override public void reset() {}
  });
  mScene.attachChild(spinningRect);
  pOnPopulateSceneCallback.onPopulateSceneFinished();
}
```

How it works...

In step one, we define the normal `BaseGameActivity` variables as well as a square `Rectangle` object, `spinningRect`, that will spin in place and a float variable, `totalElapsedSeconds`, to keep track of how many seconds have elapsed since the start of our update handler. Step two creates the standard `BaseGameActivity` methods. For more information on creating AndEngine activities, see the *Know the life cycle* recipe in *Chapter 1, AndEngine Game Structure*.

In step three, we create the `spinningRect` rectangle defined in step one by calling the `Rectangle` constructor with a location at the center of the screen. The `Rectangle` object is then set to a black color via the `setColor()` method. Next, it has our update handler registered with it that records the elapsed time and removes the rectangle from the screen if more than 5 seconds have elapsed since the start of the activity. Notice that the way we detach the rectangle from the scene is by calling `runOnUpdateThread()`. This method passes the `Runnable` parameter to the engine to be run at the completion of the update cycle.

- ▸ *Getting started with update handlers* in this chapter.
- ▸ *Know the life cycle* in *Chapter 1, AndEngine Game Structure*.
- ▸ *Applying primitives to a layer* in *Chapter 2, Working with Entities*.

Adding game timers

Many games count down time and challenge the player to complete a task within the given amount of time. Such challenges are rewarding for the player, and often add replay value to a game. In the previous recipe, we kept track of the total elapsed time. In this recipe, we will start with a time and subtract from it the elapsed time provided by the update handler.

Getting ready...

Create a new class named `GameTimerActivity` that extends `BaseGameActivity`. We will use this class to create a game timer from an update handler.

How to do it...

Follow these steps to create a game timer using an update handler:

1. Place these variable definitions in our new activity class:

```
public static int cameraWidth = 800;
public static int cameraHeight = 480;
public Scene mScene;
public Font fontDefault32Bold;
public Text countingText;
public float EndingTimer = 10f;
```

2. Next, insert the following standard, overridden methods:

```
@Override
public EngineOptions onCreateEngineOptions() {
  return new EngineOptions(true,
    ScreenOrientation.LANDSCAPE_SENSOR,
    new FillResolutionPolicy(), new Camera(0, 0,
    cameraWidth, cameraHeight)).setWakeLockOptions(
    WakeLockOptions.SCREEN_ON);
}
@Override
public void onCreateResources(OnCreateResourcesCallback
    pOnCreateResourcesCallback) {
```

```
    fontDefault32Bold = FontFactory.create(
      mEngine.getFontManager(),
      mEngine.getTextureManager(), 256, 256,
      Typeface.create(Typeface.DEFAULT, Typeface.BOLD),
      32f, true, Color.BLACK_ARGB_PACKED_INT);
    fontDefault32Bold.load();
    pOnCreateResourcesCallback.onCreateResourcesFinished();
  }
  @Override
  public void onCreateScene(OnCreateSceneCallback
      pOnCreateSceneCallback) {
    mScene = new Scene();
    mScene.setBackground(new Background(0.9f,0.9f,0.9f));
    pOnCreateSceneCallback.onCreateSceneFinished(mScene);
  }
```

3. Finally, add this overridden onPopulateScene() method to the GameTimerActivity class:

```
  @Override
  public void onPopulateScene(Scene pScene,
      OnPopulateSceneCallback pOnPopulateSceneCallback) {
    countingText = new Text(400f, 240f,
      fontDefault32Bold, "10", 10,
      this.getVertexBufferObjectManager());
    mScene.attachChild(countingText);
    mScene.registerUpdateHandler(new IUpdateHandler() {
      @Override
      public void onUpdate(float pSecondsElapsed) {
        EndingTimer-=pSecondsElapsed;
        if(EndingTimer<=0) {
          // The timer has ended
          countingText.setText("0");
          mScene.unregisterUpdateHandler(this);
        } else {
          countingText.setText(String.valueOf(
            Math.round(EndingTimer)));
        }
      }
      @Override public void reset() {}
    });
    pOnPopulateSceneCallback.onPopulateSceneFinished();
  }
```

How it works...

In step one, we define common `BaseGameActivity` variables as well as an `EndingTimer` float variable set at `10` seconds. Step two creates the common methods for our activity. For more information on creating a BaseGameActivity class, see the *Know the life cycle* recipe in *Chapter 1, AndEngine Game Structure*.

In step three, we create the `countingText` entity, and use our scene to register an update handler, which counts down the `EndingTimer` variable using the `pSecondsElapsed` variable until it reaches `0`. When it reaches `0`, we simply unregister the update handler from the scene by calling the scene's `unregisterUpdateHandler()` method. In an actual game, the timer ending could end a level or even call the next wave of enemies to attack the player.

See also

- ▸ *Getting started with update handlers* in this chapter.
- ▸ *Know the life cycle* in *Chapter 1, AndEngine Game Structure*.
- ▸ *Applying text to a layer* in *Chapter 2, Working with Entities*.

Setting entity properties based on the time passed

Consistency across devices is one of the more important aspects of mobile game development. Players expect a game to scale properly for their device's screen, but another important, and often overlooked, aspect of game development is basing movements and animations on time instead of engine updates. In this recipe, we will set an entity's property using an update handler.

Getting ready...

Create a new class named `SettingEntityPropertiesBasedOnTimePassedActivity` that extends `BaseGameActivity`. We will use this class to demonstrate how to set entity properties in time with an update handler.

How to do it...

Follow these steps to see how we can set an entity's property based on how much time has passed in an update:

1. Define the following variables in the activity:

```
public static int cameraWidth = 800;
public static int cameraHeight = 480;
public Scene mScene;
public Rectangle spinningRect;
```

2. Then, place these overridden methods in the class:

```
@Override
public EngineOptions onCreateEngineOptions() {
  return new EngineOptions(true,
  ScreenOrientation.LANDSCAPE_SENSOR,
  new FillResolutionPolicy(), new Camera(0, 0,
  cameraWidth, cameraHeight)).setWakeLockOptions(
  WakeLockOptions.SCREEN_ON);
}
@Override
public void onCreateResources(OnCreateResourcesCallback
    pOnCreateResourcesCallback) {
  pOnCreateResourcesCallback.onCreateResourcesFinished();
}
@Override
public void onCreateScene(OnCreateSceneCallback
    pOnCreateSceneCallback) {
  mScene = new Scene();
  mScene.setBackground(new Background(0.9f,0.9f,0.9f));
  pOnCreateSceneCallback.onCreateSceneFinished(mScene);
}
```

3. Lastly, insert this `onPopulateScene()` method at the end of the activity to complete it:

```
@Override
public void onPopulateScene(Scene pScene,
    OnPopulateSceneCallback pOnPopulateSceneCallback) {
  spinningRect = new Rectangle(400f, 240f, 100f, 20f,
    this.getVertexBufferObjectManager());
  spinningRect.setColor(Color.BLACK);
  spinningRect.registerUpdateHandler(new IUpdateHandler() {
    @Override
```

```
public void onUpdate(float pSecondsElapsed) {
    spinningRect.setRotation(
        spinningRect.getRotation() +
        ((pSecondsElapsed*360f)/2f));
    }
    @Override public void reset() {}
});
mScene.attachChild(spinningRect);
pOnPopulateSceneCallback.onPopulateSceneFinished();
}
```

How it works...

As with the other recipes in this chapter, we first create common `BaseGameActivity` variables. For this recipe, we also define a `Rectangle` object, `spinningRect`, that will spin at specific revolutions per second. For more information on creating AndEngine activities, see the *Know the life cycle* recipe in *Chapter 1, AndEngine Game Structure*.

In step three, we fill the `onPopulateScene()` method by first creating our `spinningRect` rectangle, which we then use to register our update handler. Inside the update handler's `onUpdate()` method, we set the rotation of the rectangle to equal its current rotation, via the `getRotation()` method, plus a calculation that adjusts the `pSecondsElapsed` variable to a set number of rotations per second. The following diagram shows how the updates in our games do not have equal durations and thus must take advantage of the `pSecondsElapsed` parameter instead of a constant value:

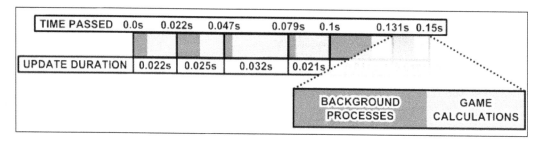

There's more...

The calculation that we use in the onUpdate() method of our update handler sets the Rectangle object to rotate at half of a rotation per second. If we were to multiply the (pSecondsElapsed*360f) portion of the calculation by 4, the rectangle would spin at 4 revolutions per second. For linear movements based on time, simply multiply the desired pixels per second with the pSecondsElapsed variable.

See also

- ▸ *Getting started with update handlers* in this chapter.
- ▸ *Know the life cycle* in *Chapter 1, AndEngine Game Structure.*

8
Maximizing Performance

In this chapter, we're going to cover some of the best practices to improve the performance of our AndEngine applications. The topics included are as follows:

- ▶ Ignoring entity updates
- ▶ Disabling background window rendering
- ▶ Limiting simultaneous sound streams
- ▶ Creating sprite pools
- ▶ Cutting down render time with sprite groups
- ▶ Disabling rendering with entity culling

Introduction

Game optimization plays a critical role in the success of a game on Google Play. It is likely that a user will rate a game negatively if it doesn't run well on their device. Unfortunately, with there being so many different devices out there and no way to effectively mass-restrict low-end devices on Google Play, it's best to optimize Android games as much as possible. Ignoring ratings, it's fair to assume that a game with poor performance across the mid-level devices will not reach its full potential as far as downloads and active users go. This chapter is going to cover some of the most helpful solutions for performance issues related to AndEngine. This will help us to improve performance for mid- to low-end devices, eliminating the need to sacrifice quality.

While the recipes in this chapter can greatly improve the performance of our games, it is important to keep in mind that clean and efficient code goes equally as far. Game development is a very performance-critical task and, as with all languages, there are plenty of little things to do or avoid. There are many resources online that cover the majority of the good versus bad topics related to both Java general practices as well as Android-specific tips and tricks.

Ignoring entity updates

One of the most important rules for game development when it comes to optimizing a game is, *don't do work that does not need to be done!*. In this recipe, we're going to talk about how we can use the setIgnoreUpdate() method on our entities in order to restrict the update thread to only update what should be updated, rather than constantly updating all of our entities whether we're using them or not.

How to do it...

The following setIgnoreUpdate(boolean) methods allow us to control which entities will be updated via the engine's update thread:

```
Entity entity = new Entity();

// Ignore updates for this entity
entity.setIgnoreUpdate(true);

// Allow this entity to continue updating
entity.setIgnoreUpdate(false);
```

How it works...

As we've discussed in the previous chapters, each child's onUpdate() method is called via its parent. The engine first updates, calling the update method for the main Scene object. The scene then proceeds to call all of the update methods of its children. Next, the children of the scene will call the update method to their children respectively and so on in that fashion. With this in mind, by calling setIgnoreUpdate() on our main Scene object, we can effectively ignore updates to all entities on the scene as well.

Ignoring updates to entities which are not in use, or even entities which should not react unless a certain event occurs, can save quite a bit of CPU time. This is especially true on a scene with a large number of entities. It may not seem like much work, but keep in mind that for each entity with an entity modifier or update handler, those objects must be updated as well. On top of that, each of the entities' children then proceed to update due to the parent/child hierarchy.

It is best practice to set `setIgnoreUpdate(true)` to all entities which are offscreen or do not require constant updates. For sprites which may not require any updates at all, such as the background sprite of a scene, we can ignore updates indefinitely and not cause any problems. In situations where the entity needs to be updated, but not very frequently, such as a bullet being fired from a turret, we can enable the updates to that bullet while it is traveling from the turret to the destination, disabling it when it's no longer needed.

See also

▸ The *Understanding AndEngine entities* section in *Chapter 2, Working with Entities*

Disabling background window rendering

In most games, developers generally lean toward full-screen modes. This may not seem obvious since we see no real difference visually, but the Android OS doesn't realize which applications are running in full-screen. What this means is that the background window will continue to be drawn underneath our application unless otherwise specified in the `AndroidManifest.xml`. In this topic, we're going to cover how to disable background rendering to improve application FPS, mainly benefiting lower-end devices.

Getting ready...

The first thing we must do in order to stop the background windows from rendering is create a theme for our application. We will do this by adding a new xml file to our project's `res/values/` folder, called `theme.xml`.

Overwrite all code in the default xml file with the following code and save the file:

```xml
<?xml version="1.0" encoding="UTF-8"?>
<resources>
    <style name="Theme.NoBackground" parent="android:Theme">
        <item name="android:windowBackground">@null</item>
    </style>
</resources>
```

How to do it...

Once we've created and filled out the `theme.xml` file, we can disable background window rendering by applying the theme to our application tag in the `AndroidManifest.xml` file of our project. The application tag's attributes might look similar to this:

```
<application
        android:theme="@style/Theme.NoBackground"
        android:icon="@drawable/ic_launcher"
        android:label="@string/app_name"
        >
```

Note that we can also apply the theme to specific activities, rather than on an application-wide basis by adding the `android:theme="@style/Theme.NoBackground"` code to individual activity tags. This would be most relevant for hybrid games which require both the AndEngine view as well as native Android views across multiple activities.

How it works...

Disabling the background window rendering is a simple task and can offer a few percentages of performance gain, mostly in older devices. The main line of code which takes care of the background window is found in the `theme.xml` file. By nullifying the `android:windowBackground` item, we're notifying the device that, rather than drawing the background window, we want to completely remove it from being rendered.

Limiting simultaneous sound streams

Sound playback is generally not a problem when it comes to game performance with AndEngine. However, there are situations where a large number of sounds may play in a very short time-span which can cause a noticeable amount of lag on older and sometimes newer devices depending on how many sounds are playing. AndEngine allows up to five simultaneous sound streams, of the same `Sound` object, to play at any given time by default. In this topic, we're going to work with `EngineOptions` in order to change the number of simultaneous sound streams in order to better accommodate our application's needs.

How to do it...

In order to increase or decrease the number of simultaneous streams per Sound object, we must make a simple adjustment to `EngineOptions` in the `onCreateEngineOptions()` method of our activity:

```
@Override
public EngineOptions onCreateEngineOptions() {
```

```
    mCamera = new Camera(0, 0, 800, 480);

    EngineOptions engineOptions = new EngineOptions(true,
              ScreenOrientation.LANDSCAPE_FIXED, new
              FillResolutionPolicy(),mCamera);

    engineOptions.getAudioOptions().setNeedsSound(true);
    engineOptions.getAudioOptions().getSoundOptions().
    setMaxSimultaneousStreams(2);

    return engineOptions;
}
```

How it works...

The `Engine` object's `AudioOptions` is set to allow five simultaneous sound streams for each `Sound` object created within our applications by default. In most cases, this will not cause any noticeable performance loss for applications which do not rely heavily on sound playback. On the other hand, games which tend to produce sounds on collision or forces applied to bodies may be susceptible to large numbers of sound streams being played at the same time, especially in games with more than 100 sprites on the scene at any given time.

Limiting the number of simultaneous sound streams is an easy task to accomplish. By simply calling `getAudioOptions().getSoundOptions().setMaxSimultaneousStreams(n)` on our `EngineOptions`, where n is the number of maximum streams per `Sound` object, we can reduce the number of unnecessary sounds to be played during gameplay at inconvenient times.

See also

▶   The *Introducing sounds and music* section in *Chapter 1, AndEngine Game Structure*

Creating sprite pools

The `GenericPool` classes are an incredibly important part of AndEngine game design considering mobile platforms are relatively limited when it comes to hardware resources. In Android game development, the key to a smooth gameplay experience throughout a lengthy session is to create the least amount of objects as possible. This does not necessarily mean we should limit ourselves to four or five objects on the screen, it means we should consider the option of recycling objects which have already been created. This is where object pools come into play.

Getting started..

Refer to the class named `SpritePool` in the code bundle.

How to do it...

The `GenericPool` classes make use of a few useful methods, which make recycling objects for later use very easy. We will cover the main methods to be used here.

Constructing the `SpritePool` class:

```
public SpritePool(ITextureRegion pTextureRegion,
VertexBufferObjectManager pVertexBufferObjectManager){
  this.mTextureRegion = pTextureRegion;
  this.mVertexBufferObjectManager = pVertexBufferObjectManager;
}
```

1. Allocating pool items:

```
@Override
protected Sprite onAllocatePoolItem() {
  return new Sprite(0, 0, this.mTextureRegion, this.
mVertexBufferObjectManager);
}
```

2. Obtaining pool items:

```
public synchronized Sprite obtainPoolItem(final float pX, final
float pY) {
  Sprite sprite = super.obtainPoolItem();

  sprite.setPosition(pX, pY);
  sprite.setVisible(true);
  sprite.setIgnoreUpdate(false);
  sprite.setColor(1,1,1);

  return sprite;
}
```

3. Recycling pool items:

```
@Override
protected void onHandleRecycleItem(Sprite pItem) {
  super.onHandleRecycleItem(pItem);

  pItem.setVisible(false);
  pItem.setIgnoreUpdate(true);
  pItem.clearEntityModifiers();
  pItem.clearUpdateHandlers();
}
```

How it works...

The idea of the `GenericPool` class is very simple. Rather than creating new objects when we need them and discarding them when we're finished with them, we can tell the pool to allocate a limited number of objects and store them for later use. We can now call the `obtainPoolItem()` method from the pool to obtain one of the stored allocated objects for use in our levels, possibly as an enemy. Once that enemy is destroyed by the player, for example, we can now call `recyclePoolItem(pItem)` to send that enemy object back into the pool. This allows us to avoid garbage collection invocations and gives us the potential to greatly reduce the memory needed for new objects.

The four methods in the *How to do it...* section are all that is needed when working with your average pool. We must obviously create the pool before we can use it. Then the following three methods define what happens in the event of object allocation, obtaining an object for use, and what happens once an object is recycled, or sent back to be stored in the pool when we are finished with it until we need a new object. Object pools can be used for more than just sprite recycling, though, so we're going to go a little bit more in-depth about what each of these methods does, how they do it, and why they do it, starting with the constructor.

In step one, we must pass any objects needed for the pool object's constructor. In this case, we need to obtain a `TextureRegion` and `VertexBufferObjectManager` in order to create the Sprite objects. This is nothing new, but keep in mind that the `GenericPool` class is not limited to creating pools for sprites. We can create pools for any type of object or datatype. The key note is to use the pool's constructor as a method to obtain the necessary parameters to be passed to the pool's object allocations.

In step two, we're overriding the `onAllocatePoolItem()` method. The pool will call this method any time it needs to allocate a new object. Two instances are if there are initially no objects in the pool or if all of the recycled objects have been obtained and are in use. All we need to take care of in this method is that we return a new instance of the object.

Step three involves the `obtain` method used in order to retrieve an object from the pool to be used in our game. We can see that the `obtainPoolItem()` method in this case requires us to pass in `pX` and `pY` parameters to be used by the sprite's `setPosition(pX, pY)` method in order to reposition the sprite. We proceed to set the sprite's `visibility` to `true`, allow updates to the sprite, as well as setting the color back to its initial value, white. In any case, this method should be used to reset the values of the object back to a default state or otherwise define the necessary *new* properties of the object. In the code, we might obtain a new sprite from the pool as shown in the following code snippet:

```
// obtain a sprite and attach it to the scene at position (10, 10)
Sprite sprite = pool.obtainPoolItem(10, 10);
mScene.attachChild(sprite);
```

In the final method, we will use from the `GenericPool` class the `recyclePoolItem(pItem)` method, where `pItem` is the object to recycle back into the pool. This method should take care of all aspects related to disabling the object from use within our game. In terms of sprites, in order to increase performance while sprites are stored in the pool, we set the visibility to false, ignore updates to the sprite, clear any entity modifiers and update handlers so that they are not still running once we obtain a new sprite.

 Even if not using pools, an option to consider is to use `setVisible(false)` alongside `setIgnoreUpdate(true)` on an `Entity`, which is no longer needed. Constantly attaching and detaching `Entity` objects may provide opportunities for the garbage collector to run and potentially cause noticeable hiccups in frame rate during gameplay.

There's more...

Creating pools to handle object recycling is very important to aid in the reduction of performance hiccups, but when a game is first initialized the pool will not have any objects ready for use. This means that, depending on how many objects the pool will need to allocate in order to satisfy the maximum number of objects throughout a full level, a player may notice sudden bursts of frame rate interruption during the first few minutes of gameplay. In order to avoid an issue such as this, it is a good idea to preallocate pool objects during level loading to avoid any object creation during gameplay.

In order to allocate a large number of pool items during loading, we can call `batchAllocatePoolItems(pCount)` on any class extending `GenericPool`, where `pCount` is the number of items we wish to allocate. Keep in mind it is a waste of resources to load any more items than we need, but it can also cause hiccups in frame rate if we don't allocate enough items. For example, in order to determine how many enemy objects should be allocated within our game, we can come up with a formula such as default enemy count multiplied by level difficulty. However, all games are different and so too will be the formula needed for object creation.

See also

▸ The *Bringing a scene to life with sprites* section in *Chapter 2, Working with Entities*

Cutting down render time with sprite groups

Sprite groups are a great addition to any AndEngine game which deals with hundreds of visible sprites on the scene at any given time. The `SpriteGroup` class allows us to eliminate a large amount of overhead by grouping many sprite rendering calls into a limited number of OpenGL calls. If a school bus were to pick up a single child, drop them off at school, then pick up the next child, repeating until all children were at school, the process would take a far greater time to complete. The same goes for drawing sprites with OpenGL.

Getting started...

Refer to the class named `ApplyingSpriteGroups` in the code bundle. This recipe requires an image named `marble.png`, which is 32 pixels in width by 32 pixels in height.

How to do it...

When creating a `SpriteGroup` for use in our games, we can treat them as an `Entity` layer which is specifically meant for `Sprite` objects only. The following steps explain how to create and attach `Sprite` objects to a `SpriteGroup`.

1. Creating a sprite group can be achieved with the following code:

   ```
   // Create a new sprite group with a maximum sprite capacity of
   500
     mSpriteGroup = new SpriteGroup(0, 0, mBitmapTextureAtlas, 500,
   mEngine.getVertexBufferObjectManager());

     // Attach the sprite group to the scene
     mScene.attachChild(mSpriteGroup);
   ```

2. Attaching sprites to the sprite group is an equally simple task:

   ```
   // Create new sprite
     Sprite sprite = new Sprite(tempX, tempY,
   spriteWidth, spriteHeight, mTextureRegion, mEngine.
   getVertexBufferObjectManager());

     // Attach our sprite to the sprite group
     mSpriteGroup.attachChild(sprite);
   ```

How it works...

In this recipe, we're setting up a scene which applies roughly 375 sprites to our scene, all drawn through the use of the `mSpriteGroup` object. Once the sprite group is created, we can basically treat it as an ordinary entity layer, attaching sprites as needed.

▸ Create a `BuildableBitmapTextureAtlas` for our sprite in the `onCreateResources()` method of our activity:

```
// Create texture atlas
mBitmapTextureAtlas = new BuildableBitmapTextureAtlas(mEngine.
getTextureManager(), 32, 32, TextureOptions.BILINEAR);

// Create texture region
mTextureRegion = BitmapTextureAtlasTextureRegionFactory.createFrom
Asset(mBitmapTextureAtlas, getAssets(), "marble.png");

// Build/load texture atlas
mBitmapTextureAtlas.build(new BlackPawnTextureAtlasBuilder<IBitmap
TextureAtlasSource, BitmapTextureAtlas>(0, 0, 0));
mBitmapTextureAtlas.load();
```

Creating the textures for use in a `SpriteGroup` can be handled as we would an ordinary Sprite.

▸ Construct our `mSpriteGroup` object and apply it to the scene:

```
// Create a new sprite group with a maximum sprite capacity of 500
mSpriteGroup = new SpriteGroup(0, 0, mBitmapTextureAtlas, 500,
mEngine.getVertexBufferObjectManager());

// Attach the sprite group to the scene
mScene.attachChild(mSpriteGroup);
```

`SpriteGroup` requires two new parameters that we've not dealt with yet. `SpriteGroup` is an `Entity` subtype, so we already know that the first two parameters are the x and y coordinates to position `SpriteGroup`. For the third parameter, we're passing a `BitmapTextureAtlas`. *The sprite group can only contain sprites which share the same texture atlas as the sprite group!* The fourth parameter is the maximum capacity that `SpriteGroup` is able to draw. If the capacity is 400, then we can apply up to 400 sprites to `SpriteGroup`. It is important to limit the capacity to the maximum number of sprites we wish to draw. *Exceeding the limit will cause a force-closure of the application.*

▸ The final step is to apply the sprites to the sprite group.

In this recipe, we have set a loop up in order to apply the sprites to various positions on the screen. However, what we're really interested in here is the following code used to create a `Sprite` and attach it to the `SpriteGroup`:

```
Sprite sprite = new Sprite(tempX, tempY, spriteWidth, spriteHeight,
mTextureRegion, mEngine.getVertexBufferObjectManager());

// Attach our sprite to the sprite group
mSpriteGroup.attachChild(sprite);
```

We can create our sprite as we would create any other sprite. We can set the position, scale, and texture region as usual. Brace for the tricky part now! We must call `mSpriteGroup.attachChild(sprite)` in order to allow the `mSpriteGroup` object to handle drawing of the sprite object. That's all it takes!

Following these steps, we can successfully allow our sprite groups to draw many, many sprites onto the screen before even noticing a drop in performance within our application. The difference is huge compared to individually drawing sprites with separate buffers. In many cases, users have claimed to achieve an improvement of up to 50 percent when working with games which include large amounts of entities on the scene at one time.

There's more...

It's not time to run off and convert all of your projects to use sprite groups just yet! The benefits to using sprite groups speak for themselves, but that's not to say there are no negative side effects either. The `SpriteGroup` class is not supported directly by OpenGL. The class is more or less a 'hack', which allows us to save some time with additional rendering calls. Setting up sprite groups in more complex projects can be a hassle due to the 'side effects'.

There are some situations after attaching and detaching many sprites which take advantage of alpha modifiers and modified visibility, causing some of the sprites on the sprite group to 'flicker'. This outcome is most noticeable after more and more sprites have been attached and detached or set to invisible/visible multiple times. There is a way around this that will not hurt performance too much, which involves moving sprites off the screen rather than detaching them from the layer or setting them to invisible. However, for larger games that only take advantage of one activity and swap scenes based on the current level, moving the sprites off the screen might only lead to future problems.

Take this into account and plan wisely before deciding to use a sprite group. It might also help to test the sprite group in terms of how you plan to use your sprites before incorporating it into your game. The sprite group will not always cause problems, but it's something to keep in mind. Additionally, AndEngine is an open source project which is continuously being updated and enhanced. Keep up to date with the latest revisions for fixes or improvements.

See also

▸ The *Understanding AndEngine entities* section in *Chapter 2, Working with Entities*

▸ The *Bringing a scene to life with sprites* section in *Chapter 2, Working with Entities*

Disabling rendering with entity culling

Culling entities is a method used to prevent unnecessary entities from being rendered. This can result in improved performance in cases where a sprite is not visible within the viewing area of an AndEngine `Camera`.

How to do it...

Make the following method call to any preexisting `Entity` or `Entity` subtype:

```
entity.setCullingEnabled(true);
```

How it works...

Culling entities disallows certain entities from being rendered depending on their position on the scene relative to the portion of the scene visible by the camera. This is useful when we have many sprites on a scene that might occasionally move out of view of the camera. With culling enabled, those entities which are outside of the camera view will not be rendered in order to save us from unnecessary calls to OpenGL.

Note that culling only takes place on those entities which are entirely out of view of the camera. This takes into account the full area of the entity, from the bottom left corner to the top right corner. Culling is not applied to portions of an entity, which may be outside of the camera's view.

There's more...

Culling will only stop rendering those entities which move out of visibility of the Camera. Because of this, it is not a bad idea to enable culling on all game objects (items, enemies, and so on.) that are constantly moving out of the Camera area. For instances with large backgrounds made up of smaller textures, culling can also greatly improve performance, especially considering the size of background images.

Culling can really help us save some rendering time, but that doesn't necessarily mean that we should enable it on all entities. After all, there's a reason why it's not enabled by default. It is a bad idea to enable culling on HUD entities. It might seem like a viable option to include it for pause menus or other large entities which might transition in and out of the camera view, but this can lead to problems when moving the camera. AndEngine works in such a way that the HUD never really moves with the camera, so if we enable culling on HUD entities, then move our camera 800 pixels to the right (assuming our camera width is 800 pixels) our HUD entities would still physically respond as if they were in the proper position on our screen but they will not render. They would still react with touch events and other various scenarios, but we simply won't see them on the screen.

Additionally, culling requires an added layer of visibility-checking before an Entity is drawn on the Scene. Because of this, older devices have the potential to actually notice a performance loss while Entity culling is enabled while those entities are not being culled. It may not sound like much, but when we've got players running on devices that are just barely capable of running at 30 frames per second, there's a good chance that those additional visibility checks on, for example, 200 sprites may be just enough to tilt the scale toward 'inconvenient gameplay'.

See also

▸ The *Understanding AndEngine entities* section in *Chapter 2, Working with Entities*.

9
AndEngine Extensions Overview

In this chapter, we're going to cover the purpose and usage of some of AndEngine's most popular extensions. The following topics are included in this chapter:

- Creating live wallpapers
- Networking with the multiplayer extension
- Creating high-resolution graphics with **scalable vector graphics** (**SVG**)
- Color mapping with SVG texture regions

Introduction

In the extensions overview chapter, we're going to begin to work with a number of classes that don't come packaged with AndEngine. There are many extensions that can be written to add various improvements or extra features to any default AndEngine game. In this chapter, we're going to be working with three main extensions that will allow us to create live wallpapers with AndEngine, create online games that allow multiple devices to connect directly to each other or a dedicated server, and finally, incorporate SVG files into our games as texture regions, allowing for high resolution and scalable graphics within our games.

AndEngine includes a relatively long list of extensions which can be included in our projects in order to make certain tasks easier to complete. Unfortunately, due to the number of extensions and the current state of some of them, we are limited in the number of extensions, which can be included within this chapter. However, most AndEngine extensions are relatively easy to use and include example projects which can be acquired from Nicolas Gramlich's public GitHub repository – `https://github.com/nicolasgramlich`. The following is a list of additional AndEngine extensions, as well as a brief description describing its purpose:

  ▶ `AndEngineCocosBuilderExtension`: This extension allows developers to create games through the use of the **WYSIWYG** or **what you see is what you get** concept. This approach allows developers to build applications in a GUI based drag-and-drop environment using the CocosBuilder software for desktop computers. This extension can help make menu and level design as simple as placing objects on a screen and exporting the setup to a file which can be read in via the `AndEngineCocosBuilderExtension` extension.

  ▶ `AndEngineAugmentedRealityExtension`: The augmented reality extension allows developers to easily convert an otherwise ordinary AndEngine activity into an augmented reality activity, which will display the device's physical camera view on the screen. We are then able to attach entities over the top of the camera's view displayed on the screen.

  ▶ `AndEngineTexturePackerExtension`: This extension allows developers to import sprite sheets created through the use of the TexturePacker program for desktop computers. This program makes creating sprite sheets remarkably easy by allowing us to drag-and-drop our images into the program, export the finished sprite sheet into an AndEngine-readable format, and simply load it into our project with the `AndEngineTexturePackerExtension` extension.

  ▶ `AndEngineTMXTiledMapExtensions`: This extension can greatly increase productivity in games based on the tiled map style of gameplay. With the use of a TMX tiled map editor, developers can simply drag-and-drop sprites/tiles onto a grid-based level editor in order to create levels. Once a level is created in the editor, simply export it to the `.tmx` file format and from there use the `AndEngineTMXTiledMapExtension` to load the level into our project.

Creating live wallpaper

The live wallpaper extension is a great addition to the AndEngine lineup of available Android development resources. With this extension, we can easily create wallpapers through the use of all the normal AndEngine classes we're used to using for our game development. In this topic, we're going to create a live wallpaper containing a simple particle system that spawns particles at the top of the screen. The wallpaper settings will include a value that allows a user to increase the speed of particle movement.

This recipe assumes that you have at least a basic knowledge of the Android SDK's `Activity` class as well as a general understanding of Android view objects, such as `SeekBars` and `TextViews`.

Getting ready

Live wallpapers are not your typical Android activity. Instead, they are a service, which requires a slightly different approach in terms of setting a project up. Before visiting the code, let's go ahead and create the necessary folders and files for the live wallpaper.

 Refer to the project named `LiveWallpaperExtensionExample` in the code bundle.

We will cover the code to reside in each file in the following section:

1. Create or overwrite the current `main.xml` file in the `res/layout` folder, naming it `settings_main.xml`. This layout file will be used to create the settings activity layout where the wallpaper's properties are adjusted by the user.

2. Create a new folder named `xml` in the `res` folder. Within this folder, create a new xml file and name it `wallpaper.xml`. This file will be used as a reference to the wallpaper's icon, description, as well as a reference to the setting's activity which will be used to modify the wallpaper properties.

How to do it...

We will start off by populating all of the XML files in order to accommodate a live wallpaper service. These files include `settings_main.xml`, `wallpaper.xml`, and finally `AndroidManifest.xml`.

1. Create the `settings_main.xml` layout file:

   The first step involves defining the `settings_main.xml` file as a layout for the settings activity of the wallpaper. There are no rules limiting a developer to a specific layout style, but the most common approach for a live wallpaper is a simple `TextView` with a corresponding `Spinner` used to provide a means of modification to the live wallpaper's adjustable values.

2. Open the `wallpaper.xml` file in the `res/xml/` folder. Import the following code to `wallpaper.xml`:

```xml
<?xml version="1.0" encoding="utf-8"?>
<wallpaper xmlns:android="http://schemas.android.com/apk/res/
android"
    android:settingsActivity="com.Live.Wallpaper.Extension.
Example.LiveWallpaperSettings"
    android:thumbnail="@drawable/ic_launcher"/>
```

3. Modify `AndroidManifest.xml` to suit the wallpaper service needs:

In the third step, we must modify `AndroidManifest.xml` in order to allow our project to run as a wallpaper service. In the project's `AndroidManifest.xml` file, replace all code inside of the `<manifest>` tags with the following:

```xml
<uses-feature android:name="android.software.live_wallpaper" />

<application android:icon="@drawable/ic_launcher" >
    <service
        android:name=".LiveWallpaperExtensionService"
        android:enabled="true"
        android:icon="@drawable/ic_launcher"
        android:label="@string/service_name"
        android:permission="android.permission.BIND_WALLPAPER" >
        <intent-filter android:priority="1" >
            <action android:name="android.service.wallpaper.
WallpaperService" />
        </intent-filter>

        <meta-data
            android:name="android.service.wallpaper"
            android:resource="@xml/wallpaper" />
    </service>

    <activity
        android:name=".LiveWallpaperSettings"
        android:exported="true"
        android:icon="@drawable/ic_launcher"
        android:label="@string/live_wallpaper_settings"
        android:theme="@android:style/Theme.Black" >
    </activity>
```

Once the three xml files have been taken care of, we can create the classes needed for the live wallpaper. We will be using three classes to handle the live wallpaper's execution. These classes are `LiveWallpaperExtensionService.java`, `LiveWallpaperSettings.java`, and `LiveWallpaperPreferences.java`, which will be covered in the following steps:

1. Create the live wallpaper preferences class:

   The `LiveWallpaperPreferences.java` class is similar to that of the preferences class we covered in the *Saving and loading game data* section in *Chapter 1, AndEngine Game Structure*. The main purpose of the preference class in this case is to handle the speed value of the spawned particles. The following methods are used for saving and loading the particle's speed value. Note that we negate the `mParticleSpeed` value as we want the particles to travel toward the bottom of the screen:

   ```
   // Return the saved value for the mParticleSpeed variable
   public int getParticleSpeed(){
     return -mParticleSpeed;
   }


   // Save the mParticleSpeed value to the wallpaper's preference
   file
   public void setParticleSpeed(int pParticleSpeed){
     this.mParticleSpeed = pParticleSpeed;
     this.mSharedPreferencesEditor.putInt(PARTICLE_SPEED_KEY,
   mParticleSpeed);
     this.mSharedPreferencesEditor.commit();
   }
   ```

2. Create the live wallpaper settings activity:

   The live wallpaper's settings activity extends Android SDK's `Activity` class, using the `settings_main.xml` file as the activity's layout. This activity's purpose is to obtain a value for the `mParticleSpeed` variable depending on the progress of the `SeekBar` object. Once the settings activity is exited, the `mParticleSpeed` value is saved to our preferences.

3. Create the live wallpaper service:

   The final step involved for setting up our live wallpaper is to create the `LiveWallpaperExtensionService.java` class, containing the code for the live wallpaper service. In order to specify that we would like the class to use the live wallpaper extension class, we simply add `extends BaseLiveWallpaperService` to the `LiveWallpaperExtensionService.java` declaration. Once this is done we can see that setting up a `BaseLiveWallpaperService` class is very much the same as setting up a `BaseGameActivity` class from this point on, allowing us to load resources, apply sprites, or any other common AndEngine task we're already used to.

How it works...

This recipe is a rather big one if we look at the whole project, but fortunately most of the code related to the class files has already been discussed in previous sections, so don't be worried! For the sake of brevity we are going to omit the classes which have already been discussed in previous chapters. Take a look at the topics mentioned in the *See more...* subsection for a refresher if needed.

In the first step, all we're doing is creating a minimal Android `xml` layout to be used for the settings activity. It is quite possible to skip this step and use AndEngine's `BaseGameActivity` for the settings activity, but to keep things simple we are using a very basic `TextView/SeekBar` approach. This makes things convenient for both the developer, time-wise, as well as the user, for convenience. Try to keep this screen as clutter free as possible as it is meant to be a simple screen, with a simple purpose.

In step two, we are creating the `wallpaper.xml` file to be used as a reference to a few specifications needed for the live wallpaper service in the `AndroidManifest.xml` file. This file is simply in place to store the service's properties, which include the package and class name or "link" to the settings activity to be launched by pressing the **Settings...** button during the wallpaper preview. `wallpaper.xml` also includes a reference to the icon to be used in the wallpaper selection window.

In step three, we are modifying the `AndroidManifest.xml` file to allow us to run the live wallpaper service as the main component for this project, rather than launching an activity. Within the `<service>` tags, we are including the `name`, `icon`, and `label` attributes for the wallpaper service. These attributes have the same purpose as they would for an activity. The other two attributes are `android:enabled="true"`, meaning that we'd like the wallpaper service to be enabled by default, as well as the `android:permission="android.permission.BIND_WALLPAPER"` attribute, meaning only the Android OS can bind to the service. The activity's attributes are similar, except we're including the `exported` and `theme` attributes and excluding the `enabled` and `permission` attributes. The `android:exported="true"` attribute states that the activity can be launched through outside processes while the theme attribute will alter the appearance of the settings activity UI.

Step four involves creating the preferences class that we will be using to store the values available for adjustment by the user. In this recipe, we're including a single value called `mParticleSpeed` within the preferences class with corresponding getter and setter methods. In a more complex live wallpaper we can build on this class, allowing us to easily add or remove variables for as many customizable properties to our wallpaper as we'd like.

In step five, we are creating the `Activity` class shown when a user presses the **Settings...** button on the live wallpaper preview screen. In this particular `Activity`, we're obtaining the `settings_main.xml` file to be used as our layout, containing two `TextView` view types used to display labels and corresponding values, and one `SeekBar` to allow manipulation of the wallpaper's adjustable values. The most important task for this `Activity` is to be able to save to the preference file once a user has selected their ideal speed. This is done by adjusting the `mParticleSpeed` variable when `SeekBar` realizes a user has moved the `SeekBar` slider:

```
// OnProgressChanged represents a movement on the slider
  @Override
  public void onProgressChanged(SeekBar seekBar, int progress,
      boolean fromUser) {
    // Set the mParticleSpeed depending on the SeekBar's
position(progress)
    mParticleSpeed = progress;
```

As well as updating the `mParticleSpeed` value, the associating `TextView` is updated within this event. This value, however, is not actually saved to the preference file until the user leaves the settings activity, to avoid unnecessary overwriting to the preference file. In order to save the new value to the preference file, we can call `setParticleSpeed(mParticleSpeed)` from the `LiveWallpaperPreferences` singleton during minimization of the `Activity` class:

```
@Override
protected void onPause() {
  // onPause(), we save the current value of mParticleSpeed to the
preference file.
  // Anytime the wallpaper's lifecycle is executed, the mParticleSpeed
value is loaded
  LiveWallpaperPreferences.getInstance().setParticleSpeed(mParticleSp
eed);
  super.onPause();
}
```

In the sixth and final step, we can finally start to code the visual aspects of our live wallpaper. In this particular wallpaper, we're keeping it simple in terms of visual appeal, but we do cover what all necessary information for developing a wallpaper. If we take a look at the `LiveWallpaperExtensionService` class, a few of the key variables to pay attention to, include the following:

```
private int mParticleSpeed;

// These ratio variables will be used to keep proper scaling of
entities
// regardless of the screen orientation
private float mRatioX;
private float mRatioY;
```

While we've already discussed the `mParticleSpeed` variable throughout the other class explanations, it should be obvious at this point that we'll be using this variable to finally determine the speed of the particles, as this is the class that will handle the `ParticleSystem` object. The other two 'ratio' variables declared above are to help us keep a proper scaling ratio for our entities. These variables are needed in the event that a user tilts their device from landscape to portrait or vice versa, so that we can calculate the scale of the particles depending on the width and height of the surface view. This is to prevent our entities from being stretched or distorted upon orientation changes. Skipping to the bottom overridden method of this class, the following code determines the values for `mRatioX` and `mRatioY`:

```
@Override
public void onSurfaceChanged(GLState pGLState, int pWidth, int
pHeight) {

  if(pWidth > pHeight){
      mRatioX = 1;
      mRatioY = 1;
    } else {
      mRatioX = ((float)pHeight) / pWidth;
      mRatioY = ((float)pWidth) / pHeight;
    }

    super.onSurfaceChanged(pGLState, pWidth, pHeight);
}
```

We can see here that the `if` statement is checking whether or not the device is in landscape or portrait mode. If `pWidth` is greater than `pHeight`, it means the orientation is currently in landscape mode, setting the x and y scale ratios to the default 1 value. On the other hand, if the device is set to portrait mode, then we must recalculate the scale ratio for our particle entities.

Once the onSurfaceChanged() method is taken care of, let's continue on to the remaining key points with the next up being preference management. Taking care of preferences is a fairly trivial task. First and foremost, we should initialize the preference file, in case it is the first time the wallpaper is launched. We do this by calling the initPreferences(this) method from the LiveWallpaperPreferences instance in onCreateEngineOptions(). We also need to override the onResume() method in order to load the mParticleSpeed variable with the value stored in the preference file by calling the getParticleSpeed() method from the LiveWallpaperPreferences instance.

Finally, we come to the remaining setup step for the live wallpaper, which is setting up the particle system. This particular particle system is none too fancy, but it does include a ParticleModifier object, which includes some points to note. Since we're adding an IParticleModifier interface to the particle system, we are given access to individual particles spawned by the system on every update to each particle. In the onUpdateParticle() method, we'll be setting the particle's speed based on the mParticleSpeed variable loaded in from the preference file:

```
// speed set by the preferences...
if(currentVelocityY != mParticleSpeed){
   // Adjust the particle's velocity to the proper value
   particlePhysicsHandler.setVelocityY(mParticleSpeed);
}
```

We must also adjust the scale of the particle if its scale is not equal to the mRatioX/ mRatioY values to compensate for device orientation:

```
// If the particle's scale is not equal to the current ratio
if(entity.getScaleX() != mRatioX){
   // Re-scale the particle to better suit the current screen ratio
   entity.setScale(mRatioX, mRatioY);
}
```

That's all it takes to set up a live wallpaper with AndEngine! Try playing around with the particle system, adding new customizable values to the settings, and see what you can come up with. With this extension, you'll be up and running, creating new live wallpapers in no time at all!

See also...

- The _Saving and loading game data_ section in _Chapter 1, AndEngine Game Structure._
- The _Working with particle systems_ section in _Chapter 2, Working with Entities._

Networking with the multiplayer extension

Here we come to the undoubtedly most popular aspect of game design. This is of course multiplayer gaming. In this project recipe, we're going to work with AndEngine's multiplayer extension in order to create a fully functional client and server directly onto the mobile device. Once we cover the range of classes and features that this extension includes to make network programming easier, you will be able to take your online gaming ideas and turn them into reality!

Getting ready

Creating a multiplayer game can require quite a few components in order to satisfy the readability of the project.

 Refer to the project named `MultiplayerExtensionExample` in the code bundle.

For this reason, we're going to separate these different components into five classes.

Create a new Android project, naming it `MultiplayerExtensionExample`. Once the project is ready to go, create four new class files with the following names:

  ▶ `MultiplayerExtensionExample.java`: The `BaseGameActivity` class for the recipe

  ▶ `MultiplayerServer.java`: The class containing the main server component

  ▶ `MultiplayerClient.java`: The class containing the main client component

  ▶ `ServerMessages.java`: The class containing messages meant to be sent from the server to clients

  ▶ `ClientMessages.java`: The class containing messages meant to be sent from clients to the server

Open the project's `AndroidManifest.xml` file and add the following two `<uses-permission>` attributes:

```
<uses-permission android:name="android.permission.ACCESS_WIFI_STATE"/>
<uses-permission android:name="android.permission.INTERNET"/>
```

How to do it...

For the sake of keeping things relative throughout this recipe, we're going to work with each class in the order they were mentioned in the *Getting ready* section, starting with the `MultiplayerExtensionExample` class.

1. Declare and register the server/client messages for `mMessagePool`:

```
this.mMessagePool.registerMessage(ServerMessages.SERVER_MESSAGE_
ADD_POINT, AddPointServerMessage.class);
this.mMessagePool.registerMessage(ClientMessages.CLIENT_MESSAGE_
ADD_POINT, AddPointClientMessage.class);
```

2. Configure the scene touch listener to allow the sending of messages to and from the server:

```
if (pSceneTouchEvent.getAction() == TouchEvent.ACTION_MOVE) {
  if (mServer != null) {

    if(mClient != null){
      // Obtain a ServerMessage object from the mMessagePool
      AddPointServerMessage message = (AddPointServerMessage)
MultiplayerExtensionExample.this.mMessagePool.
obtainMessage(ServerMessages.SERVER_MESSAGE_ADD_POINT);
      // Set up the message with the device's ID, touch
coordinates and draw color
      message.set(SERVER_ID, pSceneTouchEvent.getX(),
pSceneTouchEvent.getY(), mClient.getDrawColor());
      // Send the client/server's draw message to all clients
      mServer.sendMessage(message);
      // Recycle the message back into the message pool
      MultiplayerExtensionExample.this.mMessagePool.
recycleMessage(message);
    return true;
    }
    // If device is running as a client...
  } else if(mClient != null){
    /* Similar to the message sending code above, except
     * in this case, the client is *not* running as a server.
     * This means we have to first send the message to the server
     * via a ClientMessage rather than ServerMessage
     */
    AddPointClientMessage message = (AddPointClientMessage)
MultiplayerExtensionExample.this.mMessagePool.
obtainMessage(ClientMessages.CLIENT_MESSAGE_ADD_POINT);
    message.set(CLIENT_ID, pSceneTouchEvent.getX(),
pSceneTouchEvent.getY(), mClient.getDrawColor());
    mClient.sendMessage(message);
    MultiplayerExtensionExample.this.mMessagePool.
recycleMessage(message);

    return true;
  }
}
```

3. Create the dialog *switch* statement prompting users to select to either act as the server or client. In the event a server or client component is selected, we will initialize one of the two components:

```
mServer = new MultiplayerServer(SERVER_PORT);
mServer.initServer();


// or...


mClient = new MultiplayerClient(mServerIP,SERVER_PORT, mEngine,
mScene);
mClient.initClient();
```

4. Override the activity's `onDestroy()` method to terminate both the server and client components when the activity is destroyed:

```
@Override
protected void onDestroy() {
  // Terminate the client and server socket connections
  // when the application is destroyed
  if (this.mClient != null)
    this.mClient.terminate();

  if (this.mServer != null)
    this.mServer.terminate();
  super.onDestroy();
}
```

Once all of the main activity's functionality is in place, we can move on to writing the server-side code.

5. Create the server's initialization method—creating the `SocketServer` object, which handles connections to the server's clients:

```
// Create the SocketServer, specifying a port, client listener and
// a server state listener (listeners are implemented in this
class)
MultiplayerServer.this.mSocketServer = new SocketServer<SocketConn
ectionClientConnector>(
    MultiplayerServer.this.mServerPort,
    MultiplayerServer.this, MultiplayerServer.this) {

    // Handle client connection here...
};
```

6. Handle the client connection to the server. This involves registering client messages and defining how to handle them:

```
// Called when a new client connects to the server...
@Override
protected SocketConnectionClientConnector newClientConnector(
    SocketConnection pSocketConnection)
    throws IOException {
        // Create a new client connector from the socket connection
        final SocketConnectionClientConnector clientConnector = new
SocketConnectionClientConnector(pSocketConnection);

        // Register the client message to the new client
        clientConnector.registerClientMessage(ClientMessages.CLIENT_
MESSAGE_ADD_POINT, AddPointClientMessage.class, new IClientMessage
Handler<SocketConnection>(){

        // Handle message received by the server...
        @Override
        public void onHandleMessage(
            ClientConnector<SocketConnection> pClientConnector,
            IClientMessage pClientMessage)
            throws IOException {
        // Obtain the client message
        AddPointClientMessage incomingMessage =
(AddPointClientMessage) pClientMessage;

        // Create a new server message containing the contents of
the message received
        // from a client
        AddPointServerMessage outgoingMessage = new AddPointSe
rverMessage(incomingMessage.getID(), incomingMessage.getX(),
incomingMessage.getY(), incomingMessage.getColorId());

        // Reroute message received from client to all other clients
        sendMessage(outgoingMessage);
    }
});

    // Return the new client connector
    return clientConnector;
}
```

7. Once the `SocketServer` object has been declared and initialized, we need to call its `start()` method:

```
// Start the server once it's initialized
MultiplayerServer.this.mSocketServer.start();
```

8. Create the `sendMessage()` server broadcasting method:

```
// Send broadcast server message to all clients
public void sendMessage(ServerMessage pServerMessage){
  try {
    this.mSocketServer.sendBroadcastServerMessage(pServerMessage);
  } catch (IOException e) {
    e.printStackTrace();
  }
}
```

9. Create the `terminate()` method to shut down the connection:

```
// Terminate the server socket and stop the server thread
public void terminate(){
  if(this.mSocketServer != null)
  this.mSocketServer.terminate();
}
```

With the server-side code out of the way, we will continue on to implement the client-side code in the `MultiplayerClient` class. The class is quite similar to the `MultiplayerServer` class, so we'll be omitting the unnecessary client-side steps from here.

10. Create the `Socket`, `SocketConnection`, and finally the `ServerConnector` to establish the connection with the server:

```
// Create the socket with the specified Server IP and port

Socket socket = new Socket(MultiplayerClient.this.mServerIP,
MultiplayerClient.this.mServerPort);

// Create the socket connection, establishing the input/output
stream

SocketConnection socketConnection = new SocketConnection(socket);

// Create the server connector with the specified socket
connection

// and client connection listener

MultiplayerClient.this.mServerConnector = new SocketConnectionServ
erConnector(socketConnection, MultiplayerClient.this);
```

11. Handling the messages received from the server:

```
// obtain the class casted server message
AddPointServerMessage message = (AddPointServerMessage)
pServerMessage;

// Create a new Rectangle (point), based on values obtained via
the server
// message received
Rectangle point = new Rectangle(message.getX(), message.getY(), 3,
3, mEngine.getVertexBufferObjectManager());

// Obtain the color id from the message
final int colorId = message.getColorId();
```

12. Creating client and server messages:

    `ClientMessage` and `ServerMessage` are meant to act as bundles of data that are able to be sent and received to and from the server as well as to and from clients. In this recipe, we're creating a message for both the client and server to handle sending information about where to draw points on the client devices. The variables stored in these messages include:

```
// Member variables to be read in from the server and sent to
clients
private int mID;
private float mX;
private float mY;
private int mColorId;
```

While reading and writing the data for communication is as simple as the following:

```
// Apply the read data to the message's member variables
@Override
protected void onReadTransmissionData(DataInputStream
pDataInputStream)
    throws IOException {
  this.mID = pDataInputStream.readInt();
  this.mX = pDataInputStream.readFloat();
  this.mY = pDataInputStream. readFloat();
  this.mColorId = pDataInputStream.readInt();
}

// Write the message's member variables to the output stream
@Override
protected void onWriteTransmissionData(
    DataOutputStream pDataOutputStream) throws IOException {
  pDataOutputStream.writeInt(this.mID);
```

```
        pDataOutputStream.writeFloat(this.mX);
        pDataOutputStream.writeFloat(this.mY);
        pDataOutputStream.writeInt(mColorId);
    }
```

How it works...

In this recipe's implementation of server/client communication, we're building an application that allows a server to be deployed directly on a mobile device. From here, other mobile devices are able to act as a client and connect to the aforementioned mobile server. Once the server has been established with at least one client, the server will begin to relay messages to all clients if a touch event is created by any client, drawing points on the screens of all connected clients. If this sounds a bit confusing, have no fear. It will all come together shortly!

In the first five steps, we're writing the `BaseGameActivity` class. This class is simply the entry point to the server and client, as well as a means to provide touch event capabilities for clients to draw onscreen.

In the first step, we're registering the necessary `ServerMessage` and `ClientMessage` objects to our `mMessagePool`. The `mMessagePool` object is an extension of the `MultiPool` class in AndEngine. See the *Creating sprite pools* section in *Chapter 8, Maximizing Performance*, for how to use the `MessagePool` class to recycle messages sent and received across the network.

In step two, we are setting up the scene with a scene touch listener interface whose purpose is to send messages across the network. Within the touch listener, we can use simple conditional statements to check whether or not the device is running as a client or a server with the line, `if(mServer != null)`, returning true if the device is running as a server. Additionally, we can call `if(mClient != null)` to check if the device is running as a client. A nested client check inside a server check would return true in the event of a device operating as both a client and a server. If a device is operating as a client, sending a message is as easy as obtaining a new message from `mMessagePool`, calling the `set(device_id, touchX, touchY, colorId)` method on the said message, then calling `mClient.sendMessage(message)`. Once the message is sent, we should always recycle it back into the pool so as to not waste memory. One final point to mention before moving on; in the nested client conditional, we're sending a server message rather than a client message. This is because the client, in this case, is also the server. This means we can skip over sending a client message to the server since the server already contains the touch event data.

Step three will most likely not be an ideal situation for most developers as we're using dialogs as a means to choose whether the device will act as a server or a client. This scenario is simply used to display how to initialize the components, so a dialog is not necessarily important. Choosing whether users should be able to host games or not is very much dependent on the game type and developer's idea, but this recipe at least covers how to set up a server if need be. Just keep in mind, when initializing a server, all we need to know is the **port number**. A client, on the other hand, needs to know a valid **server IP** and server port in order to establish a connection. Once the `MultiplayerServer` and/ or `MultiplayerClient` classes have been constructed with these parameters, we can initialize the components. The purpose of the initialization will be covered shortly.

The fourth and final step for the `BaseGameActivity` class is to allow the activity to terminate the `MultiplayerServer` and `MultiplayerClient` connections in the event that the activity calls `onDestroy()`. This will shut down the communication threads and sockets before the application is destroyed.

Moving on to the `MultiplayerServer` code, let's take a look at the initialization of a server in step five. When creating a `SocketServer` object that a server uses in order to listen for new client connections, we must pass in the server's port number, as well as a `ClientConnectorListener` and a `SocketServerListener`. The `MultiplayerServer` class implements those two listeners, logging whenever the server starts up, stops, when a client connects to the server, and when a client disconnects.

In the sixth step, we're implementing the system which handles how the server will respond to incoming connections, and how to handle messages received by clients. The following points cover the process involved in the order they should be implemented:

- `protected SocketConnectionClientConnector newClientConnector(...)` is called when a new client has connected to the server.

- Create a new `SocketConnectionClientConnector` is for the client to use as a means of communication between the new client and the server.

- Register the `ClientMessages` you wish the server to recognize via `registerClientMessage(flag, message.class, messageHandlerInterface)`.

- Within the `onHandleMessage()` method of the `messageHandlerInterface` interface, we handle any messages received from across the network. In this case, the server is simply relaying the client's message back to all connected clients.

- Return the new `clientConnector` object.

These points outline the main functionality of server/client communication. In this recipe, we're using a single message in order to draw points on client devices, but for a more broad range of messages we can continue to call the `registerClientMessage()` method so long as the flag parameter matches up with the message type we're obtaining in the `onHandleMessage()` interface. Once all of the appropriate messages have been registered and we're finished with the client handling code, we can continue on to step seven and call `start()` on the `mSocketServer` object.

In step eight, we create the `sendMessage(message)` method for the server. The server's variation of `sendMessage(message)` sends a broadcast message to all clients by simply looping through the client connector list, calling `sendServerMessage(message)` to each connector. If we wish to send a server message to individual clients, we can simply call `sendServerMessage(message)` on an individual ClientConnector. On the other end, we have the client's variation of `sendMessage(message)`. The client's `sendMessage()` method does not actually send a message to other clients; in fact, the client doesn't communicate with other clients at all. A client's job is to communicate with the server, which then communicates to the other clients. See the following figure for a better understanding of how our network communication works:

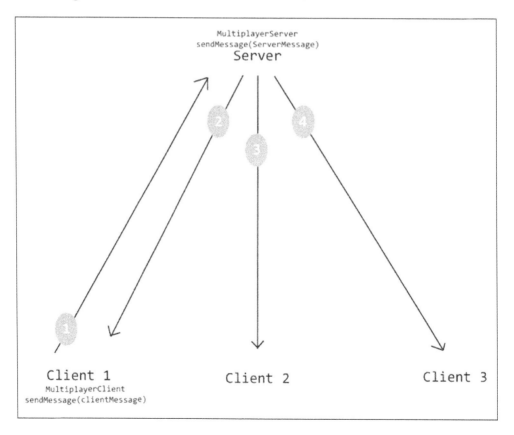

In the preceding figure, the process is outlined by the numbers. First, a client sends the message to the server. Once the server receives the message, it will loop through each of the `ClientConnector` objects in its client list, sending the broadcast to all clients.

The final step involved in creating the `MultiplayerServer` component is to create a method for terminating the `mSocketServer`. This method is called by `onDestroy()` in our main activity in order to destroy the communication thread when we are finished with it.

With all of the server-side code in place, we can move on to writing the client-side. The `MultiplayerClient` code is somewhat similar to the server's, with a few differences. When establishing a connection with the server, we must be a little bit more specific than in the server's initialization. First, we must create a new Socket with a specified IP address to connect to, along with a server port number. We then pass the `Socket` to a new `SocketConnection` object, used to establish an input/output stream on the socket. Once this is done we can then create our `ServerConnector`, whose purpose is to make the final connection between the client and the server.

We're coming close to a full client/server communication project now! Step eleven is where the real magic happens—the client receiving server messages. In order to receive a server message, similar to the server implementation of receiving messages, we simply call `mServerConnector.registerServerMessage(...)` which then gives us the opportunity to fill in an interface for `onHandleMessage(serverConnector, serverMessage)`. Again, similar to the server-side implementation, we can class-cast the `serverMessage` object to an `AddPointServerMessage` class, allowing us to obtain the custom values stored in the message.

Now, with all of the server and client code out of the way, we come to the final step. This is, of course, creating the messages that will be used for `MessagePool` as well as the objects that we've been sending and receiving all over the place. There are two different types of Message objects that we need to be aware of. The first type is `ServerMessage`, which consists of messages that are meant to be *sent from the client and received/read by the server*. The other type of message is, you've guessed it, `ClientMessage`, which is meant to be *sent from the server and received/read by the client(s)*. By creating our own message classes, we can easily package together chunks of data represented by primitive datatypes and send them across the network. The primitive datatypes include `int`, `float`, `long`, `boolean`, and so on.

In the messages used in this recipe, we're storing an ID, which is meant to tell us whether the message is sent from a client or the server, the x and y coordinates of every client touch event, and the currently selected color id for drawing. Each value should have its own corresponding *get* method so that we're able to obtain message details whenever a message is received. Additionally, by overriding a client or server message, we must implement the `onReadTransmissionData(DataInputStream)` method which allows us to obtain the datatypes from the input stream and copy them to our member variables. We must also implement the `onWriteTransmissionData(DataOutputStream)`, which is used to write the member variables to the data stream and send it across the network. One thing we need to be aware of when creating the server and client messages is that data read into our receiving member variables are obtained in the same order they were sent. See the order of our server message read and write methods:

```
// write method
pDataOutputStream.writeInt(this.mID);
pDataOutputStream.writeFloat(this.mX);
pDataOutputStream.writeFloat(this.mY);
pDataOutputStream.writeInt(this.mColorId);

// read method
this.mID = pDataInputStream.readInt();
this.mX = pDataInputStream.readFloat();
this.mY = pDataInputStream. readFloat();
this.mColorId = pDataInputStream.readInt();
```

Keeping the preceding code in mind, we can be sure that if we write a message containing an `int`, `float`, `int`, `boolean`, and a `float` into the output stream, any device receiving the message will read in an `int`, `float`, `int`, `boolean`, and a `float` respectively.

Creating high-resolution graphics with SVG

The ability to incorporate **scalable vector graphics** (**SVG**) into our mobile games is a serious benefit to development, and even more so when working with Android. The biggest benefit, and the one we'll be covering in this topic, is the fact that SVG's can be scaled to suit the device running our applications. No more having to create multiple PNG sets for larger displays, and even more importantly, no more having to deal with terribly pixelated graphics on large screen devices! In this topic we're going to use the `AndEngineSVGTextureRegionExtension` extension to create high-resolution texture regions for our sprites. See the following screenshot for a standard resolution image scaled on the left-hand side, versus SVG on the right-hand side:

While SVG assets can be very convincing when it comes to creating high-resolution graphics across multiple screen sizes, there are some downsides to them as well, in the SVG extension's current state. The SVG extension will not render all of the elements available, such as text and 3D shapes, for example. However, most of the necessary elements are available and will properly load during runtime, such as paths, gradients, fill-colors, and some shapes. Elements which fail to load will be displayed via the Logcat during SVG loading.

It is a wise choice to remove the elements which are not supported by the SVG extension from SVG files as they can influence loading times, which is the other negative aspect when it comes to using the SVG extension. The SVG textures will take considerably longer to load than PNG files as they must first be converted to PNG before loading to memory. It is not uncommon to see SVG textures take up to two or three times longer than the equivalent PNG images, depending on how many elements are included in each SVG. The most common workaround is to save the SVG textures to the device in PNG format during the first launch of the application. Every subsequent launch would then load the PNG images in order to reduce load time while keeping device-specific image resolutions.

Getting ready

Refer to the project named WorkingWithSVG in the code bundle.

How to do it...

Creating a SVG texture region is an easy task to accomplish with big results.

1. Similar to your average `TextureRegion`, first we require a `BuildableBitmapTextureAtlas`:

   ```
   // Create a new buildable bitmap texture atlas to build and
   contain texture regions
   BuildableBitmapTextureAtlas bitmapTextureAtlas = new Buildabl
   eBitmapTextureAtlas(mEngine.getTextureManager(), 1024, 1024,
   TextureOptions.BILINEAR);
   ```

2. Now that we've got a texture atlas setup, we can create the SVG texture regions through the use of the `SVGBitmapTextureAtlasTextureRegionFactory` singleton:

   ```
   // Create a low-res (32x32) texture region of svg_image.svg
   mLowResTextureRegion = SVGBitmapTextureAtlasTextureRegionFactory.
   createFromAsset(bitmapTextureAtlas, this, "svg_image.svg", 32,32);

   // Create a med-res (128x128) texture region of svg_image.svg
   mMedResTextureRegion = SVGBitmapTextureAtlasTextureRegionFactory.
   createFromAsset(bitmapTextureAtlas, this, "svg_image.svg", 128,
   128);

   // Create a high-res (256x256) texture region of svg_image.svg
   mHiResTextureRegion = SVGBitmapTextureAtlasTextureRegionFactory.cr
   eateFromAsset(bitmapTextureAtlas, this, "svg_image.svg", 256,256);
   ```

How it works...

As we can see, creating an SVG texture region is not much different from your average `TextureRegion`. The only real difference between the two in terms of instantiation is the fact that we have to enter a `width` and `height` value as the final two parameters. This is because, unlike your average raster image format whose width and height are more or less hardcoded due to the fixed pixel positions, SVG pixel positions can be scaled up or down to any size we'd like. If we scale the SVG texture region, the vector's coordinates will simply adjust themselves in order to continue to produce a clear, precise image. Once the SVG texture region is built, we can apply it to a sprite as we would any other texture region.

That's all fine and dandy, knowing how to create the SVG texture region, but there's more to it than that. After all, the beauty of being able to use SVG images in our games is the ability to scale the image depending on the device's display size. In this way we can avoid having to load larger images for smaller screened devices in order to accommodate for tablets, and we won't have to make our tablet users suffer by creating small texture regions in order to conserve memory. The SVG extension actually makes it quite simple for us to deal with the idea of scaling depending on display size. The following code shows us how we can implement a mass-scaling factor to all SVG texture regions created. This will allow us to avoid having to create different sized texture regions manually, depending on display size:

```
float mScaleFactor = 1;

// Obtain the device display metrics (dpi)
DisplayMetrics displayMetrics = this.getResources().
getDisplayMetrics();

int deviceDpi = displayMetrics.densityDpi;

switch(deviceDpi){
case DisplayMetrics.DENSITY_LOW:
  // Scale factor already set to 1
  break;

case DisplayMetrics.DENSITY_MEDIUM:
  // Increase scale to a suitable value for mid-size displays
  mScaleFactor = 1.5f;
  break;

case DisplayMetrics.DENSITY_HIGH:
  // Increase scale to a suitable value for larger displays
  mScaleFactor = 2;
  break;

case DisplayMetrics.DENSITY_XHIGH:
  // Increase scale to suitable value for largest displays
  mScaleFactor = 2.5f;
  break;

default:
  // Scale factor already set to 1
  break;
}

SVGBitmapTextureAtlasTextureRegionFactory.
setScaleFactor(mScaleFactor);
```

The preceding code can be copied and pasted into the `onCreateEngineOptions()` method of an activity. All that needs to be done is to decide on the scale factors you'd like to apply to the SVG's depending on device size! From this point on, we can create a single `SVG` texture region and, depending on the display size, the texture region will scale accordingly. For example, we can load up a texture region like the following:

```
mLowResTextureRegion = SVGBitmapTextureAtlasTextureRegionFactory.cre
ateFromAsset(bitmapTextureAtlas, this, "svg_image.svg", 32,32);
```

We may define the texture region's width and height values to `32`, but by adjusting the scale factor in the factory class, the texture region would be built to `80x80` by multiplying the specified value by the scale factor for a `DENSITY_XHIGH` display. Just be careful when handling texture regions with autoscaling factors. The scale will also increase the space they consume within the `BuildableBitmapTextureAtlas` object and may cause errors if exceeded, as with any other `TextureRegion`.

See also...

> ▸ The *Different types of textures* section in *Chapter 1, AndEngine Game Structure*.

Color mapping with SVG texture regions

A useful aspect of `SVG` texture regions is the fact that we are able to easily map the texture's colors. This technique is common in games that allow users to select custom colors for their player's character, be it clothing and accessory color, hair color, skin color, terrain themes, and much more. In this topic, we're going to use the `ISVGColorMapper` interface while building our `SVG` texture regions in order to create customized color sets for our sprites.

Getting ready

Before we get into the coding side of color mapping, we need to create an SVG image with preset colors. We can think of these preset colors as our *map*. One of the most preferred SVG editors amongst many developers is called **Inkscape**, which is a free, very easy to use, and full-featured editor. Inkscape can be downloaded from the following link, `http://inkscape.org/download/`, or feel free to work with another SVG editor of your choice.

How to do it...

Color mapping might sound like it will be a tedious job, but in reality it's actually very easy to accomplish. All we need is to keep a little bit of consistency between the `SVG` image and the code. Keeping this in mind, the idea of creating multicolored, single source textures can be a very quick task. The steps below include the process starting from drawing the `SVG` image to allow for easy color mapping, as well as writing the code for mapping colors to specific areas of the `SVG` image within our application.

▶ Drawing our SVG image:

In order to easily map colors to an SVG texture region during runtime, we need to draw an SVG image in the editor of our choice. This involves color-coding the different segments of our images for easy recognition in our ISVGColorMapper interface. The following figure depicts a shape with defined color values that are displayed on the left of the figure.

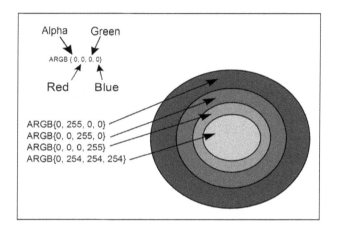

▶ Implementing the ISVGColorMapper interface:

Just prior to creating the SVG texture region via SVGBitmapTextureAtlasTextureRegionFactory, we will define our ISVGColorMapper interface in relation to our SVG image. If we look at the conditionals in the following code, we can see that we are checking for the same color values found in the preceding figure:

```
ISVGColorMapper svgColorMapper = new ISVGColorMapper(){
  @Override
  public Integer mapColor(final Integer pColor) {
    // If the path contains no color channels, return null
    if(pColor == null) {
      return null;
    }

    // Obtain color values from 0-255
    int alpha = Color.alpha(pColor);
    int red = Color.red(pColor);
    int green = Color.green(pColor);
    int blue = Color.blue(pColor);

    // If the SVG image's color values equal red, or
ARGB{0,255,0,0}
```

```
            if(red == 255 && green == 0 && blue == 0){
              // Return a pure blue color
              return Color.argb(0, 0, 0, 255);


            // If the SVG image's color values equal green, or
          ARGB{0,0,255,0}
            } else if(red == 0 && green == 255 && blue == 0){
              // Return a pure white
              return Color.argb(0, 255, 255, 255);


            // If the SVG image's color values equal blue, or
          ARGB{0,0,0,255}
            } else if(red == 0 && green == 0 && blue == 255){
              // Return a pure blue color
              return Color.argb(0, 0, 0, blue);


            // If the SVG image's color values are white, or
          ARGB{0,254,254,254}
            } else if(red == 254 && blue == 254 && green == 254){
              // Return a pure red color
              return Color.argb(0, 255, 0, 0);


            // If our "custom color" conditionals do not apply...
            } else {
              // Return the SVG image's default color values
              return Color.argb(alpha, red, green, blue);
            }
          }
        };


      // Create an SVG texture region
      mSVGTextureRegion = SVGBitmapTextureAtlasTextureRegionFactory.
      createFromAsset(bitmapTextureAtlas, this, "color_mapping.svg",
      256,256, svgColorMapper);
```

▶ Lastly, once the interface has been defined, we can pass it in as the final parameter
  when creating the texture region. Once this is done, creating a new sprite with the
  SVG texture region will yield the color values defined within the color mapper.

How it works...

Just a brief lesson on colors before we start; if you're looking at this recipe's code and are confused about the *random* values selected for our conditionals and color results, it's very simple. Each color component, red, green and blue, can be supplied a color value anywhere between 0 and 255. passing a value of 0 to a color component would result in no contribution from that color, while passing 255 would be considered to be *full* color contribution. With this in mind, we know that if all color components return a value of 0, we will be passing the color black to our texture region's path. If we pass a value of 255 to the red component, while passing 0 for both green and blue, we know that the texture region's path will be a bright red color.

If we take a look back at the figure in the *How to do it...* section, we can see **alpha, red, green, and blue** (**ARGB**) color values with arrows pointing to the area on the circle that they represent. These will not directly affect the end result of our texture region's colors; they are simply in place so that we can gain a reference to each portion of the circle within our color mapper interface. Note that the very first, most outer portion of the circle, is bright red at a value of 255. With that in mind, see the following condition within our color mapper:

```
// If the SVG image's color values equal red, or ARGB{0,255,0,0}
} else if(red == 255 && green == 0 && blue == 0){
  // Return a pure blue color
  return Color.argb(0, 0, 0, 255);

// If the SVG image's color values equal green, or ARGB{0,0,255,0}
}
```

The conditional statement in the preceding code will check for any path of the SVG image which contains a pure red value with no contributions from green or blue, returning a pure blue color instead. This is how the swapping of colors occurs, and this is how we can map colors to our images! Knowing this, it is entirely possible to create many different sets of colors for our SVG images, but for each color set, we must provide a separate texture region.

One important key point to note is that we should include a returning value that will return the default path's color values in the event that none of our conditions are met. This allows us to leave out conditionals for smaller details such as the SVG image's outline, or other colors, and instead fill them in as they appear in the image if we were to open it in our favorite SVG editor. This should be included as the final `else` statement in the color mapper:

```
// If our "custom color" conditionals do not apply...
} else {
  // Return the SVG image's default color values
  return Color.argb(alpha, red, green, blue);
}
```

There's more...

In the *How it works...* section of this recipe, we covered how to change the colors of static SVG image paths. Without putting too much thought into the idea of creating color themes as mentioned above, it might sound like this is the be-all-end-all to creating more objects, terrain, characters, and so on. The truth is that, in this day and age, a lot of games need variance in order to create an appealing asset. By variance, we are of course referring to gradients. If we think back to the conditionals we'd written above, we are checking for absolute color values before returning a customized color.

Thankfully, working with gradients is not too difficult as we can adjust the gradient's **Stop Color** and the interpolation between colors will automatically be handled for us! We can think of a *stop* as a color-defining point of the gradient which interpolates between other *stops* as distance increases. This is what causes the gradient's blending effect and this also plays a role in the ease of creating color themes through the use of the same method described in this recipe. See the following screenshot for a gradient that starts out as a pure red color RGB{255, 0, 0}, to pure green RGB{0, 255, 0}, and finally to blue RGB{0, 0, 255}:

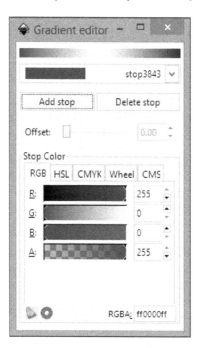

If we were to use the above gradient in an SVG image, we could easily apply color mapping with proper interpolation between the color stops by simply modifying the specific color at the position of each stop. The following code will change the gradient to appear red, green, and yellow, rather than having blue as the third color stop:

```
} else if(red == 0 && green == 0 && blue == 255){
  // Return a pure blue color
  return Color.argb(0, 255, 255, 0);
  }
```

See also...

▶ The *Creating high-resolution graphics with SVG* section.

10
Getting More From AndEngine

This chapter will cover additional recipes that have a more specific application than those in previous chapters. These recipes include:

- ▶ Loading all textures from a folder
- ▶ Using textured meshes
- ▶ Applying a sprite-based shadow
- ▶ Creating a physics-based moving platform
- ▶ Creating a physics-based rope bridge

Loading all textures from a folder

When creating a game that has a large amount of textures, loading each texture individually can become tedious. Creating a method to load and retrieve textures in such a game can be not only timesaving during development, but also reduce the overall loading times during runtime. In this recipe, we will create a way to load a large amount of textures using only a single line of code.

Getting ready...

First, create a new activity class named `TextureFolderLoadingActivity` that extends the `BaseGameActivity` class. Next, create a folder named `FolderToLoad` in the `assets/gfx/` folder. Finally, place five images in the `assets/gfx/FolderToLoad/` folder with the names: `Coin1`, `Coin5`, `Coin10`, `Coin50`, and `Coin100`.

Follow these steps to fill our `TextureFolderLoadingActivity` activity class:

1. Place the following, simple code in our activity to make it functional:

```
@Override
public EngineOptions onCreateEngineOptions() {
  return new EngineOptions(true,
    ScreenOrientation.LANDSCAPE_SENSOR,
    new FillResolutionPolicy(),
    new Camera(0, 0, 800, 480))
    .setWakeLockOptions(WakeLockOptions.SCREEN_ON);
}
@Override
public void onCreateResources(OnCreateResourcesCallback
    pOnCreateResourcesCallback) {
  pOnCreateResourcesCallback.onCreateResourcesFinished();
}
@Override
public void onCreateScene(OnCreateSceneCallback
    pOnCreateSceneCallback) {
  Scene mScene = new Scene();
  mScene.setBackground(new Background(0.9f,0.9f,0.9f));
  pOnCreateSceneCallback.onCreateSceneFinished(mScene);
}
@Override
public void onPopulateScene(Scene pScene,
    OnPopulateSceneCallback pOnPopulateSceneCallback) {
  pOnPopulateSceneCallback.onPopulateSceneFinished();
}
```

2. Next, place this `ArrayList` variable and `ManagedStandardTexture` class inside of the activity:

```
public final ArrayList<ManagedStandardTexture> loadedTextures =
  new ArrayList<ManagedStandardTexture>();
public class ManagedStandardTexture {
  public ITextureRegion textureRegion;
  public String name;
  public ManagedStandardTexture(String pName,
      final ITextureRegion pTextureRegion) {
    name = pName;
    textureRegion = pTextureRegion;
  }
  public void removeFromMemory() {
```

```
            loadedTextures.remove(this);
            textureRegion.getTexture().unload();
            textureRegion = null;
            name = null;
        }
    }
```

3. Then, add the next two methods to the activity class to allow us to load a texture by passing only the `TextureOptions` parameter and the filename:

```
public ITextureRegion getTextureRegion(TextureOptions
        pTextureOptions, String pFilename) {
  loadAndManageTextureRegion(pTextureOptions,pFilename);
  return loadedTextures.get(
    loadedTextures.size()-1).textureRegion;
}
public void loadAndManageTextureRegion(TextureOptions
        pTextureOptions, String pFilename) {
  AssetBitmapTextureAtlasSource cSource =
    AssetBitmapTextureAtlasSource.create(
    this.getAssets(), pFilename);
  BitmapTextureAtlas TextureToLoad =
    new BitmapTextureAtlas(mEngine.getTextureManager(),
      cSource.getTextureWidth(),
      cSource.getTextureHeight(),
      pTextureOptions);
  TextureRegion TextureRegionToLoad =
    BitmapTextureAtlasTextureRegionFactory.
      createFromAsset(TextureToLoad, this,
        pFilename, 0, 0);
  TextureToLoad.load();
  loadedTextures.add(new ManagedStandardTexture(
    pFilename.substring(
      pFilename.lastIndexOf("/")+1,
      pFilename.lastIndexOf(".")),
    TextureRegionToLoad));
}
```

4. Now insert the following method that allows us to load all of the textures within either one folder or multiple folders:

```
public void loadAllTextureRegionsInFolders(TextureOptions
        pTextureOptions, String... pFolderPaths) {
  String[] listFileNames;
  String curFilePath;
  String curFileExtension;
```

```
     for (int i = 0; i < pFolderPaths.length; i++)
       try {
         listFileNames = this.getAssets().
           list(pFolderPaths[i].substring(0,
           pFolderPaths[i].lastIndexOf("/")));
         for (String fileName : listFileNames) {
           curFilePath =
             pFolderPaths[i].concat(fileName);
           curFileExtension =
             curFilePath.substring(
             curFilePath.lastIndexOf("."));
           if(curFileExtension.
             equalsIgnoreCase(".png")
             || curFileExtension.
             equalsIgnoreCase(".bmp")
             || curFileExtension.
             equalsIgnoreCase(".jpg"))
             loadAndManageTextureRegion(
               pTextureOptions,
               curFilePath);
         }
       } catch (IOException e) {
         System.out.print("Failed to load textures
           from folder!");
         e.printStackTrace();
         return;
       }
   }
```

5. Next, place the following methods into the activity to let us unload all
   ManagedStandardTexture classes or retrieve a texture by its short filename:

```
public void unloadAllTextures() {
  for(ManagedStandardTexture curTex : loadedTextures) {
    curTex.removeFromMemory();
    curTex=null;
    loadedTextures.remove(curTex);
  }
  System.gc();
}

public ITextureRegion getLoadedTextureRegion(String pName) {
  for(ManagedStandardTexture curTex : loadedTextures)
    if(curTex.name.equalsIgnoreCase(pName))
      return curTex.textureRegion;
  return null;
}
```

6. Now that we have all of our methods in the activity, place the following line of code in the `onCreateResources()` method:

    ```
    this.loadAllTextureRegionsInFolders(TextureOptions.BILINEAR, "gfx/
    FolderToLoad/");
    ```

7. Finally, add the following code to the `onPopulateScene()` method to show how we can retrieve a loaded texture by name:

    ```
    pScene.attachChild(new Sprite(144f, 240f,
      getLoadedTextureRegion("Coin1"),
      this.getVertexBufferObjectManager()));
    pScene.attachChild(new Sprite(272f, 240f,
      getLoadedTextureRegion("Coin5"),
      this.getVertexBufferObjectManager()));
    pScene.attachChild(new Sprite(400f, 240f,
      getLoadedTextureRegion("Coin10"),
      this.getVertexBufferObjectManager()));
    pScene.attachChild(new Sprite(528f, 240f,
      getLoadedTextureRegion("Coin50"),
      this.getVertexBufferObjectManager()));
    pScene.attachChild(new Sprite(656f, 240f,
      getLoadedTextureRegion("Coin100"),
      this.getVertexBufferObjectManager()));
    ```

How it works...

In step one, we set up our `TextureFolderLoadingActivity` activity class by implementing the standard, overridden `BaseGameActivity` methods that most AndEngine games use. For more information on setting up an activity for use with AndEngine, see the *Understanding the life cycle* recipe in *Chapter 1, AndEngine Game Structure*.

In step two, we create an `ArrayList` variable of `ManagedStandardTexture` objects, which is defined directly following the definition of the `ArrayList` variable. `ManagedStandardTextures` are simple containers that hold a pointer to an `ITextureRegion` region and a string variable that represents the `ITextureRegion` object's name. The `ManagedStandardTexture` class also includes a method to unload `ITextureRegion` and prepare the variables to be removed from memory upon the next garbage collection.

The third step includes two methods, `getTextureRegion()` and `loadAndManageTextureRegion()`:

▶ The `getTextureRegion()` method calls the `loadAndManageTextureRegion()` method and returns the recently-loaded texture from the `ArrayList` variable named `loadedTextures` defined in step two.

▸ The `loadAndManageTextureRegion()` method creates an
`AssetBitmapTextureAtlasSource` source named `cSource`, which is only
used to pass the texture's width and height in the following definition of the
`BitmapTextureAtlas` object, `TextureToLoad`.

The `TextureRegion` object, `TextureRegionToLoad`, is created by calling the
`BitmapTextureAtlasTextureRegionFactory` object's `createFromAsset()` method.
`TextureToLoad` is then loaded, and the `TextureRegionToLoad` object is added to the
`loadedTextures ArrayList` variable by creating a new `ManagedStandardTexture`
class. For more information on textures, see the *Different types of textures* recipe in *Chapter
1, AndEngine Game Structure*.

In step four, we create a method that parses the list of files in each folder passed in the
`pFolderPaths` array and loads the image files as textures with the `TextureOptions`
parameter being applied to each image. The `listFileNames` string array holds the list of
files in each of the `pFolderPaths` folders, and the `curFilePath` and `curFileExtension`
variables are used to store the filepaths and their relative extensions for use in determining
which files are AndEngine-supported images. The first `for` loop simply runs the parsing and
loading process for each folder path given. The `getAssets().list()` method throws an
`IOException` exception and thus needs to be enclosed in a `try-catch` block. It is used
to retrieve a list of all of the files within the passed `String` parameter. The second `for`
loop sets `curFilePath` to the current i value's folder path concatenated with the current
filename from the `listFileNames` array. Next, the `curFileExtension` string variable
is set to the `curFilePath` variable's last index of ".", to return the extension, using the
`substring()` method. Then, we check to make sure that the current file's extension is equal
to one that is supported by AndEngine and call the `loadAndManageTextureRegion()`
method if `true`. Finally, we catch the `IOException` exception by sending a message to the
log and printing a `StackTrace` message from the `IOException` exception.

The fifth step includes two methods, `unloadAllTextures()` and
`getLoadedTextureRegion()`, that assist our managing of the textures loaded by our
previous methods:

▸ The `unloadAllTextures()` method runs through all
`ManagedStandardTextures` in the `loadedTextures ArrayList` object and
unloads them using the `removeFromMemory()` method before removing them
from `loadedTextures` and requesting a garbage collection from the system

▸ The `getLoadedTextureRegion()` method checks every
`ManagedStandardTexture` in the `loadedTextures` variable against the `pName`
string parameter and returns the current `ManagedStandardTexture` class'
`ITextureRegion` region if the names are equal, or `null` if no match is made

Step six calls the `loadAllTextureRegionsInFolders()` method from inside the `onCreateResources()` activity method by passing a `BILINEAR TextureOption` parameter and the asset folder path of our `FolderToLoad` folder. For more information on `TextureOptions`, see the *Applying options to our textures* recipe in *Chapter 1, AndEngine Game Structure*.

In our final step, we attach five sprites to our scene inside of the `onPopulateScene()` activity method. Each of the sprite constructors calls the `getLoadedTextureRegion()` method and passes the respective short name of the sprite's image file. The locations of each of the sprites place them in a horizontal line across the screen. The display of our sprites with textures loaded all at once should look similar to the following image. For more information on creating sprites, see the *Adding sprites to a layer* recipe in *Chapter 2, Working with Entities*.

See also

- ▸ *Understanding the life cycle* in *Chapter 1, AndEngine Game Structure*.
- ▸ *Different types of textures* in *Chapter 1, AndEngine Game Structure*.
- ▸ *Applying options to our textures* in *Chapter 1, AndEngine Game Structure*.
- ▸ *Adding sprites to a layer* in *Chapter 2, Working with Entities*.

Using textured meshes

Textured meshes, which are simply triangulated polygons with a texture applied, are becoming more popular in mobile games because they allow for the creation and manipulation of non-rectangular shapes. Having the ability to work with textured meshes often creates an extra layer of game mechanics that were previously too costly to implement. In this recipe, we will learn how to create a textured mesh from a predetermined set of triangles.

Getting ready...

First, create a new activity class named `TexturedMeshActivity` that extends `BaseGameActivity`. Next, place a seamless-tiling texture named `dirt.png` with the dimensions 512 x 128 in the `assets/gfx/` folder of our project. Finally, import the `TexturedMesh.java` class from the code bundle into our project.

Follow these steps to build our `TexturedMeshActivity` activity class:

1. Place the following code in our activity to give us a standard AndEngine activity:

```
@Override
public EngineOptions onCreateEngineOptions() {
    return new EngineOptions(true,
        ScreenOrientation.LANDSCAPE_SENSOR,
        new FillResolutionPolicy(),
        new Camera(0, 0, 800, 480))
        .setWakeLockOptions(WakeLockOptions.SCREEN_ON);
}
@Override
public void onCreateResources(OnCreateResourcesCallback
        pOnCreateResourcesCallback) {
    pOnCreateResourcesCallback.onCreateResourcesFinished();
}
@Override
public void onCreateScene(OnCreateSceneCallback
        pOnCreateSceneCallback) {
    Scene mScene = new Scene();
    mScene.setBackground(new Background(0.9f,0.9f,0.9f));
    pOnCreateSceneCallback.onCreateSceneFinished(mScene);
}
@Override
public void onPopulateScene(Scene pScene,
        OnPopulateSceneCallback pOnPopulateSceneCallback) {
    pOnPopulateSceneCallback.onPopulateSceneFinished();
}
```

2. Add the following code snippet to the `onPopulateScene()` method:

```
BitmapTextureAtlas texturedMeshT = new BitmapTextureAtlas(
    this.getTextureManager(), 512, 128,
    TextureOptions.REPEATING_BILINEAR);
ITextureRegion texturedMeshTR =
    BitmapTextureAtlasTextureRegionFactory.
    createFromAsset(texturedMeshT, this, "gfx/dirt.png", 0, 0);
texturedMeshT.load();
float[] meshTriangleVertices = {
    24.633111f,37.7835047f,-0.00898f,113.0324447f,
    -24.610162f,37.7835047f,0.00387f,-37.7900953f,
    -103.56176f,37.7901047f,103.56176f,37.7795047f,
    0.00387f,-37.7900953f,-39.814736f,-8.7311953f,
    -64.007044f,-83.9561953f,64.00771f,-83.9621953f,
    39.862562f,-8.7038953f,0.00387f,-37.7900953f};
```

```
float[] meshBufferData = new float[TexturedMesh.VERTEX_SIZE *
    (meshTriangleVertices.length/2)];
for( int i = 0; i < meshTriangleVertices.length/2; i++) {
  meshBufferData[(i * TexturedMesh.VERTEX_SIZE) +
    TexturedMesh.VERTEX_INDEX_X] =
    meshTriangleVertices[i*2];
  meshBufferData[(i * TexturedMesh.VERTEX_SIZE) +
    TexturedMesh.VERTEX_INDEX_Y] =
    meshTriangleVertices[i*2+1];
}
TexturedMesh starTexturedMesh = new TexturedMesh(400f, 225f,
    meshBufferData, 12, DrawMode.TRIANGLES, texturedMeshTR,
    this.getVertexBufferObjectManager());
pScene.attachChild(starTexturedMesh);
```

How it works...

In step one, we prepare our `TexturedMeshActivity` class by inserting into it the standard, overridden `BaseGameActivity` methods that most AndEngine games use. For more information on setting up an activity for use with AndEngine, see the *Understanding the life cycle* recipe in *Chapter 1, AndEngine Game Structure*.

In step two, we first define `texturedMeshT`, a `BitmapTextureAtlas` object, with the final parameter of the constructor being a `REPEATING_BILINEAR` `TextureOption` parameter to create a texture that will tile seamlessly within the triangles that make up our textured mesh. For more information on `TextureOptions`, see the *Applying options to our textures* recipe in *Chapter 1, AndEngine Game Structure*.

After creating the `texturedMeshTR` `ITextureRegion` object and loading our `texturedMeshT` object, we define an array of float variables that specify the relative and consecutive x and y positions of each of the vertices of each triangle that make up our textured mesh. See the following image for a better idea of how the vertices of a triangle are used in a textured mesh:

Next, we create the `meshBufferData` float array and set its size to the vertex size of the `TexturedMesh` class multiplied by the number of vertices in the `meshTriangleVertices` array—one vertex occupies two indices in the array, `X` and `Y`, so we must divide the length by 2. Then, for each of the vertices in the `meshTriangleVertices` array, we apply the vertex's position to the `meshBufferData` array. Finally, we create the `TexturedMesh` object, named `starTexturedMesh`. The parameters of the `TexturedMesh` constructor are the following:

 ▸ The first two parameters of the constructor are the x and y location of `400f, 225f`

 ▸ The next two parameters are the `meshBufferData` buffer data and the number of vertices, `12`, that we placed in the `meshBufferData` array

 ▸ The final three parameters of the `TexturedMesh` constructor are `DrawMode` of `Triangles`, `ITextureRegion` for the mesh, and our `VertexBufferObjectManager` object.

For more information on creating `Meshes`, from which the `TexturedMesh` class is derived, see the *Applying primitives to a layer* recipe in *Chapter 2, Working with Entities*.

See also

 ▸ *Understanding the life cycle* in *Chapter 1, AndEngine Game Structure.*
 ▸ *Applying options to our textures* in *Chapter 1, AndEngine Game Structure.*
 ▸ *Applying primitives to a layer* in *Chapter 2, Working with Entities.*

Applying a sprite-based shadow

The addition of shadows to a game can increase the visual depth and give the game a more appealing appearance. Simply placing a sprite with a shadow texture below an object is a fast and efficient way to handle shadow creation. In this chapter, we will be learning how to do that while keeping the shadow properly aligned with its parent object.

Getting ready...

First, create a new activity class named `SpriteShadowActivity` that extends `BaseGameActivity` and implements `IOnSceneTouchListener`. Next, place a shadow image with a size of 256 x 128 and named `shadow.png` into the `assets/gfx/` folder. Finally, place a character image of size 128 x 256 and named `character.png` into the `assets/gfx/` folder.

How to do it...

Follow these steps to build our `SpriteShadowActivity` activity class:

1. Place the following standard AndEngine activity code in our activity class:

```
@Override
public EngineOptions onCreateEngineOptions() {
  EngineOptions engineOptions = new EngineOptions(true,
    ScreenOrientation.LANDSCAPE_SENSOR,
    new FillResolutionPolicy(),
    new Camera(0, 0, 800, 480))
    .setWakeLockOptions(WakeLockOptions.SCREEN_ON);
  engineOptions.getRenderOptions().setDithering(true);
  return engineOptions;
}
@Override
public void onCreateResources(OnCreateResourcesCallback
    pOnCreateResourcesCallback) {
  pOnCreateResourcesCallback.onCreateResourcesFinished();
}
@Override
public void onCreateScene(OnCreateSceneCallback
    pOnCreateSceneCallback) {
  Scene mScene = new Scene();
  mScene.setBackground(new Background(0.8f,0.8f,0.8f));
  pOnCreateSceneCallback.onCreateSceneFinished(mScene);
}
@Override
public void onPopulateScene(Scene pScene, OnPopulateSceneCallback
    pOnPopulateSceneCallback) {
  pScene.setOnSceneTouchListener(this);
  pOnPopulateSceneCallback.onPopulateSceneFinished();
}
@Override
public boolean onSceneTouchEvent(Scene pScene,
    TouchEvent pSceneTouchEvent) {
  return true;
}
```

2. Next, place these variables in our activity to give us specific control over the shadow:

```
Static final float CHARACTER_START_X = 400f;
static final float CHARACTER_START_Y = 128f;
static final float SHADOW_OFFSET_X = 0f;
static final float SHADOW_OFFSET_Y = -64f;
static final float SHADOW_MAX_ALPHA = 0.75f;
static final float SHADOW_MIN_ALPHA = 0.1f;
static final float SHADOW_MAX_ALPHA_HEIGHT = 200f;
static final float SHADOW_MIN_ALPHA_HEIGHT = 0f;
static final float SHADOW_START_X = CHARACTER_START_X + SHADOW_
OFFSET_X;
static final float SHADOW_START_Y = CHARACTER_START_Y + SHADOW_
OFFSET_Y;
static final float CHARACTER_SHADOW_Y_DIFFERENCE =
  CHARACTER_START_Y - SHADOW_START_Y;
static final float SHADOW_ALPHA_HEIGHT_DIFFERENCE =
  SHADOW_MAX_ALPHA_HEIGHT - SHADOW_MIN_ALPHA_HEIGHT;
static final float SHADOW_ALPHA_DIFFERENCE =
  SHADOW_MAX_ALPHA - SHADOW_MIN_ALPHA;
Sprite shadowSprite;
Sprite characterSprite;
```

3. Now place the following method in our activity to make the shadow's alpha inversely proportional to the distance of the character from the shadow:

```
public void updateShadowAlpha() {
  shadowSprite.setAlpha(MathUtils.bringToBounds(
    SHADOW_MIN_ALPHA, SHADOW_MAX_ALPHA,
    SHADOW_MAX_ALPHA - ((((characterSprite.getY()-
    CHARACTER_SHADOW_Y_DIFFERENCE)-SHADOW_START_Y) /
    SHADOW_ALPHA_HEIGHT_DIFFERENCE) *
    SHADOW_ALPHA_DIFFERENCE)));
}
```

4. Insert the following code snippet into the onSceneTouchEvent() method:

```
if(pSceneTouchEvent.isActionDown() ||
    pSceneTouchEvent.isActionMove()) {
  characterSprite.setPosition(
    pSceneTouchEvent.getX(),
    Math.max(pSceneTouchEvent.getY(),
      CHARACTER_START_Y));
}
```

5. Finally, fill the `onPopulateScene()` method with the following snippet:

```
BitmapTextureAtlas characterTexture =
  new BitmapTextureAtlas(this.getTextureManager(), 128, 256,
    TextureOptions.BILINEAR);
TextureRegion characterTextureRegion =
  BitmapTextureAtlasTextureRegionFactory.createFromAsset(
    characterTexture, this, "gfx/character.png", 0, 0);
characterTexture.load();
BitmapTextureAtlas shadowTexture =
  new BitmapTextureAtlas(this.getTextureManager(), 256, 128,
    TextureOptions.BILINEAR);
TextureRegion shadowTextureRegion =
  BitmapTextureAtlasTextureRegionFactory.createFromAsset(
    shadowTexture, this, "gfx/shadow.png", 0, 0);
shadowTexture.load();
shadowSprite = new Sprite(SHADOW_START_X, SHADOW_START_Y,
  shadowTextureRegion,this.getVertexBufferObjectManager());
characterSprite = new Sprite(CHARACTER_START_X, CHARACTER_START_Y,
  characterTextureRegion,this.getVertexBufferObjectManager())
  {
  @Override
  public void setPosition(final float pX, final float pY) {
    super.setPosition(pX, pY);
    shadowSprite.setPosition(
      pX + SHADOW_OFFSET_X, shadowSprite.getY());
    updateShadowAlpha();
  }
};
pScene.attachChild(shadowSprite);
pScene.attachChild(characterSprite);
updateShadowAlpha();
```

How it works...

In step one, we set up our `SpriteShadowActivity` activity class by implementing the standard, overridden `BaseGameActivity` methods that most AndEngine games use. For more information on setting up an activity for use with AndEngine, see the *Understanding the life cycle* recipe in *Chapter 1, AndEngine Game Structure*.

The following image shows how this recipe places our shadow sprite in relation to the character sprite:

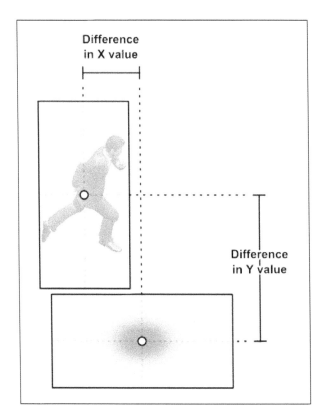

In step two, we define several constants that will control how the shadow sprite, `shadowSprite`, is aligned to the character sprite, `characterSprite`:

- ▸ The first two constants, `CHARACTER_START_X` and `CHARACTER_START_Y`, set the initial position of `characterSprite`

- ▸ The next two constants, `SHADOW_OFFSET_X` and `SHADOW_OFFSET_Y`, control the distance on the x and y axis as to how far the shadow will be initially positioned in relation to the character sprite

- ▸ The `SHADOW_OFFSET_X` constant is also used to update the shadow sprite's position when the character sprite is moved

The next four constants control how, and to what level, the shadowSprite sprite's alpha will be controlled:

- SHADOW_MAX_ALPHA and SHADOW_MIN_ALPHA set the absolute minimum and maximum alpha, which is changed according to the character's distance on the y axis from the shadow. The further the distance, the lower the alpha of the shadowSprite sprite will be until the minimum level is reached.

- The SHADOW_MAX_ALPHA_HEIGHT constant represents the maximum distance of the character from the shadow that the shadowSprite sprite's alpha will be affected before defaulting to SHADOW_MIN_ALPHA.

- The SHADOW_MIN_ALPHA_HEIGHT constant represents the minimum distance of the character from the shadow that the shadow's alpha should change. If SHADOW_MIN_ALPHA_HEIGHT is greater than 0, the shadow's alpha will be at its maximum while the character's distance from the shadow is below SHADOW_MIN_ALPHA_HEIGHT.

The remaining constants are calculated automatically from the previous set. SHADOW_START_X and SHADOW_START_Y represent the starting position of the shadowSprite sprite. They are calculated by adding the shadow's offset values to the character's starting position. The CHARACTER_SHADOW_Y_DIFFERENCE constant represents the initial starting distance between the character and the shadow on the y axis. The SHADOW_ALPHA_HEIGHT_DIFFERENCE constant represents the difference between the minimum and maximum heights and acts to modulate the shadow's alpha at runtime. The final constant, SHADOW_ALPHA_DIFFERENCE, represents the difference between the minimum and maximum alpha levels of the shadowSprite sprite. Similar to the SHADOW_ALPHA_HEIGHT_DIFFERENCE constant, it is used at runtime to determine the alpha level of the shadow.

The final two variables in step two, shadowSprite and characterSprite, represent the shadow and character in our scene.

In the third step, we create a method that will update the shadow's alpha. We call the shadowSprite.setAlpha() method with the MathUtils.bringToBounds() method as the parameter. The MathUtils.bringToBounds() method takes a minimum and maximum value and ensures that the third value is within that range. We pass the SHADOW_MIN_ALPHA and SHADOW_MAX_ALPHA constants as the first two parameters of the bringToBounds() method.

The third parameter is the algorithm for determining the alpha of the shadow based on the distance of the `characterSprite` sprite from the `shadowSprite` sprite. The algorithm starts by subtracting the `CHARACTER_SHADOW_Y_DIFFERENCE` constant from the character's position on the y axis. This gives us the current ceiling of the y value that affects the shadow's alpha. Next, we subtract the shadow's starting position on the y axis to get the current, ideal distance of the character from the shadow. Next, we divide that distance by `SHADOW_ALPHA_HEIGHT_DIFFERENCE` to get the unit ratio of constrained-distance to alpha and multiply the ratio by the `SHADOW_ALPHA_DIFFERENCE` constant to get the unit ratio of constrained-distance to constrained-alpha. Currently, our ratio is inverted and will increase the alpha with distance, which opposes our goal of decreasing alpha as the character moves further, so we subtract it from the `SHADOW_MAX_ALPHA` constant to give us a proper ratio that decreases alpha as distance increases. Completing the algorithm, we then use the `bringToBounds()` method to ensure that the alpha value produced by the algorithm is constrained within the range of `SHADOW_MIN_ALPHA` to `SHADOW_MAX_ALPHA`.

Step four sets the position of the `characterSprite` sprite when the screen is first touched, or if the touch is moved, by checking the touch event's `isActionDown()` and `isActionMove()` properties. The `setPosition()` method, in this case, simply sets the x value to the touched x value and the x value to the touched y value or the character's starting y value, whichever is greater.

In the final step, we load the `TextureRegions`, `characterTextureRegion`, and `shadowTextureRegion` objects, for the character and shadow. For more information on `TextureRegions`, see the *Different types of textures* recipe in *Chapter 1, AndEngine Game Structure*. Then, we create the `shadowSprite` and `characterSprite` sprites using their starting constants as the positions in the constructors. For `characterSprite`, we override the `setPosition()` method to also set the `shadowSprite` sprite's position with the x offset applied and then call the `updateShadowAlpha()` method to set the proper alpha for the shadow after the character has moved. Finally, we attach the `shadowSprite` and `characterSprite` sprites to our scene and call the `updateShadowAlpha()` method to set the initial alpha of the shadow. The following image shows how the shadow's alpha level is changed in relation to the distance from the character:

▸ *Understanding the life cycle* in *Chapter 1, AndEngine Game Structure.*

▸ *Different types of textures* in *Chapter 1, AndEngine Game Structure.*

Creating a physics-based moving platform

Most platform-style games have some sort of moving platform, which challenges the player to land with accurate timing. From a developer's standpoint, the platform is simply a physics-enabled body that moves from one location to another. In this recipe, we will see how to create a horizontally-moving platform.

Getting ready...

Create a new activity class named `MovingPhysicsPlatformActivity` that extends `BaseGameActivity`.

How to do it...

Follow these steps to build our `MovingPhysicsPlatformActivity` activity class:

1. Insert the following code snippet into our activity to make it functional:

```
@Override
public Engine onCreateEngine(final EngineOptions pEngineOptions) {
  return new FixedStepEngine(pEngineOptions, 60);
}
@Override
public EngineOptions onCreateEngineOptions() {
  return new EngineOptions(true,
    ScreenOrientation.LANDSCAPE_SENSOR,
    new FillResolutionPolicy(),
    new Camera(0, 0, 800, 480)
    ).setWakeLockOptions(WakeLockOptions.SCREEN_ON);
}
@Override
public void onCreateResources(OnCreateResourcesCallback
    pOnCreateResourcesCallback) {
  pOnCreateResourcesCallback.onCreateResourcesFinished();
}
@Override
public void onCreateScene(OnCreateSceneCallback
    pOnCreateSceneCallback) {
```

```
      Scene mScene = new Scene();
      mScene.setBackground(new Background(0.9f,0.9f,0.9f));
      pOnCreateSceneCallback.onCreateSceneFinished(mScene);
    }
    @Override
    public void onPopulateScene(Scene pScene, OnPopulateSceneCallback
       pOnPopulateSceneCallback) {
      pOnPopulateSceneCallback.onPopulateSceneFinished();
    }
```

2. Add the following code snippet to the `onPopulateScene()` method:

```
    FixedStepPhysicsWorld mPhysicsWorld =
      new FixedStepPhysicsWorld(60,
      new Vector2(0,-SensorManager.GRAVITY_EARTH*2f),
      false, 8, 3);
    pScene.registerUpdateHandler(mPhysicsWorld);
    Rectangle platformRect = new Rectangle(400f, 200f, 250f, 20f,
      this.getVertexBufferObjectManager());
    platformRect.setColor(0f, 0f, 0f);
    final FixtureDef platformFixtureDef =
      PhysicsFactory.createFixtureDef(20f, 0f, 1f);
    final Body platformBody = PhysicsFactory.createBoxBody(
      mPhysicsWorld, platformRect, BodyType.KinematicBody,
      platformFixtureDef);
    mPhysicsWorld.registerPhysicsConnector(
      new PhysicsConnector(platformRect, platformBody));
    pScene.attachChild(platformRect);
    float platformRelativeMinX = -200f;
    float platformRelativeMaxX = 200f;
    final float platformVelocity = 3f;
    final float platformMinXWorldCoords =
      (platformRect.getX() + platformRelativeMinX) /
      PhysicsConstants.PIXEL_TO_METER_RATIO_DEFAULT;
    final float platformMaxXWorldCoords =
      (platformRect.getX() + platformRelativeMaxX) /
      PhysicsConstants.PIXEL_TO_METER_RATIO_DEFAULT;
    platformBody.setLinearVelocity(platformVelocity, 0f);
```

3. Insert the following code directly below the preceding code in the `onPopulateScene()` method:

```
    pScene.registerUpdateHandler(new IUpdateHandler() {
      @Override
      public void onUpdate(float pSecondsElapsed) {
        if(platformBody.getWorldCenter().x >
```

```
                    platformMaxXWorldCoords) {
                platformBody.setTransform(
                    platformMaxXWorldCoords,
                    platformBody.getWorldCenter().y,
                    platformBody.getAngle());
                platformBody.setLinearVelocity(
                    -platformVelocity, 0f);
            } else if(platformBody.getWorldCenter().x <
                    platformMinXWorldCoords) {
                platformBody.setTransform(
                    platformMinXWorldCoords,
                    platformBody.getWorldCenter().y,
                    platformBody.getAngle());
                platformBody.setLinearVelocity(
                    platformVelocity, 0f);
            }
        }
        @Override
        public void reset() {}
    });
```

4. Finish the `onPopulateScene()` method and our activity by placing the following
    code after the preceding code to create a physics-enabled box that rests on
    the platform:

```
Rectangle boxRect = new Rectangle(400f, 240f, 60f, 60f,
    this.getVertexBufferObjectManager());
boxRect.setColor(0.2f, 0.2f, 0.2f);
FixtureDef boxFixtureDef =
    PhysicsFactory.createFixtureDef(200f, 0f, 1f);
mPhysicsWorld.registerPhysicsConnector(
    new PhysicsConnector(boxRect,
        PhysicsFactory.createBoxBody( mPhysicsWorld, boxRect,
        BodyType.DynamicBody, boxFixtureDef)));
pScene.attachChild(boxRect);
```

How it works...

In the first step, we prepare our `MovingPhysicsPlatformActivity` class by inserting into it the standard, overridden `BaseGameActivity` methods that most AndEngine games use. For more information on setting up an activity for use with AndEngine, see the *Understanding the life cycle* recipe in *Chapter 1, AndEngine Game Structure*. The following image shows how our platform moves on a single axis, in this case to the right, while keeping the box on top of it:

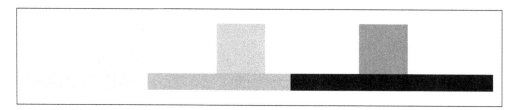

In step two, we first create a `FixedStepPhysicsWorld` object and register it as an update handler with our scene. Then, we create a `Rectangle` object, named `platformRect`, that will represent our moving platform and place it near the center of the screen. Next, we set the color of the `platformRect` rectangle to black using the `setColor()` method with a value of `0f` for the red, green, and blue float parameters. We then create a fixture definition for the platform. Notice that the friction is set to `1f` to prevent objects on it from sliding too much while it is moving.

Next, we create the `Body` object, named `platformBody`, for the platform. Then, we register a `PhysicsConnector` class to connect the `platformRect` rectangle to the `platformBody` body. After attaching `platformRect` to our scene, we declare and set the variables that will control the moving platform:

- The `platformRelativeMinX` and `platformRelativeMaxX` variables represent how far to the left and right that the platform will move from its starting location in scene units.

- The `platformVelocity` variable represents the speed in meters per second for our physics platform body.

- The next two variables, `platformMinXWorldCoords` and `platformMaxXWorldCoords`, represent the absolute position of the `platformRelativeMinX` and `platformRelativeMaxX` variables and are calculated from the platform's initial x position scaled by the default `PIXEL_TO_METER_RATIO_DEFAULT`.

- Finally, we set the initial velocity of our `platformBody` body to the `platformVelocity` variable to make the body actively mobile as soon as the scene is first drawn. For more information on creating physics simulations, see the *Introduction to the Box2D physics extension* and the *Understanding different body types* recipes in *Chapter 6, Applications of Physics*.

The third step registers a new `IUpdateHandler` handler with our scene. In the `onUpdate()` method, we test if the platform's location is beyond the absolute bounds that we previously defined, `platformMinXWorldCoords` and `platformMaxXWorldCoords`. Depending on which absolute bound is reached, we set the location of the `platformBody` body to the reached bound and set its velocity to move away from the boundary. For more information on conditional update handlers, see the *Update handlers and conditionals* recipe in *Chapter 7, Working with Update Handlers*.

In step four, we create and attach a box body to rest on the platform. For more information on creating a physics-enabled box, see the *Understanding different body types* recipe in *Chapter 6, Applications of Physics*.

See also

- ▶ *Understanding the life cycle* in *Chapter 1, AndEngine Game Structure*.
- ▶ *Introduction to the Box2D physics extension* in *Chapter 6, Applications of Physics*.
- ▶ *Understanding different body types* in *Chapter 6, Applications of Physics*.
- ▶ *Update handlers and conditionals* in *Chapter 7, Working with Update Handlers*.

Creating a physics-based rope bridge

With the Box2D physics extension, creating complex physics-enabled elements is simple. One example of such a complex element is a rope bridge that reacts to collisions. In this recipe, we will see how to implement a method that creates a rope bridge tailored to specific parameters that control the bridge's size and physical properties.

Getting ready...

Create a new activity class named `PhysicsBridgeActivity` that extends `BaseGameActivity`.

How to do it...

Follow these steps to build our `PhysicsBridgeActivity` activity class:

1. Place the following code in our activity to give us a standard AndEngine activity:

```
@Override
public Engine onCreateEngine(final EngineOptions pEngineOptions) {
  return new FixedStepEngine(pEngineOptions, 60);
}
@Override
public EngineOptions onCreateEngineOptions() {
```

```
        return new EngineOptions(true,
          ScreenOrientation.LANDSCAPE_SENSOR,
          new FillResolutionPolicy(),
          new Camera(0, 0, 800, 480))
          .setWakeLockOptions(WakeLockOptions.SCREEN_ON);
    }
    @Override
    public void onCreateResources(OnCreateResourcesCallback
        pOnCreateResourcesCallback) {
      pOnCreateResourcesCallback.onCreateResourcesFinished();
    }
    @Override
    public void onCreateScene(OnCreateSceneCallback
        pOnCreateSceneCallback) {
      Scene mScene = new Scene();
      mScene.setBackground(new Background(0.9f,0.9f,0.9f));
      pOnCreateSceneCallback.onCreateSceneFinished(mScene);
    }
    @Override
    public void onPopulateScene(Scene pScene, OnPopulateSceneCallback
        pOnPopulateSceneCallback) {
      pOnPopulateSceneCallback.onPopulateSceneFinished();
    }
```

2. Next, place the following, incomplete method in our activity. This method will facilitate the creation of our bridge:

```
public void createBridge(Body pGroundBody,
        final float[] pLeftHingeAnchorPoint,
        final float pRightHingeAnchorPointX,
        final int pNumSegments,
        final float pSegmentsWidth,
        final float pSegmentsHeight,
        final float pSegmentDensity,
        final float pSegmentElasticity,
        final float pSegmentFriction,
        IEntity pScene, PhysicsWorld pPhysicsWorld,
        VertexBufferObjectManager
          pVertexBufferObjectManager) {
      final Rectangle[] BridgeSegments =
        new Rectangle[pNumSegments];
      final Body[] BridgeSegmentsBodies = new Body[pNumSegments];
      final FixtureDef BridgeSegmentFixtureDef =
        PhysicsFactory.createFixtureDef(
        pSegmentDensity, pSegmentElasticity,
```

```
    pSegmentFriction);
  final float BridgeWidthConstant = pRightHingeAnchorPointX -
    pLeftHingeAnchorPoint[0] + pSegmentsWidth;
  final float BridgeSegmentSpacing = (
    BridgeWidthConstant / (pNumSegments+1) -
    pSegmentsWidth/2f);
  for(int i = 0; i < pNumSegments; i++) {


  }
}
```

3. Insert the following code inside of the `for` loop of the `createBridge()` method above:

```
BridgeSegments[i] = new Rectangle(
  ((BridgeWidthConstant / (pNumSegments+1))*i) +
    pLeftHingeAnchorPoint[0] + BridgeSegmentSpacing,
  pLeftHingeAnchorPoint[1]-pSegmentsHeight/2f,
  pSegmentsWidth, pSegmentsHeight,
  pVertexBufferObjectManager);
BridgeSegments[i].setColor(0.97f, 0.75f, 0.54f);
pScene.attachChild(BridgeSegments[i]);
BridgeSegmentsBodies[i] = PhysicsFactory.createBoxBody(
  pPhysicsWorld, BridgeSegments[i], BodyType.DynamicBody,
  BridgeSegmentFixtureDef);
BridgeSegmentsBodies[i].setLinearDamping(1f);
pPhysicsWorld.registerPhysicsConnector(
  new PhysicsConnector(BridgeSegments[i],
    BridgeSegmentsBodies[i]));
final RevoluteJointDef revoluteJointDef = new RevoluteJointDef();
if(i==0) {
  Vector2 anchorPoint = new Vector2(
    BridgeSegmentsBodies[i].getWorldCenter().x -
      (BridgeSegmentSpacing/2 + pSegmentsWidth/2)/
      PhysicsConstants.PIXEL_TO_METER_RATIO_DEFAULT,
    BridgeSegmentsBodies[i].getWorldCenter().y);
  revoluteJointDef.initialize(pGroundBody,
    BridgeSegmentsBodies[i], anchorPoint);
} else {
  Vector2 anchorPoint = new Vector2(
    (BridgeSegmentsBodies[i].getWorldCenter().x +
      BridgeSegmentsBodies[i-1]
      .getWorldCenter().x)/2,
    BridgeSegmentsBodies[i].getWorldCenter().y);
  revoluteJointDef.initialize(BridgeSegmentsBodies[i-1],
```

```
        BridgeSegmentsBodies[i], anchorPoint);
    }
    pPhysicsWorld.createJoint(revoluteJointDef);
    if(i==pNumSegments-1) {
      Vector2 anchorPoint = new Vector2(BridgeSegmentsBodies[i].
    getWorldCenter().x + (BridgeSegmentSpacing/2 + pSegmentsWidth/2)/
    PhysicsConstants.PIXEL_TO_METER_RATIO_DEFAULT,
    BridgeSegmentsBodies[i].getWorldCenter().y);
      revoluteJointDef.initialize(pGroundBody,
    BridgeSegmentsBodies[i], anchorPoint);
      pPhysicsWorld.createJoint(revoluteJointDef);
    }
```

4. Finally, add the following code inside of our `onPopulateScene()` method:

```
final FixedStepPhysicsWorld mPhysicsWorld = new
FixedStepPhysicsWorld(60, new Vector2(0,-SensorManager.GRAVITY_
EARTH), false, 8, 3);
pScene.registerUpdateHandler(mPhysicsWorld);

FixtureDef groundFixtureDef = PhysicsFactory.createFixtureDef(0f,
0f, 0f);
Body groundBody = PhysicsFactory.createBoxBody(mPhysicsWorld, 0f,
0f, 0f, 0f, BodyType.StaticBody, groundFixtureDef);

createBridge(groundBody, new float[] {0f,240f}, 800f, 16,
40f, 10f, 4f, 0.1f, 0.5f, pScene, mPhysicsWorld, this.
getVertexBufferObjectManager());

Rectangle boxRect = new Rectangle(100f,400f,50f,50f,this.
getVertexBufferObjectManager());
FixtureDef boxFixtureDef = PhysicsFactory.createFixtureDef(25f,
0.5f, 0.5f);
mPhysicsWorld.registerPhysicsConnector(new
PhysicsConnector(boxRect, PhysicsFactory.
createBoxBody(mPhysicsWorld, boxRect, BodyType.DynamicBody,
boxFixtureDef)));
pScene.attachChild(boxRect);
```

How it works...

In step one, we set up our `PhysicsBridgeActivity` activity class by implementing the standard, overridden `BaseGameActivity` methods that most AndEngine games use. For more information on setting up an activity for use with AndEngine, see the *Understanding the life cycle* recipe in *Chapter 1, AndEngine Game Structure*. The following image shows what our physics-enabled bridge looks like with a physics-enabled square resting on it:

In the second step, we implement the beginning of a method, named `createBridge()`, that will create our physics-enabled bridge. The first parameter, pGroundBody, is the ground Body object to which the bridge will be attached. The second parameter, pLeftHingeAnchorPoint, represents the x and y location of the upper-left side of the bridge. The third parameter, pRightHingeAnchorPointX, represents the x location of the right-hand side of the bridge. The next three parameters, pNumSegments, pSegmentsWidth, and pSegmentsHeight, represent how many segments the bridge will consist of and the width and height of each segment. The pSegmentDensity, pSegmentElasticity, and pSegmentFriction parameters will be directly passed to a fixture definition that will be applied to the segments of the bridge. For more information on fixture definitions, see the *Introduction to the Box2D physics extension* recipe in *Chapter 6, Applications of Physics*. The next two parameters, pScene and pPhysicsWorld, tell our method what the bridge segment rectangles and bridge segment bodies should be attached to. The final parameter is our VertexBufferObjectManager object and will be passed to the rectangles that represent each segment of our bridge.

The first two variables, BridgeSegments and BridgeSegmentsBodies, defined in the createBridge() method, are arrays that will hold the segment rectangles and segment bodies. They are defined to have a length passed by the pNumSegments parameter. The next variable, BridgeSegmentFixtureDef, is the fixture definition that each segment of the bridge will have. The BridgeWidthConstant variable represents the width of the bridge, calculated by finding the difference between the left and right anchors added to the width of a single segment of the bridge. The last variable, BridgeSegmentSpacing, represents how much space should be between each segment and is determined by dividing the width of the bridge by one more than the number of segments, and subtracting from that the half-width of the segments. We then create a for loop that will create and position the number of segments passed in the pNumSegments parameter.

In the third step, we fill the previously created for loop. First, we create the current segment's rectangle, BridgeSegments[i], that will act as the visual representation of the segment. We place it on the x axis using the BridgeWidthConstant variable divided by one more than the number of segments, and multiply that by the current segment number before adding the left hinge's x position, pLeftHingeAnchorPoint[0] and the amount of spacing between the segments, BridgeSegmentSpacing. For the y axis position of the current segment's rectangle, we place it at the left hinge's y position minus the segments' height divided by 2f to make it flush with the hinge position.

Next, we set the color of each segment to a light orange, `0.97f` red, `0.75f` green, and `0.54f` blue. After attaching the `Rectangle` object to the passed scene, we create the current segment's body by passing the segment's rectangle and a `BodyType` value of `Dynamic` to the standard `PhysicsFactory.CreateBoxBody()` method. We then set the linear damping to `1f` to smoothen the rhythmic movements caused by a collision. Next, we register a `PhysicsConnector` class to connect the current segment's rectangle to the current segment's body.

Now that we have established a position and created corresponding rectangles and bodies for each segment, we create a `RevoluteJointDef` object, `revoluteJointDef`, to attach each segment to the bridge via a revolute joint. We test to see if the current segment is the first and, if so, attach the segment to the ground `Body` object instead of a previous segment. For the first bridge segment, the definition of the `Vector2 anchorPoint` places the `RevoluteJointDef` definition's anchor at an x location of the segment's x value, `BridgeSegmentsBodies[i].getWorldCenter().x`, minus the segment spacing, `BridgeSegmentSpacing`, divided by 2, plus the segment width, `pSegmentsWidth`, divided by 2, and scaled to the `PIXEL_TO_METER_RATIO_DEFAULT` default. The y location of the first segment's anchor point is simply the current segment's y value, `BridgeSegmentsBodies[i].getWorldCenter().y`. For the remaining segments, the anchor point's x location is computed by averaging the x position of the current segment with the x position of the previous segment.

Then, `revoluteJointDef` is initialized using the `initialize()` method with the first body either set to the ground body, `pGroundBody`, if the current segment is the first, or the previous segment's body, `BridgeSegmentsBodies[i-1]`, if the current segment is not the first. The second body of `revoluteJointDef` is set to the current segment's body, and, after exiting the `if` statement, the joint is created with the `pPhysicsWorld` object's `createJoint()` method. We then test if the current segment will be the last created and, if so, create another revolute joint to attach the segment to the ground body to the right-hand side of the segment using a similar anchor point x location formula as for the first segment. For more information on physics simulations, see the *Introduction to the Box2D physics extension* and the *Understanding different body types* recipes in *Chapter 6, Applications of Physics*.

In the final step, we first create a `FixedStepPhysicsWorld` object inside of the `onPopulateScene()` method and register it as an update handler with our scene. Then, we create a ground body to which our bridge will be attached. Next, we create our bridge by calling the `createBridge()` method. We pass `groundBody` as the first parameter, a position of `0f,240f` to represent the mid-left side of the screen as the left anchor point, and an x position representing the right-hand side of the screen as the right anchor point. We then pass an integer of `16` as the number of segments to create and a segment width and height of `40f` and `10f`. Next, we pass a segment density of `4f`, a segment elasticity of `0.1f`, a segment friction of `0.5f`, our scene to which the segment rectangles will be attached, our physics world, and our `VertexBufferObjectManager` object. Now that our bridge is created, we create a simple box body to show that the bridge reacts to collisions properly.

See also

- ▸ *Understanding the life cycle* in *Chapter 1, AndEngine Game Structure.*
- ▸ *Introduction to the Box2D physics extension* in *Chapter 6, Applications of Physics.*
- ▸ *Understanding different body types* in *Chapter 6, Applications of Physics.*

A

Source Code for MagneTank

This chapter provides a short description of and references for all of the classes used in the game **MagneTank**. MagneTank is available on the Google Play Store (`http://play.google.com/store/apps/details?id=ifl.games.MagneTank`), formerly known as **Android Market**, and the source code can be found in the code bundle for this book. The gameplay includes aiming the tank's turret by touching where the turret should point and tapping in the same location to fire the turret. For the sake of demonstrating physics-enabled vehicles, the tank can be pulled to the left-hand side or the right-hand side by first touching it and then sliding in the desired direction.

The game's classes are spread across the following topics:

- ▶ Game level classes
- ▶ Input classes
- ▶ Layer classes
- ▶ Manager classes
- ▶ Menu classes
- ▶ Activity and engine classes

The following image is an in-game screenshot from MagneTank's second level:

Game level classes

These classes are present in the playable portion of the game:

ManagedGameScene.java

MagneTank's `ManagedGameScene` class builds upon the `ManagedGameScene` class presented in *Chapter 5, Scene and Layer Management*, by adding a stepped loading screen to show what the game is loading for each level. The idea behind using loading steps is the same as showing a loading screen for one frame before loading the game, much like how the `SceneManager` class functions when showing a new scene, but the loading screen is updated for each loading step instead of just once at the first showing of the loading screen.

This class is based on the following recipes:

- *Applying text to a layer* in Chapter 2, *Working with Entities*
- *Creating the scene manager* in Chapter 5, *Scene and Layer Management*
- *What are update handlers?* in Chapter 7, *Working with Update Handlers*

GameLevel.java

The `GameLevel` class brings all of the other in-game classes together to form the playable part of MagneTank. It handles the construction and execution of each actual game level. It extends a customized `ManagedGameScene` class that incorporates a list of `LoadingRunnable` objects, which create the level in steps that allow each progression of the level construction to be shown on the screen. The `GameLevel` class also determines the completion or failure of each game level using the `GameManager` class to test for win or lose conditions.

This class is based on the following recipes:

- *Understanding AndEngine entities* in *Chapter 2, Working with Entities*
- *Bringing a scene to life with sprites* in *Chapter 2, Working with Entities*
- *Applying text to a layer* in *Chapter 2, Working with Entities*
- *Overriding the onManagedUpdate method* in *Chapter 2, Working with Entities*
- *Using modifiers and entity modifiers* in *Chapter 2, Working with Entities*
- *Using parallax backgrounds to create perspective* in *Chapter 3, Designing Your Menu*
- *Introducing the camera object* in *Chapter 4, Working with Cameras*
- *Limiting camera area with the bound camera* in *Chapter 4, Working with Cameras*
- *Taking a closer look with zoom cameras* in *Chapter 4, Working with Cameras*
- *Applying a HUD to the camera* in *Chapter 4, Working with Cameras*
- *Customizing managed scenes and layers* in *Chapter 5, Scene and Layer Management*
- *Introduction to the Box2D physics extension* in *Chapter 6, Applications of Physics*
- *What are update handlers?* in *Chapter 7, Working with Update Handlers*
- *Creating sprite pools* in *Chapter 8, Maximizing Performance*

LoadingRunnable.java

The `LoadingRunnable` class acts as a `Runnable` object while also updating the loading screen in the `ManagedGameScene` class. An `ArrayList` type of `LoadingRunnable` objects is present in each `ManagedGameScene` class to give the developer as much or as little control over how much loading progression is shown to the player. It is important to note that, while the updating of the loading screen is not processor-intensive in MagneTank, a more complicated, graphically complex loading screen may take a large toll on the loading times of each level.

Levels.java

The `Levels` class holds an array of all of the levels that can be played in the game as well as helper methods to retrieve specific levels.

BouncingPowerBar.java

The `BouncingPowerBar` class displays a bouncing indicator to the player that indicates how powerful each shot from the vehicle will be. It transforms the visible location of the indicator to a fractional value, which then has a cubic curve applied to add even more of a challenge when trying to achieve the most powerful shot. The following image shows what the power bar looks like after being constructed from three separate images:

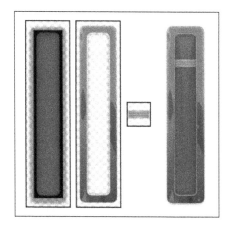

The `BouncingPowerBar` class is based on the following recipes:

▶ *Understanding AndEngine entities* in *Chapter 2, Working with Entities*

▶ *Bringing a scene to life with sprites* in *Chapter 2, Working with Entities*

▶ *Overriding the onManagedUpdate method* in *Chapter 2, Working with Entities*

▶ *Applying a HUD to the camera* in *Chapter 2, Working with Entities*

MagneTank.java

The `MagneTank` class creates and controls the vehicle that the game is based on. It pieces together Box2D bodies using joints to create the physics-enabled vehicle, and uses the player's input, via `BoundTouchInputs`, to control how each part of the vehicle moves and functions. The following image shows the MagneTank before and after construction:

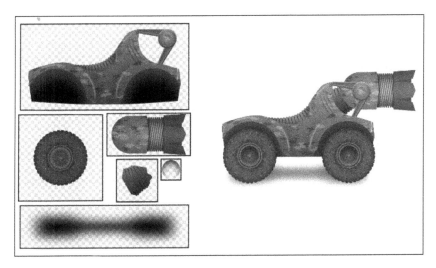

The `MagneTank` class is based on the following recipes:

- *Understanding AndEngine entities in Chapter 2, Working with Entities*
- *Bringing a scene to life with sprites in Chapter 2, Working with Entities*
- *Using relative rotation in Chapter 2, Working with Entities*
- *Overriding the onManagedUpdate method in Chapter 2, Working with Entities*
- *Limiting camera area with the bound camera in Chapter 4, Working with Cameras*
- *Introduction to the Box2D physics extension in Chapter 6, Applications of Physics*
- *Understanding different body types in Chapter 6, Applications of Physics*
- *Creating unique bodies by specifying vertices in Chapter 6, Applications of Physics*
- *Using forces, velocities, and torque in Chapter 6, Applications of Physics*
- *Working with joints in Chapter 6, Applications of Physics*
- *What are update handlers? in Chapter 7, Working with Update Handlers*
- *Applying a sprite-based shadow in Chapter 10, Getting More From AndEngine*

MagneticCrate.java

The `MagneticCrate` class extends the `MagneticPhysObject` class. It creates and handles the various types of crates available to launch from the MagneTank vehicle. Each crate is displayed in the form of a tiled sprite, with the tiled sprite's image index set to the crate's type. The `MagneticCrate` class makes use of Box2D's `postSolve()` method from the physics world's `ContactListener`. The following image shows the various sizes and types of crates available in the game:

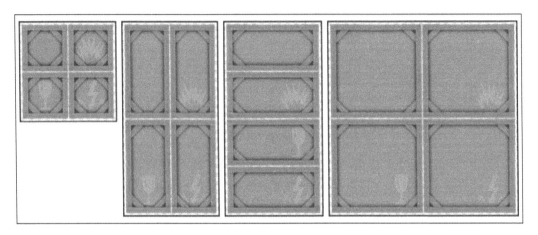

The `MagneticCrate` class is based on the following recipes:

- ▶ *Understanding AndEngine entities* in *Chapter 2, Working with Entities*
- ▶ *Bringing a scene to life with sprites* in *Chapter 2, Working with Entities*
- ▶ *Overriding the onManagedUpdate method* in *Chapter 2, Working with Entities*
- ▶ *Introduction to the Box2D physics extension* in *Chapter 6, Applications of Physics*
- ▶ *Understanding different body types* in *Chapter 6, Applications of Physics*
- ▶ *Using preSolve and postSolve* in *Chapter 6, Applications of Physics*
- ▶ *What are update handlers?* in *Chapter 7, Working with Update Handlers*

MagneticOrb.java

The `MagneticOrb` class creates a visual effect around MagneTank's current projectile. It rotates two swirl images (see the following image) in opposite directions to give the illusion of a spherical force. The `MagneticOrb` class forms and fades as projectiles are loaded and shot.

The `MagneticOrb` class is based on the following recipes:

- ▸ *Understanding AndEngine entities* in *Chapter 2, Working with Entities*
- ▸ *Bringing a scene to life with sprites* in *Chapter 2, Working with Entities*
- ▸ *Using relative rotation* in *Chapter 2, Working with Entities*
- ▸ *Overriding the onManagedUpdate method* in *Chapter 2, Working with Entities*

MagneticPhysObject.java

The `MagneticPhysObject` class extends the `PhysObject` class to allow an object to be grabbed, or released, by the MagneTank vehicle. When grabbed, the object has anti-gravity forces applied as well as forces that pull the object toward the MagneTank turret.

The `MagneticPhysObject` class is based on the following recipes:

- ▸ *Introduction to the Box2D physics extension* in Chapter 6, *Applications of Physics*
- ▸ *Understanding different body types* in Chapter 6, *Applications of Physics*
- ▸ *Using forces, velocities, and torque* in Chapter 6, *Applications of Physics*
- ▸ *Applying anti-gravity to a specific body* in Chapter 6, *Applications of Physics*
- ▸ *What are update handlers?* in Chapter 7, *Working with Update Handlers*

MechRat.java

The `MechRat` class extends the `PhysObject` class to take advantage of the `postSolve()` method that gets called when it collides with another physics-enabled object. If the force is great enough, MechRat is destroyed, and previously loaded particle effects are immediately shown. MechRat also has wheels connected by revolute joints, which add to the challenge of destroying it. The following image shows the visual composition of MechRat:

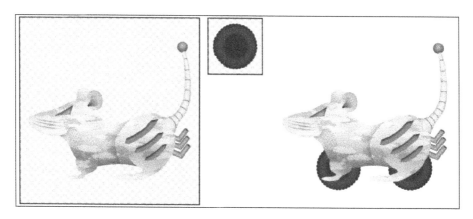

This class is based on the following recipes:

- *Understanding AndEngine entities* in *Chapter 2, Working with Update Handlers*
- *Bringing a scene to life with sprites* in *Chapter 2, Working with Update Handlers*
- *Overriding the onManagedUpdate method* in *Chapter 2, Working with Update Handlers*
- *Working with particle systems* in *Chapter 2, Working with Update Handlers*
- *Introduction to the Box2D physics extension* in *Chapter 6, Applications of Physics*
- *Understanding different body types* in *Chapter 6, Applications of Physics*
- *Creating unique bodies by specifying vertices* in *Chapter 6, Applications of Physics*
- *Working with joints* in *Chapter 6, Applications of Physics*
- *Using preSolve and postSolve* in *Chapter 6, Applications of Physics*
- *Creating destructible objects* in *Chapter 6, Applications of Physics*
- *What are update handlers?* in *Chapter 7, Working with Update Handlers*

MetalBeamDynamic.java

This class represents the non-static, physics-enabled girders seen in the game. The length of each beam can be set thanks to its repeating texture.

The `MetalBeamDynamic` class is based on the following recipes:

- *Understanding AndEngine entities* in *Chapter 2, Working with Entities*
- *Bringing a scene to life with sprites* in *Chapter 2, Working with Entities*
- *Using relative rotation* in *Chapter 2, Working with Entities*
- *Overriding the onManagedUpdate method* in *Chapter 2, Working with Entities*
- *Introduction to the Box2D physics extension* in *Chapter 6, Applications of Physics*
- *Understanding different body types* in *Chapter 6, Applications of Physics*

MetalBeamStatic.java

Similar to the `MetalBeamDynamic` class above, this class also represents a girder, but the `BodyType` option of this object is set to `Static` to create an immobile barrier.

The `MetalBeamStatic` class is based on the following recipes:

- *Understanding AndEngine entities* in *Chapter 2, Working with Entities*
- *Bringing a scene to life with sprites* in *Chapter 2, Working with Entities*
- *Using relative rotation* in *Chapter 2, Working with Entities*
- *Introduction to the Box2D physics extension* in *Chapter 6, Applications of Physics*
- *Understanding different body types* in *Chapter 6, Applications of Physics*

ParallaxLayer.java

The `ParallaxLayer` class, which was written and released by the co-author of this book, Jay Schroeder, allows for the easy creation of `ParallaxEntity` objects that give the perception of depth when the `Camera` object is moved across a scene. The level of parallax effect can be set, and the `ParallaxLayer` class takes care of correctly rendering each `ParallaxEntity` object. The following image shows the background layers of MagneTank that are attached to a `ParallaxLayer` class:

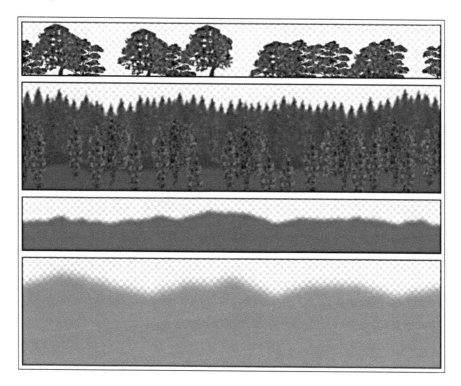

The `ParallaxLayer` class is based on the following recipes:

- ▸ *Understanding AndEngine entities* in *Chapter 2, Working with Entities*
- ▸ *Working with OpenGL* in *Chapter 2, Working with Entities*
- ▸ *Overriding the onManagedUpdate method* in *Chapter 2, Working with Entities*
- ▸ *Using parallax backgrounds to create perspective* in *Chapter 3, Designing Your Menu*

PhysObject.java

The `PhysObject` class is used in MagneTank to delegate contacts received from the physics world's `ContactListener`. It also facilitates a `destroy()` method to make destroying physics objects easier.

The `PhysObject` class is based on the following recipes:

- ▸ *Understanding AndEngine entities* in *Chapter 2, Working with Entities*
- ▸ *Introduction to the Box2D physics extension* in *Chapter 6, Applications of Physics*
- ▸ *Understanding different body types* in *Chapter 6, Applications of Physics*
- ▸ *Using preSolve and postSolve* in *Chapter 6, Applications of Physics*
- ▸ *What are update handlers?* in *Chapter 7, Working with Update Handlers*

RemainingCratesBar.java

The `RemainingCratesBar` class gives a visual representation to the player of which crates are left to be shot by MagneTank. The size, type, and number of crates left in each level are retrieved from the `GameLevel` class and vary from level to level. When one crate is shot, the `RemainingCratesBar` class animates to reflect the change in the game state.

This class is based on the following recipes:

- ▸ *Understanding AndEngine entities* in *Chapter 2, Working with Entities*
- ▸ *Bringing a scene to life with sprites* in *Chapter 2, Working with Entities*
- ▸ *Working with OpenGL* in *Chapter 2, Working with Entities*
- ▸ *Overriding the onManagedUpdate method* in *Chapter 2, Working with Entities*
- ▸ *Using modifiers and entity modifiers* in *Chapter 2, Working with Entities*

TexturedBezierLandscape.java

The `TexturedBezierLandscape` class creates two textured meshes and a physics body that represent the ground of the level. As the name implies, the landscape is comprised of Bezier curves to show rising or falling slopes. The textured meshes are made from repeating textures to avoid any visible seams between landscaped areas. The following image shows the two textures used to create the landscape as well as an example of how the combined meshes appear after a Bezier slope has been applied:

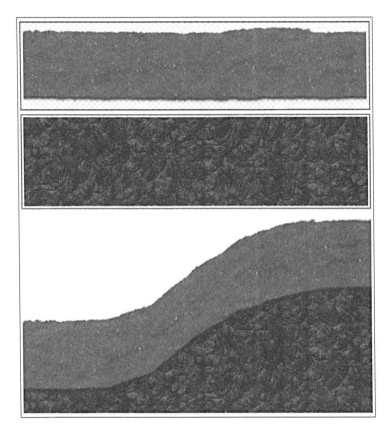

The `TexturedBezierLandscape` class is based on the following recipes:

- ▸ *Understanding AndEngine entities* in *Chapter 2, Working with Entities*
- ▸ *Working with OpenGL* in *Chapter 2, Working with Entities*
- ▸ *Introduction to the Box2D physics extension* in *Chapter 6, Applications of Physics*
- ▸ *Understanding different body types* in *Chapter 6, Applications of Physics*
- ▸ *Creating unique bodies by specifying vertices* in *Chapter 6, Applications of Physics*
- ▸ *Textured meshes* in *Chapter 10, Getting More From AndEngine*

TexturedMesh.java

This class is the same `TexturedMesh` class as found in the recipe, *Textured meshes* in *Chapter 10, Getting More From AndEngine*.

WoodenBeamDynamic.java

This class is similar to the `MetalBeam` classes, but adds a health aspect that causes the `WoodenBeamDynamic` class to be replaced with a particle effect once its health reaches zero.

The `WoodenBeamDynamic` class is based on the following recipes:

- *Understanding AndEngine entities in Chapter 2, Working with Entities*
- *Bringing a scene to life with sprites in Chapter 2, Working with Entities*
- *Using relative rotation in Chapter 2, Working with Entities*
- *Overriding the onManagedUpdate method in Chapter 2, Working with Entities*
- *Working with particle systems in Chapter 2, Working with Entities*
- *Introduction to the Box2D physics extension in Chapter 6, Applications of Physics*
- *Understanding different body types in Chapter 6, Applications of Physics*
- *Using preSolve and postSolve in Chapter 6, Applications of Physics*
- *What are update handlers? in Chapter 7, Working with Update Handlers*

Input classes

Each of these classes handles a specific input method used in the game:

BoundTouchInput.java

The `BoundTouchInput` class facilitates the delegation of inputs, which are then bound to the `BoundTouchInput` class. This can be easily seen in-game when moving MagneTank to aim at the turret. When the touch enters another touchable area, it stays tied to the original area.

GrowButton.java

The `GrowButton` class simply shows an image that grows to a specific scale when the player is touching it and returns to its original scale when the touch is lifted or lost.

This class is based on the following recipes:

- *Understanding AndEngine entities* in *Chapter 2, Working with Entities*
- *Bringing a scene to life with sprites* in *Chapter 2, Working with Entities*
- *Overriding the onManagedUpdate method* in *Chapter 2, Working with Entities*
- *Using modifiers and entity modifiers* in *Chapter 2, Working with Entities*

GrowToggleButton.java

Based on the `GrowButton` class, this class adds the functionality to show one or two `TiledTextureRegion` indices, depending on the state of a condition.

The `GrowToggleButton` class is based on the following recipes:

- *Understanding AndEngine entities* in *Chapter 2, Working with Entities*
- *Bringing a scene to life with sprites* in *Chapter 2, Working with Entities*
- *Overriding the onManagedUpdate method* in *Chapter 2, Working with Entities*
- *Using modifiers and entity modifiers* in *Chapter 2, Working with Entities*

GrowToggleTextButton.java

Based on the `GrowToggleButton` class, this class uses a `Text` object instead of a `TiledTextureRegion` object to show the state of a condition.

The `GrowToggleTextButton` class is based on the following recipes:

- *Understanding AndEngine entities* in *Chapter 2, Working with Entities*
- *Bringing a scene to life with sprites* in *Chapter 2, Working with Entities*
- *Applying text to a layer* in *Chapter 2, Working with Entities*
- *Overriding the onManagedUpdate method* in *Chapter 2, Working with Entities*
- *Using modifiers and entity modifiers* in *Chapter 2, Working with Entities*

Layer classes

These classes represent the layers that are present within the game:

LevelPauseLayer.java

The `LevelPauseLayer` class represents the layer that is shown to the player when a level is paused. It displays the current level number, score, and high score, as well as buttons to go back to the game, back to the level-select screen, restart the level, or skip to the next level.

This class is based on the following recipes:

- ▶ *Understanding AndEngine entities* in *Chapter 2, Working with Entities*
- ▶ *Bringing a scene to life with sprites* in *Chapter 2, Working with Entities*
- ▶ *Applying text to a layer* in *Chapter 2, Working with Entities*
- ▶ *Customizing managed scenes and layers* in *Chapter 5, Scene and Layer Management*
- ▶ *What are update handlers?* in *Chapter 7, Working with Update Handlers*

LevelWonLayer.java

The `LevelWonLayer` class represents the layer that is shown to the player when a level is completed successfully. It displays the current level number, score, and high score, as well as the star rating that the player received. It also includes buttons to go back to the level-select screen, replay the level, or go on to the next level. The following image shows the `LevelWonLayer` class textures and what they look like when assembled in the game:

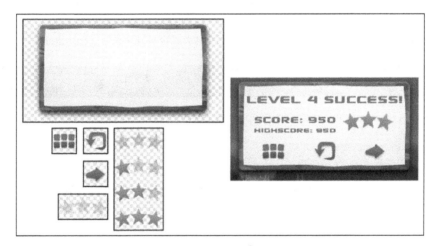

The `LevelWonLayer` class is based on the following recipes:

- ▶ *Understanding AndEngine entities* in *Chapter 2, Working with Entities*
- ▶ *Bringing a scene to life with sprites* in *Chapter 2, Working with Entities*
- ▶ *Applying text to a layer* in *Chapter 2, Working with Entities*
- ▶ *Using modifiers and entity modifiers* in *Chapter 2, Working with Entities*
- ▶ *Customizing managed scenes and layers* in *Chapter 5, Scene and Layer Management*
- ▶ *What are update handlers?* in *Chapter 7, Working with Update Handlers*

ManagedLayer.java

This class is the same `ManagedLayer` class as found in the *Creating the scene manager* recipe in *Chapter 5, Scene and Layer Management*.

OptionsLayer.java

This layer is accessible from the `MainMenu` scene and allows the player to enable or disable music and sounds as well as choose a graphics quality or reset the level completion data that they have achieved.

The `OptionsLayer` class is based on the following recipes:

- *Understanding AndEngine entities* in *Chapter 2, Working with Entities*
- *Bringing a scene to life with sprites* in *Chapter 2, Working with Entities*
- *Applying text to a layer* in *Chapter 2, Working with Entities*
- *Customizing managed scenes and layers* in *Chapter 5, Scene and Layer Management*
- *What are update handlers?* in *Chapter 7, Working with Update Handlers*

Manager classes

These classes each manage a specific aspect of the game:

GameManager.java

The `GameManager` class simply facilitates the checking of two conditions to determine if a level is completed or failed. Using that information, the game manager then calls the appropriate methods set in the `GameLevel` class.

This class is based on the following recipes:

- *Creating the game manager* in *Chapter 1, AndEngine Game Structure*
- *What are update handlers?* in *Chapter 7, Working with Update Handlers*

ResourceManager.java

The `ResourceManager` class is very similar to the one found in *Chapter 1, AndEngine Game Structure*, but adds the ability to use a set of lower quality textures, if desired. It also includes methods for determining an accurate font texture size to prevent wasting valuable texture memory.

This class is based on the following recipes:

- *Applying texture options* in *Chapter 1, AndEngine Game Structure*
- *Using AndEngine font resources* in *Chapter 1, AndEngine Game Structure*
- *Creating the resource manager* in *Chapter 1, AndEngine Game Structure*
- *Working with OpenGL* in *Chapter 2, Working with Entities*
- *Setting up the resource manager for scene resources* in *Chapter 5, Scene and Layer Management*

SceneManager.java

This class is identical to the `SceneManager` class found in the *Creating the scene manager* recipe in *Chapter 5, Scene and Layer Management*.

SFXManager.java

This simple class handles the playback of music and sounds as well as their muted state.

The `SFXManager` class is based on the following recipe:

- *Introducing sounds and music* in *Chapter 1, AndEngine Game Structure*

Menu classes

These classes are used only for the menus in the game.

LevelSelector.java

This class closely resembles the level selector found in *Chapter 3, Designing Your Menu*, but uses a series of `LevelSelectorButton` objects instead of sprites.

This class is based on the following recipes:

- *Understanding AndEngine entities* in *Chapter 2, Working with Entities*
- *Bringing a scene to life with sprites* in *Chapter 2, Working with Entities*
- *Creating our level selection system* in *Chapter 3, Designing Your Menu*

LevelSelectorButton.java

The `LevelSelectorButton` class visually shows the player the state of a level, locked or unlocked, and the number of stars achieved if the level is unlocked.

This class is based on the following recipes:

- *Understanding AndEngine entities* in *Chapter 2, Working with Entities*
- *Bringing a scene to life with sprites* in *Chapter 2, Working with Entities*
- *Applying text to a layer* in *Chapter 2, Working with Entities*
- *Overriding the onManagedUpdate method* in *Chapter 2, Working with Entities*
- *Using modifiers and entity modifiers* in *Chapter 2, Working with Entities*

MainMenu.java

The `MainMenu` class holds two `Entity` objects, one representing the title screen and one representing the level-select screen. The movement between the two screens is achieved using entity modifiers. During the first showing of the main menu, a loading screen is shown while the game's resources are being loaded.

The `MainMenu` class is based on the following recipes:

- *Understanding AndEngine entities* in *Chapter 2, Working with Entities*
- *Bringing a scene to life with sprites* in *Chapter 2, Working with Entities*
- *Overriding the onManagedUpdate method* in *Chapter 2, Working with Entities*
- *Using modifiers and entity modifiers* in *Chapter 2, Working with Entities*
- *Customizing managed scenes and layers* in *Chapter 5, Scene and Layer Management*

ManagedMenuScene.java

This class is the same `ManagedMenuScene` class as presented in the *Creating the scene manager* recipe in *Chapter 5, Scene and Layer Management*.

ManagedSplashScreen.java

This class is based on the `ManagedMenuScene` class found in the *Customizing managed scenes and layers* recipe in Chapter 5, *Scene and Layer Management*. It adds code to unload `Entity` objects after the splash screen is hidden.

SplashScreens.java

The `SplashScreen` class uses entity modifiers and resolution-independent positioning to show the splash screens of the game. Each logo is clickable and starts an intent related to the logo.

This class is based on the following recipes:

- *Bringing a scene to life with sprites* in *Chapter 2, Working with Entities*
- *Applying text to a layer* in *Chapter 2, Working with Entities*
- *Using modifiers and entity modifiers* in *Chapter 2, Working with Entities*
- *Customizing managed scenes and layers* in *Chapter 5, Scene and Layer Management*
- *What are update handlers?* in *Chapter 7, Working with Update Handlers*

Activity and Engine Classes

These classes act as the backbone of the game.

MagneTankActivity.java

This activity class builds upon the standard AndEngine `BaseGameActivity` class with the addition of ads, some advanced resolution-scaling performed in the `onCreateEngineOptions()` method, and shared preference methods to save and restore options and scores.

This class is based on the following recipes:

- *Know the life cycle* in *Chapter 1, AndEngine Game Structure*
- *Choosing our engine type* in *Chapter 1, AndEngine Game Structure*
- *Saving and loading game data* in *Chapter 1, AndEngine Game Structure*
- *Setting up an activity to use the scene manager* in *Chapter 5, Scene and Layer Management*

MagneTankSmoothCamera.java

This class extends the `SmoothCamera` object, but includes the ability to pan to the enemy base for a specified amount of time, as well as track the `MagneTank` object.

This class is based on the following recipes:

- *Introducing the camera object* in *Chapter 4, Working with Cameras*
- *Creating smooth moves with a smooth camera* in *Chapter 4, Working with Cameras*
- *What are update handlers?* in *Chapter 7, Working with Update Handlers*

ManagedScene.java

This class is the same `ManagedScene` class as presented in the *Creating the scene manager* recipe in *Chapter 5, Scene and Layer Management*.

SwitchableFixedStepEngine.java

This `Engine` object acts exactly like a `FixedStepEngine` object when the `EnableFixedStep()` method has been called.

This class is based on the following recipes:

- *Choosing our engine type* in *Chapter 1, AndEngine Game Structure*
- *What are update handlers?* in *Chapter 7, Working with Update Handlers*

Index

B

background
about 113, 155
applying 114, 115
EntityBackground class 115, 116
RepeatingSpriteBackground class 117-119
SpriteBackground class 116, 117
stitching 155, 156, 157, 158
background window rendering
about 265
disabling 266
BaseGameActivity class 183
beginContact() 235
Bilinear texture option 35
BitmapTextureAtlasTextureRegionFactory
class 29
BlendFunctionParticleInitializer 98
body type
specifying 194-196
BouncingPowerBar class 338
BouncingPowerBar.java class 338
bound camera
used, for camera area limiting 148
working 148
BoundTouchInput.java class 347
Box2D physics extension
about 187, 188
body types 193
force, using 206
joints 211
torque, using 206
using 188-191
velocities, using 206
working 191-193
BoxBody.setTransform() method 244
bringToBounds() method 322
BuildableBitmapTextureAtlas 31, 32
buttons
adding, to menu 105-108

C

camera
about 146
chase entity functionality 148
height, adjusting 147
HUD, applying 158, 159
positioning 146
visibility, checking 147
width, adjusting 147
working 146
CardinalSplineMoveModifier modifier 87
category-filtered bodies
about 196
creating 197, 198
working 198
CircleOutlineParticleEmitter 96
CircleParticleEmitter 96
collideConnected property 224
collidesWith(pOtherEntity) method 56
collisions
about 227
working with 227-231
color mapping
SVG texture regions used 300-305
ColorModifier 84
ColorParticleInitializer 99
ColorParticleModifier 101
computeTriangles() method 205
conditionals
update handler, using with 251, 253
working 253
controller
applying to display 159-161
coordinate conversion
about 162
using 162, 163
working 164
createBridge() method 333
createFromAsset() method 41
createJoint() method 332
create() method 41
createStrokeFromAsset() method 41
createStroke() method 41
culling 275

D

DelayModifier 84
destructible objects
about 236
creating 237-239
working 240

Thank you for buying
AndEngine for Android Game
Development Cookbook

About Packt Publishing

Packt, pronounced 'packed', published its first book *"Mastering phpMyAdmin for Effective MySQL Management"* in April 2004 and subsequently continued to specialize in publishing highly focused books on specific technologies and solutions.

Our books and publications share the experiences of your fellow IT professionals in adapting and customizing today's systems, applications, and frameworks. Our solution based books give you the knowledge and power to customize the software and technologies you're using to get the job done. Packt books are more specific and less general than the IT books you have seen in the past. Our unique business model allows us to bring you more focused information, giving you more of what you need to know, and less of what you don't.

Packt is a modern, yet unique publishing company, which focuses on producing quality, cutting-edge books for communities of developers, administrators, and newbies alike. For more information, please visit our website: www.packtpub.com.

About Packt Open Source

In 2010, Packt launched two new brands, Packt Open Source and Packt Enterprise, in order to continue its focus on specialization. This book is part of the Packt Open Source brand, home to books published on software built around Open Source licences, and offering information to anybody from advanced developers to budding web designers. The Open Source brand also runs Packt's Open Source Royalty Scheme, by which Packt gives a royalty to each Open Source project about whose software a book is sold.

Writing for Packt

We welcome all inquiries from people who are interested in authoring. Book proposals should be sent to author@packtpub.com. If your book idea is still at an early stage and you would like to discuss it first before writing a formal book proposal, contact us; one of our commissioning editors will get in touch with you.

We're not just looking for published authors; if you have strong technical skills but no writing experience, our experienced editors can help you develop a writing career, or simply get some additional reward for your expertise.

open source
community experience distilled

[PACKT]
PUBLISHING

Unity iOS Game Development Beginner's Guide

ISBN: 978-1-84969-040-9   Paperback: 314 pages

Develop iOS games from concept to cash flow using Unity

1. Dive straight into game development with no previous Unity or iOS experience

2. Work through the entire lifecycle of developing games for iOS

3. Add multiplayer, input controls, debugging, in app and micro payments to your game

4. Implement the different business models that will enable you to make money on iOS games

Creating Games with cocos2d for iPhone 2

ISBN: 978-1-84951-900-7   Paperback: 388 pages

Master cocos2d through building nine complete games fro the iPhone

1. Games are explained in detail, from the design decisions to the code itself

2. Learn to build a wide variety of game types, from a memory tile game to an endless runner

3. Use different design approaches to help you explore the cocos2d framework

Please check **www.PacktPub.com** for information on our titles

Marmalade SDK Mobile Game Development Essentials

ISBN: 978-1-84969-336-3   Paperback: 318 pages

Get to grips with the Marmalade SDK to develop games fro a wide range of mobile devices, including iOS, Android, and more

1. Easy to follow with lots of tips, examples and diagrams, including a full game project that grows with each chapter

2. Build video games for all popular mobile platforms, from a single codebase, using your existing C++ coding knowledge

3. Master 2D and 3D graphics techniques, including animation of 3D models, to make great looking games

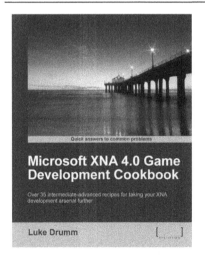

Microsoft XNA 4.0 Game Development Cookbook

ISBN: 978-1-84969-198-7   Paperback: 356 pages

Over 35 intermediate-advanced recipes for taking your XNA development arsenal further

1. Accelerate your XNA learning with a myriad of tips and tricks to solve your everyday problems

2. Get to grips with adding special effects, virtual atmospheres and computer controlled characters with this book and e-book

3. A fast-paced cookbook packed with screenshots to illustrate each advanced step by step task

www.ingramcontent.com/pod-product-compliance
Lightning Source LLC
Chambersburg PA
CBHW080148060326
40689CB00018B/3899